Classical Conditioning:

A Symposium

THE CENTURY PSYCHOLOGY SERIES

Richard M. Elliott, Gardner Lindzey & Kenneth MacCorquodale

Editors

EDITED BY

WILLIAM F. PROKASY

The Pennsylvania State University

Classical Conditioning:
A Symposium

APPLETON - CENTURY - CROFTS
DIVISION OF MEREDITH PUBLISHING COMPANY
New York

ACKNOWLEDGMENTS FOR ILLUSTRATIONS

1-4 *from* E. R. Behrend & M. E. Bitterman. Avoidance conditioning in the fish: Further studies of the *CS-US* interval. *Amer. J. Psychol.*, 1964, 77, 15-28. By permission of *The American Journal of Psychology.*

1-7, 1-8, 1-9, 1-10, 1-11, 1-12 *from* M. E. Bitterman. Classical conditioning in the goldfish as a function of the *CS-US* interval. *J. comp. physiol. Psychol.*, 1964, 58, 359-366. By permission.

2-1, 2-2 *from* A. H. Black & W. M. Lang. Cardiac conditioning and skeletal responding in curarized dogs. *Psychol. rev.*, 1964, 71, 80-85. By permission.

3-1 *from* J. W. Moore & I. Gormezano. Yoked comparisons of instrumental and classical eyelid conditioning. *J. exp. Psychol.*, 1961, 62, 552-559. By permission.

3-2 *from* I. Gormezano, J. W. Moore, & E. Deaux. Supplementary report: Yoked comparisons of classical and avoidance conditioning under three UCS intensities. *J. exp. Psychol.*, 1962, 64, 551-552. By permission.

3-5 *from* W. N. Runquist, J. Sidowski, & I. Gormezano. Yoked comparisons of classical and avoidance conditioning in differential conditioning of the eyelid response. *Psychol. Rep.*, 1962, 11, 43-50. By permission.

4-1, 4-2 *from* W. W. Grings & R. A. Lockhart. Effects of "anxiety-lessening" instructions and differential set development on the extinction of GSR. *J. exp. Psychol.*, 1963, 66, 292-299. By permission.

4-3 *from* W. W. Grings & A. Zeiner. Autonomic responses to words modified by sensitizing and conditioning experiences. *J. psychosom. Res.*, in press. By permission.

7-1, 7-2, 7-3 *from* L. J. Kamin & R. E. Schaub. Effects of conditioned stimulus intensity on the conditioned emotional response. *J. comp. physiol. Psychol.*, 1963, 56, 502-507. By permission.

7-5 *from* L. J. Kamin & C. J. Brimer. The effects of intensity of conditioned and unconditioned stimuli on a conditioned emotional response. *Can. J. Psychol.*, 1963, 17, 194-198. By permission.

8-1, 8-4, 8-11 *from* H. D. Kimmel. Further analysis of GSR conditioning: A reply to Stewart, Stern, Winokur, and Fredman. *Psychol. rev.*, 1964, 71, 160-166. By permission.

9-1 *from* W. R. McAllister & D. E. McAllister. Increase over time in the stimulus generalization of acquired fear. *J. exp. Psychol.*, 1963, 65, 576-582. By permission.

9-8, 9-9 *from* W. R. McAllister & D. E. McAllister. Role of the CS and of apparatus cues in the measurement of acquired fear. *Psychol. Rep.*, 1962, 11, 749-756. By permission.

15-1 *from* G. D. Ellison. Differential salivary conditioning to traces. *J. comp. physiol. Psychol.*, 1964, 57, 373-380. By permission.

16-5 *from* D. D. Wickens, D. G. Born, & C. D. Wickens. Response strength to a compound conditioned stimulus as a function of the element interstimulus interval. *J. comp. physiol. Psychol.*, 1963, 56, 727-731. By permission.

16-6 *from* C. K. Allen, F. A. Hill, & D. D. Wickens. The orienting reflex as a function of the interstimulus interval of compound stimuli. *J. exp. Psychol.*, 1963, 65, 309-316. By permission.

16-7 *from* D. D. Wickens & H. A. Cross. Resistance to extinction as a function of temporal relations during sensory preconditioning. *J. exp. Psychol.*, 1963, 65, 206-211. By permission.

19-1 *from* D. Zeaman, G. Deane, & N. Wegner. Amplitude and latency characteristics of the conditioned heart response. *J. Psychol.*, 1954, 38, 235-250. By permission.

19-2, 19-3 *from* G. E. Deane & D. Zeaman. Human heart rate during anxiety. *Percept, Motor Skills*, 1958, 8, 103-106. By permission.

19-4, 19-5, 19-6, 19-7 *from* G. E. Deane. Human heart rate responses during experimentally induced anxiety. *J. exp. Psychol.*, 1961, 61, 489-493. By permission.

19-16, 19-17 *from* M. R. Westcott & J. Huttenlocher. Cardiac conditioning: The effects and implications of controlled and uncontrolled respiration. *J. exp. Psychol.*, 1961, 61, 353-359. By permission.

19-26 *from* R. S. Jenks & G. E. Deane. Human heart rate during experimentally induced anxiety: A follow-up. *J. exp. Psychol.*, 1963, 65, 109-112. By permission.

PREFACE

In August, 1963, a group of nineteen investigators interested in classical conditioning met at the Nittany Lion Inn on the campus of The Pennsylvania State University to participate in a symposium sponsored by Grant GB-275 to the editor from the National Science Foundation. This volume is a direct outgrowth of the symposium.

In the hope of obtaining about a dozen contributors, twenty-six individuals were invited to participate. Of these, two did not respond to the initial invitation, one declined, and four who had planned to attend later withdrew because of unanticipated conflicts. The remaining nineteen participants, though more than anticipated, do not, of course, exhaust the field of all the individuals who are contributing to our knowledge of classical conditioning. They do, however, represent the fulfillment of an original goal for the symposium: a wide diversity in response measure, experimental methodology, and theoretical predisposition. The result is, in a sense, a "state of the art" in the United States and Canada, with emphasis placed more on what individual investigators are doing and thinking than on an organizing theme more specific than "classical conditioning."

Publication of the volume was delayed until all authors had had an opportunity to modify and update their papers based upon the conference proceedings. Rather than publish the proceedings, tapes of the discussions were sent to the participants for their use in writing the final versions of their papers. This not only had the virtue of eliminating an extremely difficult and time-consuming editorial chore, but also tended to insure that commentary relevant to a particular paper was used to improve it.

In addition to acknowledging the National Science Foundation for its support, two individuals should be acknowledged for their assistance. First, Richard E. Grubb, who was the conference coordinator from The Pennsylvania State University Conference Center and who both anticipated and efficiently handled all details of organization and administration. Second, L. Edwin Brown of the Nittany Lion Inn, who served as our host during the symposium, putting the facilities of the Inn at our disposal. Our thanks go to both of these men and to their staffs for their contributions to the success of the symposium.

                                                                                            W.F.P.

CONTENTS

M. E. BITTERMAN
Bryn Mawr College

1

The CS-US Interval in Classical and Avoidance Conditioning [1]

This paper is divided into three parts. The first part reviews some experiments on avoidance conditioning in the goldfish as a function of the *CS-US* interval. The second part reviews some parallel experiments on classical aversive conditioning in the goldfish. The classical experiments were designed to test certain hypotheses about the role of the *CS-US* interval which were suggested by the avoidance data. The third part describes the earliest of a new series of experiments on classical appetitive conditioning in the pigeon. The purpose of the pigeon work is to assess the generality of the results obtained with the fish.

I. AVOIDANCE CONDITIONING IN THE FISH AS A FUNCTION OF THE *CS-US* INTERVAL

A shuttlebox for the fish is diagrammed in Fig. 1-1. It consists of an elongated compartment which is divided into two smaller compartments by a hurdle. The hurdle is so constructed that the animal can cross easily from one side to the other but is not likely to loiter in the region of the hurdle. Crossing is detected by photocells, and the location of the animal is monitored by a rachet-relay. (In the current version of the apparatus, six such chambers are in operation simultaneously, the entire experiment being programmed automatically, with latency of response recorded on tape.) The *CS* is a light which is turned on at the end of the apparatus occupied by the fish, and, after a predetermined *CS-US*

[1] The research described here was supported in part by Grant MH-02857 from the Public Health Service and in part by Contract Nonr 2829(01) with the Office of Naval Research.

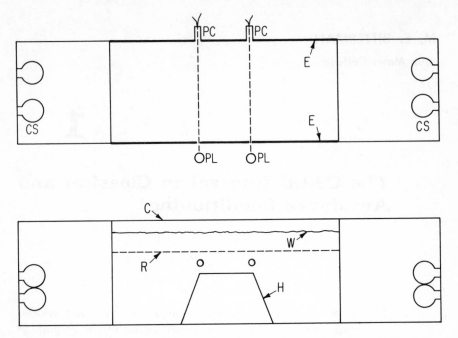

Fig. 1-1. A shuttlebox for the fish. *Top,* plan; *bottom,* side view; *PC,* photocell; *PL,* photo-cell lamp; *E,* electrode; *CS,* lamps whose onset serve as *CS; H,* hurdle; *R,* roof; *W,* water level; *C,* cover.

interval, shock is scheduled. Response to the light turns off the light and forestalls shock. Response after the onset of shock turns off both light and shock. A trial terminates independently of the animal's behavior 15 sec. after the onset of shock if (as happens occasionally early in training) the animal has not made the required response in that time. In the standard procedure, 10 trials per day are given, with a mean intertrial interval of 3 min. Let us now consider an experiment in which independent groups of animals were trained at each of a number of different *CS-US* intervals to a criterion of nine avoidances in the 10 trials of a given day. This experiment, as well as the other experiments on avoidance conditioning which I shall review here, was done in collaboration with Erika R. Behrend (Behrend & Bitterman, 1962, 1964).

Mean trials to criterion as a function of the *CS-US* interval is plotted in Fig. 1-2. The curve declines in negatively accelerated fashion from a high value at short intervals to what seems to be an asymptote at about 20 sec. What can this result mean? Why should performance be so much better at 60 sec. than at, say, 2.5 sec.? The answer is obvious. In this ex-periment, opportunity for response was confounded with *CS-US* interval: animals trained at 60 sec. had 60 sec. in which to avoid, while animals trained at 2.5 sec. had only 2.5 sec. Although the escape-latencies of prac-

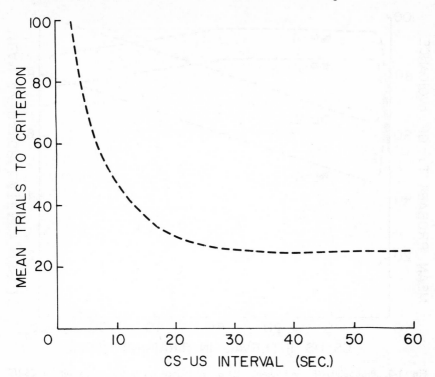

Fig. 1-2. Rate of avoidance conditioning as a function of the *CS-US* interval (confounded design).

ticed animals may be no more than a fraction of a second, and although avoidance-latencies on the order of 2 sec. or so, often are recorded, animals *required* to make low-latency responses are placed at a disadvantage. Clearly, then, we must unconfound training interval and opportunity for response if we are to measure the effect of the training interval alone. Although the point is an obvious one, it has often been ignored in experiments on the *CS-US* interval.

One way to unconfound training interval and opportunity for response is to use a transfer design: train independent groups of goldfish at different *CS-US* intervals, and then test all groups at the same (relatively long) interval. The pooled results of a number of such experiments are schematized in Fig. 1-3. One set of groups was trained for two days at the different intervals and tested on the third day at 20 sec. Another set of groups was trained for four days at the different intervals and tested on the fifth day at 20 sec. The curves shown are plotted in terms of probability of avoidance and latency of avoidance on the testing day. The probability curves rise sharply to a maximum in the early seconds, remain level for a time, and then seem to fall off gradually, although the decline

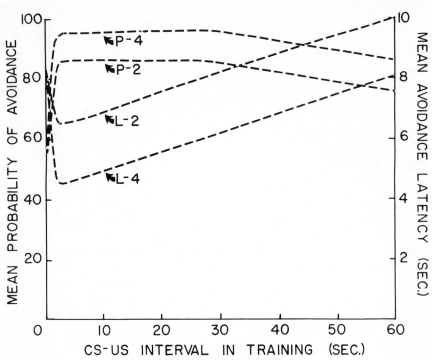

Fig. 1-3. Probability (P) and latency (L) of avoidance on testing trials with a CS-US interval of 20 sec. after two or four days of training at each of a variety of CS-US intervals (transfer design).

is not statistically significant. The latency curves fall sharply in the early seconds and then rise significantly in essentially linear fashion as the CS-US interval increases. The shapes of the functions are only roughly indicated here, but there can be no doubt that the maxima of the probability functions and the minima of the latency functions are reached in 1-2 sec. The curves for the two different amounts of training are quite parallel, more practice yielding a higher probability of avoidance and a lower latency of avoidance at each interval except zero. The performance of the 0-sec. groups did not differ from the performance of various sensitization-controls.

How are these results to be understood? Consider first the right-hand portion of each function in the light of the Pavlovian assumptions (1) that what is conditioned is the afferent state of affairs immediately antedating the onset of the US and (2) that what is necessary to elicit the conditioned response is an afferent state similar in some degree to that which has been conditioned. It follows from these assumptions that latency will increase with CS-US interval; an animal trained with a longer interval must wait longer for the requisite state of affairs to develop than an animal trained at a shorter interval, although both animals will tend to respond with latencies shorter than their training intervals because of stimulus-generalization. It also follows from these assumptions that probability of response will remain relatively constant over a wide range of intervals if the testing interval is sufficiently long. An animal trained with a longer interval must wait longer for the afferent state requisite to response, but eventually that state will develop and the animal will respond. With short testing intervals, probability of response may be expected to decline in animals trained at longer intervals because there is insufficient time for the development of the requisite afferent state, and it may be that the tendency for the probability function to fall off at the longer training intervals is due to our use of a 20-sec. testing interval. Even with longer testing intervals, however, some decline in probability might be expected from the generalization of extinction.

These relations are schematized in Fig. 1-4. The abscissa represents CS-duration, while the ordinate represents the strength of some hypothetical excitatory process established by conditioning, with the probability of avoidance at any given moment assumed to be proportional to the level of excitation. Curves A and B represent temporal gradients of excitation generated by training at two different CS-US intervals, T_2 and T_4. If R is a level of excitation that will produce avoidance with some substantial probability, then it is clear that the animal trained at T_2 will tend to avoid earlier on each trial than the animal trained at T_4, but the

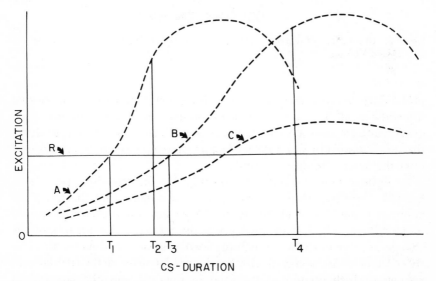

Fig. 1-4. Hypothetical results of equal amounts of training at two different CS-US intervals (curves A and B) and of unequal amounts of training at the same interval (curves B and C). See text for explanation. (Behrend & Bitterman, 1964)

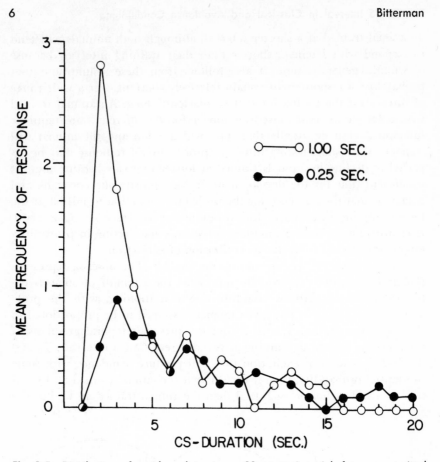

Fig. 1-5. Distributions of avoidance-latencies on 20-sec. testing trials for groups trained at 0.25 and 1.00 sec.

probability of avoidance will be high in both animals if the testing interval exceeds T_3. Curve C, which represents the gradient of excitation generated by a lesser amount of training at T_2 than does Curve B, shows that lower probability and longer latency of avoidance are to be expected after the lesser amount of training.

Consider now the left-hand portions of the functions plotted in Fig. 1-3—the sharp rises in probability of avoidance and the sharp declines in latency of avoidance as the *CS-US* interval is increased from 0 to 1 or 2 sec. The fall in latency may be treated as an artifact of the change in probability. As probability increases, more and more relatively short latencies are averaged with the longer latencies of the spontaneous responses which occur in substantial number. If only the latencies of "true" avoidances could be measured, they might not be very different for animals trained, say, at 0.25 sec. than for animals trained at 1 sec.

This point is illustrated by Fig. 1-5, which shows the temporal distribution of avoidances in ten 20-sec. testing trials made by groups trained at 0.25 and at 1.00 sec.; the two groups differ only in the number of short-latency (2-4 sec.) avoidances. The dramatic increase in probability of avoidance as the *CS-US* interval is increased from 0 to 1 or 2 sec. is open to a number of interpretations. Fig. 1-5 suggests that conditioning at the different short intervals generates excitatory gradients of different heights with maxima at essentially the same locus on the temporal continuum. It might be proposed that what is conditioned at a very short interval such as 0.25 sec. is a highly transient afferent state, quite unlike the state which exists after the *CS* has been on for a few seconds. The conditioned state may be so different and so fleeting that there simply is no time for the development of an excitatory process of substantial magnitude.

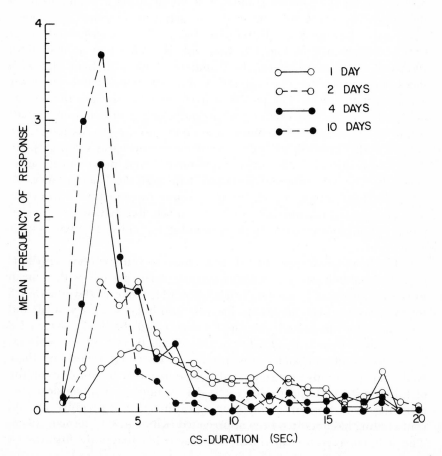

Fig. 1-6. Distributions of avoidance-latencies on 20-sec. testing trials in groups trained for one, two, four, and ten days at 2.5 sec.

It may be well also to look at the way in which the distribution of avoidance-latencies is affected by amount of training. Fig. 1-6 shows the temporal distribution of avoidances in ten 20-sec. testing trials for groups previously given 1, 2, 4, or 10 days of training at 2.5 sec. The increasing frequency of short-latency responses is precisely what would be expected from Fig. 1-4. The change in curve-shape, which would not be expected from Fig. 1-4, suggests that the excitatory gradient not only reaches a higher level as training proceeds, but that it falls more sharply in the region beyond the training interval.

II. CLASSICAL CONDITIONING IN THE FISH AS A FUNCTION OF THE *CS-US* INTERVAL

For a closer examination of the excitatory process which is assumed to underlie avoidance, and which the measures available to us in the shuttlebox reflect only indirectly, we may turn to some experiments on classical conditioning (Bitterman, 1964).[2] The experimental situation is diagrammed in Fig. 1-7. Each fish is confined in a small dark compartment in which it can be stimulated both with light and with shock while its activity is monitored by a paddle inserted into the water a short distance away. The paddle is fixed on a rod set into the needle-holder of a phonograph cartridge whose output (amplified and integrated) is used to drive a print-out counter and an event-recorder. Actually there are six such chambers arranged end-to-end in which six animals are studied concurrently, the entire experiment being programmed automatically. The basic procedure is to pair light with shock, and to measure the generalized activity which the light comes in consequence to evoke. The graphic records obtained look very much like Pavlov's records of salivary conditioning, with the pips standing for units of activity rather than drops of saliva.

The first experiment which I shall report to you was done with four groups of goldfish. Each group was given 20 trials per day with a mean intertrial interval of 3 min. On Trials 1-9 and 11-19 of each day, the *CS-US* interval was 0 sec. for one group, 1 sec. for another, 3 sec. for a third, and 9 sec. for a fourth; in each case the *CS* overlapped the brief (0.6-sec.) *US* and terminated with it. On Trials 10 and 20, the *CS-US* interval was 20 sec. for all groups, and it was in terms of their performance on these trials that the groups were compared. Please note that the unconfounding of training interval and testing interval is as important in classical conditioning as in avoidance conditioning, although the necessity for unconfounding has not often been appreciated (Klinman & Bitterman, 1963). The design of a second experiment was exactly like that of the first, except

---

2 This work was done with the able assistance of Beverly Berger.

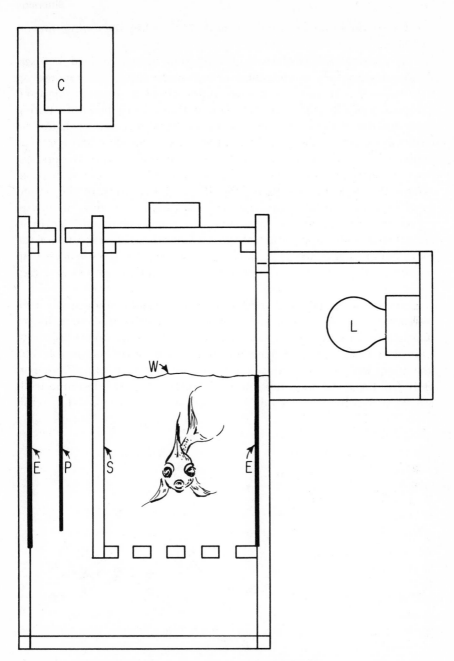

Fig. 1-7. A classical aversive conditioning situation for the fish. *C*, cartridge; *E*, electrode; *P*, paddle; *S*, slatted wall; *W*, water level; *L*, CS-lamp. (Bitterman, 1964)

that the training intervals were 1, 9, and 27 sec., while the testing interval was 40 sec.

As training proceeded, each group except the one trained at 0 sec. showed a negatively accelerated increase in magnitude of response on testing trials. The asymptotic magnitudes varied to some extent from group to group, but it was in this distribution of activity within testing trials that the effect of variation in *CS-US* interval was most evident. The results are given in Fig. 1-8. The curves on the left show the temporal gradients of activity measured on the 20-sec. testing trials of the first experiment after all groups except the one trained at 0 sec. had reached asymptote. Analogous results for the 40-sec. testing trials of the second experiment are shown on the right. In each case, the gradient of activity reflects the training interval, each curve reaching a maximum 5 sec. or so after the scheduled appearance of the *US* in training. The results for the 0-sec. group of the first experiment suggest that whatever tendency to respond in the light it acquired was due to the reinforced 20-sec. testing trials.

To determine whether the 0-sec. interval would produce any conditioning at all in the absence of reinforced testing trials at a longer interval, a third experiment was performed. Three groups of fish were trained—a 10-sec. group, a 0-sec. group, and a sensitization-control. The first group was given 10 trials per day, the first nine with a *CS-US* interval of 10 sec. For a second group, the *CS-US* interval on the first nine trials was 0 sec., but the *CS* stayed on for 10 sec. as in the first case. The tenth

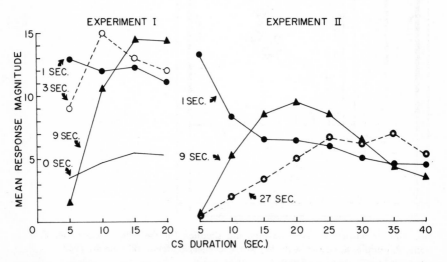

Fig. 1-8. Gradients of activation on later (20-sec. and 40-sec.) testing trials for independent groups classically conditioned at the designated *CS-US intervals.* (Bitterman, 1964)

trial of each day for both groups was an *un*reinforced 40-sec. presentation of the *CS*. For the third group, unreinforced 10-sec. presentations of light alone and unheralded brief shocks were scheduled in random order at an average intertrial interval of 1.5 min. (half that used for the other two groups); on the last trial of each day, the *CS* was presented alone for 40 sec. just as it was for the other two groups.

In Fig. 1-9, mean magnitude of response to light on testing trials is plotted for each of the three groups. The curve of the 10-sec. group shows the characteristic negatively accelerated growth, while those of the other two groups do not. It seems clear, then, that strictly simultaneous pairing of light and shock produces no tendency to respond to the light. It also seems clear that the response measured in this situation is not sensitized by the unpaired presentation of light and shock as it is in the shuttlebox. In the shuttlebox, 0-sec. groups and sensitization-controls respond at the same relatively high level, while here they show hardly any response at all. The difference may be accounted for by the fact that the response measured in the shuttlebox is repeatedly reinforced in training by the shock-termination.

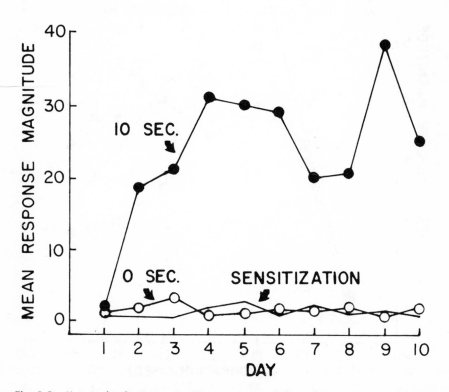

Fig. 1-9. Magnitude of response on 40-sec. testing trials for a sensitization-control group and for groups classically conditioned at 0 sec. and 10 sec. (Bitterman, 1964)

Fig. 1-10 shows the temporal gradients of activity on testing trials at various stages in the training of the 10-sec. group. As Fig. 1-9 indicates, the over-all level of response on Days 7-10 was very much the same in this group as on Days 2-5, yet the pattern of activity was different. In six more days of training given the 10-sec. group, the over-all level of activity remained the same, but the progressive change in the within-trials pattern continued—that is, there was a further peaking of the function in the period immediately following the scheduled presentation of shock on training trials (see the curve for Days 13-16). The change in pattern is strongly reminiscent of that which appears in the distributions of avoidance-latencies plotted in Fig. 1-6.

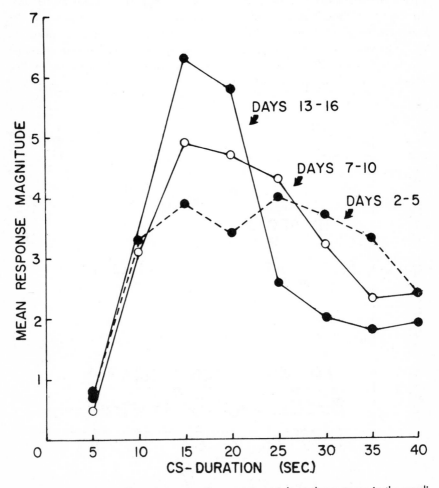

Fig. 1-10. Gradients of activation on 40-sec. testing trials at three stages in the conditioning of a 10-sec. group. (Bitterman, 1964)

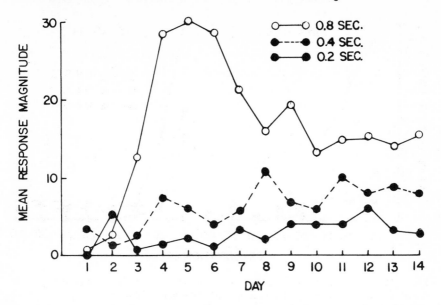

Fig. 1-11. Magnitude of response on 40-sec. testing trials for groups classically conditioned at the designated CS-US intervals. (Bitterman, 1964)

A fourth experiment on classical conditioning was performed to study the effects of training at very short CS-US intervals. Three groups of fish were given 10 trials per day with a mean intertrial interval of 3 min. On nine of each day's trials, the CS-US interval was 0.2 sec. for one group, 0.4 sec. for a second group, and 0.8 sec. for a third group; in each case, the CS overlapped the brief (0.6-sec. shock) and terminated with it. On the remaining trial of each day (the third, fifth, or eighth in balanced order), there was an unreinforced 40-sec. presentation of the CS.

Mean magnitude of response on testing trials is plotted in Fig. 1-11, which shows a progressive increase in level of response with increasing CS-US interval. Within-trials patterns of activity for Days 4-6, when the 0.8-sec. group was responding at a high level, and for Days 10-14, when all groups seemed to be at asymptote, are plotted in Fig. 1-12. The shape of the within-trials function for the 0.8-group is quite like that for the 1-sec. groups of previous experiments. The 0.4-sec. and 0.2-sec. groups show the same general within-trials pattern but at a lower over-all level. The steepening of all the functions with continued training reflects a developing temporal discrimination. The right-hand set is not very different than we should have been led to expect from the latency-distributions plotted in Fig. 1-5.

Two implications of these results should be noted briefly. Consider first their bearing on our conception of avoidance conditioning: A process

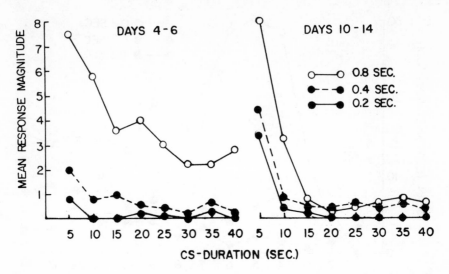

Fig. 1-12. Gradients of activation on 40-sec. testing trials at two stages in the conditioning of 0.2-sec., 0.4-sec., and 0.8-sec. groups. (Bitterman, 1964)

of classical conditioning long has been assumed to underlie avoidance—the notion being that what triggers the avoidance response is a stimulus which has acquired certain activating properties by virtue of its pairing with shock—but here we have begun to inquire into the details of relationship, and it now becomes quite clear that independent measures of classical conditioning provide a basis for understanding certain quantitative features of avoidance conditioning. If the probability of avoidance at any moment is proportional to the magnitude of activation at that moment, then the probability of avoidance in any testing period will increase with the level of activation developed in that period, and the latency of avoidance will be inversely related to the slope of the activation gradient (rate of activation).

That there is no avoidance conditioning when the *CS-US* interval used in training is 0 sec. can be predicted from the fact that there is no classical conditioning at that interval. The precipitous increase in probability of avoidance and decline in latency of avoidance as the training interval increases from 0-1 sec. can be predicted from the progressively steeper gradients of activation measured in classical conditioning over the same range of intervals. That the probability of avoidance on testing trials is as great when the *CS-US* interval used in training is long as when it is short, while the latency of avoidance increases as the training interval increases, can be predicted from the fact that the activation gradients produced by classical conditioning at longer intervals ultimately reach the same levels as do those produced by classical conditioning at shorter intervals, but the rate of activation is less. As avoidance training at a given CS-US interval continues, probability of avoidance on testing trials increases and latency of avoidance decreases; these changes are exactly what might be expected from the progressive peaking with continued training of the activation gradients produced by classical conditioning.

The results which have been presented here bear also on our thinking about the role of the CS-US interval in classical conditioning. Despite the fact that the work of Pavlov (1927) showed the question to be a fruitless one, many investigators have continued to ask about the "optimal" CS-US interval for conditioning. The question implies that the same two events are associated at the different CS-US intervals, with variation only in the degree to which they are associated. The present results point again to the validity of Pavlov's conclusion that what is conditioned is the afferent state of affairs which exists when the US is introduced. From this point of view, earlier events are important only insofar as they determine the nature of the state which is conditioned, and they come to elicit the conditioned response only insofar as they generate states resembling the one which has been conditioned.

When the CS-US interval is 20 sec., what is conditioned is the afferent state generated by a CS which has been on for 20 sec. The onset of the CS elicits the CR only to the degree that it generates a similar state. When the CS-US interval is 0 sec., what is conditioned is an afferent state characteristic of the intertrial interval. As the CS-US interval increases progressively from 0-1 sec., the conditioned state is progressively less similar to the intertrial state, and progressively more like that characteristic of the CS in its early seconds of operation. The CS-onset state probably has some unique properties, however, and the low level of response on testing trials after training with very brief CS-US intervals may reflect that uniqueness.

III. CLASSICAL CONDITIONING IN THE PIGEON AS A FUNCTION OF THE CS-US INTERVAL

Questions about conditioning usually are phrased in such a way as to suggest that perfectly general answers are expected—general over species and general over method. In practice, however, systematic work on conditioning has been limited to a few species and a few methods, with species and methods usually being confounded. Until our inquiry ranges more widely over these variables, it will be difficult to decide which of our findings have general significance and which are products of the special conditions of our experiments. Why do the results reported in the second section of this paper look so different from what we might have been led to expect from a consideration of the data on eyelid conditioning in man? Which set of results provides a more representative picture of the role of the *CS-US* interval in conditioning? We shall only know when we have studied a wider sample of species by a wider variety of methods.

It may be of interest to look now at the results of an experiment on classical appetitive conditioning in the pigeon (Longo, Klempay, & Bitterman, 1964) which was patterned after those described in the second section of this paper. In the appetitive experiment, a signal is paired, not with shock, but with the discharge of a few pieces of grain into a feeding dish, and what is measured is the anticipatory activity which the signal soon begins to evoke. Although this appetitive technique was used decades ago by Popov (Razran, 1933), I was led to it independently by observations of the behavior of pigeons at feeding time, when the removal of the cover of the grain bucket or the approach of the experimenter to a rack of cages provokes a fury of anticipatory activity. Very much the same sort of behavior can be observed in fish at feeding time, and I hope soon to make it the subject of some formal experiments; but the development of the pigeon technique has proceeded at a more rapid rate, and we must be content now with the familiar confounding of difference in method with difference in species.

The chamber used in the pigeon experiment is diagrammed in Fig. 1-13. The pigeon stands on a spring-mounted platform which is connected by a short length of rod to a phonograph cartridge. As in work with the fish, the output of the cartridge is amplified and integrated to provide a measure of activity; in fact, the same type of programmer is used for the experiments with both species. In work with the pigeon, the *CS* is compound—the colored house light goes off and the buzzer is turned on. The *CS* terminates with the presentation of food, which is accompanied by the sound of a heavy solenoid and the flash of a white magazine-light which briefly illuminates the feeding dish.

In our first experiment with this technique, two groups of pigeons were studied. Both groups were given ten trials per day with a mean inter-trial interval of about 20 min. On nine of these trials, the *CS-US* interval was 1 sec. for one of the groups and 10 sec. for the other. On the tenth (testing) trial, whose position was varied in quasi-random fashion from session to session, the *CS-US* interval was 40 sec. for both groups. In each session, too, a determination of basal activity was made at a point which varied from session to session. For these determinations, the integrator was connected to the chambers just as it was on the 40-sec. testing trials, but no stimuli were presented. Such determinations are no longer made routinely in our work with the fish because long experience has shown that the interval activity of those animals is essentially nil, but pilot work with the pigeon technique showed that interval activity might be sub-

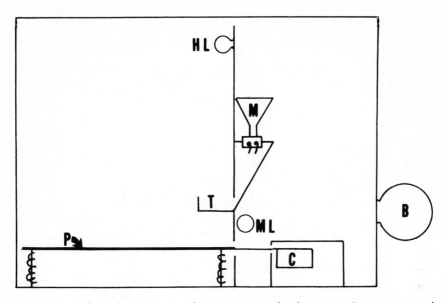

Fig. 1-13. A classical appetitive conditioning situation for the pigeon. *P,* spring-mounted platform; *C,* phonograph cartridge; *T,* food tray; *M,* magazine; *ML,* magazine light; *HL,* house light; *B,* blower.

stantial. With short intertrial intervals, almost continuous activity was produced in some birds, and, even with longer intertrial intervals, the probability of interval activity was found to be high enough to make monitoring essential. From experiments with pigeons in which shock was used as the *US* (Longo, Milstein, & Bitterman, 1962), my guess is that the difference is due to the *US* employed rather than to the species.

As training proceeded, the magnitude of response in both groups increased in negatively accelerated fashion. The magnitude of response to the *CS* on testing trials was significantly greater in the 10-sec. group than in the 1-sec. group. The response of the 10-sec. group to the *CS* on testing trials also was greater in magnitude than its basal activity, but the response of the 1-sec. group was about the same whether or not the *CS* was presented. These relationships are illustrated in Fig. 1-14, which shows the distribution of response in both groups on 40-sec. tests (with and without the *CS*) given on Days 11-16, when all measures had stabilized. Two discrepancies between these curves and those of Fig. 1-8 (Experiment II) are immediately apparent. First, the 10-sec. pigeons do not show the temporal discrimination which is found in the 9-sec. fish. Second, relative to the performance of longer-interval groups of the same species, the 1-sec. pigeons show a much lower level of conditioning than the 1-sec.

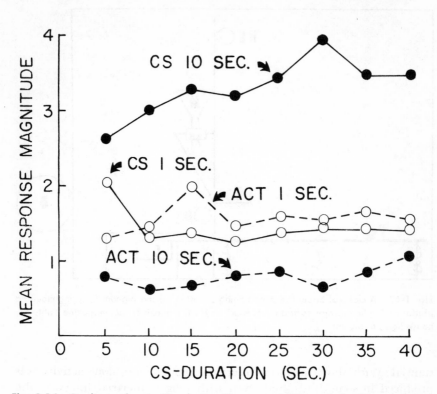

Fig. 1-14. Gradients of activation during 40-sec. presentations of the CS and during 40-sec. periods of no stimulation (ACT) in groups of pigeons classically conditioned with CS-US intervals of 1 and 10 sec. (Longo, Klempay, & Bitterman, 1964)

fish; comparisons with basal activity suggest, in fact, that the 1-sec. pigeons acquired no tendency at all to respond to the *CS*.

Whether these discrepancies are due to species or to method or to both cannot now, of course, be said. My own guess is that method is the more important variable. I take seriously the possibility that much of the activity which develops in the appetitive situation is instrumental in character, a product of adventitious reinforcement—there is evidence that general activity of the kind here measured can function as an operant (Graf & Bitterman, 1963)—and I can believe that the 10-sec. interval would afford much more opportunity than the 1-sec. interval for its development. Whatever the correctness of this interpretation, the results suggest that more attention might well be given than has been given in the past to parameters of species and method.

References

BEHREND, E. R., & BITTERMAN, M. E. Avoidance conditioning in the goldfish: Exploratory studies of the CS-US interval. *Amer. J. Psychol.,* 1962, *75,* 18-34.

BEHREND, E. R., & BITTERMAN, M. E. Avoidance conditioning in the fish: Further studies of the CS-US interval. *Amer. J. Psychol.,* 1964, *77,* 15-28.

BITTERMAN, M. E. Classical conditioning in the goldfish as a function of the CS-US interval. *J. comp. physiol. Psychol.,* 1964, *58,* 359-366.

GRAF, V., & BITTERMAN, M. E. General activity as instrumental: Applications to avoidance training. *J. exp. Anal. Behav.,* 1963, *6,* 301-305.

KLINMAN, C. S., & BITTERMAN, M. E. Classical conditioning in the fish: The CS-US interval. *J. comp. physiol. Psychol.,* 1963, *56,* 578-583.

LONGO, N., KLEMPAY, S., & BITTERMAN, M. E. Classical appetitive conditioning in the pigeon. *Psychonom. Science,* 1964, *1,* 19-20.

LONGO, N., MILSTEIN, S., & BITTERMAN, M. E. Classical conditioning in the pigeon: Exploratory studies of partial reinforcement. *J. comp. physiol. Psychol.,* 1962, *55,* 983-986.

RAZRAN, G. H. S. Conditioned responses in animals other than dogs. *Psychol. Bull.,* 1933, *30,* 261-324.

A. H. BLACK
McMaster University

2

Cardiac Conditioning in Curarized Dogs: The Relationship Between Heart Rate and Skeletal Behaviour [1]

One of the persistent problems which has arisen in our work on classical heart rate conditioning is the relationship between heart rate and skeletal responding. It is this problem which I would like to discuss in the present paper.

Originally, we were interested in the heart rate response as an index of a conditioned emotional or fear response (CER). This CER was assumed to play a crucial role in many avoidance theories (Solomon & Brush, 1956), but instead of being observed independently it was typically inferred from the same avoidance behaviour that it was supposed to explain. We hoped to achieve an independent measure of the CER by recording heart rate during avoidance conditioning. The results of the first experiment were ambiguous (Black, 1959). There seemed to be a relationship between heart rate and avoidance responding, but this relationship was difficult to interpret; we could not decide, in some cases, whether the heart rate response was an independent measure of the CER or a reflexive response to skeletal movement. After this experiment, we temporarily abandoned the avoidance situation, and began a series of parametric studies of classical heart rate conditioning. We found, however, that the effects of other responses (particularly skeletal responses) on heart rate created difficulties for the interpretation of the classical conditioning data just as they had done in avoidance conditioning (Lang & Black, 1963). Thus, in order to interpret the results of other avoidance and classical conditioning experiments, the relationship between heart

[1] The research described in this paper was supported by United States Public Health Service Grant MH-0274. C. Batenchuk, A. Dalton, L. de Toledo and W. Lang collaborated with the author on this work.

rate and skeletal responding had to be explored in more detail. The way in which we attacked this problem was to compare conditioning when skeletal responding could occur, with conditioning when it could not occur. We prevented skeletal responding by employing curare-like drugs to produce paralysis of the skeletal musculature. If skeletal responding does influence heart rate conditioning, marked differences between the conditioned heart rate response in the normal and curarized states should occur. In the present paper, we will first discuss the general nature of the relationship between heart and skeletal responding during conditioning, and then turn to the relevant data.

HEART RATE CONDITIONING AND SKELETAL ACTIVITY

Heart rate responses are produced by a wide variety of internal and external stimuli. Because of the complex homeostatic relationships involving the circulatory system, these stimuli can affect the heart rate in many different ways (Eichna & McQuarrie, 1960). The heart rate, in this sense, is a promiscuous response and as one might expect, often embarrasses those who are involved with it. This embarrassment, however, arises not from moral considerations, but rather from difficulties in experimenting on heart rate conditioning. There are two types of difficulties. The first is a methodological one. Because the heart rate is so open to influence, the variability of the data can be high. The second difficulty— and the one which is our concern—is the specification of the variables and internal mechanisms which are involved in producing a given change in heart rate during conditioning.

First of all, a change in heart rate can be reflexively elicited by proprioceptive feedback from some other non-cardiac response. It might be, as Smith (1954) has suggested, that only skeletal responses can be conditioned, and that heart rate responses are no more than artifacts elicited by feedback from these skeletal responses. Such considerations lead to the question, "Can a heart rate response be conditioned directly, or is it simply an artifact of some other response which is conditioned directly, and which reflexively produces changes in heart rate?" Shearn (1961), for example, has discussed this problem in some detail in an article entitled "Does the heart really learn?" without seeming to come to a definite conclusion.

Secondly, even if one concludes that the heart can be conditioned directly, changes in heart rate reflexively produced by other responses can, of course, still occur at the same time. For example, if heart rate and respiratory responses were conditioned simultaneously, the observed heart rate change might be a contaminated amalgam produced by two factors— one, direct conditioning, the other, feedback from the conditioned or (for that matter) unconditioned respiratory responses.

In both of the situations described above, the heart rate response (or some component of it) is supposed to be elicited by feedback from another response, and the relationship between the two types of responses is assumed to be "innate." In the third case the relationship between heart rate and skeletal activity is assumed to depend on conditioning, and one response is supposed to mediate or be chained to the other. Either feedback from a heart rate response acts as a CS for skeletal activity, or feedback from skeletal activity acts as a CS for a subsequent heart rate response. There are a wide variety of situations where a relationship of this type might occur; we will limit ourselves to avoidance conditioning in this discussion since much of the relevant research and theorizing has been done on this topic. Also, we will assume that heart rate can act as an index of a classically conditioned emotional response (CER) to the CS in avoidance conditioning.

Examples of theories which emphasize the role of feedback from the CER as a CS or motivator for the avoidance response are those of Mowrer (1947) and Solomon and Wynne (1954). First the CER is conditioned to the CS; then, termination of the CER reinforces the avoidance response, and feedback stimuli from the CER becomes CSs for the avoidance response. In this sense, the CER feedback acts as a drive stimulus to which avoidance behaviour is conditioned.

Mowrer (1960), in a more recent theory, emphasizes the opposite side of the coin. In this theory, the feedback from the avoidance response acts as a CS for a classically conditioned emotional response—the conditioned "relief" response. Termination of the CER acts as a UCS for the conditioning of the "relief" response to the feedback from the avoidance response. Thus the sequence of events for a well learned avoidance response involves two conditioned responses—firstly, the occurrence of a CER to the CS, and secondly, a conditioned "relief" response to feedback from avoidance.

Recently Soltysik and Kowalska (1960) have presented a theory of avoidance conditioning stemming from Konorski's (1948) earlier analysis in which both types of chaining are involved. The CER elicited by the CS is assumed to mediate the avoidance response, and feedback from the avoidance response is supposed to act as a stimulus leading to conditioned inhibition of the CER.

From this cursory review of avoidance theories it becomes clear that two types of chaining or mediation between the CER and the avoidance response are assumed to occur. In one, feedback from the classical CER acts as a stimulus for the operant avoidance response. In the other, feedback from the operant avoidance response acts as a CS for classically conditioned "relief" responses, or as a conditioned inhibitor of the CER.

For such theories, which assign a crucial role to the conditioning of one response to feedback from another, it would be important to determine which of the various types of relationships described above might be occurring. One example of a correlation between heart rate (as one index of a CER) and avoidance is that the heart rate is higher on trials during which an avoidance response occurs than on trials during which no avoidance response occurs (Black, 1959). This might be taken as support for the theories outlined above which argue that the CER mediates avoidance. If, however, one could find no evidence for direct conditioning of heart rate, one would be hesitant about such a conclusion; rather, one would be more likely to believe that the heart rate response was a reflex product of feedback from the skeletal operant response. Furthermore, even if direct heart rate conditioning did occur, a particular result might be produced by an amalgam of direct conditioning and feedback from skeletal responding. In order to interpret a result such as the one described above, the way in which a particular heart rate response was produced must be known. Thus, there are three questions which must be considered in attempting to understand the relationship between conditioned heart rate and skeletal responses:

1. Is the heart rate response nothing but an artifact of other responses—in particular, skeletal activity?
2. If the heart rate is directly conditioned, to what extent does feedback from other responses also affect the observed heart rate conditioned response?
3. Does the heart rate as a component of a classically conditioned emotional response enter into a response chain controlling or mediating operant skeletal behaviour, or vice versa?

In the experiments which are described below, we hoped to find evidence which would throw some light on these questions.

IS THE CONDITIONED HEART RATE RESPONSE AN ARTIFACT OF SKELETAL RESPONDING?

In our earlier work we found that heart rate conditioning did occur when observable skeletal responses were prevented by curare-like drugs (Black, Carlson, & Solomon, 1962). This research can be criticized, however, in that skeletal activity which was not detected by a gross visual examination could have occurred in the curarized dogs (Smith, 1964). Therefore, in the present experiment EMG was employed during heart rate conditioning as a measure of skeletal activity, and an attempt was made to observe heart rate conditioned responses when no skeletal responding as defined by the EMG was detected. Figure 2-1 shows data for a single dog conditioned under curare using a 4000 cycle tone as CS+, and a 4 ma. shock UCS. For this dog CS+ and UCS were paired on all trials. Record A shows acquisition trial 3, and record B acquisition trial

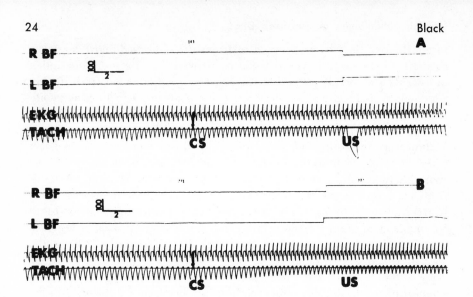

Fig. 2-1. Heart rate (channels 3 and 4) and muscle potentials (channels 1 and 2) during Pavlovian conditioning in the curarized state for dog S-4. *Record A:* Acquisition trial 1. This trial followed the administration of 36 mg. of d-Tubocurarine Chloride over 90 minutes. *Record B:* Acquisition trial 16. This trial followed the administration of 102 mg. of d-Tubocurarine Chloride over 210 minutes. *Calibrations:* Time, 2 seconds; EMG amplitude, 100 uv. (Black & Lang, 1964)

16. In each record the top two channels present muscle potential (EMG), the third heart rate (EKG), and the fourth presents a tachographic recording of the heart rate. A signal marker is superimposed on the fourth channel. The tachograph presents each interbeat interval as a vertical distance. The shorter the interval between beats (and the faster the heart rate), the less is the vertical displacement of the pen. The onset of the CS is represented by an arrow above the signal marker, and the occurrence of the UCS is represented by a solid bar on the signal marker line. In order to avoid 60 cycle noise the muscle potential channels were switched off during shock presentation.

On the 16th acquisition trial (record B) there was a clear-cut heart rate response (the difference in rate during the 10″ CS-UCS interval and the 10″ preceding CS onset was approximately 33 beats per minute) but no apparent change in the EMG. For this dog a cardiac conditioned response occurred with no detectable movement.

Even if one assumes that some form of skeletal behaviour which we failed to detect does occur in curarized dogs, there is some further evidence of the independence of skeletal and heart rate responding. If skeletal and heart rate responses are intimately related, then we would expect a change in one to occur when a change in the other occurred. Thus, if we drastically affect skeletal activity, we would also expect to find a change in cardiac activity, and vice versa. Figure 2-2 presents evi-

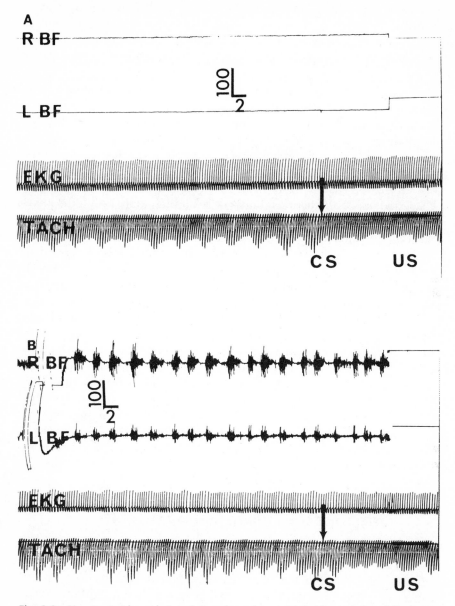

Fig. 2-2. Heart rate (channels 3 and 4) and muscle potentials (channels 1 and 2), during Pavlovian conditioning in dog S-3. *Record A:* A conditioning trial under complete curarization. This trial followed the administration of 42 mg. of d-Tubocurarine Chloride over 140 minutes. *Record B:* A conditioning trial after the administration of Tensilon which produced partial recovery of skeletal activity. This trial occurred approximately three hours following the trial shown in Record A. *Calibrations:* Time, 2 seconds; EMG amplitude, 100 uv. (Black & Lang, 1964)

dence on this point. Record A shows a conditioned cardiac response in a curarized dog. The procedure was the same as that described above in Figure 2-1. There is an obvious heart rate response to the CS but no apparent EMG response. Three hours after completion of the conditioning phase of the experiment, Tensilon was administered in order to counteract the effects of curare, and further conditioning trials were run. One such trial is shown in record B. The amount of Tensilon injected permitted partial recovery of skeletal responding. At this stage of recovery, the skeletal activity consisted mainly of bursts of trembling and shivering in phase with the respiratory cycle. This behaviour pattern is common among dogs recovering from curare paralysis when body temperature drops.

In the top channel of record B, skeletal activity is higher during the CS period (especially between bursts of trembling) than during the pre-CS period. In the bottom channel, there is a heart rate response during the CS-UCS interval. However, there is no such parallel between the skeletal activity and cardiac responses in the curarized state (record A). Furthermore, if the heart rate response were completely determined by skeletal activity, we would expect *similar patterns* of skeletal activity in the two states shown in A and B, since the cardiac responses were similar. This was not the case; thus it would seem that there is considerable independence between the skeletal and heart rate responses. Research on normal dogs in which both cardiac and skeletal classically conditioned responses are measured also shows that the two types of responses do change independently during conditioning. (Gantt, 1960; Jaworska, Kowalska, & Soltysik, 1962). These data are in accord with the results just described.

While we, of course, have not proved that skeletal activity of some vestigial sort does not occur in curarized subjects, these data do suggest that heart rate responding and skeletal behaviour are not necessarily correlated.

TO WHAT EXTENT DOES FEEDBACK FROM SKELETAL BEHAVIOUR AFFECT THE CONDITIONED CARDIAC RESPONSE?

While individual examples such as those presented in the previous section are relevant to an extreme position which maintains that cardiac responses are nothing but artifacts, they do not provide us with adequate information concerning the extent to which concomitant skeletal behaviour influences heart rate responding to a CS. If these skeletal responses play a significant role in determining the heart rate response in the normal state we would expect conditioning in the normal and curarized states to be different, since the skeletal responses are prevented in the curarized state. Differences of two types could occur. First of all, if the skeletal behaviour contributes to the variability of the heart rate responses in the normal state, we would expect a reduction in variability under curare. Secondly, if a *stable* [2] skeletal response elicited by the CS contributes to the heart rate response in the normal state, we might expect a change in the magnitude or in the pattern of the heart rate response under curare. In order to compare conditioning in the normal and curarized states we performed the following experiment.

Method. In these experiments a discriminative conditioning procedure was employed. Ten dogs were conditioned in the normal state and compared to ten dogs conditioned in the curarized state. Five dogs in each group were conditioned with a high intensity white noise as the CS+ and low intensity white noise as the CS−; five with a low intensity white noise as the CS+ and a high intensity white noise as the CS−. The UCS was a 4.0 ma. shock. Control dogs were also run (six in the normal state and six in the curarized state) and received presentations of the CS+, CS−, and UCS but the CSs were never paired with the UCS. Only 15 presentations of each CS were given to the control dogs. On each trial, the CS-UCS interval was 10 sec. and the UCS duration 5 sec. A delayed conditioning procedure was employed with the UCS and CS terminating at the same time. The intertrial interval averaged 2 minutes.

The experimental session was divided into three phases. First of all, auditory stimuli which were to be used as CSs were presented alone. These presentations were followed by 10 paired presentations of the CS+ and UCS. Then followed differential conditioning. The CS which had been previously paired with shock continued to be paired with shock (CS+). Another CS was presented and never paired with shock (CS−). The presentations of CS+ and CS− occurred in a fixed irregular order. Each dog received 65 trials of differential conditioning. Two blocks of thirty trials (each containing 15 CS+ and 15 CS− trials) were separated by a block of five CS− trials. The 5 CS− trials were not included in the analysis of the data.

Heavy dose levels of d-Tubocurarine were employed in order to prevent skeletal activity. They ranged from 40 to 92 mg. Curarization was

[2] All of this is complicated further by the research of Sołtysik and Jaworska (1962) which provides evidence for stable classical conditioning of skeletal responses using aversive reinforcers. Results such as these create problem of distinguishing between skeletal classical conditioned responses, and skeletal operant conditioned responses to the CS. If the skeletal response which is reflexively producing a heart rate change is under the control of classical conditioning variables, the problem would not be serious; both directly and indirectly controlled heart rate responses would reflect the same underlying process. If, however, the skeletal response which is producing a heart rate change is under the control of operant conditioning variables, errors in interpretation might occur. The heart rate response which we assume to be controlled by classical conditioning would be influenced by operant conditioning.

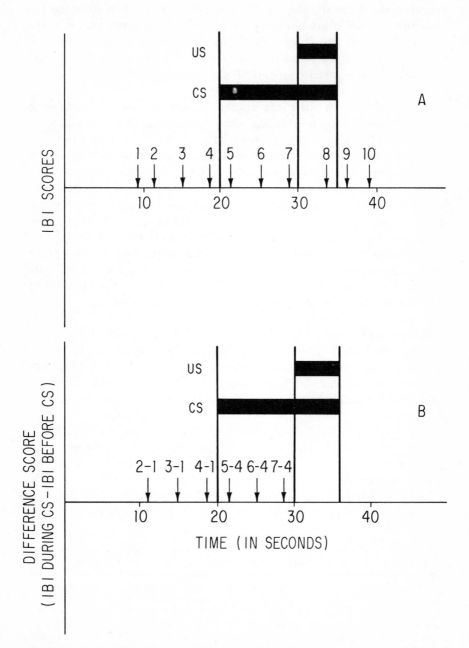

Fig. 2-3. (A) The points in time during a single trial when heart rate measurements were taken. (B) The pairs of differences used to measure the response to the CS (5-4), (6-4), (7-4), and the response during a control period before CS onset, (2-1), (3-1), (4-1).

carried out by injecting d-Tubocurarine Chloride [3] intravenously through a polyethylene catheter. The d-Tubocurarine was injected slowly until respiratory failure occurred. An endotracheal tube was then inserted, and artificial respiration begun. Drug injections were continued throughout the course of the experiment in order to maintain the proper depth of curarization.

Measurement—The law of initial values and the form of the heart rate response. The time required for two complete beats (identified by the QRS complex) was the basic measurement. This was calculated to the nearest .01 sec., and was called the IBI (interbeat interval). The heart rate was measured in this way just before CS onset, 1 sec. after CS onset, 5 sec. after CS onset, and just before CS termination; also just before UCS termination, 1 sec. after UCS termination, and 5 sec. after UCS termination. In addition a point 10 sec. before CS onset was identified and measurements were made just before this point, 1 sec. after and 5 sec. after it. Thus 10 measurements were made on each trial, as shown in Figure 2-3A.

The differences between the measurements during the CS and the measurement immediately preceding CS onset (5-4), (6-4), (7-4), give an index of the response to the CS at different times during the CS-UCS interval. The differences between measurements all of which occur before CS onset, (2-1), (3-1), and (4-1), give us the response when no stimulus is present (Figure 2-3B).

In this experiment "heart rate response" is used as a general term. In order to distinguish which particular measure is being discussed, the time required for the occurrence of two beats will be called the IBI score, and its reciprocal, which is actually a rate measure, the R score. The relationship between them is as follows: $R = \dfrac{1200}{IBI}$. The R score is given in beats per minute, and the IBI score in $\dfrac{milliseconds}{50}$.

Problems concerning the appropriate methods for measuring heart rate in this experiment stem from two sources—the differences between groups in baseline level of heart rate (the rate when no stimuli are being applied), and differences in the form of the conditioned response (the changes in direction of the heart rate during the CS-UCS interval).

There was a significant difference between curarized and normal groups in the level of the baseline heart rate. As can be seen from Figure 2-4, curarized dogs had a higher baseline than normal dogs. This baseline heart rate effect makes it difficult to compare groups using the measures of differences between the heart rate at 2 points in time or measures of

[3] The d-Tubocurarine Chloride was supplied by E. R. Squibb and Sons of Canada Ltd.

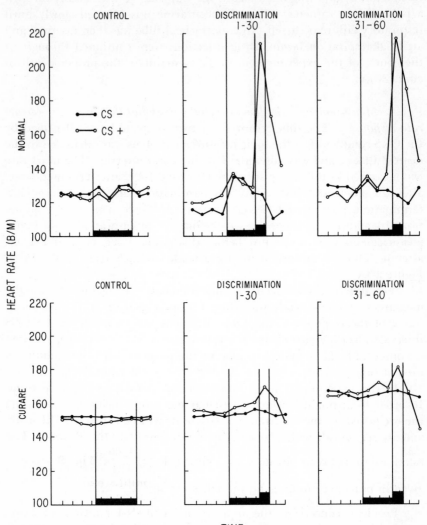

Fig. 2-4. Heart rate responses for control dogs receiving no pairings of CS and UCS, and experimental dogs receiving pairings of CS+ and UCS. Data are shown for both normal and curarized dogs. For the experimental dogs the first and last thirty discriminative conditioning trials are presented separately. The lower solid bar represents CS duration; the upper solid bar UCS duration. The measurements of heart rate were taken at the points in time shown in Fig. 2-3A.

variability. When there is a difference in baseline rate, the results will depend on the particular measure that is employed. For example, the response to the CS is often measured by taking a difference score (e. g., rate during the CS-UCS interval minus rate during the pre-CS period). That the magnitude of this difference score can be drastically affected by choosing appropriately transformed measures of heart rate is illustrated in Figure 2-5 where the relationship between the IBI and R measures is plotted, and two hypothetical examples of heart rate responses are shown. In one example the pre-CS level (B_1) is 20 IBI units and the level during the CS-UCS interval (C_1) is 16 units; the difference score for the response during the CS-UCS interval is 4 IBI units. In the other example the pre-CS level (B_2) is 10 IBI units and the level during the CS-UCS interval (C_2) is 8 units; the difference score for the response during the CS-UCS interval is 2 IBI units. When the original scores are transformed to rates (R scores), then as can be seen from Figure 2-5, the larger difference now becomes the smaller difference. Thus, in this particular example, the rank order of the magnitude of the difference scores was reversed by the transformation. It is obvious then that the results of a comparison of the magnitude of difference scores is specific to the particular measure of heart rate that is employed. This argument also holds for measures of variability of baseline heart rate levels (as is illustrated, of course, in variance equalizing transformations).

A number of remedies for this difficulty can be suggested. First, of course, one can simply count the number of CR's (provided that a CR can be unambiguously defined). Second, one can use the difference score, as described above, but express this as a ratio using some measure of each subject's own variability as the denominator. Since the variability changes with the baseline, we might be able to use it to provide a control for the baseline effect. Finally, one can use an order statistic derived from a within-subject analysis of the difference scores over a series of trials (provided the baseline rate stays constant over those trials). Normally we would use order statistics to make a significance test. However, just as we often use the Z both as a transformation for a given measure and as a statistic in a significance test, we can use these order statistics in the same manner. We explored the last of these alternatives in analyzing the results of the present paper.

The index which we employed to measure the response to the CS was Wilcoxon's T statistic. This statistic depends on the sign and the magnitude of the difference between pairs of correlated measures. If the differences all have the same sign, T is 0. If there are only a few small differences with one sign, T has a low positive value. If there are a few large differences with one sign, T has a larger positive value. If there are the same number of positive and negative differences, and if these are of the same magnitude, T is 60. (T was computed in each case using 15 observations; zero scores were divided evenly between positive and negative differences.) T was computed for the difference between the IBI score during the CS and IBI score immediately preceding CS onset. T,

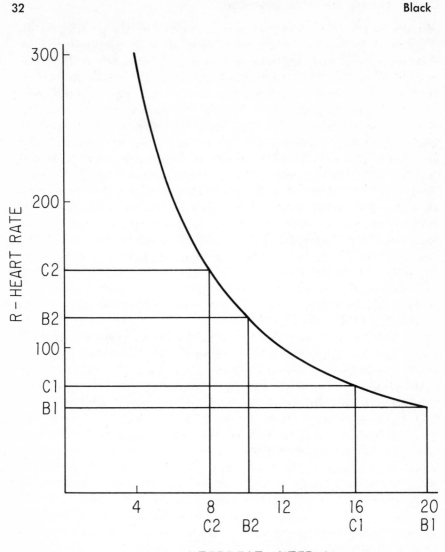

Fig. 2-5. The relationship of the time between the QRS complexes (IBI) and the heart rate (R). R is the reciprocal of IBI. See text for explanation of C and B points.

used in this way, tells us whether a given dog tends to respond to the CS in a consistent manner from trial to trial.

The Mann-Whitney U statistic was employed as an index of discrimination. This statistic gives a measure of overlap between two independent sets of observations—in this case responses to the CS+ and to the CS−. If all the CS+ responses are greater than the CS− responses, U is 0.

If the CS+ and CS− responses overlap so that neither is greater, U is 112.5 (for 15 observations on CS+ and 15 observations on CS− which were the values employed in our calculations; in those cases where observations were missing, corrections were made by adding an observation at the median value). If all the CS− responses are greater in magnitude than the CS+ responses, U is 225.

The second methodological difficulty is concerned with the form of the conditioned response (the direction of the response and the pattern of rate changes during the CS-UCS interval). In the present experiment there were considerable individual differences [4] in the form of the response. Of the 20 experimental dogs, 11 showed an increase in rate during the CS-UCS interval, 5 showed a decrease in rate, and 4 showed some pattern involving both increases and decreases. These individual differences add to the variability of the data in between-group comparisons of some measure of magnitude of response. For example, in Figure 2-6, data are shown for 2 dogs conditioned in the normal state using a 3 ma. UCS. The CS+ was a 4000 cycle per second tone; the CS− a 400 cycle per second tone. (This was a relatively easy discrimination.) The difference between the mean heart rate during the 10″ CS-UCS interval and the 10″ preceding CS onset is plotted for each trial. As can be seen a stable differentiation rapidly developed in both dogs; however, the response to the CS+ was an acceleration in one case, and a deceleration in the other. If the mean difference between CS+ and CS− for each dog in Figure 2-6 were taken, and the data averaged over both dogs, it would look as though no differentiation had occurred. One way of avoiding this problem is to disregard the direction of the conditioned response. Thus, one dog's T score of 0 for which every response to the CS was an acceleration would be considered equal to another dog's T score of 0 for which every response to the CS was a deceleration. This makes a certain intuitive sense, provided, of course, the responses were consistent within a given subject even though they differed in direction. This procedure was employed in the present experiment for all comparisons except those for which the form of the response was being considered.

Turning now to the results, we will consider first the baseline heart rate and its variability, and then the conditioned heart rate response.

[4] The form of the conditioned heart rate response is a function not only of individual difference among dogs; it is also affected by the parameters of conditioning. We first observed this during heart rate conditioning in curarized dogs (Black, Carlson, & Solomon, 1962). Trace conditioning procedures seemed more likely to produce a deceleration during the CS-US interval than delayed conditioning procedures. Leaf (1963) has subsequently reported that this effect has been confirmed in his research. More recently we have been working on the effects of UCS intensity, and this variable also seems to affect the form of the response. In experiments using normal dogs and shock intensities of 3, 4, and 8 ma. there seemed to be more decelerative responses at the low shock intensities than at the high shock intensities (Lang & Black, 1963).

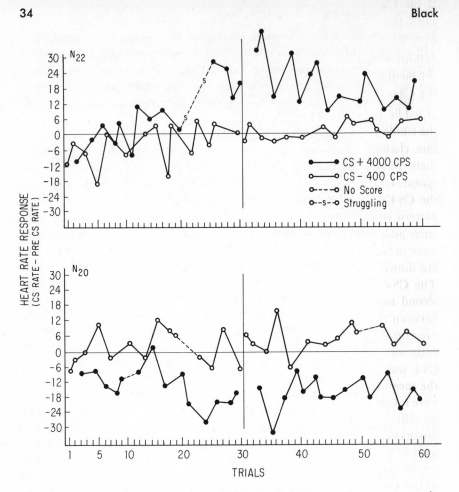

Fig. 2-6. Heart rate responding during differential conditioning. The response to the CS+ and CS− are plotted for each of 2 dogs conditioned at 3 ma.

The baseline rate under curare was higher than in the normal state (Figure 2-4). There were also differences between curarized and normal dogs in variability of the baseline. The curarized dogs showed less variability (both between subject variability and within subject variability from trial to trial) than the normal dogs on the IBI measure. As was pointed out earlier the results of comparisons such as those on variability are specific to the particular rate measure employed. There is, however, further evidence that suggests that curarized dogs do have less variable heart rates than normal dogs. As can be seen from Figure 2-4, the heart rate of curarized dogs was higher than that of normals during the intertrial interval and lower than that of normals during UCS presentations. Thus, the effect of curare was not simply to increase the baseline heart rate; rather it was to "lock" the heart rate at a high level so that even very strong stimuli such as electric shock could not elevate the heart rate to the level which occurred to shock in the normal state. This suggests that the variability of the heart rate in curarized subjects is less—at least, in response to stimulation.

There were no apparent differences between curarized and normal dogs in the form of the heart rate response to the CS+. Five normal and six curarized dogs maintained an increase in rate throughout the CS-UCS interval; three normal and two curarized dogs maintained a decreased rate throughout the CS-UCS interval; two normal and two curarized dogs showed a pattern combining increases and decreases in rate throughout the CS-UCS interval.

The data on the T measures of stability or consistency of response are shown in Figure 2-7. A score of 0 indicates maximum stability; 60 indicates an unstable response. An analysis of the T scores during the CS+ shows no significant difference between curarized and normal dogs. The results for CS— are different. Between group comparison of the T scores during the CS— shows a significant difference. The normal dogs displayed more stable responding to the CS— than the curarized dogs. It would seem that normal dogs showed a consistent response to both the CS+ and CS— while curarized dogs showed a consistent response only to the CS+.

Finally, the normal and curarized dogs were compared on the overlap between the response to the CS+ and CS— in order to determine whether the groups differed on discrimination. For each dog the difference between the IBI scores during the CS and the IBI score immediately preceding CS onset was computed for the 15 CS+'s and 15 CS—'s; then the overlap between these CS+ and CS— difference scores was determined using the Mann Whitney U statistic. This was done for each of the difference scores shown in Figure 2-3B. The mean of the U indices is shown in Table 2-1 for the control dogs, and for the first and last 30 discrimination training trials of the experimental dogs separately. As can be seen from Table 2-1 the U scores were high during the last thirty trials of discriminative conditioning among both control and experimental dogs; the discrimination had not been well established by the end of the experiment for either normal or curarized groups. The curarized dogs, however, did seem to show less overlap between CS+ and CS— than normal dogs during the first 30 trials of discriminative conditioning.

In discussing these results, I would like to deal first with the lack of difference between normal and curarized dogs in the form of the response and consistency of the response to the CS+. One explanation for these results is related to the level of curarization which was reached in the present experiment. Large doses of d-Tubocurarine have effects beyond the simple prevention of skeletal behaviour—effects which could interfere

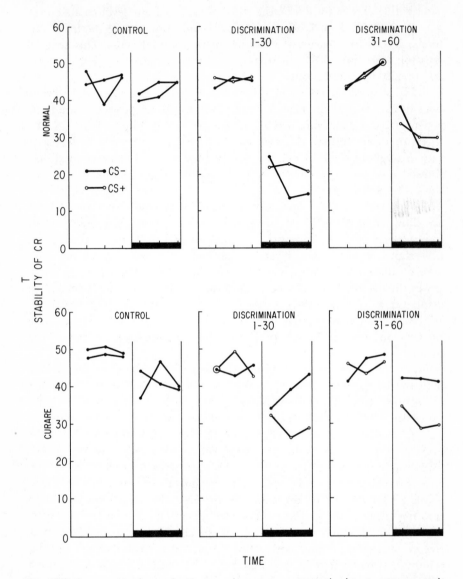

Fig. 2-7. T scores (the lower the T score, the more consistent the heart rate response) for control dogs receiving no pairing of CS and UCS, and experimental dogs receiving pairings of CS and UCS. Data are shown for normal and curarized dogs. For the experimental dogs the first and last thirty discriminative conditioning trials are presented separately. The solid bar represents CS duration. Scores were taken for the differences shown in Fig. 2-3B.

with conditioning (Miner, 1951). Thus, it may be that our curare procedure, which was originally designed to overcome artifacts occurring in

Table 2-1———U indices of overlap between CS+ and CS− during discriminative conditioning for both normal and curarized dogs

CONTROL

	Pre-CS			During CS-UCS Interval		
NORMAL	103.4	83.4	98.2	97.0	97.4	109.8
CURARIZED	98.5	101.2	101.1	96.5	86.8	101.9

DISCRIMINATIVE CONDITIONING
(Trials 1-30)

	Pre-CS			During CS-UCS Interval		
NORMAL	102.3	103.2	114.9	121.3	112.6	100.0
CURARIZED	95.2	101.3	95.9	104.1	79.6	74.3

DISCRIMINATIVE CONDITIONING
(Trials 31-60)

	Pre-CS			During CS-UCS Interval		
NORMAL	104.6	105.1	107.5	109.4	89.3	85.4
CURARIZED	92.9	98.2	98.0	85.8	87.6	81.1

the normal state, produces artifacts of its own which disrupt conditioning. In the normal state we assumed that problems arose because the heart rate was too variable or noisy because of struggling. In the curarized state it may be that problems arose when overdoses were given and the heart rate became unresponsive. There is some support for this hypothesis in that the three normal dogs (out of 10) which failed to show a stable response to the CS+ ranked 1, 2 and 7 in amount of baseline heart rate variability when compared with the other normal dogs; the three curarized dogs (out of 10) which failed to show a stable heart rate response to the CS+ ranged 6.5, 9, and 10 in amount of baseline heart rate variability when compared with other curarized dogs. Dogs which failed to condition in the normal state seemed to have the highest variability in their group, while dogs which failed to condition in the curarized state seemed to have the lowest variability in their group. (Further evidence supporting a lack of responsiveness under curare was presented in discussing the response to the UCS.) If the above conjectures are correct we might expect lightly curarized dogs to show the best conditioning since both interference from struggling in the normal state and interference from too much curare are prevented. We are presently carrying out research on such dogs.

In the light of these data showing no difference between curarized and normal dogs, it was somewhat surprising to find that curarized dogs seemed to show a more stable response to the CS+ than to the CS— and also displayed less overlap between CS+ and CS— than normal dogs at first. The basis for this is not clear. It might be that feedback from struggling, barking, etc. which occur in the normal state interfere with the discrimination between the CS's at first; in the curarized state no such interference would, of course, occur. Or it may be that the effect of curare is to reduce variability in exteroceptive input since the dog cannot move its head, and is, therefore, exposed to a more constant auditory CS. Either of these factors might have acted to decrease generalization under curare early in discriminative conditioning.

In summary, the experiment reported above compared conditioning in the normal and curarized states in order to study the effect of skeletal behaviour on heart rate conditioning. There was little difference between normal and curarized dogs on the form and stability of the heart rate response to the CS+. There was, however, less variability under curare in the sense that the magnitude of response to UCS was less. Also, curarized dogs showed a less stable response to the CS— and, initially, seemed to show less overlap between the CS+ and CS— than normal dogs. It would seem then that concomitant skeletal responses do not affect the form and stability of the heart rate response; this conclusion, however, can be made only tentatively until further data (especially on the effects of curare) are obtained.

WHAT IS THE RELATIONSHIP BETWEEN CONCOMITANT HEART RATE AND AVOIDANCE BEHAVIOUR?

There have been a number of attempts to study the correlation between the CER and avoidance—some using the conditioned suppression technique (Hoffman & Fleshler, 1962; Kamin, Brimer, & Black, 1963), and others employing heart rate (Black, 1959; Soltysik & Kowalska, 1960; Wenzel, 1961; Stern & Ward, 1962; Perez-Cruet, Tolliver, Dunn, Marvin, & Brady, 1963). In these experiments two types of relationships have been explored—the CER as a CS for, or mediator of, subsequent avoidance, and the avoidance as a determiner of the subsequent changes in the CER. In the latter case an additional source of control over the CER can occur— that is, CS termination. In this paper, because of the limitations of space, we will discuss only the relationship between the avoidance response and subsequent changes in the CER using the heart rate as an index of the CER. We will first discuss the evidence for a correlation betwen avoidance responding and subsequent heart rate responding, and then turn to a comparison of the relative importance of CS termination and feedback from the avoidance response in controlling the subsequent heart rate response.

In the theories of avoidance which we described earlier, the reduction of the CER was assumed to play a major role as a source of reinforcement: either as a form of drive reduction reinforcing the operant avoidance response (Mowrer, 1947; Solomon & Wynne, 1954), or as a UCS leading to the conditioning of "relief" responses to feedback from the avoidance response (Mowrer, 1960). In a third theory, feedback from the avoidance response was assumed to act as a conditioned inhibitor (Soltysik & Kowalska, 1960) which produced a decrease in the magnitude of the CER. All three theories would predict a decrease in the CER following the termination of the CS and the simultaneous occurrence of the avoidance response.

Thus, if these theories are correct, and if the heart rate is a component of the CER, we might expect a rapid drop in the heart rate response following CS termination. (In the following section we will use the phrase "CS termination" to mean "CS termination and/or avoidance" since the two always occurred together.) Previous research has not confirmed this expectation. In an experiment on avoidance conditioning in dogs (Black, 1959) the heart rate response to the CS (when measured just after the dog had begun to avoid on every trial) did not reach its maximum and begin to decline until 2 to 3 seconds after CS termination. Soltysik and Kowalska (1961), studying a well established avoidance, found that after CS termination there was a rapid drop in heart rate for two dogs, a fairly slow deceleration for one dog, and an acceleration for a fourth dog. These results suggest that CS termination does not produce an immediate decrement in the heart rate response, as the theories described above would have predicted. It may be, however, that the delay in the heart rate decrease following CS termination simply reflects a delay in reinforcement. Avoidance conditioning was slow in the experiments in which heart rate was measured, and delay of reinforcement may be one of the reasons. Thus, we would expect that certain manipulations that affect the rate at which avoidance conditioning occurs would also affect the heart rate response following CS termination. Presumably the delay in reinforcement would be less when acquisition of avoidance was rapid, and more when avoidance acquisition was slow. Thus, for avoidance procedures leading to rapid acquisition, the decrement in the heart rate following CS termination should occur more quickly than for avoidance procedures leading to slow acquisition.

The following experiment which was designed to test this hypothesis is being conducted in our laboratory. Rats were trained to avoid shock by running from the black to the white compartment of a one-way Miller avoidance box. Heart rate was recorded from electrodes placed under the skin over the rib cage; insulated wires ran from the electrodes to an Amphenol connector which was firmly cemented to the skull. Speed of acquisition of the avoidance response was controlled by preshocking the rats in the Miller box. Three groups of rats were employed. Rats in one group (the conflict group) were preshocked in the white compartment of the Miller box. This was the compartment into which the rats were required to run during subsequent avoidance conditioning; consequently, the preshocks hindered acquisition. Rats in a second group (the facilitation group) were preshocked in the black compartment. This was the compartment from which the rats ran during subsequent avoidance conditioning; consequently the preshocks facilitated acquisition. A third group was given no preshocks; this produced a rate of acquisition midway between the first two groups.

Preliminary results are shown in Figure 2-8. Data are shown for the final criterion trial (the 10th consecutive avoidance). The heart rate for each of the three groups on the 10 seconds following CS termination is shown. The group which learned most slowly (the "conflict" group) had a high heart rate with a long delay before the heart rate began to decrease; the intermediate group (given no preshock) showed a more rapid decrease in the heart rate response; the group which learned most quickly (the "facilitation" group) showed an increase in the heart rate and then a rapid decrease.

These data show a relationship between speed of acquisition of avoidance and heart rate responding following CS termination. The relationship, however, is not the simple one which was predicted originally. The decrease in heart rate occurred more quickly in the no preshock group than in the conflict group as predicted; the facilitation group which learned the avoidance most quickly and, therefore, should have shown a rapid decrease in heart rate, displayed instead an increase followed by a decrease. It is still too soon to determine the variables which control these patterns of responding; it seems unlikely, however, that the patterns of responding shown in Figure 2-8 can be attributed to artifacts produced by skeletal behaviour, since all the rats made the avoidance response, there were no significant differences in latency of avoidance, and there were no obvious differences in the amount of activity following avoidance.

Supposing that one does accept that there is a correlation between avoidance and heart rate and that this correlation is not a spurious one produced by skeletal activity. The question still remains as to the roles of CS termination and of the avoidance response and its feedback as CSs for the subsequent heart rate response. Although the evidence is fragmentary and incomplete, we do have data which suggest that CS termination is more important than the occurrence of the avoidance response in controlling the subsequent heart rate response. These data come from current research on the extinction of avoidance under curare in dogs, an

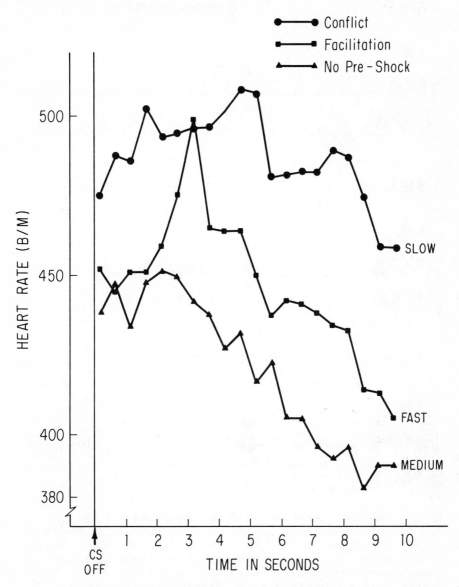

Fig. 2-8. The heart rate response following termination of a CS which was contingent on an avoidance response. The heart rate was measured at half-second intervals. (The first interbeat interval after each half second was measured.) Data are shown for three groups of rats which differed in the preshock procedure to which they were subjected before avoidance training began. Rats in the "facilitation" group learned the avoidance response quickly (labeled "fast"). Rats in the no-preshock control group learned the avoidance response at an intermediate rate (labeled "medium"). Rats in the "conflict" group learned the avoidance response most slowly (labeled "slow").

41

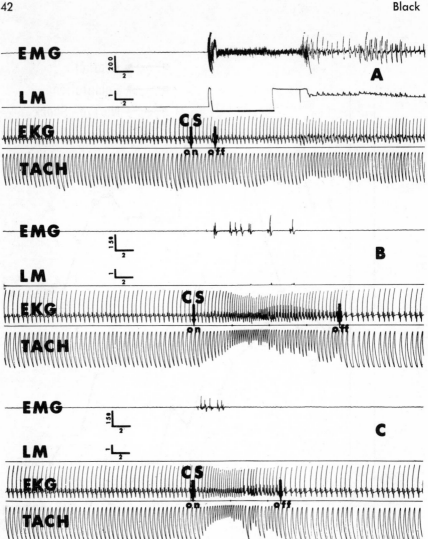

Fig. 2-9. Heart rate (channels 3 and 4), muscle potentials (channel 1), and leg movements (channel 2) for dog C-2 during avoidance conditioning. Data are shown for 3 trials. *Record A:* The last avoidance trial in the normal state. *Records B and C:* The first and second trials in the curarized state. In channel 2, both vertical leg movements and pedal presses are presented; when a pedal press occurs the marker drops below the baseline and remains there until the pedal is released. CS termination was contingent on a pedal press in the normal state, and on a five-second period with no EMG response in the curarized state. *Calibration:* Time, 2 seconds; EMG amplitude, (normal) 200 uv., (curarized) 150 uv., vertical leg movements, 1 cm. (this scale is nonlinear). (Black & Dalton, 1965)

attempt to extend our and Solomon's earlier work on this problem (Black, 1958; Solomon & Turner, 1962).

Results bearing on this point are shown in Figures 2-9 and 2-10. Each figure shows data for a single dog. The dogs were first conditioned to avoid shock by depressing a foot pedal in the normal state. The CS was a white noise, and the CS-UCS interval was 10 seconds. Once the avoidance response was well established, the dogs were curarized and given 50 trials under curare. The dogs were curarized lightly in order to permit small EMG responses, and prevent movement of the foreleg (on some trials very slight movements of 2 or 3 mms. did occur). Following curarization the dogs were allowed to recover and given extinction trials in the normal state. The only difference between the two dogs was in the procedure employed under curare. For one dog CS termination (Figure 2-10) occurred only after an EMG response; for the other dog CS termination (Figure 2-9) occurred after 5 seconds with no EMG response. We expected that reinforcement of the EMG response by CS termination would increase resistance to extinction of pedal pressing in the normal state, and that the 5 second delay of CS termination would speed up extinction of pedal dressing.

In Figures 2-9 and 2-10, the records A and D show data for the last trial in the normal state; records B and E, the first trial under curare; and records C and F, the 2nd trial under curare. In each record, channel 1 shows the EMG, channel 2 the vertical movement of the leg and the pedal press, channel 2 the EKG, and channel 4 the cardiotachograph.

For both dogs there was very little heart rate responding to the CS on the last avoidance trial in the normal state (record A in Figure 2-9, and record D in Figure 2-10). When CS termination occurred immediately after an EMG response in the curarized state there was still very little heart rate responding (records E and F, Figure 2-10). However, when CS termination was delayed until 5 seconds had passed without an EMG response, a full-blown heart rate response occurred (records B and C, Figure 2-9).

These data suggest that it is CS termination more than feedback from avoidance behaviour which controls the subsequent heart rate response. In both dogs the avoidance response failed to occur under curare; if only feedback from the avoidance response were controlling heart rate, then we would expect no prevention or diminution in the heart rate response. When CS termination occurred shortly after CS onset there was little heart rate responding. The heart rate response was similar to that occurring in the normal state. A heart rate response, however, did occur when CS termination was delayed. This suggests that CS termination prevents or diminishes the CER, and delay of CS termination allows the heart rate response to occur; further, whether the avoidance response occurred or not seemed to have little effect.

There is some evidence to suggest that the EMG response could act in much the same way as the complete pedal pressing response. When CS

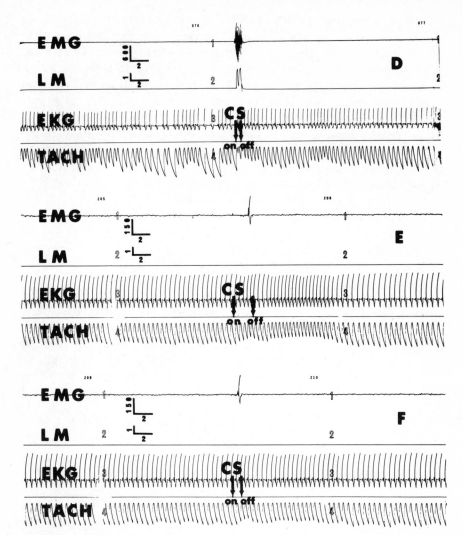

Fig. 2-10. Heart rate (channels 3 and 4), muscle potentials (channel 1), and leg movements (channel 2) for dog NC-7 during avoidance conditioning. Data are shown for 3 trials. *Record D:* The last avoidance trial in the normal state. *Records E and F:* The first and second trials in the curarized state. In channel 2, both vertical leg movements and pedal presses are presented; when a pedal press occurs the marker drops below the baseline and remains there until the pedal is released. CS termination was contingent on a pedal press in the normal state, and on an EMG response in the curarized state. *Calibrations:* Time, 2 seconds; EMG amplitude (normal) 600 uv., (curarized) 150 uv.; vertical leg movements, 1 cm. (this scale is nonlinear). (Black & Dalton, 1965)

termination was made contingent on the EMG response, the pedal pressing response failed to extinguish in 400 trials in the normal state. When the termination of the CS was made contingent on a five second period with *no* EMG response, the pedal pressing response extinguished in 65 trials in the normal state. It would seem that reinforcement of the EMG or of some response incompatible with the EMG had an effect on pedal pressing which was similar to reinforcement of pedal pressing or of responses incompatible with it. If this is true, then the full occurrence of a response and its associated feedback is not necessary for the modification of that response by operant reinforcement.[5] One might be tempted to conclude that the reinforcement of "intentions to respond" is effective in much the same way as reinforcement of the response itself in this situation.

Thus, one could argue that the EMG response was a component of the avoidance response, and as such provided enough feedback to elicit the "relief response" or to act as a conditioned inhibitor. But this does not seem likely since the EMG response occurred in both dogs and we would, therefore, have expected the heart rate response to be similar in both dogs. Instead, the heart rate response was different, and was correlated with the delay of CS termination.

It would seem then that while there are correlations between avoidance behaviour and subsequent heart rate responses, the avoidance response and its feedback do not seem to control the occurrence of subsequent heart rate changes. Rather, the heart rate response seems to be under the control of CS termination. Thus for this particular correlation, chaining of responses or the mediation of one response by another does not seem to play an important role.

SUMMARY AND CONCLUSIONS

In the present paper the following points were made in discussing the relationship between heart rate and skeletal behaviour. First of all, the evidence does not support the hypothesis that heart rate responses are only artifacts of skeletal responses. Secondly, there is little difference in the form and stability of heart rate responses to the CS+ between dogs conditioned in the curarized and normal states. The interpretation of these results was made difficult because factors interfering with the heart rate conditioning occurred in the curarized state as well as in the normal state. The curarized preparation, however, seemed to have an advantage with respect to the normal; curarized dogs showed less stable responding to the CS−, and also a suggestion of less overlap between CS+ and CS− during the early stages of discriminative conditioning. Finally, the role of the avoidance response as a CS for heart rate responses was discussed.

---

[5] There is further evidence that feedback from the avoidance response is not necessary for the maintenance of that response. Gorska and Jankowska (1961) have shown that deafferentation does not result in a loss of the avoidance response.

While the two are correlated, they do not seem to be chained. The prevention of the avoidance response does not seem to affect heart rate responding which occurs after CS termination.

References

BLACK, A. H. The extinction of avoidance responses under curare. *J. comp. physiol. Psychol.*, 1958, *51*, 519-524.

BLACK, A. H. Heart rate changes during avoidance learning in dogs. *Canad. J. Psychol.*, 1959, *13*, 229-242.

BLACK, A. H., CARLSON, N. J., & SOLOMON, R. L. Exploratory studies of the conditioning of autonomic responses in curarized dogs. *Psychol. Monogr.*, 1962, V. *76*, whole no. 548.

BLACK, A. H., & DALTON, A. J. The relationship between the avoidance response and subsequent changes in heart rate. *Acta Biol. Exp.*, 1965, *25*, in press.

BLACK, A. H., & LANG, W. M. Cardiac conditioning and skeletal responding in curarized dogs. *Psychol. rev.*, 1964, *71*, 80-85.

EICHNA, L. W., & McQUARRIE, D. G. (Eds.) Central nervous system control of circulation. *Physiol. Rev.*, 1960, *40*, Suppl. #4.

GANTT, W. H. Cardiovascular component of the conditional reflex to pain, food and other stimuli. *Physiol. Rev.*, 1960, *40*, Suppl. #4, Part 2, 266-291.

GORSKA, T., & JANKOWSKA, E. The effects of deafferentation on instrumental (Type II) conditioned reflexes in cats. *Acta Biol. Exp.*, 1961, *21*, 219-233.

HOFFMAN, H. S., & FLESHLER, M. The course of emotionality in the development of avoidance. *J. exp. Psychol.*, 1962, *64*, 288-294.

JAWORSKA, K., KOWALSKA, M., & SOLTYSIK, S. Studies on the aversive classical conditioning. 1. Acquisition and differentiation of motor and cardiac conditioned classical defensive reflexes in dog. *Acta Biol. Exp.*, 1962, *22*, 23-24.

KAMIN, L. J., BRIMER, C. J., & BLACK, A. H. Conditioned suppression as a monitor of fear of the CS in the course of avoidance training. *J. comp. physiol. Psychol.*, 1963, *56*, 497-501.

KONORSKI, J. Conditioned reflexes and neuron organization. New York: Cambridge University Press, 1948.

LANG, W., & BLACK, A. H. Cardiac conditioning in dogs as a function of U.S. intensity and difficulty of differentiation. Paper presented at Eastern Psychological Association meetings, 1963.

LEAF, R. Personal communication.

MINER, R. W. (Ed.) Curare and anti-curare agents. *Ann. N. Y. Acad. Sci.*, 1951, *54*, 297-530.

MOWRER, O. H. On the dual nature of learning: A reinterpretation of "conditioning" and "problem solving." *Harvard Educ. Rev.*, 1947, *17*, 102-148.

MOWRER, O. H. *Learning theory and behaviour.* New York: John Wiley & Sons, 1960.

PEREZ-CRUET, J., TOLLIVER, C., DUNN, C., MARVIN, S., & BRADY, J. V. Concurrent measurement of heart rate and instrumental avoidance behaviour in the Rhesus monkey. *J. exp. Anal. Behav.,* 1963, *6,* 61-64.

SHEARN, D. Does the heart learn? *Psychol. Bull.,* 1961, *58,* 452-458.

SMITH, K. Conditioning as an artifact. *Psychol. Rev.,* 1954, *61,* 217-225.

SMITH, K. Curare drugs and total paralysis. *Psychol. Rev.,* 1964, *71,* 77-79.

SOLOMON, R. L., & BRUSH, E. S. Experimentally derived conceptions of anxiety. In *Nebraska Symposium on Motivation,* Lincoln, Neb.: Univ. of Nebraska Press, 1956.

SOLOMON, R. L., & TURNER, L. H. Discriminative classical conditioning in dogs paralyzed by curare can later control discriminative avoidance responses in the normal state. *Psychol. Rev.,* 1962, *69,* 202-219.

SOLOMON, R. L., & WYNNE, L. C. Traumatic avoidance learning: The principle of anxiety conservation and partial irreversibility. *Psychol. Rev.,* 1954, *61,* 353-385.

SOLTYSIK, S., & JAWORSKA, K. Studies on the aversive classical conditioning #2. On the reinforcing role of shock in classical leg flexion conditioning. *Acta Biol. Exp.,* 1962, *22,* 181-191.

SOLTYSIK, S., & KOWALSKA, M. Studies on the avoidance conditioning #1. Relations between cardiac (Type I) and motor (Type II) effects in the avoidance reflex. *Acta Biol. Exp.,* 1960, *22,* 157-170.

STERN, J. A., & WORD, T. J. Heart rate changes during avoidance conditioning in the male albino rat. *J. Psychosom. Res.,* 1962, *6,* 167-175.

WENZEL, B. M. Changes in heart rate associated with responses based on positive and negative reinforcement. *J. comp. physiol. Psychol.,* 1961, *54,* 638-644.

I. GORMEZANO

Indiana University

3

Yoked Comparisons of Classical and Instrumental Conditioning of the Eyelid Response; and an Addendum on "Voluntary Responders" [1]

The operational distinction between instrumental and classical conditioning rests on whether or not *S*'s response determines the occurrence of an empirically derived reinforcing event. Although a variety of instrumental conditioning paradigms exist, comparisons of classical and instrumental conditioning have involved the use of the avoidance procedure with a homogeneous UCS (i.e. the UCS determines the response to be conditioned) to presumably insure measurement of the same response under the two procedures. Apparently, Storytzin in 1926 at Bechterev's laboratory performed the first experiment explicitly designed to compare the two procedures. He employed the leg flexion response of dogs to shock and found as did the majority of later Russian studies that the avoidance procedure was superior (Razran, 1956).

In the American laboratories comparisons of the two procedures with dogs (Brogden, 1939; Whatmore, Morgan, & Kleitman, 1946) and rats (Kappauf & Schlosberg, 1937; Schlosberg, 1936) failed to reveal *reliable* differences on rate or level of conditioning of the leg flexion response. However, Girden (1938) noted a potential complication in conditioning the leg flexion response of dogs under the classical procedure that would question the validity of the assumption that the use of a homogeneous UCS assures conditioning of the same response under both procedures. He noted that under the classical conditioning procedure the application of shock when a conditioned leg flexion occurred frequently led to exten-

[1] The research reported was supported by Grants GB-2843, GB-145 and G16030 from the National Science Foundation.

sion of the leg. Schlosberg (1936) and Brogden (1939) had also incidentally noted the occurrence of an incompatible extension response under the classical procedure.

A study by Brogden, Lipman and Culler (1938) and a later replication by Sheffield (1948) comparing classical and instrumental avoidance procedures with a running response, generated considerable interest. It will be recalled that in the Brogden *et al.* study the running response in guinea pigs was conditioned under the avoidance and classical procedures to a tone presented 2 seconds before shock, and the avoidance procedure was found to be superior. Sheffield by analyzing the behavior more completely noted that an important difference in the effects of the two procedures resided in the behavior of the animal at the time of shock onset. He observed that under the classical conditioning procedure when a conditioned running response occurred the introduction of shock frequently elicited behavior incompatible with running (e.g. crouching) and that there was a decrease in the probability of the running response to the CS on the next trial. But, for those trials where the animals continued running when the shock came on, there was an increase in the probability of running on the next trial. On the other hand Sheffield's analysis revealed that under the avoidance procedure successive avoidance responses led to extinction rather than a further strengthening of the conditioned response.

Despite the fact that in American laboratories comparisons of the two procedures had revealed significant superiority of avoidance conditioning only for the running response, it is frequently assumed that avoidance conditioning is superior for any response (e.g., Brogden, 1951, p. 580). This assumption appears, in part, to have provided the impetus for the development of a variety of two-factor interpretations of avoidance conditioning (e.g., Schlosberg, 1937; Mowrer, 1940; Hilgard & Marquis, 1940) in the opposition to unifactor reinforcement (Hull, 1943, 1952) and contiguity interpretations (Guthrie, 1940; Sheffield, 1948). Put most simply what distinguishes these two types of theoretical formulations is whether or not learning occurs on avoidance trials. For unifactor theory omission of the UCS on an avoidance trial is the condition for extinction and thus weakens the response. Whereas, for two-factor theory learning occurs not only on CS-UCS trials but also on avoidance trials where the omission of the UCS leads to a further strengthening of the response through some reward mechanism such as anxiety reduction (Mowrer, 1940). Furthermore, two-factor theories have also strongly implied that a successful avoidance of the aversive UCS may provide greater reinforcement of the response than its presentation. However, it is possible that counter-conditioning of the running or leg flexion response under the classical procedure accounts for those instances in which no differences have been observed or where the avoidance procedure has been found to be superior. Although other factors could be responsible, an effective comparison of the two procedures minimally requires the utilization of a response system devoid of the possibility of counter-conditioning an incompatible response. As noted by Logan (1951), the eyelid response appears to satisfy this condition since presentation of the UCS, when anticipatory CRs of eyelid closures occur results only in a further closure.

Logan (1951), Kimble, Mann and Dufort (1955) and Hansche (1959) employing the eyelid response in comparisons of classical and instrumental avoidance conditioning, have in fact observed results opposite to those commonly assumed for such comparisons (viz., a higher level of conditioning under the classical procedure). In the interpretation of their findings Logan (1951) and Kimble *et al.* (1955) attributed the inferior level of conditioning of the avoidance procedure to its partial reinforcement schedule. Kimble, Mann and Dufort further suggested that the observed differences may reflect some nonassociative effects of the UCS (i.e., each UCS occurrence develops an increment of acquired drive) and not an associative factor. Since in avoidance conditioning the CR prevents the occurrence of the UCS these interpretations, consistent with unifactor reinforcement theory, imply that classical conditioning is superior because of the greater number of reinforcements and higher motivational level of S. Contiguity theory would also predict superior conditioning under the classical procedure because it assures the occurrence of a vigorous response on every trial.

Presumably then, if an experimental comparison of classical and avoidance conditioning were made in which the *pattern* and *number* of UCS occurrences (and their possible nonassociative effects) were the same, the above interpretations would lead one to expect no differences in performance under classical and avoidance procedures. In the first series of studies to be presented we have effectively made these comparisons by introducing an innovation in classical conditioning involving the use of a yoked control procedure for comparisons of classical and instrumental avoidance conditioning. Essentially the procedure consists in running pairs of Ss concurrently, where if one of the Ss designated as the avoidance S, makes a CR the UCS is omitted for both Ss on that trial. If the avoidance S fails to make a CR, the UCS is presented to both Ss at the usual CS-UCS interval. Thus, the non-contingent yoked S is being conditioned under a classical procedure in which the reinforcement schedule is determined by the performance of the avoidance S.

YOKED COMPARISONS OF CLASSICAL AND AVOIDANCE CONDITIONING

In order to run two Ss simultaneously we simply employ a multiple channel oscillograph, two recording head gears, two S enclosures, and a Y-joint with flexible tubing leading from the air source to the Ss' air jets.

A differential amplifier in parallel with the recording amplifier of the avoidance S is used to activate an avoidance circuit constructed so that eyeblinks that occur within the CR latency range (i.e., 150 or 200 msec. after CS onset to the usual time of UCS onset) can prevent the occurrence of the UCS by gating out the relay that activates the air solenoid. (By feeding the output of the differential amplifier through the contacts of an electronic timer, control is exercised over the latency range of eyeblinks defined as CRs which can activate the avoidance circuit). Thus, under such a procedure the pattern and number of UCS occurrences for pairs of instrumentally and classically conditioned Ss remain identical.

In our first reported yoked comparison study (Moore & Gormezano, 1961) run under a CS-UCS interval of 500 msec. and 70 acquisition and 20 extinction trials, we employed two instrumental contingency techniques: occurrence of the CR on a particular acquisition trial resulted in either omission of the UCS (Group A) or delayed its onset for 3000 msec. after CS onset (Group AD). For each of the Ss in the instrumental groups there was a yoked classical S designated avoid-yoke (Group AY) and avoid-delay-yoke (Group ADY) respectively. A conventional classical conditioning group (Group C) that received the UCS on every trial, was also employed. A plot of the percentage CRs in acquisition and extinction for the five experimental groups (24 Ss each) is presented in Fig. 3-1. In agreement with the previous observations of Logan (1951), Kimble, Mann and Dufort (1955) and Hansche (1959) the figure reveals that the conventional classical conditioning group (Group C) attained a level of performance that was significantly higher than that of the avoidance group (Group A), and in fact it attained a level that was significantly superior to all other groups. However, when the avoidance and classical comparison is made in which the pattern and number of UCS occurrences are the same (i.e., Group A vs. Group AY) the avoidance condition led to significantly superior performance in both acquisition and extinction. But, under the UCS-delay procedure the instrumental group (Group AD) was not significantly different from its yoked-classical group (Group ADY).

In another study (Gormezano, Moore & Deaux, 1962) we assessed the effects of UCS intensity on yoked comparisons of classical and instrumental avoidance conditioning. Twenty Ss were assigned to each of the 6 cells of a 2 x 3 factorial design in which classical and avoidance procedures were made orthogonal to three UCS air puff intensities of 40, 80 and 160 mm. of mercury (calibrated at its point of delivery to the eye). All other parameters of the conditioning situation were the same as in the first study. Fig. 3-2 presents the results of plotting the percentage of CRs in acquisition and extinction. The figure indicates that the acquisition performance of the three avoidance groups (Groups A160, A80 and A40) were superior to each of their respective yoked-classical groups (i.e., A160 vs. Y160, A80 vs. Y80, and A40 vs. Y40). A split-plot analysis of

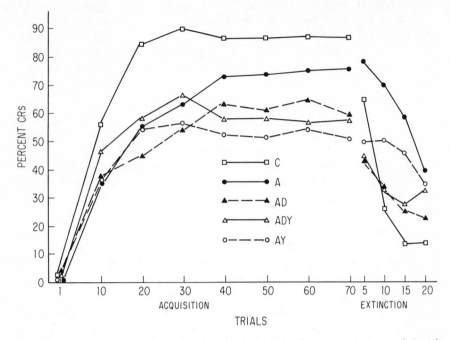

Fig. 3-1. The percentage CRs plotted in 10-trial blocks during acquisition and 5-trial blocks during extinction. (Moore & Gormezano, 1961)

variance for the 70 acquisition and 20 extinction trials revealed significantly superior performance of the avoidance procedure in the avoidance vs. yoked-classical comparisons in both acquisition and extinction. The UCS intensity dimension failed to reveal significant differences but a significant effect was obtained in acquisition for the classical-avoidance × UCS intensity interaction, reflecting the fact that as UCS intensity increased, performance of the avoidance groups increased while the performance of the yoked-classical groups decreased. This interaction appears to be a function of the negative correlation between the performance levels of the paired Ss.[2]

In a more recent study (Gormezano, Fuentes & Erickson, 1963) the effects of the CS-UCS interval parameter on the avoidance and yoke-classical procedure was assessed. Again 20 Ss were assigned to each of the six cells of a 2 x 3 factorial design in which the avoidance (A) and yoked-classical (Y) dimension was made orthogonal to three CS-UCS intervals of 500, 1000 and 1500 msec. All Ss received 80 acquisition and 20 extinction trials with the UCS air puff at a sufficient intensity to support a 100 mm.

---

[2] However, the significant interaction is heavily weighted by the low level of responding of Group Y160. If the performance of Group Y160 is not a sampling error, its performance relative to Y80 suggests a partial reinforcement × UCS intensity interaction.

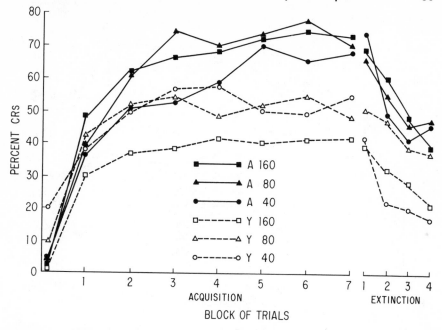

Fig. 3-2. The percentage CRs plotted in 10-trial blocks during acquisition and 5-trial blocks in extinction. (Gormezano, Moore, & Deaux, 1962)

column of mercury. A plot of the percentage CRs for the six groups in acquisition and extinction in shown in Fig. 3-3. Examination of the figure will reveal that for each of the CS-UCS intervals the avoidance group demonstrated a higher level of performance (i.e., A500 vs. Y500, A1000 vs. Y1000 and A1500 vs. Y1500) in acquisition, and their higher levels of responding persisted in extinction. Split-plot analysis of variance for the 80 acquisition and 20 extinction trials revealed significant differences for the avoid vs. yoked-classical comparison in both stages but no significant differences for the CS-UCS interval dimension nor for the avoid-yoke × CS-UCS interval interaction.

Gormezano, Fuentes and Erickson (1963) also investigated the effects of CS-UCS interval under the avoidance and yoked-classical procedure employing the nictitating membrane (third eyelid) response of the albino rabbit. Since our conditioning work with the rabbit may not be too well known a brief review of our activities may be appropriate. Recently, Schneiderman, Fuentes and Gormezano (1962) conditioned the eyelid, Gormezano, Schneiderman, Deaux and Fuentes (1962) the nictitating membrane and Deaux and Gormezano (1963) the eyeball (i.e., eyeball retraction) in the albino rabbit employing an auditory CS and a corneal air puff or shock to the infraorbital region of the eye as the UCS. These studies as well as others from the Indiana laboratory (Bruner, 1963; Paps-

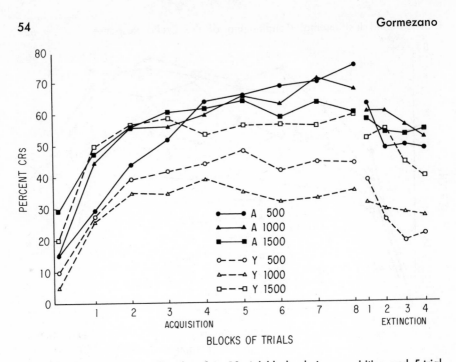

Fig. 3-3. The percentage CRs plotted in 10-trial blocks during acquisition and 5-trial blocks during extinction.

dorf, Gormezano & Prokasy, 1964; Schneiderman & Gormezano, 1964), have revealed that the albino rabbit has certain behavioral characteristics that appear to make it more ideally suited for conditioning studies than those of other infrahuman species previously conditioned. The albino rabbit when properly restrained will remain relatively passive in the conditioning situation for extended periods of time; the eyelid, nictitating membrane and eyeball retraction response have extremely low rates of spontaneous occurrence (about 1 to 3 responses per hour); and for the eyelid and nictitating membrane there is an apparent absence of alpha responses to an auditory CS.

Structurally the nictitating membrane consists of a fold of conjunctiva supported by a triangular sheet of cartilage which moves from the inner canthus of the eye laterally across the surface of the cornea. Although the mechanism of movement of the membrane is not clearly understood, it is reliably extended by a corneal air puff or shock with a latency of about 25 to 50 msec. Furthermore, the membrane when activated rarely extends past the midline of the pupil, thus leaving a portion of the receptor surface of the cornea exposed. This property of the response thus appears to provide the investigator with a high degree of control over the sensory consequences of a corneal air puff. By presenting the air puff to the temporal region of the cornea, anticipatory extensions (i.e., CRs) do not appear to modify its sensory effects. To prepare the nictitating membrane for recording, the upper and lower eyelids are pulled back while concurrently applying a slight downward pressure on the eyeball to extend the membrane out from the inner canthus of the eye. A length of 00 Ethilon monofilament nylon is then sutured through the epithelium layer of the membrane, starting in at about one-eighth of an inch from its temporal edge and coming out almost to the edge. The length of nylon is tied to form a small loop several millimeters in diameter to provide the means by which the recording of membrane movement is accomplished. By exercising care in making the loop no longer than several mm. in diameter the animal will readily adapt to its presence, and the preparation will remain stable for several weeks. If the nylon loop should become dislodged a new suture may be applied.

After preparing the nictitating membrane for recording, the animal is restrained within a plexiglass box by an adjustable back plate and the insertion of the animal's head through an adjustable stock which comprises the front of the box. A head gear containing a rotary potentiometer and a stimulus air jet is then mounted on the animal. Gross head movements of the animal are then reduced by fastening the pinna of its ears to the front of the stock with a foam-rubber coated clamp. To permit the recording of nictitating membrane movement and to insure continual exposure of the cornea the animal's upper and lower eyelids are held open by stainless steel hooks. A silk thread is attached to a rod mechanically coupled to the shaft of the potentiometer and a small metal hook connected to the other end of the silk thread is attached to the nylon loop sutured in the rabbit's nictitating membrane. The rod mechanically coupled to the potentiometer shaft is balanced and weighted to eliminate slack in the thread, and the signal from the potentiometer generated by extension of the membrane, is amplified and graphically recorded.

In the Gormezano, Fuentes and Erickson (1963) study 10 rabbits were randomly assigned to each of the 6 cells of the 2 x 3 factorial design in which the two principal dimensions were the same as in the human study (i.e., an avoidance and yoked-classical dimension and CS-UCS intervals of 500, 1000 and 1500 msec.). On the day of arrival the animal's nictitating membrane was prepared for recording, and training commenced on the following day with all Ss receiving 2 days of adaptation, 10 days of acquisition and one day of extinction. The Ss' room contained two refrigeration shells in which the animals were placed, and thus permitted two rabbits to be run simultaneously. The Ss received 80 conditioning trials on each day of acquisition and 200 CS alone presentations for the one day of extinction with trials occurring at random intervals of 15, 25 and 35 sec. (mean of 25 sec.). The CS was an 800 cps tone at 72 db SPL and the air puff measured at its point of delivery to the rabbit's eye supported a 75 mm. column of mercury. Membrane extensions of at least 1-mm.

deflection from the baseline and occurring from 50 msec. after CS onset to UCS onset were considered to be CRs. The occurrence of a CR by the *S* under the avoidance procedure precluded the occurrence of the UCS for the pair of *S*s on that trial. In the two days of adaptation a measure of spontaneous membrane movement was obtained by recording the frequency of responses in intervals corresponding to the 80 conditioning trials.

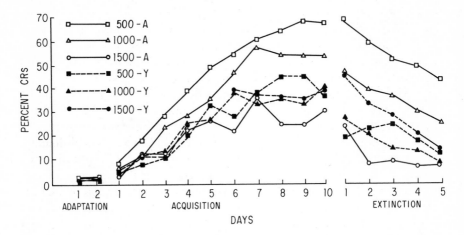

Fig. 3-4. The percentage CRs plotted in 80-trial blocks during acquisition and 40-trial blocks in extinction. The data points in adaptation are based on 80-"trial" blocks.

Fig. 3-4 presents the results of plotting the percentage CRs for the 6 groups in adaptation, acquisition and extinction. In adaptation and acquisition the data points are plotted in 80 trial blocks and for extinction in 40 trial blocks. The figure indicates that in acquisition the 500 and 1000 msec. CS-UCS interval avoidance groups were superior to their respective yoked groups (i.e., groups 500-A vs. Group 500-Y and 1000-A vs. 1000-Y), whereas there was a small inversion of the relationship for the 1500 msec. interval (i.e., Group 1500Y vs. Group 1500A). In extinction the avoidance groups rank ordered themselves in the same manner as in acquisition, but the yoked-classical groups did not demonstrate the same rank ordered separations. Split-plot analyses of variance of the percentage CRs for the last 480 trials in acquisition and the 200 trials in extinction revealed a significant effect for CS-UCS interval in acquisition and a significant CS-UCS interval × avoid-yoke interaction in acquisition and extinction. The avoid-yoke orthogonal comparisons failed to reveal significant differences in either phase of the experiment but *t*-test comparisons based on the error mean square of the analysis of variance revealed that the 500 and 1000 msec. avoidance groups were significantly superior to their respective yoked-classical groups in acquisition and extinction, but at the 1500 msec. interval the yoked-classical group was significantly superior in extinction.

In the studies presented the avoidance conditioning procedure has been found to be inferior to the conventional classical conditioning procedure (i.e., 100% reinforcement) but superior to their yoked-classical controls (with the exception of the 1500 msec. CS-UCS interval comparison with rabbits). As suggested by Logan (1951) and Kimble, Mann and Dufort (1955) the inferior performance of avoidance conditioning to conventional classical conditioning (i.e., 100% reinforcement) could be accounted for by the partial reinforcement schedule inherent in the avoidance procedure. However, versions of reinforcement or contiguity theory which have limited their formulations to the role of the UCS as a determiner of learning without taking into account the relationship of the CR and occurrence of the UCS, do not appear to be able to adequately interpret the observed superiority of the avoidance procedure over the yoked-classical procedure. Since the avoidance and yoked-classical groups were experimentally equated for pattern and number of UCS occurrences, a remaining difference is that under the avoidance procedure the UCS occurs only in the absence of the CR and under the yoked-classical procedure its occurrence is independent of the CR. If one were to assume that the reinforcing effect of the UCS is some inverse function of the strength of association between the CS and CR or varies with S's presumed conditioning state (Bower & Theois, 1964), then presentation of the UCS would have a maximum effect on response probability when the CR fails to occur and a small or no effect when the CR does occur. Since in the yoked-classical procedure any number of trials may occur in which neither the CR and UCS occur or both the CR and UCS occur, it would be expected that for an equal number of UCS presentations these contingencies would lead to inferior performance.

AVOID-YOKE COMPARISONS IN DIFFERENTIAL EYELID CONDITIONING

Although we choose to make the unifactor reinforcement interpretation that occurrence of the UCS is the reinforcing event in eyelid conditioning, an alternative interpretation is that in addition to learning occurring on reinforced trials, the occurrence of avoidance responses contributes to the further acquisition of CRs. Explicitly, it is conceivable that in human eyelid conditioning at least, verbal cues may be attached to the CR-No UCS contingency and thus, through a reward mechanism of reinforcement, lead to some degree of verbal control over the CRs. The extension of our avoid-yoke technique to differential eyelid conditioning (Runquist, Sidowski, & Gormezano, 1962) permits us to explore such a possibility. In this study 24 Ss were assigned to each of three groups. In a control group (C), the differential conditioning procedure to tones of 300 and 2000 cps at 68 db SPL was employed in which the UCS always occurred with CS+ and never with CS−. For the other two groups, avoid (A) and yoked (Y), two Ss, one from each group were run simultaneously in the yoked-chair procedure in which an eyelid response in the 150 to 550 msec. interval on the CS+ trial by the S in Group A precluded the occurrence of the UCS to both Ss on that trial. If the avoid S failed to respond, the UCS was delivered to both Ss 550 msec. after CS onset. On a CR− trial neither Ss received the UCS regardless of any response. Thus, Ss in Group A could avoid the UCS by making a CR to CS+, while placing yoked Ss on a partial reinforcement schedule. In extinction all groups were presented the CS+ and CS− without the UCS. All Ss received 90 acquisition and 18 extinction trials with the ratio of positive to negative CSs at 2:1 in both phases.

A plot of the percentage CRs of the three groups to CS+ and CS− trials is presented in Fig. 3-5. If under the avoidance procedure the S were to exercise verbal control over the CR-No UCS contingency, then one might except that extended to a differential conditioning procedure, the avoidance contingency would lead to a higher level of responding to CS+ than would a yoked-classical group. Examination of Fig. 3-5 reveals however, that Group A and Group Y did not significantly differ in the frequency of their responses to CS+. In fact, Group A failed to show significant discrimination (i.e., differential responding) whereas Groups Y and C both showed significant discrimination. The main source of failure of the avoidance group to discriminate was an increase in the percentage of CRs given to CS−.

It should be indicated at this point that our interpretation of the superiority of the avoidance procedure to the yoked-classical procedure in our previous studies is not applicable to avoidance conditioning under the differential procedure since the contingency existed only on CS+ trials. Our interpretation is that for Group A the contingency and partial reinforcement schedule on CS+ trials increased their similarity to CS− trials. If in the conditioning situation one considers the possible stimuli in control of the CR, there are in addition to the CS, stimuli produced by the occurrence of the response and the stimulus after-effects of occurrence or non-occurrence of the UCS. In the yoked-classical group a number of CS+ trials elapsed in which neither the CR nor UCS occurred. The failure of the UCS to occur would thus make the stimulus after-effects of many CS+ trials similar to CS− trials and through stimulus generalization it might be expected to increase the percentage of CRs to CS−. In the avoidance group the similarity of CS+ and CS− trials was increased not only by the failure of the UCS to occur on many CS+ trials, but also by the concomitant occurrence of the CR on these trials.

Thus, CS− trials on which a CR occurred through stimulus generalization, were because of CR occurrences, further increased in similarity to
a large proportion of the CS+ trials. The result was (relative to the
yoke-classical group) a still further increase in the percentage of CRs to
CS−, particularly on the second of two consecutive CS− trials (as indicated by sequential analyses).

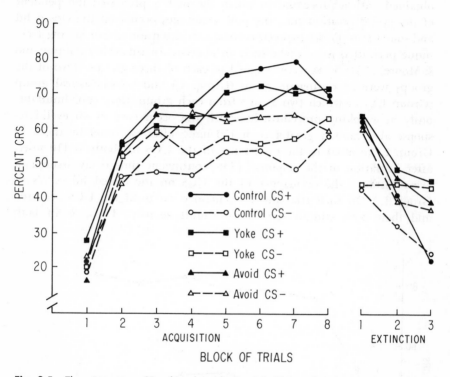

Fig. 3-5. The percentage CRs plotted in blocks of 8 CS+ and 4 CS− trials in acquisition, with the exception of the first point which is plotted on the basis of 4 CS+ and
2 CS− trials. Extinction points are plotted in blocks of 4 CS+ and 2 CS− trials. (Runquist,
Sidowski, & Gormezano, 1962)

YOKED COMPARISONS OF RESPONSE CONTINGENT UCS PRE-SENTATIONS

A common interpretation of eyelid conditioning experiments employing a corneal air puff is that the CR serves to attenuate the effects
of the puff by preventing it from falling on the cornea (Hilgard &
Marquis, 1940; Solomon & Brush, 1956). Generally implicit in such an
assumption is the notion that eyeblinks which overlap the puff are reinforced through the law of effect (i.e., rewarded by reducing the noxious-

ness of the puff). Although the mechanism of reinforcement for CRs not overlapping the puff still waits upon discovery, proponents of the law of effect would assume that puff presentations on the closed lid has a greater reinforcement effect.

A possible method for assessing the appropriateness of the law of effect analysis is to employ a contingency procedure in which the puff is always presented on the closed lid and to contrast the performance obtained with a procedure in which the puff is presented independent of the eyelid position (i.e., the puff sometimes occurs on the closed lid and sometimes on the exposed cornea). An extension of our yoking technique permitted us to make such an analysis. In this study (Gormezano & Moore, 1964) 30 Ss were assigned to each of three groups. Two of the groups were a contingent group (Group L) and yoked-classical group (Group LY) in which two Ss one from each group, were run simultaneously in a yoking procedure in which the occurrence of an eyelid response at a latency greater than 150 msec. after CS onset by the S in Group L, resulted in the occurrence of the UCS for both Ss 110 msec. after initiation of the response. (The contingent time delay assured in every instance the occurrence of the UCS on the closed lid of S's in Group L.) On each trial the CS remained on until the UCS occurred and then both stimuli terminated simultaneously. Thus, Ss in both

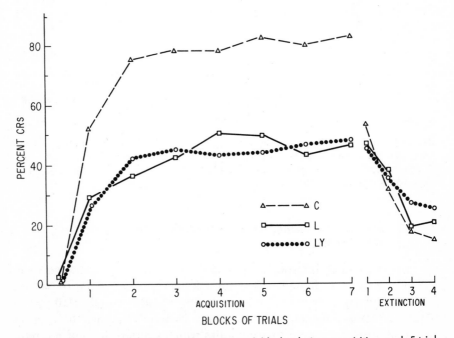

Fig. 3-6. The percentage CRs plotted in 10-trial blocks during acquisition and 5-trial blocks during extinction. The initial acquisition points are the mean percentage of responses on the first trial. (Gormezano & Moore, 1964)

groups were run under a varying CS-UCS interval in which the interstimulus interval on any trial was completely determined by the latency
of an eyeblink by the S in Group L. The third group, a conventional
classical conditioning group (Group C), received the UCS on every trial
at a CS-UCS interval of 500 msec. In extinction all groups received the
CS alone for 600 msec.

All Ss received 70 acquisition and 20 extinction trials at an average
intertrial interval of 25 sec. (timed from UCS offset); and the intensity
of a 100 msec. air puff at its point of delivery to the eye was sufficient
to support a 200 mm. column of mercury. In all groups eyeblinks were
scored as CRs in the 150 to 525 msec. interval after CS onset in acquisition and in the 150 to 600 msec. interval in extinction. Since only
anticipatory responses were scored as CRs an eyelid response by an S in
the yoked-classical group (Group LY) was scored as a CR on any given
acquisition trial only if it occurred within 25 msec. after the onset of
the UCS.

Fig. 3-6 presents a plot of the percentage CRs and Fig. 3-7 the distribution of response latencies for the three groups in acquisition and
extinction. Examination of Fig 3-6 reveals that Group C attained an
asymptotic level of approximately 80 percent whereas, Groups L and LY

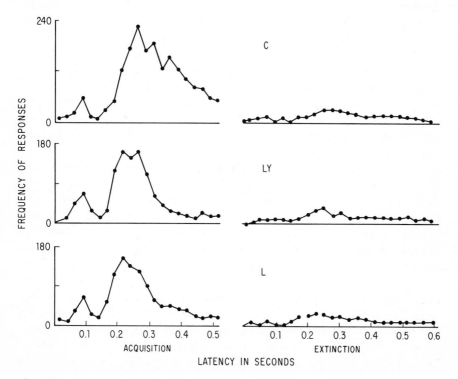

Fig. 3-7. The distribution of response latencies of eyelid responses in acquisition and
extinction.

both rose more gradually to asymptotic levels of about 42 percent. In extinction there do not appear to be appreciable differences in the frequency of response among the three groups. Examination of Fig. 3-7 indicates that the principal modes in acquisition of the contingent (Group L) and yoked-classical (Group LY) groups both had a latency of 225 msec. and that of the conventional classical conditioning group (Group C) a modal value of 275 msec. It is of particular interest to note that although all eyelid responses by Ss in Group L greater than 150 msec. after CS onset were contiguously reinforced with the UCS (no matter how late the response occurred) the unimodal distribution obtained indicated little evidence of being truncated at the 525 msec. cut-off. Furthermore, although all groups showed a considerable drop in the frequency of responses in extinction, the shorter response latencies of Groups L and LY observed in acquisition were maintained in extinction.

A modified split-plot analysis of variance revealed significant differences among the three groups on percentage and latency of CRs in acquisition but no significant differences in extinction for either measure. Multiple t-test comparisons revealed that the percentage and latency of responses of Groups L and LY were not significantly different from one another in acquisition or extinction, but were both significantly different from Group C in acquisition and extinction. Thus, though for Ss in Group L the temporal occurrence of the air puff was contingent on the time of occurrence of the eyeblink and always fell on the closed lid, this contingent relationship did not appear to produce performance (i.e., latency or frequency of responses) that differed from that of a yoked-classical group where no contingency existed. It could be argued of course by proponents of the law of effect that the comparable performance of Ss in the yoked-classical procedure arises from their having received the air puff on the closed eyelid a high percentage of the time. However, on the average this occurred on only 40 percent of the trials.

Surprising perhaps, for those who take the position that all behavior must be functionally adaptive is that Group L shows any conditioning (i.e., a progressive increase in responding within the 525 msec. interval) under a "punishment" contingency. One possible explanatory mechanism consistent with the functional point of view is that since the CS remains on until an eyeblink occurs, S responds to the CS to terminate a fear conditioned stimulus (acquired through the adventitious correlation of the CS with an air puff). If this were the reinforcing mechanism then one might expect Ss in Group L to show relative to Group LY, a greater proportion of responses within the 525 msec. interval. This is clearly not the case. However, there is little difficulty in explaining these results if one recognizes that a basic datum of both the classical and instrumental conditioning procedure is that as the strength of the association increases the response moves forward in time.

ADDENDUM: "VOLUNTARY RESPONDERS"

We have on several occasions indicated the methodological and theoretical difficulties that arise in employing the Iowa Procedure of rejecting Ss as "voluntary responders" from eyelid conditioning data (Gormezano, 1964; Gormezano & Moore, 1962; Moore & Gormezano, 1963). It is the intent of this section to review and amplify our position.

Spence and his co-workers (Spence & Ross, 1959; Spence & Taylor, 1951) have argued for the elimination of Ss from eyelid conditioning data if 50% or more of their CRs have a latency between 200 and 300 msec. Although couched in methodological terms this rejection procedure rests on the theoretical assumption that a causal relationship exists between responses characterized by sharp closure, long duration and short latency and the voluntary attempt of S to blink to the CS (Spence, 1953; Spence & Ross, 1959; Spence & Taylor, 1951). Spence and Ross (1959) have attempted to provide analogous support for this assumption by stating that *judged* voluntary responses are "...similar in form to those given by Ss instructed to blink to the CS so as to avoid the air puff and by Ss who, following conditioning, reported they were blinking voluntarily in order to avoid the puff" (p. 377). Spence and Ross (1959) have also maintained that ready agreement can be obtained between judges in the selection of "voluntary" and "nonvoluntary" eyelid responses, and that furthermore by removing the data of Ss classified as "voluntary responders" by the latency criterion one can effectively eliminate the greatest number of *judged* voluntary responses and the fewest *judged* nonvoluntary responses.

In contrast to the above contention of ready agreement in judging eyelid responses as "voluntary" or "nonvoluntary" on the basis of form, of the two studies in the literature, complete agreement between sophisticated judges (i.e., the Es) has been obtained for only 71.4% of the responses in one instance (Spence & Ross, 1959) and in the other on only 66.8% of the responses (Hartman & Ross, 1961). It is also important to note that such relatively mundane considerations as differences in "hardware" among eyelid conditioning laboratories also enters into the classification problem. The relative frequency of (as well as degree of agreement in judging) various recorded forms of the eyelid response will vary for example, as a function of the amount of peak clipping of the response signal, the paper speed at which the records are obtained and the type of hook-up employed in coupling the eyelid to the transducer. Spence and Ross (1959) presume they have demonstrated the validity of employing their latency criterion and recently Hartman and Ross (1961), their recruitment criterion for classifying Ss as "voluntary responders." However the validity of such criteria must necessarily depend upon the degree of agreement of form judgments, and the obtained degree of concordants of 71.4% and 68.8% places a serious limitation upon their validity.

Although by improving the fidelity of recording the eyelid response and standardizing apparatus one could reduce between laboratory differences in the frequency of various recorded forms of the response (and perhaps increase the coefficient of concordance of form judgments), such modifications would not mitigate more fundamental within laboratory problems. As indicated, Spence and Ross (1959) have maintained that in removing the data of Ss classified as "voluntary responders" by the latency criterion, one can effectively eliminate the greatest number of *judged* voluntary and the fewest *judged* nonvoluntary responses. But the validity of the latency criterion (or any other criterion) minimally requires demonstrating that when Ss are rejected as "voluntary responders" there is an invariant elimination of the greatest number of *judged* voluntary and fewest *judged* nonvoluntary responses. However, it has been noted for example that the latency distribution of so-called *judged* voluntary responses are affected by air puff intensity (Spence & Ross, 1959, p. 378) and by the presence or absence of a ready signal (Hartman & Ross, 1961). Similarly, the distribution of response latencies of Ss instructed to blink to the CS (in the absence of a ready signal) has been shown to vary as a function of massed or spaced conditioning trials (Hartman, Grant, & Ross, 1960) and with UCS intensity (Gormezano & Moore, 1962). Consequently, since any variable affecting the latencies of *judged* voluntary responses also affects the validity of the latency criterion employed to eliminate them, the failure of the latencies of *judged* voluntary responses to remain invariant renders the latency criterion employed to classify Ss as "voluntary responders" methodologically inadequate.

Spence has recognized one aspect of the problem of invariance in an interesting manner: "Unfortunately, investigators who did not use a ready signal took over the latency criterion to identify 'voluntary' responders without checking its appropriateness, with the consequence that all such Ss probably were not eliminated from their samples" (Spence, 1962, p. 18; Spence, 1964, p. 137). It is indeed unfortunate that despite Spence's astute observation the consultants to our journals have insisted that the latency criterion be applied to studies from laboratories in which the procedures and parameters have differed from those of the Spence and Ross (1959) study. Clearly, it has not been generally understood that the attempt of Spence and Ross (1959) to demonstrate the validity of the latency criterion was intended to have a generality restricted to an *exact* replication of their experiment. Conceivably this misconception has come from the fact that the Iowa laboratory has routinely applied the latency criterion to studies that have differed markedly from the Spence and Ross (1959) investigation (e.g., studies involving: absence of a ready signal, differential conditioning, partial reinforcement, delayed presentation of the UCS, manipulation of UCS intensity, etc.). In the absence of having demonstrated the invariance of the latencies of *judged* voluntary responses for the wide variety of procedures and parameters employed in the Iowa investigations, it must be recognized that these studies are subject to the same incisive criticism that Spence has leveled at other investigators.

Hartman and Ross (1961) have suggested employing a recruitment criterion (based upon an objective measure of speed of eyelid closure) to classify Ss as "voluntary responders." However, the recruitment measure also requires demonstrating that Ss so rejected as "voluntary responders" leads to an invariant optimal elimination of the greatest number of *judged* voluntary and fewest *judged* nonvoluntary responses. Whether or not this condition of invariance can be satisfied by the recruitment criterion remains an empirical question, but from our vantage point the logical requirements make such an outcome highly unlikely. A study by Goodrich (1964) indicated that even when a ready signal was employed that over 60% of the responses classified as "voluntary responses" by the recruitment criterion, occurred 300 msec. after CS onset. On the other hand, Spence and Ross (1959) obtained only 13.5% of their *judged* voluntary responses after 300 msec. The reported results of these two studies do not permit one to determine whether the disparity arises from the recruitment measure and/or the latencies of *judged* voluntary responses being uniquely affected by possible differences in parameters and procedures, but clearing the Goodrich results provide an empirical basis for questioning the validity of the recruitment criterion.

In considering the above methodological difficulties it must be emphasized that investigators employing a latency or recruitment criterion to reject Ss as "voluntary responders" are subject to errors of misclassification that are compounded of errors arising not only from the substantially less than perfect agreement on form judgments (on which these criteria were presumably validated) but also from those arising from the failure to meet the condition of invariance. For example, the fact that CR latency varies systematically as a function of UCS intensity (Gormezano & Moore, 1962) and with the partial reinforcement technique of omitting or delaying presentation of the UCS (Moore & Gormezano, 1963), poses immediate difficulties for investigators manipulating these variables and employing the latency criterion to reject Ss as "voluntary responders." If UCS omission rather than UCS delay is employed or if UCS intensity is systematically increased, such manipulations would classify increasing numbers of Ss as "voluntary responders." It could be maintained of course, that manipulation of such variables simply increases the incidence of "voluntary responders" but such a contention requires demonstrating that Ss so classified have the desired invariant relationship to *judged* voluntary and nonvoluntary responses. In the absence or failure to obtain such validation it must be expected that one will be misclassifying Ss as "voluntary responders" for demonstrating behavior lawfully related to the conditioning parameters employed. It is difficult to assess the consequences of erroneously classifying (or failing to classify) Ss as "voluntary responders" to the outcome of studies from Iowa or other laboratories, but Spence in attempting to demonstrate the effects of *including* the data of so-called "voluntary responders" has provided an illuminating example. "It is worthy of note that the inclusion of six voluntary responders (three in each group) ... would have reduced the reported difference of 14.2% between HA and LA Ss to 11.0%. Correspondingly, the significance of the difference would have been reduced from the .05 level to one of .16. In other words, the addition of only six voluntary Ss to the sample of 67 would have changed the conclusion from one that the difference is significant to one that it is not" (Spence, 1964, p. 138). It is unfortunate that Spence has not provided an equally illuminating example of the consequences of erroneously classifying Ss as "voluntary responders."

We wish to indicate that if an investigator is merely concerned with replicating studies from laboratories classifying Ss as "voluntary responders" then he should by all means replicate in all respects. If however, the investigator conceivably has other objectives and is yet convinced of the validity of the assumption that *judged* voluntary responses reflect S's volitional involvement he may decide that the logical though arduous approach to eliminating such Ss could be based upon the incidence of *judged* voluntary responses. Assuming that such an investigator is willing to tolerate the errors of misclassification of responses (or feels that he can improve upon the degree of judges' agreement) he must still however, address himself to the problem of establishing a criterion for when Ss are classified as a "volitional" responder. Does S become classified as a "volitional" responder if 1%, 10%, 50% or 90% of his CRs are of the *judged* voluntary form? Spence (1964, p. 138) has himself reported an instance of classifying Ss on the basis of *judged* voluntary responses, but without specifying how many *judged* voluntary responses constituted a "voluntary responder." In any event, the criterion established would be dictated by the investigator's theoretical preconceptions of the conditioning process and the functions he wishes to obtain. Furthermore, no matter what criterion were to be employed, the reliability of such a classification would necessarily vary, depending upon the number of CRs made by each S.

Spence and Ross (1959) have maintained that "The rationale behind this procedure of eliminating Ss (by the latency criterion) whose responses were primarily of the short latency, voluntary form was that such responses were governed by different laws than those obtaining in the case of the longer latency class of responses" (p. 377). Although space does not permit an extensive treatment of the theoretical implications of such a statement several points must be made explicit. Specifically, Spence and Ross (1959) maintain that the percentage of responses of "voluntary responders" are not related "... either to level of a manifest Anxiety score or to intensity of the UCS ..." (p. 377). However, if "voluntary responders" are simply Ss with higher conditioning parameters, and they are selected from different experimental groups, it might be expected that no substantial differences will appear among these groups of Ss since they would be performing near the ceiling of response measurement. Support for the proposition that rejecting Ss as "voluntary responders" simply eliminates Ss with higher conditioning rates comes from several studies. Thus, Gormezano and Moore (1962) have shown that although "voluntary responders" (classified by the latency criterion) show higher levels of performance they also demonstrate greater resistance to extinction. Hartman and Grant (1962) employing the technique of informing Ss when extinction begins observed fewer responses in these Ss than Ss not given the information. However, those Ss classified as "voluntary responders" (by the recruitment criterion) gave more responses in extinction than "nonvoluntary" Ss regardless of the information given. Furthermore, Beck (1963) has shown that the frequency of *judged* voluntary responses is positively related to intensity of the CS. If these responses do in fact reflect S's volitional involvement, it would appear to be difficult to account in any simple way for why CS intensity should increase S's volitional involvement. On the other hand, Kamin [see p. 121, below] has very nicely documented the effects of CS intensity on response probability.

In sum, we are of the opinion that the current classification procedures primarily eliminate Ss of higher learning rate parameters and whose response topography simply reflects the strength of conditioning. We do not wish to imply however, that we are not cognizant of the operation of set and self-instructional factors in conditioning (Gormezano, 1965). But we do believe that such problems are subject to direct experimental attack and control. We are in fact currently engaged in such an experimental program at the Indiana laboratories.

References

BECK, S. B. Eyelid conditioning as a function of CS intensity, UCS intensity, and manifest anxiety scale score. *J. exp. Psychol.*, 1963, *66*, 429-438.

BOWER, G. H., & THEOIS, J. A learning model for discrete performance levels. In R. C. ATKINSON (Ed.), *Studies in mathematical psychology*. Stanford: Stanford University Press, 1964.

BROGDEN, W. J. The effect of frequency of reinforcement upon the level of conditioning. *J. exp. Psychol.*, 1939, *24*, 419-431.

BROGDEN, W. J. Animal studies of learning. In S. S. STEVENS (Ed.), *Handbook of experimental psychology*. New York: John Wiley & Sons, 1951.

BROGDEN, W. J., LIPMAN, A. E., & CULLER, E. The role of incentive in conditioning and extinction. *Amer. J. Psychol.*, 1938, *5*, 109-117.

BRUNER, A. Investigations of the properties of the UCS in conditioning of the nictitating membrane response in the albino rabbit. Unpublished doctoral dissertation, Indiana University, 1963.

DEAUX, E., & GORMEZANO, I. Eyeball retraction: Classical conditioning and extinction in the albino rabbit. *Science,* 1963, *141*, 630-631.

GIRDEN, E. Conditioning and problem-solving behavior. *Amer. J. Psychol.*, 1938, *51*, 677-686.

GOODRICH, K. P. Supplementary reports: Effect of a ready signal on the latency of voluntary responses in eyelid conditioning. *J. exp. Psychol.*, 1964, *67*, 496-498.

GORMEZANO, I. Classical conditioning. In J. B. SIDOWSKI (Ed.), *Experimental methods and instrumentation in psychology*. New York: McGraw-Hill, 1965, in press.

GORMEZANO, I., FUENTES, I., & ERICKSON, R. CS-UCS interval effects on yoked comparisons of classical and avoidance conditioning of the human and infrahuman eyelid response. Midwest Psychol. Assoc., Chicago, May, 1963.

GORMEZANO, I., & MOORE, J. W. Effects of instructional set and UCS intensity on the latency, percentage, and form of the eyelid response. *J. exp. Psychol.*, 1962, *63*, 487-494.

GORMEZANO, I., & MOORE, J. W. Yoked comparisons of contingent and non-contingent US presentations in human eyelid conditioning. *Psychon. Sci.*, 1964, *1*, 231-232.

GORMEZANO, I., MOORE, J. W., & DEAUX, E. Supplementary report: Yoked comparisons of classical and avoidance conditioning under three UCS intensities. *J. exp. Psychol.*, 1962, *64*, 551-552.

GORMEZANO, I., SCHNEIDERMAN, N., DEAUX, E., & FUENTES, I. Nictitating membrane: Classical conditioning and extinction in the albino rabbit. *Science,* 1962, *138*, 33-34.

GUTHRIE, E. R. Association and the law of effect. *Psychol. Rev.*, 1940, *47*, 127-148.

HANSCHE, W. J. A comparison of operant, avoidance, and classical techniques in the conditioning of the eyelid response. Unpublished doctoral dissertation, University of Wisconsin, 1959.

HARTMAN, T. F., & GRANT, D. A. Effects of pattern of reinforcement and verbal information on acquisition, extinction and spontaneous recovery of the eyelid CR. *J. exp. Psychol.*, 1962, *63*, 217-226.

HARTMAN, T. F., GRANT, D. A., & ROSS, L. E. An investigation of the latency of "instructed voluntary" eyelid responses. *Psychol. Rep.*, 1960, 7, 305-311.

HARTMAN, T. F., & ROSS, L. E. An alternative criterion for the elimination of "voluntary" responses in eyelid conditioning. *J. exp. Psychol.*, 1961, *61*, 334-338.

HILGARD, E. R., & MARQUIS, D. G. *Conditioning and learning*, 1st ed. New York: Appleton-Century-Crofts, 1940.

HULL, C. L. *Principles of behavior: An introduction to behavior theory.* New York: Appleton-Century-Crofts, 1943.

HULL, C. L. *A behavior system.* New Haven: Yale University Press, 1952.

KAPPAUF, W. E., & SCHLOSBERG, H. Conditioned responses in the white rat. III. Conditioning as a function of the length of the period of delay. *J. Genet. Psychol.*, 1937, *50*, 27-45.

KIMBLE, G. A., MANN, L. I., & DUFORT, R. H. Classical and instrumental eyelid conditioning. *J. exp. Psychol.*, 1955, *49*, 407-417.

LOGAN, F. A. A comparison of avoidance and nonavoidance eyelid conditioning. *J. exp. Psychol.*, 1951, *42*, 391-393.

MOORE, J. W., & GORMEZANO, I. Yoked comparisons of instrumental and classical eyelid conditioning. *J. exp. Psychol.*, 1961, *62*, 552-559.

MOORE, J. W., & GORMEZANO, I. Effects of omitted versus delayed UCS on classical eyelid conditioning under partial reinforcement. *J. exp. Psychol.*, 1962, *63*, 487-494.

MOWRER, O. H. Anxiety-reduction and learning. *J. exp. Psychol.*, 1940, *27*, 497-516.

PAPSDORF, J., GORMEZANO, I., & PROKASY, W. F. Intertrial interval and UCS intensity effects on the acquisition and extinction of the classically conditioned nictitating membrane of the rabbit. Midwest Psychol. Assoc., St. Louis, May, 1964.

RAZRAN, G. Avoidant vs. unavoidant conditioning and partial reinforcement in Russian laboratories. *Amer. J. Psychol.*, 1956, *69*, 127-129.

RUNQUIST, W. N., SIDOWSKI, J., & GORMEZANO, I. Yoked comparisons of classical and avoidance conditioning in differential conditioning of the eyelid response. *Psychol. Rep.*, 1962, *11*, 43-50.

SCHLOSBERG, H. Conditioned response in the white rat: II. Conditioned responses based upon shock to the foreleg. *J. genet. Psychol.*, 1936, *49*, 107-138.

SCHLOSBERG, H. The relationship between success and the laws of conditioning. *Psychol. Rev.*, 1937, *44*, 379-394.

SCHNEIDERMAN, N., FUENTES, I., & GORMEZANO, I. Acquisition and extinction of the classically conditioned eyelid response in the albino rabbit. *Science*, 1962, *136*, 650-652.

SCHNEIDERMAN, N., & GORMEZANO, I. Conditioning of the nictitating membrane of the rabbit as a function of CS-UCS interval. *J. comp. physiol. Psychol.,* 1964, *57,* 188-195.

SHEFFIELD, F. D. Avoidance training and the contiguity principle. *J. comp. physiol. Psychol.,* 1948, *41,* 165-177.

SOLOMON, R. L., & BRUSH, E. S. Experimentally derived concepts of anxiety and aversion. In M. R. JONES (Ed.), *Nebraska symposium on motivation.* Lincoln, Neb.: University of Nebraska Press, 1956.

SPENCE, K. W. Learning and performance in eyelid conditioning as a function of the intensity of the UCS. *J. exp. Psychol.,* 1953, *45,* 57-63.

SPENCE, K. W. Anxiety (drive) level and performance in eyelid conditioning. *Off. Naval Res. tech. Rep.,* 1962, No. 7 (Contract No. ONR-1509).

SPENCE, K. W. Anxiety (drive) level and performance in eyelid conditioning. *Psychol. Bull.,* 1964, *61,* 129-139.

SPENCE, K. W., & ROSS, L. E. A methodological study of the form and latency of eyelid responses in conditioning. *J. exp. Psychol.,* 1959, *58,* 376-381.

SPENCE, K. W., & TAYLOR, J. Anxiety and strength of the UCS as determiners of the amount of eyelid conditioning. *J. exp. Psychol.,* 1951, *42,* 183-188.

WHATMORE, G. B., MORGAN, E. A., & KLEITMAN, N. The influence of avoidance conditioning on the course of non-avoidance conditioning in dogs. *Amer. J. Physiol.,* 1946, *145,* 432-435.

WILLIAM W. GRINGS
University of Southern California

4

Verbal-Perceptual Factors in the Conditioning of Autonomic Responses [1]

Presumably the focus of this symposium is to be upon the behavioral term classical conditioning as differentiated from the physiological use of the concept. Further definitional delimitation may be needed to set the stage for the specialized subtopic of verbal-perceptual determiners of conditioning. Recently the writer had occasion to review differentiating criteria for the term *classical* as a modifier to the term *conditioning* and to separate classical from other modifiers, e.g., instrumental, operant, respondent, avoidance, escape, passive, etc. (Grings, 1963). The net result of the definitional review was a conclusion that the term refers to behavior change attributable to an operational paradigm consisting of a signal (CS) in temporal conjunction with a second stimulus (UCS) with the occurrence of the UCS not contingent upon behavior of the organism being conditioned.

Although the reference cited spent considerable space discussing theories of classical conditioning, it scarcely touched upon the topic that is to be emphasized here—probably because the topic was considered to be in a region of conceptual overlap which many would exclude from classical conditioning. My inclination is to include verbal and perceptual variables as relevant determiners in the conditioning process. And a central concern is for the nature of the complications introduced into study of the traditional paradigm of classical conditioning by processes of verbalization and perception.

In part the problem is explanatory in the sense that the need is to

[1] Research was supported in part by Grant M-3916 from the National Institute of Mental Health. The author is grateful to Russell A. Lockhart and Arthur Zeiner for editorial comments and assistance in conduct of experiments.

explain a variety of learning phenomena of particular relevance to work with human Ss. And in part the problem is methodological. If the verbal-perceptual behavior involved is not considered a part of what is labelled "conditioning," some attention must be paid to the matter of control in order to prevent verbal and perceptual variables from confounding experiments designed to study "true" classical conditioning.

Both aspects are important where human learning is involved. It is well known that during conditioning experiments with human Ss the S is usually trying to figure out what is going on, so that he can feel the master of the situation in which he finds himself. He may "catch on" to the relations among stimuli, and many perceptual features of the task may influence his learning behavior. When he "catches on" should the resulting behavior change be called "classical conditioning"? If not, what form of learning is it? To what degree, if any, can classical conditioning be studied with human Ss without this "other" kind of learning complicating or confusing the picture?

The central issue becomes this. Classical conditioning is defined in terms of certain operations of stimulus pairing. Some theorists (e.g., Spence, 1956, 1960) appear to assume that these operations are sufficient for conditioning to occur as long as various limiting requirements are met (e.g., stimulus intensity, time relations, etc.). It is not clear whether these theorists would treat cognitive-perceptual variables as a special class of independent variables determining classical conditioning, or whether the use of the term "classical conditioning" should be restricted to those operations where perception of relations can be excluded. Spence seems to favor the former when he states that "extinction of the conditioned eyelid response in humans is to a considerable degree a function of cognitive factors relating to observation on the part of the subject of procedural changes with the shift to extinction. Attempts to infer the quantitative properties of an intervening theoretical variable, for example inhibition, that results from the operation of nonreinforcement, will need to take account of these potent cognitive factors" (1963, p. 1225). Razran (1955) on the other hand holds to the second view. He would divide learning into two major classes, perceptual and nonperceptual, and asserts "that the chief determinant of the division is the presence or absence of perceived—or reacted—relations between stimuli and reaction involved in learning rather than the mere nature and history of the stimulus and reaction *per se*." "Conditioning with perceived relationship is neither 'mere conditioning' or 'conditioning plus' but something else: it is relational or perceptual learning" (1955, pp. 91, 92).

Obviously it will make a great deal of difference in the direction of experimental and theoretical developments whether verbal-perceptual variables are included as a class of determining variables subsumed under classical conditioning or whether they are treated only as limiting variables lying "outside the system."

Perhaps a brief case history will be useful as an illustration at this point. For several years the writer has sought to check out with human Ss some of the assertions made by Pavlov about compound stimulus conditioning. A presupposition in some of these studies was that acquisition of the CR occurs as a simple function of a number of reinforced trials. Further, it was assumed that by misleading S about the nature of the experiment the influence of cognitive variables (knowledge of stimulus relations) could be kept at a minimum.

Throughout this series of studies (references to which are given in the bibliography) some Ss behaved with sudden shifts of behavior as if they were responding to notions about stimulus relations, whereas some Ss gave gradual acquisition curves. Complete control of various forms of verbal-perceptual trial-and-error behavior on the part of the Ss was never achieved. It became apparent that "laws" of conditioning developed on lower, nonverbal organisms might not be applicable to human Ss—at least not until some means could be devised for controlling S's perceptual participation.

The writer subscribes to the desirability of a separation between conditioning and relational learning. At the same time, he does not like to see the separation create a "wastebasket" concept of relational learning to be ignored by students of human learning. The problem cannot be ignored because there are serious difficulties in devising adequate controls for excluding relational variables in studying classical conditioning with human Ss. What is required is a direct study of verbal-perceptual determiners of human performance in the classical conditioning situation rather than a perseveration of the negative view that such variables are sources of confounding.

Material which follows will discuss four or five major areas of overlap between classical conditioning and perceptual learning as they apply to human autonomic behavior observed in the classical conditioning paradigm. The areas might be described as (a) conditioning-like behavior arising from verbal instruction or association, (b) conditioning-like behavior changes resulting from changes in perception of the total environment, (c) verbalization of stimulus relations (awareness) as a factor in autonomic "conditioning," (d) verbal association as a conditioning transfer dimension, and (e) efforts to demonstrate preparatory (perceptual) phenomena in conditioning situations.

VERBAL INSTRUCTION AND VERBAL ASSOCIATION

One of the first propositions that might be examined is that conditioning-like modification of autonomic behavior can be produced by verbal statements informing S that the CS will be followed by the

UCS. The human S is thus set to expect the UCS when the signal (CS) appears. A classic study of this question (Cook & Harris, 1937) came to the conclusion that "conditioning of the galvanic skin response in the human adult differs from the customary conditioning procedure in that ... (a) this response is established by means of a process of verbal conditioning, and (b) it is therefore not established as a result of a series of paired inadequate-adequate stimuli combinations" (p. 209). By verbal conditioning they meant "an association between two verbalizations; for example, the verbalization 'light' and the verbalization 'receive a shock'."

Since it is reasonable to assume that response to signals (CSs) may be set up by verbal instruction, many related questions arise: (a) Is this circumstance true only of the GSR or are other autonomic and skeletal responses similarly modifiable? (b) Can the effects of verbal instruction be handled as a special class of independent variables determining the conditioning process or must their presence lead to the exclusion from studies of conditioning? (c) If the latter alternate (exclusion) is chosen, are the techniques for control (elimination) of the verbal variable adequate? (d) Is verbalization of stimulus relation (awareness) a necessary condition to the behavior change? That is, can conditioning occur without verbal awareness? (e) And, is verbal instruction alone sufficient to establishment of a CS-CR relation?

Only a few answers to the first two questions will be attempted immediately. Other questions will be discussed in later sections. First, it is postulated that verbal "conditioning" like that described for the GSR will occur with other autonomic responses, like heart rate (Chatterjee & Eriksen, 1962) and blood volume, since these responses are components of a more general class of behavior ranging from simple alerting to stronger states of mobilization. It is assumed that the instruction leads to a response of expectation or of anticipation, one part of which is autonomic discharge. In addition, there is evidence that the responses of salivation (Razran, 1936, 1949); eyeblink (McAllister & McAllister, 1958); finger withdrawal (Lindley & Moyer, 1961); and a host of others (e.g., Razran, 1961) might be susceptible to such effects.

As far as handling "instructions" as an independent variable is concerned the evidence is scattered. One approach treated the variable as facilitating or inhibiting set augmenting or decreasing performance (e.g., Norris & Grant, 1948). This is similar to a more recent tendency to interpret instruction effects as related to motivation or drive concepts (Lindley & Moyer, 1961). A published study from the University of Southern California laboratory is illustrative of this problem area (Grings & Lockhart, 1963). Ss were conditioned to give a GSR to a colored light stimulus. Then half of the sample was told "There will be no more shock." The other half was told nothing. The effect of the instructional variable upon response magnitude during three extinction trials is shown in Fig. 4-1.

Attempts to observe the instruction effect as a function of number of reinforcements and UCS intensity were unsuccessful. One variable which did determine the response was an individual difference variable derived from magnitude of response to a disparity situation, suggesting that some Ss are much more sensitive to changes in an experimental situation than are others and that this difference partly determines extinction results. A significant increase in GSR magnitude during extinction was observed for Ss above the median in disparity responding, while almost complete extinction was obtained in Ss below the median (Fig. 4-2).

CONDITIONING-LIKE CHANGES RESULTING FROM PERCEPTUAL CHANGE

To quote an early discussion of the problem by Mowrer (1938) "Apparent conditioned responses can be suddenly established and equally suddenly abolished in human beings merely by controlling the subject's state of expectancy or preparatory set. Evidence from a variety of conditioning experiments suggests that many of the subsidiary facts

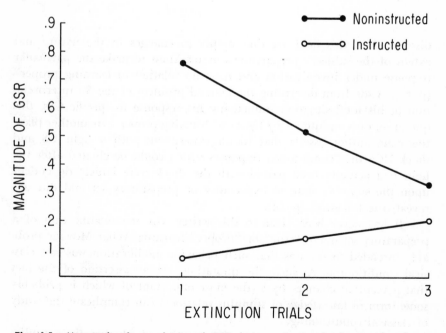

Fig. 4-1. Magnitude of second interval GSR during extinction for instructed and non-instructed groups. (Grings & Lockhart, 1963)

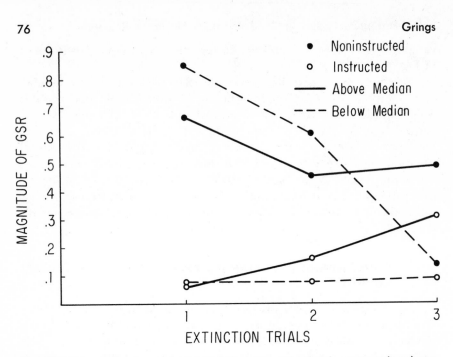

Fig. 4-2. Magnitude of second interval GSR during extinction for instructed and non-instructed Ss giving above median and below median disparity responses in a prior disparity situation. (Grings & Lockhart, 1963)

discovered in this field are due simply to changes in the nature and extent of the subject's preparedness or readiness to make the particular response under investigation and have no relation to learning proper" (p. 88). Aside from describing the general problem of the S's interpretation of his total situation influencing his response to specific CSs, this quotation puts an interesting light on "learning proper." In another place the same author asserts that in an experiment with a light CS and shock UCS the "conditioned responses which could be elicited after the light had actually been paired with the shock were largely dependent upon the subject's state of expectancy or preparatory set and did not reveal true learning" (p. 64).

It has never been clear to this writer why the modification of a preparatory set is not "true" or "proper" learning. What Mowrer probably intended to say was that such behavior modification was not classical conditioning. As such, the quotations are an assertion of the fact that perceptual changes by S (the most important of which is probably some form of knowledge of stimulus relations) can complicate the study of classical conditioning.

Putting aside for a moment the question of whether these studies are classical conditioning studies, it is possible to study them in their own right. We have chosen to do so in the hope that we might thereby better understand the total human learning (and conditioning) situation. In an already published study (Grings, Carlin, & Appley, 1962) the magnitude of GSR to a verbal cue suggesting stimulation was increased (see Table 4-1) by having this cue presented among other similar cues which were reinforced by the occurrence of the stimulation suggested by the cue (even though the "test" cue was never reinforced). The process was labelled "associated reinforcement" and was found to be related to a verbal stimulus variable described as "feasibility" of stimulation.

Table 4-1———GSRs ($\sqrt{\triangle c}$) To test cues at different levels of training

CUES	TRAINING LEVEL		
	Pretraining	14 Reinforcements	49 Reinforcements
Electric Shock			
Mean	1.03	1.34	1.14
SD	.69	.72	.67
N	80	30	30
Scalding Water			
Mean	.79	.94	.64
SD	.59	.61	.53
N	80	30	30
Pleasant Day			
Mean	.73	.64	.59
SD	.55	.53	.53
N	80	60	60

In another study comparing different determiners of response to verbal cue, verbal stimuli implying different intensities of stimulation were observed under various operations intended to "set" the subject. The four verbal stimuli ("no shock," "weak shock," "medium shock," and "strong shock") were first presented without special accompaniment. Each elicited a GSR presumably due in part to the general suggestion of noxious stimulation (see Fig. 4-3). This was followed by a series of experiences with actual shock, ranging from weak to strong, but not verbally cued. After this experience, the verbal cues were again presented and responses measured. Finally a series of conditioning trials was given in which each verbal cue was paired with the strength of stimulus implied. It will be noted that simple experience with actual shock provides differential response to the various intensity cues, differing only in level from those to the cues after paired "conditioning" experience (Grings & Zeiner, 1965).

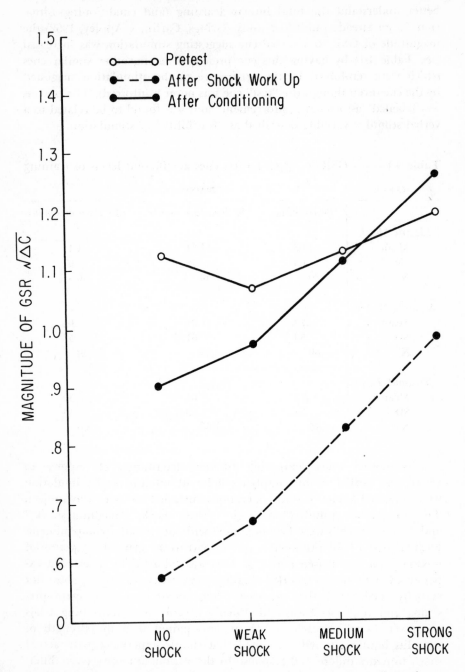

Fig. 4-3. Mean magnitude of GSR (N = 24) resulting from various "setting" experiences. (Grings & Zeiner, in press)

CONDITIONING AND VERBALIZED AWARENESS

One important implication of the "verbal-association" inter-pretation is that the experimental situation of paired stimulation is not a *necessary* condition for establishment of the autonomic response to the cue stimulus (i.e., for acquiring so-called CR). The necessary circumstance is for the cue to call upon the verbal association, and the role of paired stimulation may be merely the facilitation of learning—by providing an experience which is conducive to S's "catching on" to the CS-UCS relation.

This in turn implies that perhaps verbal-perceptual process of some sort may be a necessary feature of all classical conditioning. This is the point of view of workers who assert that conditioning of autonomic behavior occurs only when the subject is "aware" of the CS-UCS relation.

Exploration of verbal-perception-awareness problems has led us in several directions. First we used postexperimental interviews for judg-ing the extent of awareness of CS-UCS relations by Ss in discrimination conditioning situations. Ss were segregated on the basis of their verbal responses into "aware" and "unaware" groups. It was found that ver-balizations differed with manner of interrogation, learning tasks, and a host of other variables. This led eventually to doubt of the value of a definition of "awareness" so obtained. It was found that direct manipu-lation of "awareness instructions" significantly affected the degree of acquisition (Grings & Kimmel, 1959).

Another approach studied conditioning behavior of "nonverbalizing" human Ss. First, it was observed that preschool-age, deaf (nonverbal) children conditioned readily (Grings, Lowell, & Honnard, 1961). Then it was found that a group of severely mentally retarded (and nonverbal) adolescents conditioned as well as less retarded (but verbalizing) col-leagues (mean IQs of 33 vs. 66); and the mentally retarded conditioned as well as college students under similar conditions (Fig. 4-4) (Grings, Lock-hart, & Dameron, 1962; Lockhart and Grings, 1964). This work led to the conclusion that (a) conditioning does not require verbalization in the strict sense of the word and (b) the concept of "awareness" as usually de-fined is too limited to specify a necessary condition for the behavior modification (conditioning) to occur.

One of the most suggestive recent studies which bears on the "aware-ness" problem concerns instrumental conditioning of the GSR and shows that if a subject is given a shock for making a GSR to a signal cue his frequency of response to that cue will decrease. On the other hand, if he avoids shock by making a GSR to a cue, his frequency of response to that cue will increase (see Tables 4-2 and 4-3). When subjects are interrogated

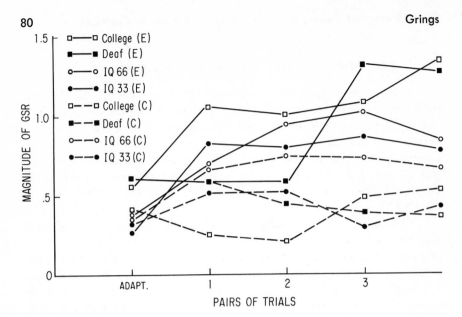

Fig. 4-4. Mean magnitudes of response of test (E) and control (C) stimuli on acquisition test trials, for different populations of Ss: College students, preschool-age deaf children, and different levels of mentally retarded adolescents.

Table 4-2————Mean frequencies (transformed to $\sqrt{F + 1}$) for three twenty-trial blocks on day one for Contingent and Noncontingent subjects of "yoked" pairs, for two types of reinforcement contingency; N = 16 Ss

	TRIALS 1-20		TRIALS 21-40		TRIALS 41-60	
	Cont.	Noncont.	Cont.	Noncont.	Cont.	Noncont.
GROUP I $GSR \rightarrow shock$	2.71	3.14	2.09	3.05	1.79	3.45
GROUP II $GSR \rightarrow no\ shock$	3.61	3.42	3.25	2.25	3.19	2.41

Table 4-3————Mean frequencies (transformed to $\sqrt{F + 1}$) for three twenty-trial blocks on each of three days, for Contingent and Noncontingent subjects of "yoked" pairs, for two types of reinforcement contingency; N = 16 Ss

	DAY 1		DAY 2		DAY 3	
	Cont.	Noncont.	Cont.	Noncont.	Cont.	Noncont.
GROUP I $GSR \rightarrow shock$	2.20	3.21	1.80	2.69	1.77	2.55
GROUP II $GSR \rightarrow no\ shock$	3.25	2.69	2.44	2.26	2.98	2.47

about their experience after three days' participation, they appear to show no knowledge of the relevant stimulus response relations.[2]

A review of what has been said thus far supports the conclusions (a) that appropriate verbal association may provide conditioning—like behavior modification in the absence of paired stimulation and (b) that conditioning will occur in the absence of verbalized awareness of stimulus relations.

VERBAL ASSOCIATION AS A CONDITIONING TRANSFER DIMENSION

All discussions of verbal factors in conditioning have concluded that when words are used as CSs the principles of meaning and of verbal learning in general become very important. For example, transfer of autonomic response from one symbolic cue to another cue related in some definable way to the original has been shown to follow verbal dimensions (Diven, 1937; Razran, 1939; Lacey & Smith, 1954; Eisen, 1954; Razran, 1949, 1952) and to vary with 'developmental level of the subject (Reiss, 1940, 1946). Transfer from a vocalized nonsense syllable to a subvocal word has been demonstrated (Noble, 1950; Menzies, 1941; Roessler & Brogden, 1943) as has generalization based on mediated verbal similarity (Branca, 1957; Phillips, 1958; Hartman, 1963; and others).

Keller (1943) after conditioning a response to a picture of an object (hat) found transfer to related objects (other hats) but not to the word hat. Harris (1960), on the other hand, found this discrimination conditioning established between pairs of words would transfer to line drawings of the objects identified by the words. He found the differences in GSRs to the object drawings of reinforced and nonreinforced words to be greater than the differences in GSRs to the original words.

The extensiveness of the work being done with semantic conditioning in the U.S.S.R. has been reviewed recently by Razran (1961) who cites studies that indicate remarkable discrimination by human subjects between positively and negatively conditioned words and their transfer stimuli. This review led Razran to point out the great significance that work in semantic conditioning has for widely different areas of psychological interest.

There are a few exploratory studies from the University of Southern California laboratory which are relevant here. All followed the same general plan. Ss were first taught to correctly anticipate words or syllables in a standard paired associates learning task. Then stimulus members of the pairs were differentially conditioned with shock as UCS, and GSRs were measured to words or syllables which had served as response mem-

[2] This study was completed with the assistance of Sidney Carlin and Tadao Uno.

bers of the pairs. In the first study (Jacobs & Grings, 1954) the strength of mediated response was observed as a function of the degree of learning of the original paired associates and the number of pairings of syllables and shock. Significant transfer occurred in the sense that GSRs to critical response syllables were greater than GSRs to noncritical response syllables. However, the transfer did not vary demonstrably as a function of either the number of shocks or the degree of original learning.

A slight modification of the study some years later (Carlin, Grings, & Jacobs, 1961) evaluated semantic transfer (based on synonym and antonym relationships) as well as the mediated transfer (based on paired associates learning). Significant semantic transfer occurred but mediated transfer did not. This was interpreted as a reflection of the importance of the strength of associate learning in providing a basis for the verbal transfer dimension.

A third study of the same questions is in progress. The general conclusion to date is twofold: (a) verbal associations provide a useful and important dimension for study of transfer of conditioned autonomic response, but (b) manipulations of the amount of such transfer as a function of variables like degree of original association and strength of conditioning are difficult to make.

PREPARATORY SET AS A CONDITIONED RESPONSE

Throughout the foregoing discussion the emphasis has been upon S's perception of the stimulus situation. Terms like "preparatory set" have been used quite loosely, although there has been some suggestion that the preparatory or perceptual set may serve as a mediating reaction. The CS may give rise to a response of preparation for receipt of the UCS. The origin of such a response might be postulated as lying in the orienting response (OR), and conditioning experience from this point of view might involve the shaping of different components of the OR. For example, the verbal component might change from "What is it?" to "Here comes such and such." Similar predictions could be made about changes in the autonomic components of the OR.

If such preparatory mediating behavior exists, it would be desirable to give it operational meaning and to study its course of development. Traditionally, this has been done to a small extent through the use of the anticipatory CR, that is the GSR occurring before onset of the UCS in long delay conditioning. Pursuit of this type of research (study of anticipatory GSRs) was reduced considerably by the general acceptance of a proposition that conditioning of the GSR does not occur with CS-UCS intervals longer than 2 seconds (White & Schlosberg, 1952; Moeller, 1954). Because of the long latency of autonomic responses, an anticipatory CR is not visible unless longer intervals (than 2 seconds) are used.

Pursuing an interest in the anticipatory CR we proceeded to observe long CS-UCS interval situations and found no difficulty in establishing differential responses during the delay intervals.[3] The existence of this "first interval response" has been interpreted as evidence for anticipatory-preparatory behavior. It has been differentiated from the OR by the fact that with CS-UCS pairings it becomes significantly greater to a reinforced CS than to a nonreinforced CS. Others have made the differentiation on the basis of latency change (Stewart, Stern, Winokur, & Freedman, 1961).

While useful as a measure of conditioned preparatory behavior this "first interval CR" has some disadvantages, one of which is the fact that magnitude of the response (or its frequency) is not a simple increasing function of number of reinforcements (it usually increases in magnitude for 7 or 8 trials, then decreases). This disadvantage has been discussed elsewhere and led to the exploration of other means for inferring the existence of preparatory (mediating) behavior during the delay interval. One of these is the *perceptual disparity response,* which compares the response to a "properly" signalled UCS and the response to the same UCS signalled by a cue associated in earlier training with a different UCS (Grings, 1960). Again, time does not permit review of different efforts to quantify preparatory behavior through the use of the "disparity" operations.

Instead, an emphasis will be placed upon how close this approach is to other work on mediating behavior in conditioning, notably that of Meryman (1954). The purpose of Meryman's research was to demonstrate that conditioned fear develops in classical defense conditioning when a long CS-UCS interval is used, and that this conditioned fear "would be revealed by changes in the amplitude of an unconditioned GSR to a probe stimulus presented during the CS-UCS interval" (p. 44). Among the results he found significant differences in anticipatory (first interval) CRs to reinforced and nonreinforced CSs (i.e., differential conditioning) but the magnitude of the CR did not increase continuously over trials. The magnitude of the unconditioned GSR to the probe stimulus showed a progressive increase over trials and was significantly greater than response on similar trials in control groups. Thus the prediction of a conditioned fear response during the trace interval was verified. However, his prediction of an increase in GSR to the probe stimulus as a function of nearness to the UCS was not confirmed.

Similar use of the probe technique has been fruitful in studies of mediating fear response in eyeblink conditioning situations (e.g., Ross, 1961; Spence & Rundquist, 1958).

---

[3] These experiments not only obtained differential responding during the delay interval but observed a second, and quite sensitive, CR occurring on test trials after the point where the UCS would normally occur (Grings, Lockhart, & Dameron, 1962; Grings & Lockhart, 1963; Lockhart & Grings, 1964).

The approach we have followed has its roots in the disparity concept yet follows a line of reasoning quite analogous to that used in the "probe" studies. In those studies the crucial assumption basic to inference of a mediating fear response is that such a response will have motivating properties and will energize the organism and hence increase level of performance on the already adequate probe stimulus. This suggests the use of a probe stimulus which is different from the UCS used in the original conditioning situation. Reasoning from the disparity notion one may create a "temporal" disparity by introducing the usual UCS at some *time* other than that used in original conditioning.

Thus, if one "probes" with the UCS at different points within the CS-UCS interval, the disparity hypothesis would predict that (1) the response to the UCS would be larger when introduced during the delay interval than when it is introduced at its original training point, (2) the magnitude of response in such "probing" should vary with nearness to the original training time of stimulus presentation, and (3) the previously mentioned effects should vary with strength of conditioning.

Data on 24 Ss are available at this time. Two colored light CSs were used, one paired with shock after a 5-sec. delay, and the other unreinforced, for a series of 20 trials on each CS. Probe trials were introduced after 1, 8, and 19 reinforcements. Three probe times were used: 1 sec., 2.5 sec., and 4.0 sec. after onset of the CS. In Table 4-4 are shown the mean responses to the UCS on the trial prior to probe test and for the probe trials, arranged according to probe interval and training level. The differences between times of probing are significant, as are also the differences between probe and non-probe UCSs, for the 8 reinforcement training level.

Table 4-4———Mean GSRs to shock on probe trials and reference (preprobe) trials as a function of probe time and training level; data in $\sqrt{\Delta c}$

TRAINING LEVEL	1-SECOND TRIALS		2.5-SECONDS TRIALS		4.0-SECONDS TRIALS	
	Ref.	*Probe*	*Ref.*	*Probe*	*Ref.*	*Probe*
8 reinforcements	1.83	2.76	1.73	2.03	1.54	1.92
20 reinforcements	2.25	2.51	2.14	2.64	2.13	2.18

The results have been interpreted as supporting the use of such "temporal disparities" to evaluate predictions about mediating reactions in long trace or delay situations. Later studies proceed from this point. However, at least two methodological problems should be mentioned.

First, when one "probes" in the delay interval, the response to the displaced UCS becomes superimposed upon the orienting response and the anticipatory CR thus introducing possible experimental confounding. Second, probing (or moving the UCS about) has an effect on conditioning making successive probing of the same S unwise. Data to support this were obtained from the fact that the GSR to a "normal" UCS on the trial before a probe is significantly less than the GSR to the "normal" UCS on the trial after the probe trial.

SUMMARY AND CONCLUSIONS

The problem discussed here begins with broad issues in human learning and centers about a class of variation not handled well in studies of autonomic response modification. The troublesome variables are, for the most part, subject variables (cognitions, perceptions, and stimulus interpretations) which are not completely definable in terms of stimulus manipulations. Efforts to response-infer the variables have not been entirely satisfactory. The result is that cognitive and perceptual variables remain to complicate the human conditioning scene. It has been asserted here that the researcher in autonomic conditioning can at the present time neither handle these variables well conceptually nor can he control them adequately by such means as disguising his experimental situation.

One alternative solution (or quasi-solution) in the context of this symposium is to label situations involving perception of stimulus relations as "not-conditioning." This is discouraged for two reasons: (a) with human Ss there is little assurance (or means of checking) for absence of perception, and (b) the danger exists of using "perception of relations" as a wastebasket concept, to explain events we cannot handle otherwise. This was not meant to imply that behavior change due to changes in perception of stimulus relations should be considered as simple conditioning, but rather that it should be studied in its own right and the concepts integrated with those of simple conditioning.

It was recognized that behavior change similar to that which occurs through classical conditioning occurs through processes of verbalization and verbal instruction; and that equally evident changes result from alterations in S's perception of the total experimental environment. Some kind of stimulus pairing (symbolic or otherwise) seems to be necessary for the behavior change to take place. However, the physical act of pairing external stimulus events is not necessary for this type of learning to occur.

At the present state of knowledge it is not possible to state (with human Ss) which levels (perceptual or nonperceptual) are operating in the "conditioning" situation unless one takes the somewhat extreme view that identifies perception with capacity to verbalize relations. Whatever criterion is used evaluation must be made of the degree of exclusion of perceptual variation that is accomplished (when the aim is to study conditioning without perception) and the restrictions placed upon informing our Ss about stimulus relations.

Assertions that conditioning occurs only if the human S is verbally aware of stimulus relations were judged to be inconclusive and lacking crucial definitions of "awareness." Evidence was presented to support the existence of conditioning without perception.

One type of learning with perception which was mentioned is that of semantic conditioning where responses are learned to meaningful (symbolic) stimuli. It was suggested that this type of conditioning situation provides a convenient area of overlap for studying principles of verbal learning and verbal association and phenomena of conditioned response transfer.

Finally, an attempt was made to point out that conditioning may involve the development of a preparatory response, the response of preparing for receipt of the UCS. Research is needed to infer the existence of preparatory sets in conditioning situations, and it was suggested, through experimental examples, that such study of learned "perception through conditioning" may contribute to important issues involving mediation behavior of human Ss.

References

ADAMS, J. K. Laboratory studies of behavior without awareness *Psychol. Bull.*, 1957, *54*, 383-405.

BRANCA, A. A. Semantic generalization at the level of the conditioning experiment. *Amer. J. Psychol.*, 1957, *70*, 541-549.

CARLIN, S., GRINGS, W. W., & JACOBS, A. Semantic and mediated generalization in autonomic conditioning. Paper presented at annual meetings of the Western Psychological Association, Seattle, Washington, June, 1961.

CHATTERJEE, B. B., & ERIKSEN, C. W. Conditioning and generalization of GSR as a function of awareness. *J. abn. soc. Psychol.*, 1960, *60*, 396-403.

CHATTERJEE, B. B., & ERIKSEN, C. W. Cognitive factors in heart rate conditioning. *J. exp. Psychol.*, 1962, *64*, 272-279.

COOK, S. W., & HARRIS, R. E. The verbal conditioning of the galvanic skin reflex. *J. exp. Psychol.*, 1937, *21*, 202-210.

DIVEN, K. Certain determinants in the conditioning of anxiety reactions. *J. Psychol.*, 1937, *3*, 291-308.

ERIKSEN, C. W. Discrimination and learning without awareness. *Psychol. Rev.*, 1960, *67*, 279-300.

GRINGS, W. W. Preparatory set variables in the classical conditioning of autonomic variables. *Psychol. Rev.,* 1960, *67,* 243-252.

GRINGS, W. W. Classical conditioning. In M. MARX, (Ed.), *Theories in Contemporary Psychology.* New York: Macmillan, 1963.

GRINGS, W. W., CARLIN, S., & APPLEY, M. Set, suggestion, and conditioning. *J. exp. Psychol.,* 1962, *63,* 417-422.

GRINGS, W. W., & KIMMEL, H. D. Compound stimulus transfer for different sense modalities. *Psychol. Reps.,* 1959, *5,* 253-260.

GRINGS, W. W., & LOCKHART, R. A. Effects of "anxiety-lessening" instructions and differential set development on the extinction of GSR. *J. exp. Psychol.,* 1963, *66,* 292-299.

GRINGS, W. W., LOCKHART, R. A., & DAMERON, L. E. Conditioning autonomic responses of mentally subnormal individuals. *Psychol. Monogr.,* 1962, *76,* No. 39 (Whole No. 558).

GRINGS, W. W., LOWELL, E. L., & HONNARD, R. R. GSR conditioning with preschool-age deaf children. *J. comp. physiol. Psychol.,* 1961, *54,* 143-148.

GRINGS, W. W., & O'DONNELL, D. E. Magnitude of response to compounds of discriminated stimuli. *J. exp. Psychol.,* 1956, *52,* 354-359.

GRINGS, W. W., & SMELEV, V. N. Changes in GSR to a single stimulus as a result of training on a compound stimulus. *J. exp. Psychol.,* 1959, *58,* 129-133.

GRINGS, W. W., & ZEINER, A. Autonomic responses to words modified by sensitizing and conditioning experiences. *J. psychosom. Res.,* in press.

HARRIS, W. Stress and perception: the effects of intense noise stimulation and noxious stimulation upon perceptual performance. PhD dissertation, Univ. Southern California, 1959.

HARTMAN, T. F. Semantic transfer of the differentially conditioned eyelid response from words to objects. *J. exp. Psychol.,* 1963, *65,* 194-200.

JACOBS, A., & GRINGS, W. W. Magnitude of GSR and associative strength as determinants of mediated transfer of GSR. Paper presented at annual meeting of the Western Psychological Association, Long Beach, Calif., 1954.

KELLER, M. Mediated generalization; the generalization of a conditioned galvanic skin response established to a picture object. *Amer. J. Psychol.,* 1943, *56,* 438-448.

KIMBLE, G. A. *Hilgard and Marquis' conditioning and learning,* 2nd ed. New York: Appleton-Century-Crofts, 1961.

LACEY, J. I., & SMITH, R. L. Conditioning and generalization of unconscious anxiety. *Science,* 1954, *120,* 1045-1052.

LACEY, J. I., SMITH, R. L., & GREEN, A. Use of conditioned autonomic responses in the study of anxiety. *Psychosom. Med.,* 1955, *17,* 208-217.

LANG, P. J., GEER, J., & HNATIOW, M. Semantic generalization of conditioned autonomic responses. *J. exp. Psychol.,* 1963, *65,* 552-558.

LINDLEY, R. H., & MOYER, K. E. Effects of instructions on the extinction of a conditioned finger-withdrawal response. *J. exp. Psychol.,* 1961, *61,* 82-88.

LOCKHART, R. A., & GRINGS, W. W. Interstimulus interval effects in GSR discrimination conditioning. *J. exp. Psychol.,* 1964, *67,* 209-214.

McAllister, W. R., & McAllister, D. E. Effect of knowledge of conditioning upon eyelid conditioning. *J. exp. Psychol.*, 1958, *55*, 579-583.

Menzies, R. Further studies in conditioned vasomotor responses in human subjects. *J. exp. Psychol.*, 1941, *29*, 457-482.

Meryman, J. J. The magnitude of an unconditioned GSR as function of fear conditioned at a long CS-UCS interval. PhD dissertation. University of Iowa, 1954.

Moeller, G. The CS-UCS interval in GSR conditioning. *J. exp. Psychol.*, 1954, *48*, 162-166.

Mowrer, O. H. Preparatory set. *Psychol. Rev.*, 1938, *45*, 62-91.

Mowrer, O. H. Preparatory set (expectancy): some methods of measurement. *Psychol. Monogr.*, 1940, *52*, No. 2, 43.

Mowrer, O. H. *Learning theory and personality dynamics.* New York: The Ronald Press, 1950.

Mowrer, O. H. *Behavior theory and learning.* New York: John Wiley & Sons, 1960.

Noble, C. E. Conditioned generalization of the galvanic skin response to a subvocal stimulus. *J. exp. Psychol.*, 1950, *40*, 15-25.

Norris, E. B., & Grant, D. A. Eyelid conditioning as affected by verbally induced inhibitory set and counter re-enforcement. *Amer. J. Psychol.*, 1948, *61*, 37-49.

Phillips, L. W. Mediated verbal similarity as a determinant of the generalization of a conditioned GSR. *J. exp. Psychol.*, 1958, *55*, 56-62.

Razran, G. Attitudinal control of human conditioning. *J. Psychol.*, 1936, *2*, 327-337.

Razran, G. A quantitative study of meaning by a conditioned salivary technique (semantic conditioning). *Science,* 1939, *90*, 89-91.

Razran, G. Attitudinal determinants of conditioning and of generalization of conditioning. *J. exp. Psychol.*, 1949, *30*, 820-829.

Razran, G. Semantic and phonetographic generalizations of salivary conditioning to verbal stimuli. *J. exp. Psychol.*, 1949, *39*, 820-829.

Razran, G. Sentential and propositional generalizations of salivary conditioning to verbal stimuli. *Science,* 1949, *109*, 447-448.

Razran, G. Some psychological factors in the generalization of salivary conditioning to verbal stimuli. *Amer. J. Psychol.*, 1949, *62*, 247-256.

Razran, G. Conditioning and perception. *Psychol. Rev.*, 1955, *62*, 83-95.

Razran, G. The observable unconscious and the inferable conscious in current Soviet psychophysiology: interoceptive conditioning, semantic conditioning and the orienting reflex. *Psychol. Rev.*, 1961, *68*, 81-147.

Reiss, B. F. Semantic conditioning involving the galvanic skin reflex. *J. exp. Psychol.*, 1940, *26*, 238-240.

Reiss, B. F. Genetic changes in semantic conditioning. *J. exp. Psychol.*, 1946, *36*, 143-152.

Roessler, R. L., & Brogden, W. J. Conditioned differentiation of vasoconstriction to subvocal stimuli. *Amer. J. Psychol.*, 1943, *56*, 78-86.

Spence, K. W. *Behavior theory and conditioning.* New Haven: Yale University Press, 1956.

Spence, K. W. *Behavior theory and learning.* Englewood Cliffs, N.J.: Prentice-Hall, 1960.

SPENCE, K. W. Cognitive factors in the extinction of the conditioned eyelid response in humans. *Science,* 1963, *140,* 1224-1225.

SPENCE, K. W., & RUNQUIST, W. N. Temporal effects of conditioned fear on the eyelid reflex. *J. exp. Psychol.,* 1958, *55,* 613-616.

STEWART, M. A., STERN, J. A., WINOKUR, G., & FREDMAN, S. An analysis of GSR conditioning. *Psychol. Rev.,* 1961, *68,* 60-67.

WHITE, C. T., & SCHLOSBERG, H. Degree of conditioning of the GSR as a function of the period of delay. *J. exp. Psychol.,* 1952, *43,* 357-362.

WOODSWORTH, R. S. Reinforcement of perception. *Amer. J. Psychol.,* 1947, *60,* 119-124.

THOMAS F. HARTMAN [1]

The Pennsylvania State University

5

Dynamic Transmission, Elective Generalization, and Semantic Conditioning

The purpose of the present paper is to summarize the literature in which verbal stimuli are used as the CS with normal human Ss in classical conditioning and "conditioning like" experiments. While the importance of work with non-normal Ss is appreciated by the author it is felt that the inclusion of these studies is impossible due to space limitations. The interested reader is referred to a volume of Russian papers (Ivanov-Smolensky, 1956) devoted exclusively to experimental research on the regulation of behavior by speech in normal and pathological children (neuroses, disease, fatigue) translated by National Science Foundation and a short summary of a 1957 Scientific Conference on this same topic held in the Institute of Higher Nervous Activity of the Academy of Sciences of the U.S.S.R. (Aslanov, 1958).

The first experimental studies using verbal stimuli as CSs were conducted in the late nineteen twenties and early thirties in the laboratories of A. G. Ivanov-Smolensky and N. I. Krasnogorsky. From these early studies of transfer between sensory stimuli and their verbal designations have evolved numerous investigations in both the United States and Russia concerned with complex relationship among word classes as well as larger verbal units. The output of conditioning studies involving verbal stimuli has increased markedly in Russia since 1950; numerous new experiments have been executed and several experiments performed in the thirties but not previously published have been disseminated. There has also been an increase in interest in the area in this

[1] Now at the Thomas J. Watson Research Center, International Business Machines, Yorktown Heights, New York.

country, probably due to a recent review of selected Russian studies of semantic conditioning by Razran (1961).

Numerous response systems have been used to investigate conditioning to verbal CSs. In addition to a wide variety of classically conditioned defensive and appetitive reflexes (e.g., eyewink, GSR, blood volume, pupillary contraction, blood coagulation, salivation, etc.), the Russians have also performed many investigations using voluntary movements (usually a bulb pressing response) conditioned by speech reinforcement. American psychologists have shown less variety than the Russians; they have typically used as CRs either the GSR or salivation.

Most American psychologists are familiar with the techniques for conditioning the various defensive reflexes, but probably few have had the opportunity to read primary literature on the conditioning of voluntary movements—Ivanov-Smolensky's "motor method of speech reinforcement." Two variations of the method currently are used. In the original version of the motor method of speech reinforcement, instructions were given prior to the experiment ("press to such and such a stimulus"); however, most recent studies have not used preliminary instructions, but rather followed each presentation of the CS by the verbal instruction (subsequent reinforcement). It was conjectured that the latter procedure was better as it allowed tracing the formation of the CR, e.g., time of first CR appearance, degree of stability of the CR, changes in correlation between the motor CR measured and its physiological concomitants, etc. The motor method of speech reinforcement with subsequent reinforcement is quite similar, if not identical to, classical conditioning. The CS can be any discriminable stimulus; the US (usually the spoken word "press") typically follows the CS by approximately two seconds. This US produces the UR, squeezing of a rubber bulb. Once a CR anticipates the US two different procedures have been used. A few investigators continue to present the US after the CS anticipates the US; most, however, give the verbal stimulus "good" to the anticipatory response and then discontinue administration of the US. The CR will not extinguish after many trials when neither the US nor any substitute stimulus is given to the S.

While the motor method of speech reinforcement may appear to have many advantages, e.g., rapid CR formation, well behaved CR latencies, easily quantified response magnitudes, etc., some data are available which question the generality of this technique. Dmitriev (1956) found that when subsequent reinforcement was used the technique was not suitable for adults; after midteens the number of Ss that showed stable conditioning decreased markedly. These data are summarized in Table 5-1. It is evident from these data that nonresponse would prove to be a considerable problem with the usual college sophomore population. Even when the technique is used with children it appears from the author's limited experience that the data obtained when the verbal stimulus "good" is given and the US omitted after the first anticipatory CR are quite different from the data obtained when the US is continued. Until more data using the technique are available its reliability and usefulness as a method of studying behavior are open to question.

Table 5-1————Percentage of children of different age groups that form CRs by motor method of speech reinforcement with subsequent verbal reinforcement (Dmitriev, 1956)

AGE IN YEARS	PERCENT Ss WITH STABLE CRs	PERCENT Ss WITH UNSTABLE CRs	PERCENT Ss WITH NO CRs
7-8	73	23	4
9-11	64	29	7
12-13	63	20	17
14-15	41	34	25
16-18	20	50	30
19-22	16	25	59

While it appears that the motor method of speech reinforcement with subsequent reinforcement cannot be used with adults, the method can be used with Ss of any age if preliminary instructions are used and the response measured is not the bulb pressing, but rather the physiological responses to the stimulus presentation concomitant to the motor response. These physiological responses are referred to in the Russian literature as "orienting reflexes," and a considerable body of literature investigating these reflexes has been developed in Russia within the past ten years. It is hypothesized in the Russian literature that the orienting reflex is a simpler, more primary, way of evaluating sensory integration and sensory analysis and is considerably more direct than the use of classical conditioning, since the orienting reflex precedes the formation of the CR in the usual conditioning experiment. The major role attributed to the CS in conditioning by the Russians and their use of typically more complex CSs than their American colleagues strengthens the relationship between these two responses in the Russian theoretical framework.

The orienting reflex is an unspecific reflex that is initiated by any qualitative or quantitative change in stimulation impinging upon the organism. There are many components of the orienting reflex, e.g., occipital EEG, GSR, respiration, vascular reactions, etc. that are highly, but not perfectly correlated. After several presentations of a stimulus to an S these physiological responses adapt or habituate at different rates. If the stimulus is changed in intensity (increased or decreased) or its other characteristics are changed the pattern of physiological response to the stimulus is essentially reinstated. The orienting reflex to a particular stimulus is *relatively* resistant to habituation, however, if that stimulus is given some special significance, such as requiring S to count to himself the number of times it is presented or requiring him to react to it in some manner such as pressing a key or squeezing a bulb. By having S perform a motor act to one stimulus, but to no other, it is possible to habituate the orienting reflex to all stimuli other than that stimulus which requires the motor act. Once the orienting reflex is "specific" to this stimulus it is possible to test for generalization of the reflex to other stimuli that are related to this stimulus. When verbal "CSs" are used the orienting reflex is habituated to a list of words and then reinstated to a single word by requiring some action to this word. Words semantically or phonetographically related to the original CS can then be tested to see if they elicit the orienting reflex.

With this brief introduction to the methodology, some representative studies using these techniques with verbal CSs will be noncritically summarized. Truly critical examination of the Russian studies is often not possible as the investigators often do not give the methodology completely enough to ascertain whether or not there was confounding of experimental variables, and the reporting of "typical protocols" rather than complete data does not allow one to determine whether or not differences found were statistically reliable. While many of the Russian studies were allegedly replicated in the laboratory before publication, in Russian, as in American, not all the data are confirmed in other laboratories (Merlin, 1957). For purposes of exposition these studies will be divided into three classes: sensory stimulus-word CR transfer, word-word CR transfer, and transfer within larger verbal units. Whenever possible developmental data will be emphasized and the results using classically conditioned CRs and those using the "conditioning like" techniques will be compared. A very brief summary will attempt limited integration of the data of the experiments discussed.

Much of the early Russian work, particularly that conducted with children, was concerned with the transfer of CRs from sensory stimuli to their word designation. Pavlov's conception of a second signaling system (speech) developing in man that takes over some of the functions of the first signaling system (sensory stimuli) made it logical to investigate developmentally the transfer of CRs from a stimulus in the first signaling system to one in the second signaling system. The Russian investigators refer to this transfer of CRs from one signal system to the other as "dynamic transmission" of a CR. Since demonstrations of the phenomenon in the thirties, e.g., Kapustnik (1930), Kotliarevsky (1935), Smolenskaya (1934), Traugott (1934), little systematic Russian work was evident until a series of papers was published in the Works of the Institute of Higher Nervous Activity in 1956.

Seredina (1956a) compared generalization in the first signaling system with generalization in the second signaling system (elective generalization) in groups of children ages 5-6, 8-9, and 11-12 using the motor method of speech reinforcement. In the first part of the experiment, the Ss were conditioned to the flash of a yellow light and generalization was tested to six other lights. Immediately following, the same Ss were conditioned to the words "yellow light" and generalization was tested to six color names as well as unrelated words. The study did not deal with transfer of a CR between the signaling systems, but rather compared the extent of the generalization within the signaling systems. Since reinforcement (the word "press") was continued throughout each experiment, the procedure was actually discrimination training, with the generalization within each signal system confounded with practice. The results of the experiment are summarized in Table 5-2. It is evident that the 5-6 and 8-9 year olds did not show the perfect correspondence between generalization in the two signaling systems that was found with the 11-12 year olds. There was only a diffuse generalization (CR transfer to unrelated words) in the 5-6 year olds in the second signaling system, and considerable diffuse generalization in the 8-9 year olds. Unfortunately, the experimental design used makes it impossible to determine how much of this diffuse generalization was present in the Ss in the first signaling system. The CR was more specific in the older children, i.e., they tended to respond only to the CS that was reinforced.

Table 5-2————Percentage of children of different age groups showing specific types of generalization of motor CRs in first and second signal systems (Seredina, 1956a)

	AGE IN YEARS		
	5-6	8-9	11-12
Generalization in 1st Signal System *Diffuse generalization in 2nd*	85	55	0
Specialization in 1st Signal System *Diffuse generalization in 2nd*	15	0	0
Generalization in 1st Signal System *Specialization in 2nd*	0	20	0
Generalization in 1st Signal System *Elective generalization in 2nd*	0	5	30
Specialization in 1st Signal System *Specialization in 2nd*	0	25	70

Korbatov (1956) studied CR transfer both from stimulus objects to words and from words to the stimulus objects. Four groups of children ages 4-6, 7-8, 12-13 and 15-16 served as Ss. Tests with stimuli from the other signaling system were made after 3, 5, 10, 20, and 30 CRs were elicited by the original CS. In addition there were control groups which did not have successive testing, but were tested only after 30 CRs were elicited by the original CS. Reinforcement of the CS was discontinued after a few CRs were made by S, so differential reinforcement to the test stimuli did not occur. The data summarizing the transfer from the first signaling system to the second appear in Fig. 5-1. It is evident that as the age of the Ss increased there was more dynamic transmission, i.e., the CR transferred from the object to its verbal representation, but not to other verbal stimuli. The younger age groups, however, showed a diffuse transfer of the CR—transfer to other verbal stimuli in addition to the one representing the object that was reinforced. Failure of the CR to transfer at all to the other signaling system (specialized CR) was not monotonically related to the age of the Ss. There appears to be some evidence that the point at which maximal transfer occurred decreased with increasing age of the Ss. Conditioned response transfer from the

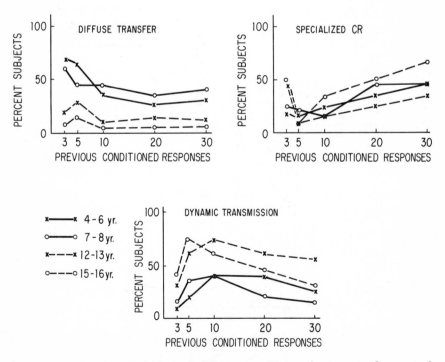

Fig. 5-1. Percentage of children of different age groups showing specific types of transfer of motor CRs from the first signal system to the second.

second signaling system to the first appear in Fig. 5-2. The most orderly data in Fig. 5-2 are those concerned with the specialization of the CR in the second signaling system; with increasing age there were more Ss that showed no CR to transfer to any stimuli in the first signaling system. Similar to the data in Fig. 5-1, the data in Fig. 5-2 show that there was more diffuse transfer in the younger Ss than the older Ss. Comparison of Figs. 5-1 and 5-2 also shows that there was, in general, less CR transfer from the second signaling system to the first than from the first to the second for all age groups.

Seredina (1956b) obtained results that were not in close agreement with those of Korbatov (1956), but the methodologies in the two studies were so different that it is not possible to determine exactly the causes of these inconsistencies. Seredina established four stable motor CRs, two to visual stimuli (a key and a pencil) and two to their verbal designations (the words "key" and "pencil"). Later the CR to one of the stimuli was extinguished by the negative reinforcement, and the transfer of extinction to the two stimuli in the other signal system was tested. No reinforcement was ever given to the test stimuli. The study was a longitudinal one; the Ss were trained and tested over a period of three

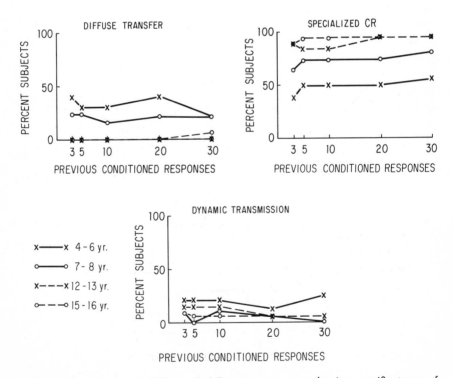

Fig. 5-2. Percentage of children of different age groups showing specific types of transfer of motor CRs from the second signal system to the first.

to four months. The results of the study are summarized in Table 5-3. These data on the transfer of CRs from the first signaling system to the second support the results found by Korbatov (1946); there was considerably more dynamic transmission with increasing age of the Ss. The discrepancy between the two studies lies in the fact that Seredina found that the CR transfer from the second signaling system to the first was approximately equal to that from the first to the second. This may have been due to the fact that her Ss had considerable experience before this transfer was tested; this was also true of similar findings in the unpublished theses of Aslanov, Kostandov, and Raeva cited by Korbatov (1956). Apparently there will be extensive transfer from the second signaling system to the first if the Ss have been previously tested for transfer from the first signaling system to the second.

Studies by Naroditskaya (1956a, 1956b) extend the studies previously cited by testing simultaneously dynamic transmission between the signaling systems and generalization within the signaling systems. In one study (Naroditskaya, 1956b), a green light was positively reinforced (the word "press") and a blue light was negatively reinforced (the words "do not press"); CR transfer was tested to related words ("grass," "sky," "sea," "leaf," etc.) and unrelated words. Increasing dynamic transmission and elective generalization were found with increasing age (5 to 12 year olds). In the other study (Naroditskaya, 1956a), the pictures of six birds were positively reinforced and the pictures of six animals

Table 5-3————Percentage of children of different age groups showing specific types of transfer of motor CRs (Seredina, 1956b)

AGE	TRANSFER FROM FIRST SIGNAL SYSTEM TO SECOND SIGNAL SYSTEM		
	Simple Diffuse Transfer	No Transfer	Dynamic Transfer
5-6	20	54	26
8-9	0	66.7	33.3
11-12	7	13	80

AGE	TRANSFER FROM SECOND SIGNAL SYSTEM TO FIRST SIGNAL SYSTEM		
	Simple Diffuse Transfer	No Transfer	Dynamic Transfer
5-6	20	40	40
8-9	20	46.7	33.3
11-12	7	13	80

were negatively reinforced. Conditioned response transfer was then tested
to the words "birds" and "beasts." With increasing age there was an
increase in the number of Ss that attained the generic verbal category
concept.

While there are several recent studies of dynamic transmission of
the orienting reflex, they are virtually identical in results so only the
experiment of Marushevsky (1957) will be cited. This paper is particularly valuable to those interested in the orienting reflex as it is
available in translation and contains one of the most complete descriptions of the technique. Marushevsky tested dynamic transmission of the
orienting reflex from the first to the second signaling system in adult
Ss and found positive results for all Ss for which data are reported. The
first signaling system stimuli were both visual and auditory (short and
long duration lights or sounds) and the verbal stimuli word phases such
as "short light," "long sound," etc. Both the occipital EEG and the GSR
were measured, but only the latter data were reported in the paper.

When defensive CRs rather than CRs conditioned by the motor
method of speech reinforcement have been used to investigate dynamic
transmission large amounts of transfer typically were not found. Branca
(1957) used conditioned GSR as the CR and found CR transfer from
stimulus objects to words in only one of eight Ss, but significant CR
transfer from words to objects in four of eight Ss. Finding more CR
transfer from the second signaling system to the first is the opposite of
what most Russian studies find—typically they report more CR transfer
from objects to words or no differences. Keller (1943) also used the GSR
and formed the CR to a picture of a boy scout hat. No significant transfer
of the CR was found to the word "hat" when compared to the control
words "duck" and "ball," but there was transfer to the picture of a
fireman's hat. The failure to find sizeable effects with the GSR may be
due to the specific response system, but the data of Korbatov (1956)
suggest another possibility—too extensive training before the transfer
tests were conducted. Some defensive reflexes have shown positive results. Markosyan (1958) found transfer of blood coagulation CRs from
the flash of a lamp to the words "lamp," "lantern," and "light," but not
to several control words.

Hartman (1962) studied the transfer of the eyelid CR from word
CSs to the objects represented by these words. It was hoped that the
existence of objective methods for separating the Ss in eyelid conditioning into voluntary and nonvoluntary responders would permit a comparison of "voluntary" and "classically conditioned" Ss in the same
experiment. The eyelid response was differential conditioned to the
words "pink" and "blue," "left" and "right," or the control words
"lion" and "deer." Transfer of this discrimination was then tested to

two laterally separated lights, one pink and one blue. While there was significantly better discrimination to the lights when the previous discrimination training was to the two pairs of word CSs relevant to the lights, the effects were very small. Despite the fact that differential conditioning was used, the differences in discrimination to the lights among the groups were due entirely to the rate of responding to the positively reinforced CS. No differences in rate of responding to the unreinforced CS were noted in the groups. While the "voluntary" Ss responded at a higher level throughout the experiment they did not appear to perform differently from the "classically conditioned" Ss with respect to the transfer of the original discrimination.

Studies of word-word CR transfer fall into three general categories: transfer to synonyms, antonyms, and homonyms; transfer within words of a general class, e.g., rural words, war words; and transfer to words related to the CS on the basis of free association tests. The pioneer work on the transfer of CRs from words to synonyms and homonyms was the study by Razran (1939). More transfer of a salivary CR from the CS words to their synonyms than their homonyms was reported; these findings were essentially confirmed by Riess (1940), who used GSR as the CR. Riess (1946) also studied CR transfer to synonyms, antonyms, and homonyms as a function of the age of the Ss. Four groups of Ss approximately eight, eleven, fourteen, and eighteen years of age were used. In the two groups of older Ss there was more CR transfer to the synonyms than to the antonyms and to the homonyms; this relationship was reversed in the youngest Ss studied. He also noted markedly less CR transfer to homonyms with increasing age. Not all investigations using the GSR have reported positive results. Eisen (1954) found no significant differences in CR transfer to synonyms, antonyms, homonyms, and neutral words in a fairly sizeable study.

Hartman (unpublished) investigated transfer of two components of the orienting reflex, GSR and occipital EEG, from words to synonyms, antonyms, and neutral words. The Ss were read a list of words at approximately 3.5 second intervals until there was no appreciable GSR elicited by five consecutive words presented to the S. At that time S was instructed to press a key when a given word was presented, but to no other words. This word was then presented either 7, 14, or 21 times before transfer was tested to synonyms, antonyms, and neutral words. Three different lists of conditioning and transfer words were used, there were no differences among the sets. The order of presentation of the test words was balanced using successive 3 x 3 Latin squares. Some of the data of the study are presented in Fig. 5-3. As expected, with successive presentations of the test stimuli the magnitude of the GSR decreased, i.e., the orienting reflex habituated to the test stimuli. What was not

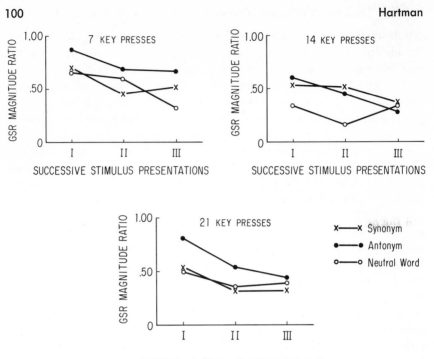

Fig. 5-3. Galvanic skin response to successive presentations of the test stimuli. The GSR measure is the ratio of the response made to the test stimuli to the mean of the responses made to the first 7 presentations of the signal stimulus.

expected was the finding that transfer of the orienting reflex was not greatest to the synonyms, but rather to the antonyms. This was especially pronounced in the groups that received either 7 or 21 "conditioning" trials. Preliminary analyses have shown the differences among the word classes and the habituation both to be statistically reliable. The differences in level of responding after 7, 14, and 21 trials was not significantly different; this was a between Ss test and, with only 15 $\overset{\text{s}}{S}s$ in each group, not a very powerful one.

Schwarz (1948, 1949, 1960) conditioned vasoconstriction and pupillary contraction to words and tested CR transfer to semantically and phonetographically related words during different stages of CR training. Phonetographic CR transfer was evident only early in training; it disappeared late in the session. Semantic transfer was evident throughout training. Marushevsky (1957) tested for transfer of a component of the orienting response (GSR) from the signal word to related and unrelated words, e.g., transfer from the word "good" to "poor," "excellent," "table," "chair." There was significant transfer to related but not to unrelated words. Branca (1957) found that few Ss showed significant transfer of the CR from a word to a related word ("freeze" to "chill," "brook" to "stream"), but considerably more transfer was found for Ss conditioned to several words ("creek," "river," and "stream") before the generalization test.

Two American studies (Diven, 1937; Lacey & Smith, 1954) conditioning "anxiety" to a word and testing CR transfer to words of the same response class are well known and need not be summarized here. Probably the most exciting similar research is the paper read by Luria to the British Psychological Society in 1957 (Luria & Vinogradova, 1959). Two studies were reported, one conducted with ten children 11-15 years old; the other with seven adults. In both experiments the response measured was blood volume in a finger and the head. These two measures have a characteristic pattern for both an orienting reflex to stimuli (contraction of blood vessels in the fingers and dilation of blood vessels in head) and as a UR to a painful stimulus (contraction of blood vessels in the fingers and the head). The study with children utilized the orienting reaction; it was found that words related to the signal stimulus produced an orienting reflex, but this reaction was not produced by phonetographically related or unrelated words. In the study with the adult Ss, the word "violin" was consistently reinforced with a painful electric shock. This reinforcement initially caused an orienting reaction to the stimulus which was gradually replaced by the pain reaction after 18-25 repetitions. At this time test words were introduced. The names of string instruments produced the same reaction at the basic stimulus; names of stringless instruments, other words connected with music, and in some cases words close to the key word in sound all produced an orienting reflex; but neutral words produced no reaction. If conditioning to the signal word was continued over an extended period it only elicited the pain reaction; words that previously produced the pain reaction then produced the orienting reflex; and no other words produced any vascular reaction.

Only one study was found that investigated transfer among words whose relation was determined from word association norms. Mednick (1957) established a conditioned GSR to the word "light," and tested generalization to the related words "dark," "lamp," "heavy," "soft," and the neutral word "square." The relationship between the four transfer words and the CS word was defined by the number of times that the CS word was given as a first association to the transfer words in free association tests. While there was, in general, more CR transfer to the related words than to the neutral test word, the CR transfer was not an orderly function of the relatedness as measured by the free association data.

Conditioning to the meaning of sentences has received attention both in this country and in the Soviet Union since the publication of Razran's paper in *Science* (Razran, 1949). In this study four Ss were trained to give salivary CRs to three short sentences ("Poverty is degrading." "Roosevelt will be elected." "Socialism is desirable.") and the transfer of the CRs was tested to nine propositionally equivalent yet sententially different sentences and to twelve sentences in which the proposition was negated. There was from 41 percent to 63 percent CR transfer to the propositionally equivalent sentences, but only 19 percent to 39 percent CR transfer to the sentences that negated the proposition.

There have also been investigations of the effectiveness of the various parts of the sentence in evoking the CR to a sentence. Razran (1952) found that the verbs and direct objects had higher probabilities of evoking the CR to the sentence than did the subject or modifiers. Elkin (1957) studied this phenomenon in 25 Ss, varying in age from ten to sixteen years with eyeblink as the CR. Younger school children took approximately twice as long to form conditioned reflexes to the sentences than did the older children. Conditioned responses were most easily formed in the younger children to sentences or phrases closely connected with the surrounding conditions, e.g., "Begins experiment." On a rainy day, the younger children developed a CR easily to the phrase "Goes rain"; on a sunny day to the phrase "Today good weather." The CRs were very difficult to condition when the sentence did not agree with the surrounding conditions. The element in the sentence that had the highest probability of eliciting CR in the younger children was the first or last word of the sentence, not the word that carried the most meaning load. If a word in the sentence was pronounced louder than the others during the conditioning to the sentence, this word also had high probability of producing the CR. Transfer to propositionally equivalent yet sententially different sentences was not observed. This latter finding was not true for children 12-14 years old. By the time a child was 15-16, transfer of the CRs to the word elements of the sentence was similar to that found in adults in an earlier study (Elkin, 1955); those words in the sentence that carried the most meaning of the sentence had the highest probability of eliciting the CR.

Two recent Russian projects (Volkova, 1953, 1957) have studied conditioning to a bipolar meaning dimension. Volkova (1953) differentially conditioned the salivary response to the words "good" (positive CS) and "bad" (negative CS). The test stimuli were sentences, which were a priori classified as being good, bad, or indifferent. There was considerable transfer to "good" sentences such as "The Soviet army was victorious," no CR transfer to "bad" sentences such as "The pupil was fresh to the teacher," and intermediate transfer to the sentence "The pupil passed the examination with a mediocre grade." In the second study (Vinogradova, 1957) both motor CRs and salivary CRs were differentially conditioned to the words "correct" (positive CS) and "error" (negative CS). When true and false statements were substituted for the CSs, they were found to be responded to in terms of the original conditioning. The sentences "Today is January 2" and "Today is January 3" were responded to as the positive or negative CS depending on which of the successive days the test was made. Acker and Edwards (1963) differentially conditioned vasoconstriction to the words "good" and "bad," and transfer was tested to fifteen words, five each from groups of words that were high, low, or intermediate on the GOOD-BAD scale of the Semantic Differential. The results were very definite; vasoconstriction increased markedly for words similar in meaning to the positive CS, decreased for words similar in meaning to the negative CS, and remained essentially unchanged for words that were neutral.

From the cursory review of the papers cited above, it is evident that transfer of classically conditioned responses on the basis of meaning does exist, but that much research remains to be done in this area. The Russian practice of reporting individual protocols for only a small proportion of the Ss in the experiment, no doubt, gives the impression of greater stability in their research than actually existed. Most studies have only attempted to demonstrate the phenomenon rather than determine precise quantitative relations. Studies using the "motor method of speech reinforcement" have shown the most orderly results, but this technique is little understood in this country and has its critics even in Russia. Merlin (1957), for example, did not find the results typically reported from Ivanov-Smolensky's laboratory; when Ss were conditioned to a light of a certain color, and the name of that color as well as other colored lights and their names were included as CSs but not reinforced, the CRs sometimes first appeared in the unreinforced signal system or appeared in one signal system only when they disappeared in the other. Thus while transfer from one signal system to the other was found for all Ss the effects were very complicated. While positive findings have been reported when defensive reflexes were used, the results have not been as definitive.

It is possible that a different set of laws governs the transfer of voluntary motor responses than governs the involuntary responses; insufficient data exist to make any conclusions. Studies utilizing both types of responses with adequate experimental controls and more sophisticated analyses are desirable. The results now available can be used to design more meaningful experiments, but the results available to date are not really more than a guide to future research.

References

ACKER, L. E., & EDWARDS, A. E. Transfer of vasoconstriction over a bipolar meaning dimension. *J. exp. Psychol.*, 1964, *67*, 1-6.

ASLANOV, A. S. Problems connected with joint activity of the first and second signal systems in normal and pathological states. *Zh. vyssh. nervn. Deyatel.*, 1958, *8*, 192-202.

BRANCA, A. A. Semantic generalization at the level of the conditioning experiment. *Amer. J. Psychol.*, 1957, *70*, 541-549.

DIVEN, E. E. Certain determinants in the conditioning of anxiety reactions. *J. Psychol.*, 1937, *3*, 291-308.

DMITRIEV, A. S. On methods of investigation of higher nervous activity in man. *Zh. vyssh. nervn. Deyatel.*, 1956, *6*, 905-912.

EISEN, N. H. The influence of set on semantic generalization. *J. abnorm. soc. Psychol.*, 1954, *49*, 491-496.

ELKIN, D. G. The characteristics of conditioned reflexes to a complex verbal stimulus. *Vop. Psikhol.*, 1955, *1*, 79-89.

ELKIN, D. G. On conditioned reflexes to complex verbal stimuli in schoolchildren. In B. G. ANAN'YEV, A. N. LEONTIEV, A. R. LURIA, N. A. MENUINSHKAIA, C. L. RUBINSTEIN, A. A. SMIRNOV, M. V. SOKOLOV, & B. M. TEPLOV (Eds.), *Materials of the conference on psychology.* Moscow: Akad. Pedag. Nauk. RSFSR, 1957. Pp. 370-379.

HARTMAN, T. F. Semantic transfer of the differentially conditioned eyelid response from words to objects. *J. exp. Psychol.*, 1963, *65*, 194-200.

IVANOV-SMOLENSKY, A. G. *Works of the institute of higher nervous activity: Pathophysiological series.* Vol. 2. Moscow: Academy of Sciences of the USSR, 1956.

KAPUSTNIK, O. P. The interrelation between direct conditioned stimuli and their verbal symbols. *Trud. Lab. Fiziol. vyssh. nervn. Deyatel. Reb.*, 1930, *2*, 11-22. (*Psychol. Abstr.*, 8:152.)

KELLER, M. Mediated generalization: the generalization of a conditioned galvanic response established to a pictured object. *Amer. J. Psychol.*, 1943, *56*, 438-448.

KORBATOV, B. M. Study of the dynamic transmission of a conditioned connection from one cortical signaling system into the other. In A. G. IVANOV-SMOLENSKY (Ed.), *Works of the institute of higher nervous activity: Pathophysiological series.* Vol. 2. Moscow: Academy of Sciences of the USSR, 1956.

KOTLIAREVSKY, L. I. Cardio-vascular conditioned reflexes to direct and to verbal stimuli. *Fiziol. Zh.*, 1936, *20*, 228-242. (*Psychol. Abstr.*, 13:4046.)

LACEY, J. U., & SMITH, R. L. Conditioning and generalization of unconscious anxiety. *Science*, 1954, *120*, 1045-1052.

LURIA, A. R., & VINOGRADOVA, O. S. An objective investigation of the dynamics of semantic systems. *Brit. J. Psychol.*, 1959, *50*, 89-105.

MARKOSYAN, A. A. Conditioned-reflex changes of blood coagulation. *Zh. vyssh. nervn. Deyatel.*, 1958, *8*, 161-167.

MARUSHEVSKY, M. On the interaction of the two signal systems in orientation reactions. *Vop. Psikhol.*, 1957, *3*, 78-87.

MEDNICK, M. T. Mediated generalization and the incubation effect as a function of manifest anxiety. *J. abnorm. soc. Psychol.*, 1957, *55*, 315-321.

MERLIN, V. S. *Vop. Psikhol.*, 1957, *3*, 53-67. Cited by A. MINTZ, Recent developments in psychology in the USSR. In P. R. FARNSWORTH (Ed.), *Annual Review of Psychology.* Vol. 9. Palo Alto: Annual Reviews, 1958.

NARODITSKAYA, G. D. The compound dynamic pattern in children of different ages. In A. G. IVANOV-SMOLENSKY (Ed.), *Works of the institute of higher nervous activity: Pathophysiological series.* Vol. 2. Moscow: Academy of Sciences of the USSR, 1956. (a)

NARODITSKAYA, G. D. A study of the question of the phenomenon of the so-called secondary excitation in the cerebral cortex of children. In A. G. IVANOV-SMOLENSKY (Ed.), *Works of the institute of higher nervous activity: Pathophysiological series.* Vol. 2. Moscow: Academy of Sciences of the USSR, 1956. (b)

RAZRAN, G. A quantitative study of meaning by a conditioned salivary technique (semantic conditioning). *Science,* 1939, *90*, 89-91.

RAZRAN, G. Sentential and propositional generalization of salivary conditioning to verbal stimuli. *Science,* 1949, *109*, 447-448.

RAZRAN, G. Experimental semantics. *Trans. NY Acad. Sci.,* 1952, *14*, 171-177.

RAZRAN, G. The observable unconscious and the inferable conscious in current Soviet psychophysiology: Introceptive conditioning, semantic conditioning, and the orienting reflex. *Psychol. Rev.,* 1961, *68*, 81-147.

RIESS, B. F. Semantic conditioning involving the galvanic skin reflex. *J. exp. Psychol.,* 1940, *26*, 238-240.

RIESS, B. F. Genetic changes in semantic conditioning. *J. exp. Psychol.,* 1946, *36*, 143-152.

SCHWARZ, L. A. Knowledge of the word and its sound form as a conditioned stimulus. *Byull. eksp. Biol. Med.,* 1948, *25*, 292-294.

SCHWARZ, L. A. Knowledge of the word and its sound form as a conditioned stimulus. *Byull. eksp. Biol. Med.,* 1949, *27*, 412-415.

SCHWARZ, L. A. Conditioned reflexes to verbal stimuli. *Vop. Psikhol.,* 1960, *6*, 86-98.

SEREDINA, M. I. Age characteristics involved in the generalization of conditioned word stimuli. In A. G. IVANOV-SMOLENSKY (Ed.), *Works of the institute of higher nervous activity: Pathophysiological series.* Vol. 2. Moscow: Academy of Sciences of the USSR, 1956. (a)

SEREDINA, M. I. Elective irradiation of the inhibitory process from the second signaling system into the first. In A. G. IVANOV-SMOLENSKY (Ed.), *Works of the institute of higher nervous activity: Pathophysiological series.* Vol. 2. Moscow: Academy of Sciences of the USSR, 1956. (b)

SMOLENSKAYA, E. P. Verbal symbols of conditioned and differential stimuli. *Trud. Lab. Fiziol. vyssh. nervn. Deyatel. Reb.,* 1934, *4*, 304-315. (*Psychol. Abstr.,* 9:1163.)

TRAUGOTT, N. N. The interrelations of immediate and symbolic projections in the process of the formation of conditioned inhibition. *Trud. Lab. Fiziol. vyssh. nervn. Deyatel. Reb.,* 1934, *4*, 273-303. (*Psychol. Abstr.,* 9:1166.)

VOLKOVA, V. D. On certain characteristics of the foundation of conditioned re-
    flexes to speech stimuli in children. *Fiziol. Zh. SSSR*, 1953, *39*, 540-548.
VOLKOVA, V. D. *Zh. Vyssh. nervn. Deyatel.*, 1957, 7, 525-533. Cited by A. MINTZ,
    Further developments in psychology in the USSR. In P. R. FARNSWORTH
    (Ed.), *Annual Review of Psychology*. Vol. 10. Palo Alto: Annual Reviews,
    1959.

HOWARD S. HOFFMAN

The Pennsylvania State University

6

Theory Construction Through Computer Simulation[1]

The formulation of a quantitative model for a given behavioral process has several advantages for the researcher. For example, the employment of a model tends to sharpen one's thinking about the variables which may play a role in the process under consideration. Of equal importance, however, is the fact that once a model has been developed, it can act as a unifying factor in the design of further research and in the interpretation of current research. This paper is concerned with the task of developing models for the mechanisms which play a role in avoidance. The work represents a joint effort of myself and the members of my laboratory staff: Mr. Morton Fleshler, Miss Sharon Toffey,[2] and Mr. John Searle. Our interest in the problem is, perhaps more than anything else, an expression of an attempt to achieve conceptual clarification of a learning process which, from every indication, is basically dynamic. The work to date has been concerned only with discriminated avoidance, but the newer conceptions of Pavlovian conditioning which recognize dynamic interactions between the subject's behavior and the prevailing stimulus conditions suggest that the approach described here may also prove useful to the contemporary student of classical conditioning.

In the avoidance paradigm with which we have been concerned, a warning signal precedes each occurrence of a noxious event. If the S

[1] This work was done in the course of a project supported by National Institute of Mental Health grant No. MH-02433-05. Access to an IBM 7074 was generously provided by the Pennsylvania State University Computation Center.

[2] Miss Toffey's work on the project was facilitated by National Science Foundation grant No. 9363 for undergraduate research participation.

performs a given response during the warning period, the signal is terminated and the noxious event fails to occur. If, however, the S fails to avoid, it must still perform the response to terminate the noxious event. Relatively few theorists (Bush & Mosteller, 1955, 1959; Hull, 1943; Miller, 1951; Mowrer, 1950; Solomon & Wynne, 1953; Spence, 1956; Theios, 1963) have sought to provide a detailed theoretical account of the behavior generated by these arrangements and only the mathematical theorists (Bush & Mosteller, 1955, 1959; Theios, 1963) have presented formal quantitative models.

The general approach of the mathematical theorists is exemplified by the two-operator linear model proposed by Bush and Mosteller. They assume that during avoidance training the events on each trial lead to progressive changes in the probability of the avoidance response. These changes in probability are represented by the action of linear operators. Thus the acquisition process is conceptualized as an increase in the probability of the avoidance response (P) that results when P is transformed by the successive application of an avoidance operator Q_1 (for trials on which the S avoids) and an escape operator Q_2 (for trials on which the S fails to avoid).

The operators Q_1 and Q_2 have the form

$$Q_i P = \alpha_i P + (1 - \alpha_i) \lambda_i$$

where the parameter λ_i represents the limit (fixed point) for repeated application of the operator, and the parameter α_i is a reflection of the effectiveness of the event in question. For example, if P_n equals the probability of avoidance on trial n and an avoidance response occurs on trial n, then

$$P_{n+1} = \alpha_1 P_n + (1 - \alpha_1) \lambda_1.$$

If, however, the S fails to avoid on trial n, then

$$P_{n+1} = \alpha_2 P_n + (1 - \alpha_2) \lambda_2.$$

To apply the model to a given set of data, either of two methods can be used to derive the learning curve. The first approach involves estimating the constants P_0, α_1, α_2, λ_1, and λ_2 and solving a series of general equations. The second approach, though less mathematically elegant, is in certain respects more interesting. It involves estimating the parameters of the operators (as in the first method) and running a group of "stat animals" using Monte Carlo methods. The technique is basically simple and is comparable to deriving an approximation to a theoretical probability distribution by throwing dice.

A given "stat S" is assigned an initial probability of avoidance on trial 1. Then a die (with the appropriate probability built in) is thrown to determine whether or not the S makes an avoidance response. If the fall of the die says that the S avoids, the avoidance operator is applied to the probability that existed on trial 1, thus transforming it to a new probability. If the fall of the die says that the S fails to avoid, the escape operator is applied. Trial 2 for this S is simulated in the same way except that the die which is thrown is arranged to represent the transformed probability. When enough "stat rats" have been run for enough trials, their data are summarized in the same fashion as the data derived in an actual experiment. The test of the model comes in the comparison between the functions yielded by the "stat Ss" and the functions obtained in the experimental laboratory.

A very different approach to the interpretation of avoidance is provided by the dual process theorists (Hull, 1943; Miller, 1951; Mowrer, 1950; Solomon & Wynne, 1953; and Spence, 1956). They suggest that the motivation for the avoidance response derives from a conditioned emotional reaction (CER) to the warning signal which develops from the pairing of the warning signal and the noxious event. The reinforcement for avoidance, on the other hand, is assumed to derive from reductions of the CER during avoidance trials. In essence, dual process theory conceives that the probability of avoidance on a given trial reflects the joint action of a motivational condition which develops on trials where the S fails to avoid and an avoidance habit which reflects reinforcements accrued on avoidance trials. It will be convenient to use the terminology of Hull and Spence to symbolize this basic notion. If we overlook mathematical details for the moment, dual process theory can be interpreted to suggest that

$$P_n = H_n \times D_n$$

where P_n = the probability of avoidance on trial n.

H_n = the avoidance habit controlled by the warning signal on trial n.
and D_n = the motivational state on trial n.

According to the model implied in this equation, the events on trial n will affect the intervening variables D or H and thus indirectly modify the probability on trial $n + 1$. In general, however, the effects of either an avoidance or nonavoidance trial will depend upon the separate levels of D_n and H_n, but not upon the level of P_n as such.

For example, there are an infinite number of ways in which $P_n = H_n \times D_n$ might equal .4:

$$P_n = .8 \times .5 = .4 \qquad P_n = .4 \times 1.0 = .4$$
$$P_n = .5 \times .8 = .4 \qquad P_n = 1.0 \times .4 = .4 \text{ etc.}$$

If the S avoids on trial n, the transformation of P will be small if the H on trial n is already close to its theoretical upper limit, but it will be large if the H on trial n is small. In essence, the effects of an avoidance response on trial n will depend not upon P_n as such, but upon the intervening variables which contribute to P_n which, in turn, reflects the nature of the trials which have preceded the n-th trial.

This set of conditions is quite distinct from those which occur in the Bush-Mosteller model, where the probability of a response on a given trial depends only upon the probability that existed just prior to the trial and upon the event which occurs on the trial. Thus, for example, if $P_n = .4$ and the S avoids on trial n, the probability on trial $n + 1$ will be transformed to a new value which will be the same, regardless of whether the S arrived at trial n through a sequence of escape responses, avoidance responses, or some combination of escape and avoidance responses. This characteristic of the model derives from the fact that the operators (Q_1 and Q_2) act directly upon P_n.

Our own work represents an effort to circumnavigate this aspect of the Bush-Mosteller model by developing an approach which employs intervening variables of the sort postulated by Hull and Spence. The need for such work arises from the fact that while both Hull and Spence have provided quantitative models for learning, neither theorist has sought to quantify the dynamic situation which arises in discriminated avoidance. In all likelihood, the reason for this omission can be found in the formidable mathematical structure which the derivation of learning curves would entail.

Our approach to the problem has been to leave the formal derivations to more mathematically sophisticated souls and instead, to program a computer to simulate the behavior that is generated by models based upon the Hull-Spence tradition. Our initial effort represented an attempt to deal with some data which we had obtained in an earlier experiment (Hoffman & Fleshler, 1962). In that study a group of rats had been run on a discriminated avoidance paradigm, while they were concurrently engaged in pressing a lever for food. The design enabled us to track the several levels of emotional behavior that occurred during the acquisition of the avoidance response. Our method was to analyze the suppression of lever pressing during each stage of the experiment.

In order to develop a quantitative model of these data, we made the simplifying assumption that the probability of avoidance on trial n was numerically equal to $H \times D$ and that while H grew on each avoidance trial, D grew on each nonavoidance trial. We were especially interested in D, however, because some of our other research (Hoffman, Fleshler, & Chorny, 1961) has suggested that although contact with the noxious event led to an increased tendency for the warning signal to evoke a CER, it also appeared to leave a lingering aftereffect which enhanced subsequent performance. For want of a better term, we have called the lingering aftereffects of contact with the noxious stimulus, "the aversive residue (AR)."

We assumed that the total drive during a given warning signal was equal to the CER evoked by that signal plus the aversive residue from previous nonavoidance trials within a given session. To keep our arithmetic straight and avoid P's with values greater than 1, we assumed that both CER and AR always had values between 0 and 1. We quantified the combined effects of the two kinds of motivation in accordance with Hull's equation for the physiological summation of habits, which in the present context reduces to

$$\text{Total D} = \text{CER} + \text{AR} - \text{CER·AR}.$$

Our equation for the development of CER was

$$\text{CER} = 1 - 10^{-jE}$$

where E is the number of prior escape trials and j is the growth constant. In essence, we were assuming that the learning curve for the CER is negatively accelerated when one examines only those trials on which the warning signal is paired with the noxious event.

The aversive residue was also assumed to grow as a function of the Ss contact with the noxious event according to the equation

$$\text{AR} = 1 - 10^{-kE'}$$

where E' is the number of prior escape trials within a given session and k is the growth constant. We assumed that the aversive aftereffects of noxious stimulation would tend to dissipate as a function of time and that given enough time (for example 24 hours) it would dissipate entirely.

The avoidance habit (H) was assumed to grow as a function of the reinforcements which presumably occur on each avoidance trial. The expression we used was

$$H = c + (1 - c)(1 - 10^{-iA})$$

where A = the number of prior avoidance trials, c is the value of H when A = 0, and i is the growth constant.

As indicated previously, the general equation for the probability of avoidance on trial n had the form $P_n = H_n \times D_n$.

When the expression is written out in its entirety, it has the form: Equation I:

$$P_n = [c + (1 - c)(1 - 10^{-iA})] [(1 - 10^{-jE}) + (1 - 10^{-kE'}) - (1 - 10^{-jE})(1 - 10^{-kE'})].$$

In the experiment upon which the model was based, 12 rats were exposed to 12 sessions of 20 trials each. Our approach to the model required that we estimate the parameters of Equation I and then program a computer to replicate this experiment.

There are a number of esoteric ways in which one might estimate the parameters in these circumstances. In order to avoid becoming immersed in the problem of estimation, we elected to specify the parameters from a visual inspection of the data itself. We, of course, tried to temper our decisions by our best guesses as to the kinds of functions which were likely to be generated by the computer.

The values which we settled upon were:

$$c = .40$$
$$i = .02$$
$$j = .04$$
$$k = .17$$

Our instructions to the computer were roughly as follows:

To run a "stat rat," set A to 0 and set E and E′ to 0. Then solve Equation I and derive a value for P_1. Next, generate a random number with a value between 0 and 1. If the number is greater than P_1, score the response as an escape. If the number is equal to or less than P_1, score the trial as an avoidance.

Then proceed to the next trial. Enter the appropriate values of A, E, and E′ (A = 0, E = 1, and E′ = 1 if the response on trial 1 was escape; A = 1, E = 0, and E′ = 0 if the response was avoidance) and solve for P. Then generate a new random number and decide whether or not an avoidance response occurs. Record the result and proceed to trial 3. At the end of every 20 trials reset E′ to 0. Proceed until the S has been exposed to 12 sessions. When the first "stat rat" has completed its run, repeat the procedure for a new S and continue until 12 Ss have been run.

Table 6-1 illustrates the kind of data generated by the computer. It shows the information printed out for the early portion of the first "stat S's" performance. As expected, the observed frequency of avoidance exhibits an increase within the session and a decline between the end of session 1 and the beginning of session 2.

The data in column three of the table are in a format which is comparable to that obtained in experiments with living organisms and could be subjected to the same kind of statistical treatment. The information shown in the rest of the table exceeds that provided by a true experiment in that the computer has reported the trial by trial levels of the several intervening variables. Obviously, such information can only be inferred in a true experiment.

The test of the model comes in the comparison between the data generated by the model and the data obtained from living organisms.

Table 6-1————A portion of the computers printout for "stat rat" no. 1; the space between trials 20 and 21 is meant to represent the end of the first session and the beginning of the second session

SEQUENTIAL PROBABILITY OF AVOIDANCE   STAT RAT NO. 1

ESCAPE RESPONSE $= 1$ AVOIDANCE RESPONSE $= 2$

Trial No.	Probability	Response	H-Value	CER-Value	AR-Value
1	0.00000	1	0.40000	0.00000	0.00000
2	0.15336	1	0.40000	0.08799	0.32392
3	0.24792	1	0.40000	0.16824	0.54291
4	0.30623	1	0.40000	0.24142	0.69097
5	0.34218	1	0.40000	0.30817	0.79197
6	0.36435	1	0.40000	0.36904	0.85875
7	0.37802	1	0.40000	0.42456	0.90450
8	0.38645	1	0.40000	0.47519	0.93543
9	0.39164	2	0.40000	0.52137	0.95635
10	0.41808	2	0.42700	0.52137	0.95635
11	0.44333	2	0.45279	0.52137	0.95635
12	0.46745	1	0.47742	0.52137	0.95635
13	0.47127	2	0.47742	0.56348	0.97049
14	0.49449	1	0.50094	0.56348	0.97049
15	0.49696	2	0.50094	0.60189	0.98005
16	0.51925	1	0.52340	0.60189	0.98005
17	0.52084	2	0.52340	0.63692	0.98651
18	0.54218	2	0.54485	0.63692	0.98651
19	0.56257	2	0.56534	0.63692	0.98651
20	0.58204	2	0.58490	0.63692	0.98651
21	0.38444	1	0.60358	0.63692	0.00000
22	0.46846	1	0.60358	0.66887	0.32392
23	0.52027	2	0.60358	0.69800	0.54291
24	0.53565	1	0.62143	0.69800	0.54291
25	0.56853	2	0.62143	0.72458	0.69097
26	0.58412	1	0.63846	0.72458	0.69097
27	0.60496	2	0.63846	0.74881	0.79107

Figure 6-1 shows the percentage avoidance response per session in the Hoffman-Fleshler experiment and also shows the comparable data generated by the computer. The overlap is striking and it is apparent that on the gross level the model provides a very good approximation to the behavior of the living subjects.

Figure 6-2 shows the percentage avoidance response per block of 5 trials for the "stat rats" and for the living rats. The two sets of curves show similar trends, but during the early sessions, the living rats exhibited much more warmup than the "stat rats."

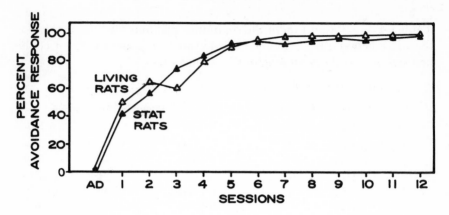

Fig. 6-1. Percentage of avoidance responses per session for living rats and for the "stat rats." (AD refers to a pre-training session with the living rats in which the warning signal was presented without an accompanying electric shock.)

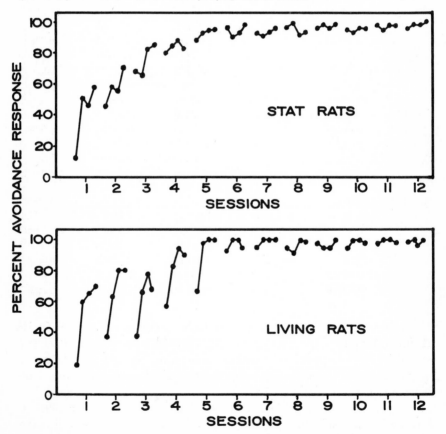

Fig. 6-2. Percentage of avoidance responses per block of 5 trials throughout the course of acquisition.

Figure 6-3 shows one of the indices of emotionality that was obtained throughout acquisition in the Hoffman-Fleshler study and also shows a comparable measure on the "stat rats." On each trial and for each rat in the Hoffman-Fleshler study we measured the rate of lever pressing (for food) during the warning signal and during a period of comparable duration which ended with the onset of the signal. These rates were then employed to compute a suppression ratio:

$$\frac{\text{Pre-tone rate}-\text{Tone rate}}{\text{Pre-tone rate}}$$

The suppression ratio serves as an index of the CER evoked by the warning signal, for it has values near 1 when suppression is nearly complete and it has values near 0 when there is little slowdown in rate. The top half of Figure 6-3 shows the median suppression ratio per session (across all Ss) for those trials on which the Ss avoided the noxious event. The second curve in the top section of Figure 6-3 shows the median CER

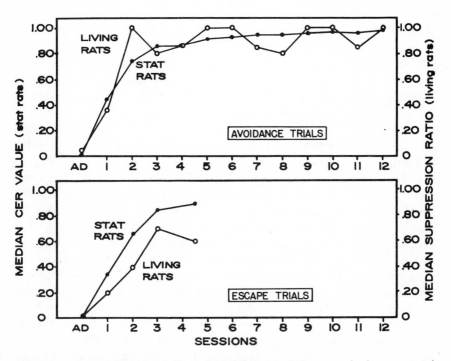

Fig. 6-3. Indices of emotionality throughout the course of acquisition for living rats and CER values during the same periods for the "stat rats." (AD refers to a pre-training session with the living rats in which the warning signal was presented without an accompanying electrical shock.)

value per session (across all "stat rats") for those trials on which an avoidance response occurred. In general, the model provides a reasonably accurate representation of the trends in the data yielded by living Ss, but the data from the "stat rats" is less variable than the data from living Ss.

The bottom section of Figure 6-3 shows the suppression ratios from living Ss and CER's from "stat Ss" on those trials during which the Ss failed to produce an avoidance response. Only the first few sessions are included in these curves because of the scarcity of nonavoidance trials in the late sessions. The same trends can be seen in both sets of data, but the function derived from the "stat Ss" is consistently higher than the function obtained from living rats. Apparently, the model provides a reasonable reproduction of reality, but the fidelity is considerably less than perfect.

It is noteworthy that the model presented in this paper was the simplest one that we could conceive to explore the quantitative implications of a dual process interpretation of avoidance. Undoubtedly, the model could be improved in several ways. We might, for example, estimate the parameters in a more rigorous fashion. Alternatively, we might try modifying some of the basic assumptions. In either case, we could readily examine the effects of the changes by running the new program through the computer.

While it is a bit early to hazard a formal evaluation of this approach, it is clear that the technique of computer simulation (via Monte Carlo methods) provides a straightforward and intuitively reasonable method for constructing and evaluating various quantitative theories of behavior. In fact, computer simulation may provide the only feasible method in certain cases. This in itself suggests that the technique is worthy of careful consideration.

There is one more intriguing possibility that deserves special comment. It would be neither time-consuming nor difficult to arrange that the data from a given set of "stat rats" be routed directly into a tabulation program and from there into one of the standard programs for analysis of variance. In short, we might find ourselves conducting, or at least pretesting, experiments by merely writing equations and asking a computer to generate the expected data and also provide a completed statistical analysis. This prospect is, to our view, awe-inspiring. Obviously, there may be dangers latent in the approach, but surely they can be kept under control as long as we have symposia like this one. Here, at least, we are focusing upon the interpretation of real experiments, conducted by real investigators on real organisms that produce real responses in real time. This paper merely wishes to suggest that computers may be able to help us in our task if we play our IBM cards right.

References

Bush, R. R., & Mosteller, F. *Stochastic models for learning*. New York: John Wiley & Sons, 1955.

Bush, R. R., & Mosteller, F. A comparison of eight models. In R. R. Bush and W. K. Estes (Eds.), *Studies in mathematical learning theory*. Stanford: Stanford University Press, 1959. Pp. 293-307.

Hoffman, H. S., & Fleshler, M. The course of emotionality in the development of avoidance. *J. exp. Psychol.*, 1962, *64*, 288-294.

Hoffman, H. S., Fleshler, M., & Chorny, H. Discriminated bar-press avoidance. *J. exp. Anal. Behav.*, 1961, *4*, 309-316.

Hull, C. L. *Principles of behavior: An introduction to behavior theory*. New York: Appleton-Century-Crofts, 1943.

Miller, N. E. Learnable drives and rewards. In S. S. Stevens (Ed.), *Handbook of experimental psychology*. New York: John Wiley & Sons, 1951.

Mowrer, O. H. *Learning theory and personality dynamics*. New York: The Ronald Press, 1950.

Solomon, R. L., & Wynne, L. C. Traumatic avoidance learning: Acquisition in normal dogs. *Psychol. Monogr.*, 1953, *67* (No. 19, Whole No. 354).

Spence, K. W. *Behavior theory and conditioning*. New Haven: Yale University Press, 1956.

Theios, John. Simple conditioning as two stage all-or-none learning. *Psychol. Review*, 1963, *70*, 403-417.

LEON J. KAMIN

McMaster University

7

Temporal and Intensity Characteristics of the Conditioned Stimulus [1]

The experiments to be discussed are concerned with the effects of various manipulations of the conditioned stimulus on the acquisition, by rats, of an Estes-Skinner (1941) conditioned emotional response (CER). The CER phenomenon consists of the suppression of on-going operant behavior in the presence of a warning signal (CS) which has preceded shock (US). Whether the study of parameters affecting the CER constitutes a study of "classical conditioning" depends, of course, upon definitions. When we adopt a completely operational view, it is clear that E's activities during a CER training procedure are identical to those involved in the Pavlovian situation. The E in each case occasionally presents to S two stimuli in succession (S_1 and S_2), and records some aspect of S's behavior in the presence of S_1. Those definitions of Pavlovian conditioning which insist that S_2 be the unconditioned stimulus for an unconditioned reflex are also satisfied by the CER paradigm, within which S_2 reliably elicits many respondents. Were the definition to include a demand that the response to S_1 "in some way resemble" the response to S_2, this condition is also satisfied. We do not, in the CER situation, routinely measure such responses as cardiac activity and pilo-erection, but responses of this class do occur both to S_2 and to S_1. To us, as to Hunt and Brady (1951), the most obvious assumption has been that the interference with behavior, which serves as our

[1] The experiments discussed were the product of collaborative work with Messrs. Charles Brimer, Thomas Gray, Anthony Hilton, and Ronald Schaub. The research was supported by a grant from the Associate Committee on Experimental Psychology of the National Research Council of Canada, and by Research Grant MY-2741 to A. H. Black, from the National Institute of Mental Health, United States Public Health Service.

measure, is largely the result of incompatibility between respondents elicited by S_1 and the on-going operant behavior. We believe that we are measuring respondent behavior indirectly, with a surprising quantitative sensitivity. We do not know why one set of the respondents elicited by S_2, rather than some other set, appears to occur to S_1. This question, however, has not been answered for *any* classical conditioning experiment. We thus see no advantage in focusing on a morphologically specific response. We know only that, as a consequence of repeated S_1-S_2 pairings, the rat's behavior in the presence of S_1 changes progressively. This fact alone seems sufficient to identify the CER with Pavlovian conditioning. The most convincing arguments, however, are in the end empirical. The fact is that parametric control over the CER more closely resembles that reported for salivary conditioning than is the case with most experimental situations which have been identified with Pavlovian conditioning. We have not doubted, from very early in this series of experiments, that we were studying the same basic associative process involved in Pavlov's experiments.

The basic procedure has been much the same in all experiments to be reported, and can be briefly described. The Ss are hooded rats, three or four months old, which have been reduced to 75 percent of ad lib. weight and which are maintained on a 24-hr. feeding rhythm. We employ eight standard Grason-Stadler "Skinner boxes," carefully sound-attenuated, with programming and recording circuits in an adjacent room. The rats receive daily two-hr. bar-pressing sessions in the Skinner box, following an initial "magazine training." The first four sessions (eight hours) develop a stable rate of bar-pressing, under a 2.5-min. variable interval (food reinforcement, Noyes pellets) schedule. The fifth preliminary session (Day P) superimposes on the basic VI schedule a pretest to assess possible unconditioned effects of the CS on bar-pressing. The CS alone is presented four times within the two hours, programmed independently of the rat's behavior. The CER acquisition days begin on the day following Day P. They consist of four superimposed CS-US sequences daily. The US is typically a .85 ma. electric shock, of .5-sec. duration.

The measure employed is the "suppression ratio." This is calculated by the formula, $B/A + B$, where "B" represents number of bar presses during the CS (or, in some studies, during a selected fraction of the CS-US interval), and "A" represents number of bar presses during the three minutes immediately preceding onset of the CS. When we are interested in a selected fraction of the CS-US interval, we take the three minutes preceding the CS as "A," and weight "B" by the appropriate multiplier. Thus, in all cases, a ratio of .50 indicates no effect of the CS on bar-pressing, and .00 indicates complete suppression of bar-pressing during the CS. We sum, for each S, the number of bar presses during the four "A" and four "B" periods of its daily session, and calculate a suppression ratio daily. We characteristically plot median ratios for experimental groups. To assess the significance of between-group differences, we calculate, for each S, a mean "overall ratio." This is simply the mean of that S's daily ratios. We have lately reduced the number of CER training days in any one experiment from ten to five; beyond five days, we do not obtain worthwhile new information. The number of days entering into the "overall ratios" in different studies is therefore variable, and figures which plot these ratios for different experiments must be compared with caution.[2]

There are some experimental treatments which have a pronounced but transient effect on CER acquisition. While many treatments produce, within a few training days, the same asymptote of complete suppression, the rates at which the asymptotes are approached may differ. To compare such treatments we have found the analysis of CER Acquisition Day 2 ratios very suitable. The analysis of overall ratios produces the same significant differences, but they appear small when the measure includes a number of days during which all groups behave similarly.

The effects in which we are interested are usually observable with eight Ss in each experimental group; all studies employ this N unless otherwise indicated. We counterbalance as completely as possible the assignment of experimental treatments to Skinner boxes and to time of day. We have already reported (Kamin, 1963; Brimer & Kamin, 1963) a number of relevant control groups. The procedure we employ produces no evidence whatever of backward conditioning. When the stimuli which we employ as CS's are presented to rats which have earlier been exposed to the US *without* a CS, the result is an increase, not a decrease, in rate of bar-pressing.

There is, however, a final precaution to be noted. The baseline CER developed by our procedure is not entirely stable from experiment to experiment. We have never failed to replicate the same *form* of relationship between variation of a parameter and CER magnitude. The exact rate at which the CER develops under a given set of experimental conditions, however, varies somewhat between experiments widely separated in time. There are doubtless many reasons for this "seasonal" variation; a major one, coming in the midst of our program, seems to have been a forced change in rat suppliers. We suspect that another is the change in the rate at which rats, in different seasons, approach 75 percent of ad lib. weight; the CER pits "hunger" against "fear." Whatever the

---

2 The overall suppression ratios calculated for very early studies generally included the data for Day 1. This day includes one trial (the first) which precedes S's first experience of the CS and US in sequence. There is generally very little suppression displayed during the remaining three trials of Day 1. We therefore now exclude this day from calculation of the overall ratio.

reasons, we have learned to suspect comparisons across experiments widely separated in time, and must caution the reader similarly. This is not really disabling; to demonstrate some effects, we have had to repeat the same control groups several times, as new experimental treatments are added.

EFFECTS OF CS INTENSITY

The first problem to be considered is that of the effect of CS intensity on acquisition of the CER. When one reflects that the most obviously manipulable variables in Pavlovian conditioning are precisely two in number, it is astonishing how little is known about the effects of varying CS intensity. There have been some American studies, almost all of human Ss, utilizing the GSR or the eye blink. These have been inconclusive; a not uncommon textbook statement is that no effect of CS intensity has been clearly demonstrated.

The Russian studies appear to be more conclusive. When summarized by Razran (1949), they seemed to indicate a direct monotonic effect of CS intensity on CR magnitude. This, however, is somewhat misleading, since Razran later pointed out (1957) that, for a given UR magnitude, the full function relating CS intensity to CR magnitude appeared to be an inverted U. This, of course, is in keeping with the full statement of Pavlov's "Law of Strength." Pavlov had indicated that, as the CS was made "too strong," protective inhibition reduced CR magnitude. Within American theorizing, Hull's (1951) principle of "stimulus intensity dynamism" plays much the same role as Pavlov's "Law of Strength." The dynamism concept, however, does not in itself provide for any curvilinear effect of CS intensity.

The first of our relevant CER studies was a simple three-group design, the groups differing only with respect to CS intensity. The CS was 3-min. white noise from a Grason-Stadler Model 901A noise generator. The CS (49, 63, or 81 db.) terminated simultaneously with the onset of the .5-sec. US. The day-by-day CER acquisition curves of all groups are presented in Figure 7-1. The groups, it should be noted, did *not* differ on the pretest day. This condition, to say the least, vastly simplifies analysis of the effects of CS intensity on acquisition.

The differences between groups in acquisition are obvious, and each group differed significantly from each. Within the range of CS intensities explored, CER acquisition varied directly with CS intensity, though all groups achieved the same asymptote. We next attempted to separate effects on "learning" from effects on "performance." To shorten the story, half the Ss trained with 49 db. were extinguished with 81 db., and half with 49 db. The Ss trained with 81 db. were similarly divided. The *only* significant effect observed during three days of extinction

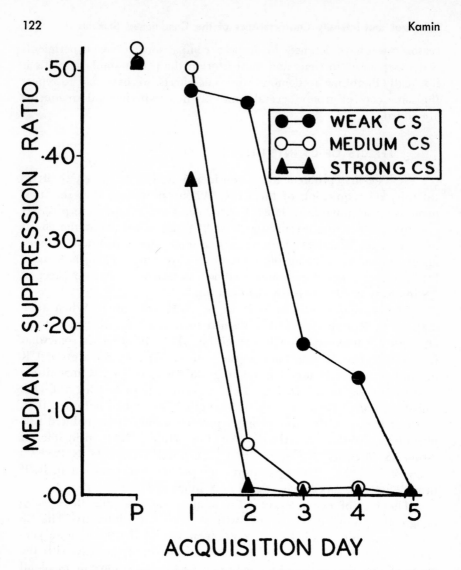

Fig. 7-1. Acquisition of trace CER as a function of CS intensity (49, 63, and 81 db). (Kamin & Schaub, 1963)

training (CS without US) was the interaction between Training CS and Extinction CS. The groups extinguished with a CS different from that with which they had been trained extinguished more rapidly. Thus, a significant generalization decrement—and nothing more—was demonstrated by the classical factorial design for disentangling learning from performance.

The effect of CS intensity may well be mediated by the level of neural activity produced by the CS. We therefore reasoned that CS intensity should be an especially potent variable in trace, as opposed to

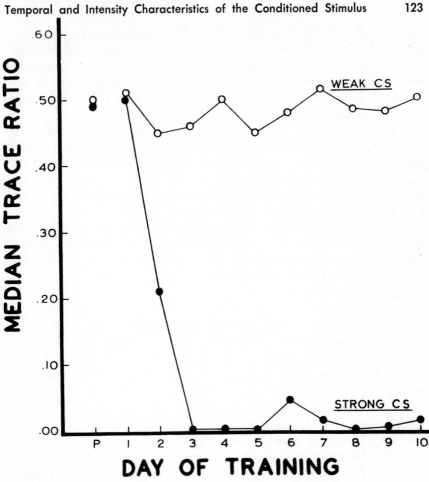

Fig. 7-2. Acquisition of trace CER as a function of CS intensity (49 and 81 db). (Kamin & Schaub, 1963)

delayed, conditioning. Presumably, trace conditioning depends upon the contiguity of a "neural trace" of the CS with the US. Thus, a weak CS might not produce a trace of sufficient magnitude to "bridge the gap" between CS and US.

The CS-US interval employed in our trace procedure was again three minutes, but the CS acted for only two minutes. There was one minute of silence between CS termination and onset of the US. We examined the effects of two CS intensities, 49 and 81 db. These are the two extreme intensities employed in the delayed conditioning study. We calculated two separate suppression ratios for each S. We were primarily concerned with the "trace ratio," which contrasts responding during the one minute of silence following the CS to responding during the three minutes preceding the CS. We calculated as well a "CS ratio," contrasting responding during the 2-min. CS to the same baseline response rate. The day-by-day acquisition curves for trace ratios are presented in Figure 7-2. The difference between groups is obvious; there was no overlap between members of different groups. With the 49 db. CS, there was no hint of a CER within 10 days of training. With the 81 db. CS, complete suppression was rapidly acquired.

The CS ratios are plotted in Figure 7-3. The picture is much the same as with trace ratios, but suppression to the 81 db. CS is considerably less than that observed during the subsequent trace interval. Thus, trace conditioning appears relatively specific to the trace interval. The majority of Ss first displayed a clear CER during the trace interval, and with repeated trials began to suppress during the CS.

The failure of a 49 db. CS to produce a CER cannot be attributed to S's inability to hear the CS. This is the same CS which, in a delayed conditioning procedure, produces complete suppression. We assume that the weak CS produces a short-lived trace, which diminishes below some critical threshold before the US is presented. There is thus no distinctive stimulus to associate with the US, and conditioning does not occur. We identify the trace in our own thinking with some sort of perseverative neural phenomenon, for which we have no independent evidence. The trace mechanism might be identified with some persisting chain of overt behaviors by S, but again there is absolutely no independent evidence for such a view.

Those of us who were early taught that "the optimal CS-US interval is 450 msec." feel compelled to stress that the rat, within six or eight pairings, can clearly associate two stimuli separated by a full minute. This kind of temporal interval is not at variance with those often employed by Pavlov in the salivary conditioning of dogs, but the very rapid acquisition is remarkable even by Pavlovian standards. We have done further work on trace conditioning, to which we shall return.

Within delayed conditioning, a monotonic effect of CS intensity can be demonstrated within a series of very weak intensities. The plot in Figure 7-4 shows the effects of 35, 45, and 50 db. The trend across these groups was significant, and the 35 db. CS produced clear conditioning. The Ss in this study received five (not the standard four) CS-US pairings daily, for only three days.

The data to this point clearly suggest monotonicity. We were captivated, however, by Razran's (1957) conception of an optimal "CS-US ratio." [3] The Razran notion, based upon Russian empirical work, suggests that the relation between CS intensity and conditioning is, for any fixed value of US intensity, an inverted U. The maximum of the U

[3] The Razran theory is actually couched in terms of the relation between CS intensity and UR magnitude. There is assumed, however, a very close relation between UR magnitude and US intensity. Manipulation of US intensity is said to be one of several ways in which UR magnitude can be manipulated.

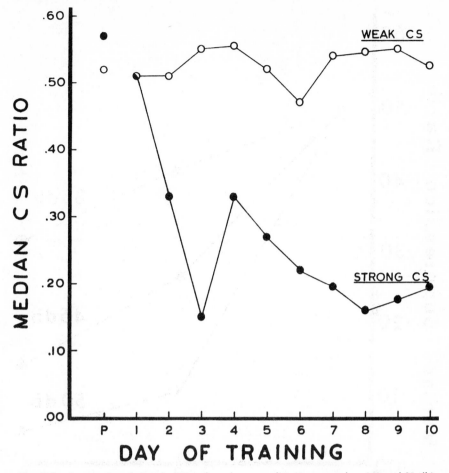

Fig. 7-3. Suppression during the CS under a trace conditioning procedure (49 and 81 db). (Kamin & Schaub, 1963)

function, further, is said to vary directly with the fixed value of US intensity. That is, for any fixed value of US intensity, there exists an optimal CS. The intensity of the optimal CS varies directly with US intensity.

We had earlier demonstrated, in single factor studies, monotonic effects both of CS and of US intensity on CER acquisition. Perhaps a factorially designed study, simultaneously varying CS and US intensities, would be illuminating. We proceeded to a 3 x 3 factorial, with three values of CS and of US intensity, and five rats in each of nine independent groups. The CS intensities were 47, 60, and 81 db; US intensities were .25, .50, and .85 ma. The data of this study are summarized in Figure 7-5, which presents mean overall suppression ratios for Days 1-10. The figure makes clear what analysis of variance demonstrated: highly significant

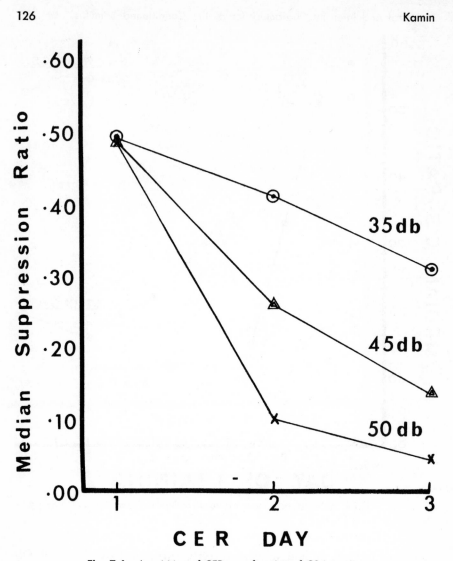

Fig. 7-4. Acquisition of CER as a function of CS intensity.

effects both of CS and of US intensity, plus a significant interaction. The interaction is not of the sort predicted by Razran's theory, which assumes nonmonotonic functions for every value of US intensity which produces conditioning. We observed no significant deviation from monotonicity. The obtained interaction was clearly due to the failure of the weakest CS to be very effective with the medium US. The same weak CS was very effective with the strongest US, and the interaction thus suggests simply that too little of one factor can be compensated for by adding more of the other.

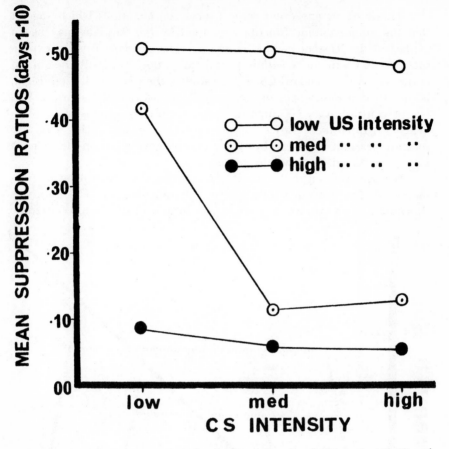

Fig. 7-5. Overall suppression ratios (days 1-10) as a function of CS intensity (47, 60, and 81 db) and of US intensity (.25, .50 and .85 ma.). (Kamin & Brimer, 1963)

We have, of course, examined only three values of CS intensity in this study. We could not have extended the range of CS intensities to very much higher values without encountering some unlearned suppression to the CS. We might, of course, have tested many more values of CS intensity within the range of values which we used. The argument can be made that such a fishing expedition might finally net something, but we are reluctant to undertake it. To *disprove* the Razran notion, we are faced with the impossible task of testing an infinite number of values in an effort to demonstrate that there is no "optimal CS." The Razran theory makes no actual use of a CS-US *ratio*. The slopes of descent on either side of the hypothetical optimum are not specified, and comparisons *across* functions obtained with different fixed values of US are thus irrelevant to the theory.

There are in any event some logical considerations which suggest that the nonmonotonic functions reported by the Russians may be an artifact of the Russian method of testing. The standard Russian experiment varies CS intensity *within* an individual dog. Typically the animal is trained with a standard CS and then, after the CR is well established, is presented with stronger or weaker CS's on occasional test trials. We, on the contrary, vary CS intensity *between* different groups of subjects. When CS intensity is varied *within*-subject (as in our earlier effort to separate learning from performance effects) generalization decrements may be expected to cloud the picture.

We can thus suggest a possible reason for the observation of nonmonotonic functions in within-subject experiments only. The notion is illustrated, in an outrageously rectilinear form, in Figure 7-6. We assume

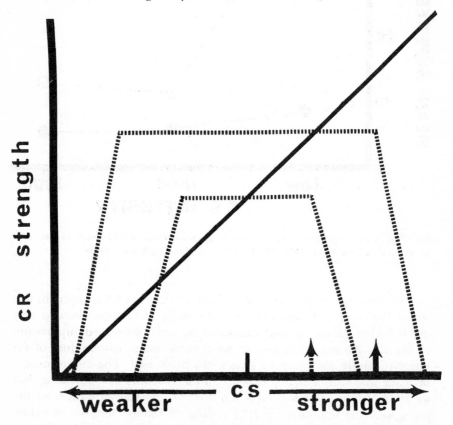

Fig. 7-6. Hypothetical summation of "intensity dynamism" and "generalization" effects in determining CR strength when CS intensity is varied *within*-subject. (Abscissa represents intensity of test CS, with training CS indicated in center. Solid diagonal line represents "dynamism" effect; broken lines represent generalization gradients for intense (upper line) and weak (lower line) US. Arrows on abscissa represent CS intensity producing maximum response with weak and with strong US.)

a monotonic "stimulus intensity dynamism" effect, represented by the solid diagonal line in the body of the figure. The CR magnitude obtained with the standard CS is determined by this simple effect. When we test an animal with CSs other than the standard, generalization effects will be superimposed on the basic intensity effect. We assume—since there has been no specific discrimination training—that the generalization gradient will be quite broad, before "breaking" sharply. Thus, relatively small variations of CS intensity on either side of the standard will not be much affected by generalization decrement, and over some range of test intensities a monotonic effect will be observed. When the test CS is very much weaker than the standard, the generalization decrement will not disturb the observed monotonic gradient. When the test CS is very much more intense than the standard, a sudden drop in CR magnitude may be observed.

We now add the assumption that, if an animal is trained with the same standard CS but with a more intense US, the generalization gradient will be further broadened. The intensity dynamism gradient would not, in theory, be affected. These considerations lead us to expect that, with the same standard CS, the "optimal CS" will vary directly with intensity of the standard US. This is precisely what the Russians are said to observe.

We cannot be certain that this model explains the discrepancy between CER results and those obtained by the Russians. The model is at least not wholly implausible, since the assumptions made are well grounded empirically. We could attempt to demonstrate that, within CER training, an "optimal CS" could be located by a within-animal testing procedure. The intensity of the optimal CS should vary with intensity of the standard CS, holding US intensity constant. The optimum should in every case be a CS more intense than the standard. We have not in fact demonstrated this.

We next began to wonder whether the concept of stimulus intensity dynamism was an adequate explanation of the effects which we had observed. The dynamism notion implies that the physical stimulus in some way "energizes" the CR. There is, however, a rather different way of interpreting the observed effects of CS intensity. This has been suggested independently by Perkins (1953) and by Logan (1954). They pointed out that, in a traditional study of CS intensity, any "energizing" effects of the CS are completely confounded with the discriminability of the CS from normal background stimulation. The "discriminability" of the CS is determined by the amount of *change* from the background stimulation level which it represents. Thus, if stimulus change rather than stimulus energy is the critical variable, we ought to be able to produce a gradient analogous to those previously observed when the CS is a *reduction* (of greater or lesser degree) in the intensity of a standard background noise.

The Perkins-Logan notion implies that better conditioning will occur to greater reductions of background noise intensity, but an unmodified dynamism concept predicts exactly the opposite. Perhaps both views are partially valid, and in this case exploration of a wide range of stimulus reductions might produce a nonmonotonic gradient. We thus tested five groups, all of which were trained with an 80 db. white noise continuously present in the Skinner box. The CS was a reduction of this noise, for three minutes, to either 70, 60, 50, 45, or 0 (ambient level) db. The day-by-day acquisition curves for these five conditions are given in Figure 7-7. The effect is clearly monotonic, with more conditioning produced by the larger stimulus reductions. The 80-45 and

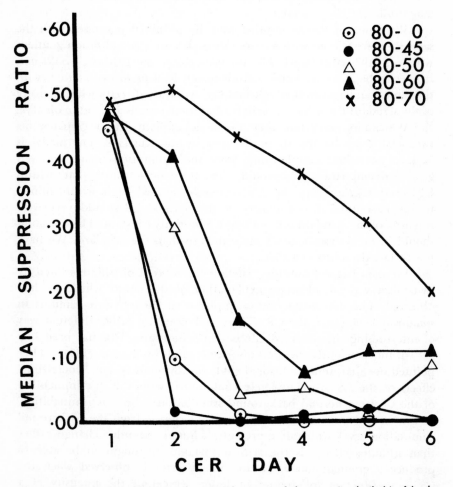

Fig. 7-7. Acquisition of CER as a function of amount of decrease (in decibels) of background noise.

80-0 groups were not distinguishable, but all other groups differed significantly from these two, and from each other.

This outcome makes it foolhardy in the extreme to ignore the role of discriminability in traditional studies. We might argue that there is no need to postulate *any* dynamism effect, but we were reluctant to give up completely any role for the "energizing" effect of physical intensity. Prompted by some earlier observations, we performed a companion study to that just reported. We had noted that, though it was impossible to produce a trace CER with a 49 db. CS, this *could* be done by utilizing what we call the "upside-down" trace procedure. This procedure involves a continuous background noise present in the Skinner box. The CS proper is the removal of this noise for two minutes, followed by a "trace" interval of one minute preceding the US. The background noise is resumed during this trace interval. With a 49 db. background noise, we obtained successful trace conditioning under the "upside-down" procedure. The normal trace procedure, with a 49 db. CS, again failed to produce a CER. Thus, since at least the change in stimulation intensity between CS and trace intervals is equated for all groups, these results may indicate some effect of the physical intensity of stimulation contiguous with the US. Further, we had trained two groups without background noise in the Skinner box. The two-segment CS consisted, for the first group, of 2 min. of 80 db. noise followed by one min. of 49 db. noise. The CS for the second group was 2 min. of 49 db. noise followed by one min. of 80 db. noise. The groups each conditioned, but the group with 80 db. contiguous with the US conditioned more rapidly. Though this group was inferior to the other in the *first* CS segment of very early trials, it soon became superior during both CS segments. The intensity contiguous with the US thus seemed to control behavior during both segments.

The companion study matched each "decrease" group of the earlier design with a corresponding "increase" group. Thus, the 80-70 group was matched by a 70-80 group, the 80-60 group by a 60-80 group, etc. Within this latter design, the CS was 80 db. for all groups, but the amount of change from the background noise varied. The outcome is portrayed in Figure 7-8. The functions depicted in this figure should scarcely be called a gradient. The 70-80 group showed significantly less conditioning than did all the others, but they in turn did not differ among themselves.

The two parts of this study can be combined into a 2 x 5 factorial design. There are two directions of stimulus change (increase vs. decrease), and five amounts of stimulus change, measured in db. This analysis showed highly significant effects of both factors, plus a significant interaction. This is clarified by Figure 7-9, which plots overall ratios for Days 2-6 for all groups. Within both the increase and decrease procedures, the significant effect of amount of stimulus change can be

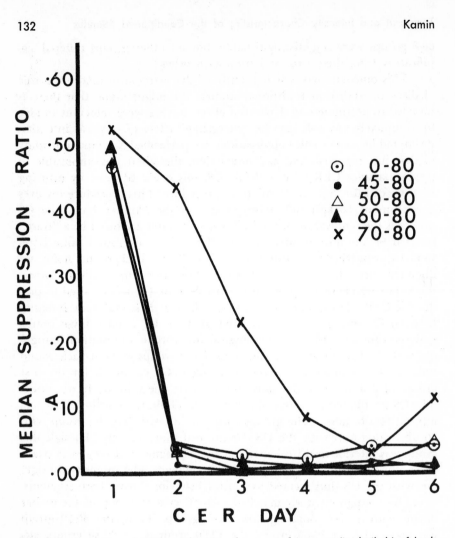

Fig. 7-8. Acquisition of CER as a function of amount of increase (in decibels) of background noise.

seen; but this effect was greater within the decrease procedure. Put another way round, the increase procedure was significantly superior when the stimulus change was small. There was no difference between the two procedures when the stimulus change was large.

Thus, when the stimulus provides a gross change from the background stimulation level, conditioning appears to be asymptotic. When the CS is a moderate change from the background stimulation, the direction of the change and/or the physical intensity contiguous with the US has a substantial effect. The structure of the experiment makes it impossible to unravel these two alternatives; whenever the direction of change was an increase, it was *to* an 80 db. stimulus. We have no

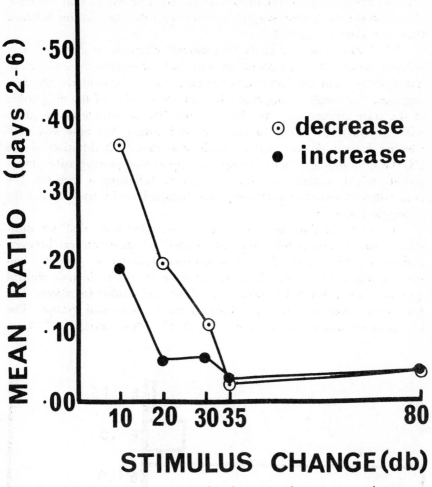

Fig. 7-9. Overall suppression ratios, within decrease and increase procedures, as a function of amount of change (in decibels) of background noise.

observations on conditioning when the CS is a reduction to 80 db. To make meaningful comparisons, we shall have to become deeply involved in the study of loudness discriminability functions for the rat.

TEMPORAL CHARACTERISTICS OF THE CS

To this point we have been concerned exclusively with the intensity of the CS. We now turn to the related problem of the temporal relations between CS and US. Previously, we have employed a constant 3-min. interval between CS onset and US onset, while varying CS intensity. We now report a series of studies in which CS intensity was held constant while temporal relations were varied. The notion that the trace of the CS decays in time suggests at once the intimate relation between these two areas of research.

We backed into the study of temporal relations in a stumblingly indirect manner. The studies of intensity had encouraged some primitive speculations about the "perseverative neural trace." Particularly, the data suggested that conditioning might be a direct function of the magnitude of the trace contiguous with the US, and that magnitude of the trace might in turn be a direct function of CS intensity. We now wondered whether magnitude of the trace might also vary with duration of the CS. We were simple-minded enough to suppose that perseverative neural activity might "reverberate" for a long time following a long CS. We thus rather expected to obtain superior acquisition of a trace CER with a long-duration CS.

To vary CS duration, however, means necessarily that we must simultaneously and reciprocally vary either the time interval between onset of the CS and the US, or that between termination of the CS and the US. Thus it was often necessary in these studies to include control groups which attempted to tease apart these confounded variations. The first study involved three experimental and two control groups. The CS, as in all studies of this series, was 60 db. white noise. We first ex-

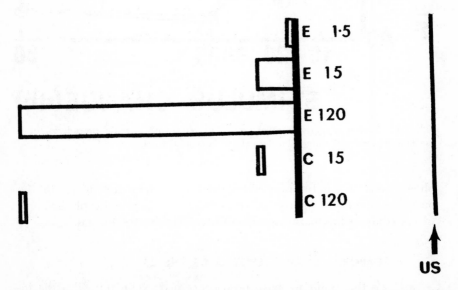

Fig. 7-10. Schematic representation of temporal relations between CS and US. Interval between two vertical lines is one minute. CS durations are 1.5, 15, or 120 sec. (E experimental, C control).

amined CS durations of 1.5, 15, and 120 sec., holding constant a 1-min. trace interval between CS termination and the US. We were concerned primarily with suppression during the 1-min. trace interval. The design is presented schematically in Figure 7-10, which also indicates the nature of the two control groups. These were both trained with a 1.5 sec. CS, with its onset either 75 or 180 sec. before the US. Thus, by including the 1.5-sec. experimental group with the controls, we have

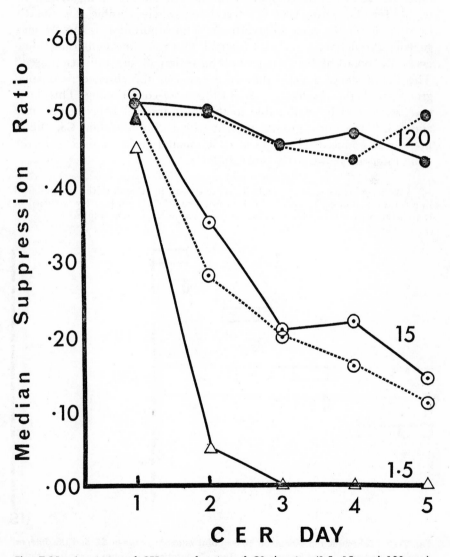

Fig. 7-11. Acquisition of CER as a function of CS duration (1.5, 15, and 120 sec.). Solid lines are experimental groups; broken lines are corresponding control groups (cf. Fig. 7-10).

three groups with the same CS duration, but which differ with respect to the temporal interval between CS onset (and CS termination!) and the US.

The day-by-day acquisition curves of all groups are portrayed in Figure 7-11, which is based on suppression ratios calculated for the 1-min. interval immediately preceding the US. We must stress that in this, as in all subsequent studies with a 60 db. CS, it makes no practical difference if ratios are computed for the last minute of the CS-US interval, for the entire CS-US interval, or, where feasible, for the CS interval or for the trace interval only. The suppression is quite homogeneous throughout the CS-US interval, and the same significant differences are obtained between groups regardless of the ratio employed.[4] The figure shows a clear difference between the three experimental groups, with the *shorter* CS's producing more conditioning. This, however, seems clearly attributable to the short interval between CS *onset* and US. The control groups, trained with a short-duration CS, almost literally reproduced the curves of experimental groups trained with the same intervals between CS onset and US.

[4] We have earlier reported a relative specificity of suppression to the trace interval in a trace conditioning procedure (cf. Figures 7-1 and 7-2). This, however, occurred in conjunction with a much more intense CS than that of the present studies.

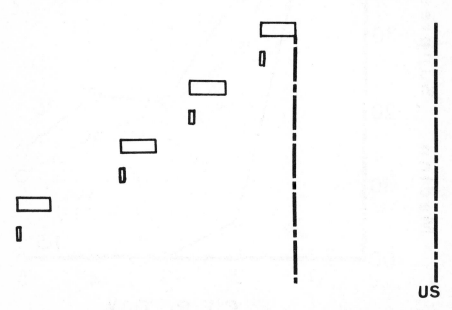

Fig. 7-12. Schematic representation of temporal relations between CS and US. Interval between two vertical lines is one minute. Two CS durations (1.5 and 15 sec.) are tested at each of four intervals between CS onset and US (180, 135, 105, and 75 sec.).

We were not yet ready to abandon the notion of an effect of CS duration, and so proceeded to complete a 2 x 4 factorial design in which two CS durations were examined in conjunction with four temporal intervals between CS onset and US. The CS durations were 1.5 and 15 sec., each employed with groups for which CS onset occurred either 75, 105, 135, or 180 sec. before the US. The design is presented schematically in Figure 7-12, and Figure 7-13 plots overall ratios for Days 2-5 for all groups. The ratios in Figure 7-13 were computed for the entire CS-US interval. The extra group plotted in the figure was trained with a 1.5-sec. CS with an onset 61.5 sec. before the US. There was no 15-sec. CS group with onset 61.5 sec. before the US, so the extra group was omitted from the analysis of variance.

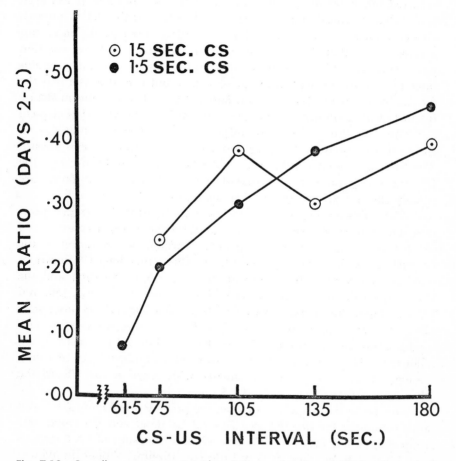

Fig. 7-13. Overall suppression ratios (days 2-5) as a function of CS duration and of interval between CS onset and US.

The analysis indicated a highly significant effect of the temporal interval between CS onset and US, but no effect whatever of CS duration, and no interaction. Within this study, CS duration and the interval between CS termination and US were confounded. Thus, the failure to obtain either an effect of CS duration or an interaction suggests that the interval between CS-termination and the US did not affect conditioning. The situation in this study differs from that in the preceding study, in which CS duration was confounded with the interval between CS-onset and the US.

The data depicted in Figure 7-13 represent a significant effect, within each CS duration, of the interval between CS onset and US. The shorter this interval, the more conditioning occurred. This fact scarcely seems astonishing, but the range of temporal values over which the effect occurred might occasion some surprise. The assertion—and it has been made—that "classical conditioning cannot occur" with CS-US intervals greater than a few seconds is clearly incorrect. Perhaps the most surprising fact is that, in the light of Pavlovian data, such an assertion was ever made. The dependence of conditioning on the interstimulus interval is clearly evident in the present data, but it is also true that the rat can very quickly learn to associate a 1.5-sec. CS of quite moderate intensity with a US which does not occur until a full minute has elapsed.

The data thus far seem to suggest that CS duration itself has no effect on conditioning. To make this statement, however, seems absurd. The limiting case of CS duration is that in which the CS overlaps the US. We surely cannot assert that delayed and trace conditioning are equally effective procedures; or then again, can we?

With this question in mind, the next study utilized seven groups of rats. The interval between CS onset and US onset was a constant 180 sec. for all groups, but the independent variable was duration of the CS within this interval. This meant, of course, that long CS durations were associated with short intervals between CS termination and the US. The CS durations studied were: 1.5, 15, 120, 175, 179.5, 180, and 185 sec. Thus, the intervals between CS termination and US onset were 178.5, 165, 60, 5, .5, 0, and −5 sec. The first five groups represent trace conditioning, though in the fifth case the trace interval is a mere .5 sec., following a 179.5 sec. CS. The last two groups represent delayed conditioning; in one case the CS terminates with onset of the US, in the other it persists for 5 sec. beyond US onset.

The day-by-day acquisition curves are presented in Figure 7-14, with ratios computed for the 180 sec. between CS onset and US onset. The groups fall clearly into three clusters. Within the range of CS durations from 1.5 to 120 sec. there is very little conditioning, though individual Ss did display some clear suppression. The two delayed conditioning groups were significantly superior to all others, but did not differ from

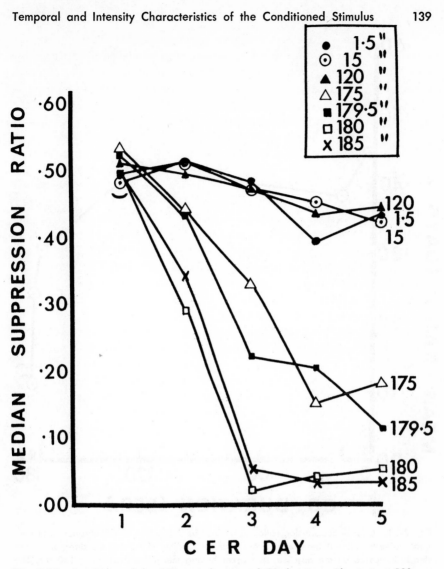

Fig. 7-14. Acquisition of the CER as a function of CS duration with constant 180-sec. interval between CS onset and US.

each other. The two "short-trace" groups in turn were superior to the three "long-trace" groups. The function is portrayed in Figure 7-15, which plots overall ratios for Days 2-5. There is no effect of the independent variable over a very wide range of values, but there is then a precipitate gradient-like effect as CS termination occurs "almost contiguously" with the US.

Perhaps the most impressive aspect of these data is the profoundly disruptive effect of introducing a relatively tiny .5-sec. time gap between

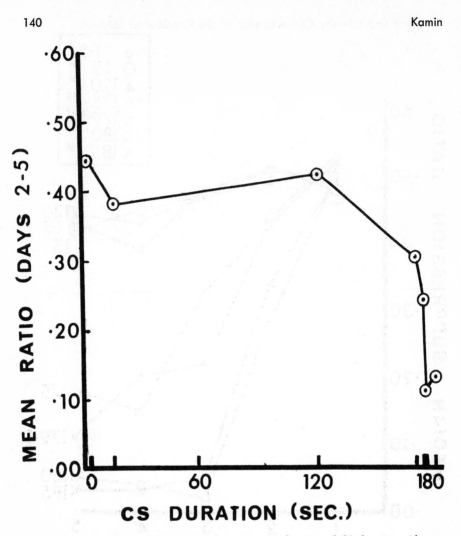

Fig. 7-15. Overall suppression ratios (days 2-5) as a function of CS duration with constant 180-sec. interval between CS onset and US. (The 179.5-sec. CS duration is not clearly indicated on the abscissa, its marker having merged with that for 180 sec. The last marker on the abscissa represents 185 sec.)

CS-termination and the US. The animals so treated are not "tricked" into believing that the CS and US are contiguous. The literal contiguity of CS and US seems to be a very important factor.

The sudden appearance of suppression within the trace procedure as CS duration was increased seems clearly due to reduction of the time gap between CS termination and US, rather than to the correlated increase of CS duration per se. When CS termination was not "almost contiguous" with the US, very large increments in CS duration produced no beneficial effect.

The inferiority of the 179.5 sec. CS duration group to the 180 sec. group cannot be attributed to any general incapacity of the rat to "bridge time gaps." The time gap between a 1.5 sec. CS of the same intensity and a US which followed after a full minute was bridged admirably. Peculiarly, a few hundred msec. seem very critical when interposed between CS termination and US, although a full minute interposed between CS onset and US produces no detectable decremental effect.

We should like to attempt some integration of these data, but we had better first examine some of the relevant interrelations. These are illustrated in Figure 7-16, which schematizes some of the conditions which we have studied in this series. The conditions labelled as A and B have in common a CS onset 61.5 sec. before the US. They differ grossly with respect to the interval between CS termination and US. The conditions labelled as C and D have in common a CS onset 180 sec. before the US, and again differ grossly with respect to the interval between CS termination and US. The condition labelled as E shares with C and D a 180 sec. interval between CS onset and US, but the very short interval between CS termination and US much more closely resembles the D than the C condition.

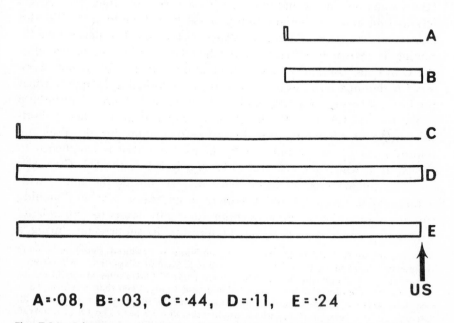

A = ·08, B = ·03, C = ·44, D = ·11, E = ·24

Fig. 7-16. Schematic representation of five experimental conditions. Intervals between CS onset and US are, for groups A through E respectively, 61.5, 61.5, 180, 180, and 180 sec. CS durations are 1.5, 61.5, 1.5, 180, and 179.5 sec., respectively. Mean overall ratios (days 2-5) are given at bottom for all groups.

The four groups A, B, C, and D may be viewed as constituting a factorial design, in which the two factors are delayed vs. trace conditioning, and interval between CS onset and US. Within such an analysis, the major effect is the interaction. When, as in A and B, CS onset is "favorably close" to the US (61.5 sec.), there is no significant difference between delayed and trace procedures. When, as in C and D, CS onset is "too far" from the US, excellent conditioning occurs with a delayed procedure, but virtually none with a trace procedure. We can thus conclude that if a 60 db. CS has its onset no more than 61.5 sec. before the US, further action of the CS is unnecessary to produce asymptotic conditioning. When the CS has its onset 180 sec. before the US, however, significant conditioning results only if the CS continues to act until at least "almost contiguity" with the US. When actual contiguity obtains, conditioning is much superior.

We believe that these data can be most simply interpreted by postulating both a basic effect of a CS-US contiguity, and a differential between the magnitudes of traces established by CS onset and by CS termination. That is, for the rat, CS termination appears to produce a much shorter-lived trace than does CS onset. We know that the time between a brief CS and a US following after one minute can be bridged; we believe the effective trace to arise from CS onset rather than from CS termination since Condition E, with a *very* short time between CS termination and US, is significantly worse than Condition A. We also know that, even with CS onset 180 sec. before the US, delayed conditioning is extremely effective even when CS termination occurs *after* the US. Thus, contiguity of CS termination with the US is not necessary for the superiority of delayed to trace conditioning to appear when the interval between CS onset and US is presumably longer than the life of the trace of CS onset. We finally feel compelled to postulate a short-lived trace of CS termination in order to account for the dramatic improvement in trace conditioning when CS duration is lengthened to the point at which the CS terminates shortly before the US (C vs. E).[5]

The argument can be made that when we provide the animal with a time gap between CS and US there is no reason why he "should" suppress during the CS. Perhaps suppression only occurs to "redundant" stimulating conditions; if we could measure it, suppression during a

[5] Parenthetically, we might note that condition B produced significantly more suppression than did D. We might attribute this to "neural adaptation" in the course of long continued noise stimulation. The present effect of CS-US interval should not be confused with the observation by Stein, Sidman, and Brady (1958) that, when the CS is *very* long relative to the intertrial interval, failure to suppress is correlated with "saving" positive reinforcements which would otherwise be lost. The CS-US intervals which we use are very brief, compared to the intertrial interval. The ratios of these intervals in our studies are outside the range for which these authors report an effect. The VI schedule is such that complete suppression during the CS would cost our rats a "nondetectable" proportion of their food reinforcements.

.5 sec. silent interval preceding the US might be complete! There are several observations within the studies already reported which argue against such a notion, but the most effective answer is contained in some experiments soon to be reported.

We should note an interesting parallelism between the differential effectiveness of CS onset and CS termination in mediating trace conditioning and the differential effectiveness of the "increase" and "decrease" procedures in *delayed* conditioning. Within delayed conditioning, an increase of background noise was a more effective CS than was the corresponding reduction of background noise. The onset and the termination of the same CS can be viewed as special cases of the increase and decrease procedures. With both delayed and trace procedures—independent of the absolute level of stimulation—the *change* in stimulation appears critical; and in each case an increase in stimulation produces more conditioning than does the corresponding reduction. The rat seems much more responsive to the onset of white noise than to its termination.

There is an obvious possible explanation for the differential effectiveness of CS onset and CS termination. Perhaps the onset of white noise produces much more neural activity than does its termination. The evidence for "off-responses" by elements in the mammalian auditory nervous system is in fact rather tenuous; in any event, no such clear cut phenomena as the off-responses within the visual system have been demonstrated. Thus conditioning might always be a direct function of the amount of neural activity produced by the stimulating events which precede the US. Trace conditioning might depend largely on the duration of the neural activities set up by the onset and termination of the CS.

We continued to investigate the effects of introducing a small "gap" between the CS and the US. With the onset of noise as the CS, the median Day 2 suppression ratios were .29 without and .43 with the gap. These ratios differed significantly. We next performed an analogous experiment with the "upside-down" procedure, employing two groups of 18 Ss each. The CS for each group was the reduction to zero of a 60 db. background noise. The interval between CS onset and US was again set at 180 sec., with a .5-sec. gap programmed for one group only. The "gap" for this group consisted of the resumption of the 60 db. background noise. The median Day 2 ratios were .45 without and .30 with the "gap." These ratios differed significantly, but in this case the "gap" *facilitated* conditioning. The "redundancy" explanation cannot itself interpret all the data. There seems to be a basic difference in the effectiveness of increase and decrease of stimulation level.

The problem remains, however, of why the facilitating effect of the "gap" in the present study should be manifested in the long *first* segment of the CS-US interval. We seem forced to conclude that the rat manages in some way to treat the entire CS-US interval as a unit. We know that he does not always do this. The very first study of trace conditioning, using onset of a 2-min., *81* db. noise as the CS, demonstrated suppression relatively specific to the trace interval. We can only hope that future experiments will help to resolve this dilemma.

The results obtained to date can be summarized by stating that when the CS consisted of a single segment, providing only an increase *or* a decrease in background stimulation, the increase produced better conditioning than did the corresponding decrease. When the CS consisted of two segments, thus providing *both* an increase *and* a decrease, conditioning could be better or worse than that obtained with a one segment CS. This presumably depends on complex interactions between intensity and temporal characteristics. We have recently studied the effects of a .5 sec.-gap when the CS is the onset of 80 db. noise 180 sec. before the US. The median Day 2 ratios were .04 without and .02 with the gap. This seems to confirm the earlier finding in delayed conditioning that there is no difference between the two directions of stimulus change when the amount of change is very large. Put in more theoretical terms, it suggests that the trace of the termination of 80 db., unlike that of the termination of 60 db., persists strongly for at least .5 sec.

SOME RECENT EXTENSIONS

The preceding studies all employed rats as subjects, the CER as the response, and white noise as the CS. We have wondered how general the effects which we have described might be. We have taken a first step toward finding out by recently employing light as a CS. The plexiglas ceiling of the Skinner box was covered with milk glass, above which a 7-w. frosted bulb, in series with a bank of resistors, was suspended. We have thus far utilized "bright," "medium," and "dim" light intensities in preliminary studies.

When the CS is to consist of the onset of light, Ss are given VI training in complete darkness during all but the first preliminary session. This training develops bar-pressing rates identical to those obtained in earlier studies. The experimental conditions are in all other details identical to those previously described. The first experiment studied the effects of the three light intensities with a delayed conditioning procedure and a 3-min. CS. The day-by-day acquisition curves are presented in Figure 7-17. There was a significant monotonic trend across the three CS intensities. These findings are thus basically similar to those depicted for three noise intensities in Figure 7-1. The "dim" light intensity, however, was somewhat less effective than 49 db.

We have also studied the effects of increase vs. decrease of illumination, each in both standard delayed conditioning and with a .5-sec. "gap." This has been done, however, only for the medium light intensity. When the CS is to be the reduction to zero of the medium light, the normal

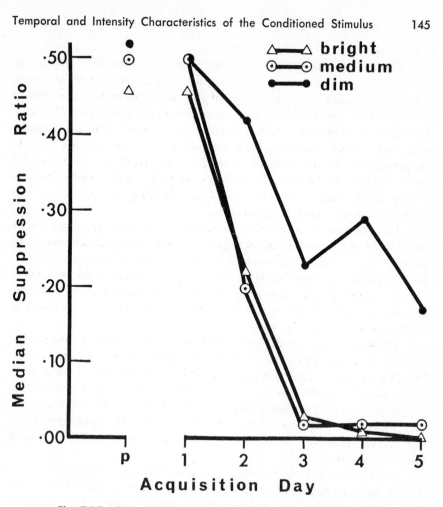

Fig. 7-17. CER acquisition as a function of intensity of a light CS.

background illumination throughout training is provided by the medium light. The median *pretest* ratio under this condition was .51. The results can be described briefly. There were no significant differences between any of the groups. The acquisition curves of all groups were very similar to that depicted for the medium light intensity in Figure 7-17. The meaning of these results is difficult to assess. We had found no difference between the increase and decrease procedures with a "loud" (81 db.) CS, and no effect of the "gap" treatment with the same noise CS. We have not yet examined reduction of our "dim" light as a CS. This might produce results analogous to those obtained with 60 db. noise. The suppression obtained under a delayed conditioning procedure with the medium light, on the other hand, was about the same as that obtained with 60 db. noise. Thus, whether or not there are basic differences between some of the CS charac-teristics of light and of noise is a question which can be answered only by future research.

The most recent effort—a study still in progress—has been an attempt to analyze "two segment" as opposed to "one segment" CSs. We view trace conditioning as a special case of the two segment CS. The stimuli we employ are the onsets of 80 db. noise and of medium light. The basic procedure is to present S with two consecutive 90 sec. CSs, the termination of the second coinciding with onset of the US. We compute separate suppression ratios for Segment 1 and for Segment 2. We have thus far examined six conditions: Noise-Noise, Noise-Light, and Noise-Nothing, as well as Light-Light, Light-Noise, and Light-Nothing. The returns are not yet all in, but this much is already clear.

The amount of suppression in Segment 1 is determined jointly by the stimuli of Segment 1 and of Segment 2. Whatever stimulus occurs in Segment 1, the most suppression occurs at that time if the stimuli in the two segments are identical. With either light or noise as the Segment 1 stimulus, intermediate suppression occurs in Segment 1 if the opposite stimulus occurs in Segment 2. The suppression in Segment 1 is minimal if there is *no* stimulus in Segment 2.

The picture is very different when we focus on suppression during Segment 2. There appears to be little if any effect of the Segment 1 stimulus on suppression during Segment 2. When the Segment 2 stimulus is either noise or light, excellent suppression occurs during Segment 2; suppression is much weaker if there is *no* Segment 2 stimulus. Put another way, we can note that within the 180-sec. test interval, suppression tends to be relatively specific to Segment 2 if the stimulating conditions during the two segments differ.

We are especially interested in the relatively poor suppression, even during Segment 2, produced by the trace conditioning procedures when 90-sec. trace intervals are employed. What would happen if we provided a very brief noise onset (a "blip") immediately prior to termination of the Segment 1 light stimulus? This might produce a trace sufficient to persist until the US. The light might at the same time be associated with the noise blip, possibly resulting in good suppression throughout both segments. What is the role of the first segment in a two segment stimulus? We can ask anthropomorphically whether the rat "knows" during the first stimulus that the second stimulus and the US are to follow, and "chooses" not to suppress, or whether the first stimulus simply has no "significance." What will happen when, as we plan to do, we present the first stimulus, and omit the second? When we present the second stimulus, having omitted the first? When, with new animals, we present only a noise blip and a light blip 90 sec. apart, with the US 90 sec. after the light blip? When we study two segment CSs, with the stimulus of Segment 1 continuing during the action of the Segment 2 stimulus? When two stimuli are presented during Segment 1, with only one remaining during Segment 2? The theoretical understanding of the associative process underlying classical conditioning is not sufficiently advanced to enable any firm predictions.

We are aware of the danger of accumulating a mountain of empirical findings without an integrating theory. We believe, however, that existing theories of classical conditioning wilfully ignore too many easily replicable facts. These facts are not very tidy, because they involve interactions which sharply limit the generality of statements about conditioning. They might, however, pave the way for much more general statements at the neurological level. Within the behavioral level, we shall surely have to cope with the interaction of generalization and discrimination and "dynamism-like" processes in determining the outcome of conditioning experiments. We simply cannot state that "conditioning is a function of the physical intensity of the stimulus." To talk very much about the effects of CS intensity on conditioning, we must at once concern ourselves with a number of interacting basic psychological processes. We might even some day decide that the category established by an operational definition of classical conditioning is not a particularly useful one.

References

BRIMER, C. J., & KAMIN, L. J. Disinhibition, habituation, sensitization and the conditioned emotional response. *J. comp. physiol. Psychol.*, 1963 *56*, 508-516.

ESTES, W. K., & SKINNER, B. F. Some quantitative properties of anxiety. *J. exp. Psychol.*, 1941, *29*, 390-400.

HULL, C. L. *Essentials of behavior.* New Haven: Yale University Press, 1951.

HUNT, H. F., & BRADY, J. V. Some effects of electro-convulsive shock on a conditioned emotional response ("anxiety"). *J. comp. physiol. Psychol.*, 1951, *44*, 88-98.

KAMIN, L. J. Backward conditioning and the conditioned emotional response. *J. comp. physiol. Psychol.*, 1963, *56*, 517-519.

KAMIN, L. J., & BRIMER, C. J. The effects of intensity of conditioned and unconditioned stimuli on a conditioned emotional response. *Can. J. Psychol.*, 1963, *17*, 194-198.

KAMIN, L. J., & SCHAUB, R. E. Effects of conditioned stimulus intensity on the conditioned emotional response. *J. comp. physiol. Psychol.*, 1963, *56*, 502-507.

LOGAN, F. A. A note on stimulus intensity dynamism (V). *Psychol. Rev.*, 1954, *61*, 77-80.

PERKINS, C. C., JR. The relation between conditioned stimulus intensity and response strength. *J. exp. Psychol.*, 1953, *46*, 225-231.

RAZRAN, G. Stimulus generalization of conditional responses. *Psychol. Bull.*, 1949, *46*, 337-365.

RAZRAN, G. The dominance-contiguity theory of the acquisition of classical conditioning. *Psychol. Bull.*, 1957, *54*, 1-46.

STEIN, L., SIDMAN, M., & BRADY, J. V. Some effects of two temporal variables on conditioned suppression. *J. exp. Anal. Behav.*, 1958, *1*, 153-162.

H. D. KIMMEL

University of Florida

8

Instrumental Inhibitory Factors in Classical Conditioning[1]

Experimenters in the area of classical conditioning are well acquainted with the pejorative use of such terms as "mechanical," "automatic," etc. to describe the behavioral events and processes they have chosen to investigate. Classical conditioning has been called "uncreative," "stupid," and regarding its seemingly involuntary aspects, even "purposeless." People are apt to become most vehement in their denial of the possibility that there might be anything machine-like about human behavior.

The most frequent reply of the classical conditioner to these assaults on his scientific efforts is a shrug of his shoulder, as he returns to his work. Occasionally a direct response is elicited, as when Gregory Razran agreed with Tolman's claim that classical conditioning may be a "dumb" kind of learning but went on to point out that its significance was established by the overwhelming proportion of adult behavior based upon it. And, of course, he also noted that the *evaluative* connotation of terms like "stupid" and "dumb" has no place in the language of science.

One of the premises of this report and the research it describes is that a considerable proportion of the antagonism and criticism directed toward classical conditioning and its investigators stems from a misunderstanding of the nature of the classical conditioning process. Furthermore, the suspicion is justified that responsibility for this misunderstanding may be found *within* as well as outside the ranks of conditions. While we have busily, and with scientific justification, sought to identify the parameters of conditioning (in our careful studies of the CS-UCS interval,

1 Done under Grant MH-6060-2, U.S.P.H.S.

CS and UCS intensity and duration, massing and spacing of conditioning trials, etc.), we have tended largely to ignore certain "dynamic" aspects of the developing CR that bear the promise of contributing to a rather different image of classical conditioning than that which is held conventionally.

It is appropriate to begin an exposition of this viewpoint by noting that Pavlov implied a similar approach, although he did not fully exploit his initial insight. In his discussion of the various types of internal inhibition, he wrote, "The experimental evidence . . . demonstrates the enormous biological importance of internal inhibition of conditioned reflexes. It is by means of internal inhibition that the signalizing activity of the hemispheres is constantly corrected and perfected." Pavlov went on, ". . . if a regular interval of sufficient duration is established between the commencement of a conditioned stimulus and its reinforcement by the unconditioned stimulus, the former becomes ineffective during the first part of its isolated action; during the second part of its action a positive excitatory effect appears, and this increases progressively in intensity as the moment approaches when the unconditioned stimulus has customarily been applied (inhibition of delay). In the above manner a continuous and most exact adaptation of the organism to its environment is effected, revealing a most delicate adjustment in the antagonistic nervous processes of the higher animals" (1927, p. 106).

A LAW OF EFFECT IN CLASSICAL CONDITIONING?

To the knowledge of the writer, no one has suggested previously [2] that the principle underlying the phenomenon of inhibition of delay might be similar to the law of effect, yet it is not difficult to draw this inference from Pavlov's remarks. When he refers to the possibility that internal inhibition is a means by which ". . . the signalizing activity of the hemispheres is constantly *corrected* and *perfected*" (*op. cit.*, italics not in original), and again, when he writes that inhibition of delay effects ". . . a continuous and most exact *adaptation of the organism to its environment*" (*op. cit.*, italics not in original), an effect similar to differential instrumental conditioning may be inferred. Simply stated, the inference is that inhibiting the salivary CR until such time as it is *more appropriate* (i.e., more likely to be of use in masticating, swallowing, and digesting the impending food UCS or in diluting an acid UCS) is differentially reinforcing in comparison to responding at the onset of the CS.

While an *ad hoc* interpretation of inhibition of delay in salivary conditioning in terms of differential reinforcement may be sufficiently

[2] It is clear that the contributions to this symposium by Professors Sheffield and Prokasy touch on these matters.

appealing to warrant its further exploration, extension of the argument to situations in which a noxious UCS is used does not suggest immediately any similarities. Some writers have pointed out that an appropriately timed lid-closure would result in partial avoidance of the air-puff in eyelid conditioning (Solomon and Brush, 1956), yet the fact that an air-puff directed to the cheek may be used successfully in eyelid conditioning tends to defeat this argument, albeit prematurely. Nevertheless, it is of some interest that eyelid conditioners seem to prefer longer latency responses over short, even to the point of only counting as CRs those blinks that "blend" with the UCR (Pennypacker, 1964).

We have taken this point of view still farther in our research and asked, "In what way could inhibition of delay in *GSR* conditioning be reinforcing in comparison with responding as quickly as possible?" How would inhibition of delay in GSR conditioning reflect ". . . a continuous and most exact *adaptation* of the organism to its environment," harking back to Pavlov? A basis for such adaptation, by means of differential reinforcement, it will be argued in this paper, may be found in a manifestation of inhibition of delay which has recently been receiving increasing experimental attention.

CONDITIONED DIMINUTION OF THE UCR

In an experiment by Kimble and Dufort (1956) Ss were given 40 eyelid conditioning trials after which (Trials 41-60) they received only the UCS. Then, on Trials 61-80, they again received the CS and UCS in paired fashion.[3] It was observed that the amplitude of the UCR immediately following omission of the CS (Trial 41) appeared to increase abruptly. Further exploration of this fortuitous discovery showed that the UCR had, in fact, systematically been reducing in amplitude during the first 40 CS-UCS trials. When the CS was omitted the UCR increased and remained relatively large while the CS was absent. As soon as the CS was restored on Trial 61, the UCR was again attenuated.

Speculating on the possibility that this reduction of the UCR in the presence of the CS was a manifestation of a conditioned inhibitory process, perhaps similar to Pavlov's inhibition of delay, Kimble and Ost (1962) studied its dependence upon the CS-UCS interval used during paired conditioning trials and found that the largest amount of recovery of the UCR produced by omitting the CS occurred in a group of Ss trained with a 0.5 second CS-UCS interval. They interpreted this result as supporting the proposition that a *conditioned* inhibitory process analogous to inhibition of delay was responsible for the UCR-diminution.

[3] The major purpose and results of this study are not immediately relevant and will be ignored.

UCR-diminution and subsequent recovery (when the CS is omitted) has since been reported by Kimmel and Pennypacker (1963) in a study of the conditioned GSR. In that study it was found that the amount of increase in UCR following CS-omission was related in negatively accelerated fashion to the number of training trials given prior to presenting the UCS alone. Again, the view that this phenomenon is the result of a learned inhibition was supported. A further study by Kimmel and Pennypacker (unpublished) revealed maximum UCR-recovery following training at 0.5 second CS-UCS interval, though this result received only marginal fiducial support and was complicated by the fact that a differential conditioning procedure had been used prior to presenting the UCS alone. It is reasonable to conclude from these studies that diminution of the UCR in the presence of the CS is an important aspect of classical conditioning and that it may be related to inhibition of delay.

Experiment No. 1: Inhibition of Delay and Disinhibition in GSR Conditioning

Of fundamental importance in elaborating an explanation of inhibition of delay in terms of an instrumental reinforcement concept is our knowledge of the empirical facts of inhibition of delay. In the light of the meagerness of the empirical evidence in this area, a fairly large study was conducted with the purpose of partly filling this void. Pilot study had shown no differences in the development of inhibition of delay among three techniques of approaching a long CS-UCS interval. For this reason it was decided to start with a long interval and use the same CS-UCS interval throughout conditioning. Furthermore, an earlier study (Kimmel, 1963) suggested that there would be a slight tendency for S to recover inhibited CR amplitude and latency, from the end of one day's training to the beginning of the next, if the study occupied more than one day. For this reason only one day per single S was employed even though some sessions required one and one-half hours of continuous data-collection from one S.

Method.[4]   Three hundred undergraduate students served as Ss in this study. They were divided randomly into six groups of 50 to receive either 0, 1, 2, 10, 25, or 50 paired presentations of a CS and UCS, following an adaptation series of presentations of the CS only and preceding test trials on which a disinhibiting stimulus was added to the CS at one of five temporal points during its presentation. The 50 Ss in each group were divided randomly into subgroups of 10 Ss each to

4 This study was conducted by W. A. Green, Ellen Kimmel, J. H. Kramer, and R. C. Martin.

receive the disinhibitor at the onset of the CS, after 25 percent of its duration, after 50 percent of its duration, after 75 percent of its duration, or at its offset. The UCS was omitted on these test trials.

The CS was a circular red light, produced by a Grayson-Stadler Multiple Stimulus Projector. Its duration was 7.5 seconds. The UCS was an electric shock to the tips of the index and middle fingers of the S's left hand. The shock intensity was 2.5 milliamperes and its duration was 0.2 second. The shock was delivered simultaneously with the offset of the CS. The disinhibitor was a 3,000 cps tone of low but noticeable intensity delivered via a speaker mounted on a wall behind the S's head and concealed by darkness. Its duration was 0.1 second.

The GSR was a DC resistance change picked up by zinc-zinc sulphate electrodes (in lucite cups filled with NaCl paste) from the palm and back of the S's right hand. It was amplified and recorded on an Esterline-Angus recorder with a paper speed of 12 inches per minute. Data were collected in a soundproof, electrically shielded room illuminated by a covered 7.5 watt lamp. E and the equipment were in an adjoining room.

After E read the noninformative instructions and attached the electrodes, a series of three electric shocks were delivered, in intensity increments up to the value used during conditioning. Then a maximum of 20 presentations of the CS alone were given, unless the S reached an adaptation criterion of two successive zero-response trials. Then the Ss received 0, 1, 2, 10, 25, or 50 CS-UCS trials. These were followed by four disinhibition test trials.

Results and Discussion

Inhibition of delay.   Two classes of data were available for examination with respect to the occurrence of inhibition of delay. These were the changes in the temporal characteristics of the response, such as the latency of its onset or of the peak deflection, and a combination of latency and magnitude, by means of inspection of individual trial-by-trial records, which, as will be demonstrated below, provided a most vivid and informative picture of both inhibition of delay and, in general, of the long-interval, delayed conditioning process.

Latency of the CR.   Figure 8-1 shows the average latency of the initial deflection following the delivery of the CS in the group of 50 Ss who received 50 conditioning trials. The number of measures contributing to each point in the figure is 50, an arbitrary latency score of 9.0 seconds being recorded in each instance of zero response throughout the CS-UCS interval (under the assumption of a 1.5 second lower limit to UCR latency). The obvious systematic increase in latency throughout

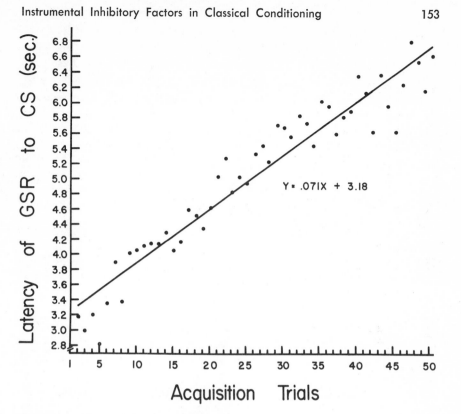

Fig. 8-1. Average CR latency (initial deflection) of Ss receiving 50 training trials. Non-response trials were scored as 9.0 seconds. (Kimmel, 1964)

training appeared to be sufficiently close to a linear trend to justify fitting the straight line which appears in the figure. Attention is drawn to the fact that the latency of the conditioned GSR is shown in this figure to change from an average value of near three seconds, at the beginning of training, to an average value of near seven seconds at the end of fifty trials. Since these data were obtained from the same 50 Ss at each data-point, we were satisfied that statistical analysis would be superfluous. However, since the procedure of using an arbitrary value of 9.0 seconds on occasions when no response at all occurred might be objectionable on various grounds, the same phenomenon is shown in Figure 8-2, with all zero responses omitted and with the data grouped into blocks of three adjacent trials to increase the stability of these averages. As can be seen in Figure 8-2, a steady (essentially linear) increase in latency of the conditioned GSR occurred even when latencies of only nonzero responses were used, although the range of the means is now reduced considerably and the longest average latency approaches only 4.0 seconds instead of 7.0 seconds.

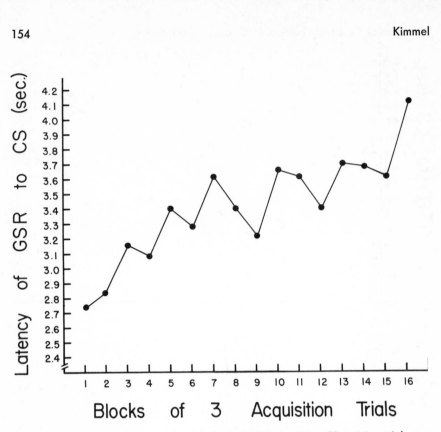

Fig. 8-2. Average CR latency (initial deflection) of Ss receiving 50 training trials, presented in blocks of 3 trials omitting Trials #1 and 50. Non-response trials were omitted.

On the basis of the data shown in Figures 8-1 and 8-2 the conclusion appears justified that the latent period of the conditioned GSR (the latency as defined above) grows steadily throughout training of the sort involved in this experiment, in a way which supports the contention that inhibition of delay was operating. These data also strongly refute the assertion made recently by Stewart, *et al.* (1961) that the "first" deflection following the CS is not a true CR but is a sensitized original response to the CS, an assertion based largely on the inability of those investigators to obtain changes in the latency of the "first" deflection in their sample of 19 Ss.

Further evidence of the operation of a process similar to inhibition of delay is shown in Figure 8-3. In this figure are shown the average latencies of the peak of the largest GSR deflection, measured from the time of onset of the CS to the time of the peak of the largest response. Again, these data come from the group of 50 Ss receiving 50 conditioning trials. If no response was made a score of 11 seconds was entered (i.e., 2 seconds more than the arbitrary maximum latency of CR onset used

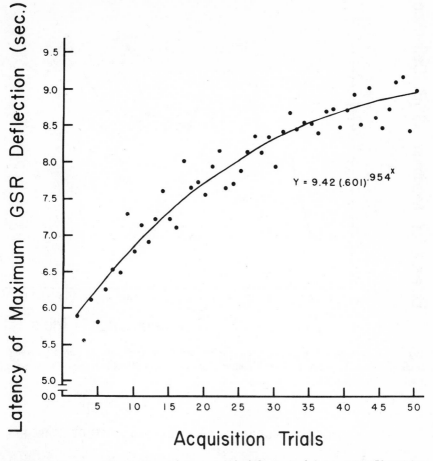

Fig. 8-3. Average CR recruitment latency (peak deflection) of Ss receiving 50 training trials. Non-response trials were scored as 11.0 seconds.

in Figure 8-1, this value being added on the assumption that at least 2 additional seconds would be needed for an hypothetical response that started at 9 seconds to reach its maximum). The equation fitted to these data is a Gompertz curve in which 9.42 is a calculated amount of growth in latency at its limit, 0.601 is a proportion giving the amount of initial growth, and 0.954 is a constant defining the rate of growth. Because of the addition of hypothetical latency scores, these data are also shown in Figure 8-4, in blocks of three trials, with zero response trials being omitted. It is clear in either representation of these data that the latency of the largest deflection shifted during training to a value close to the time of onset of the UCS (and, in Figure 8-3), perhaps to the time of occurrence of the UCR.

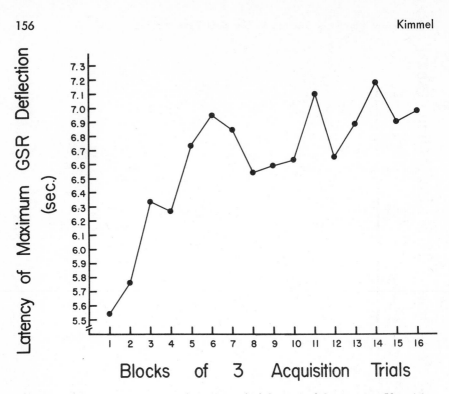

Fig. 8-4. Average CR recruitment latency (peak deflection) of Ss receiving 50 training trials, presented in blocks of 3 trials omitting Trials #1 and 50. Non-response trials were omitted. (Kimmel, 1964)

TRIAL-BY-TRIAL INDIVIDUAL RECORDS OF AMPLITUDE-TEMPORAL PATTERNS

The following series of figures shows the pattern of change in the actual GSR deflection for some of the Ss who received 50 reinforcements. In these figures, each conditioning trial is shown separately exactly as it occurred. The first (left side) vertical curved line represents the onset of the CS. The second (to the right) curved line represents the onset of the UCS. The time between these two stimuli was 7.5 seconds. Above each trial is the value of the S's basal resistance, in kilohms. In the first trial-panel, the amplitude scale used throughout is indicated.

Figure 8-5 is the record of a S who made no response to the CS on the first training trial, but who showed a CR on Trial No. 2 and, again, on Trial No. 3. Attention is drawn to the change from Trial No. 2 to Trial No. 3, the latter response appearing to occupy more of the interstimulus interval. This is a relatively typical change early in conditioning. In Trial No. 7 we see the first instance of the operation of inhibition of delay, the CR coming just before the delivery of the UCS. This is

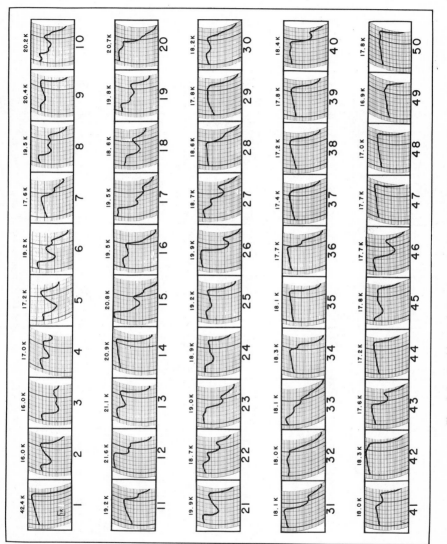

Fig. 8-5. Trial-by-trial GSR record of individual S (see text).

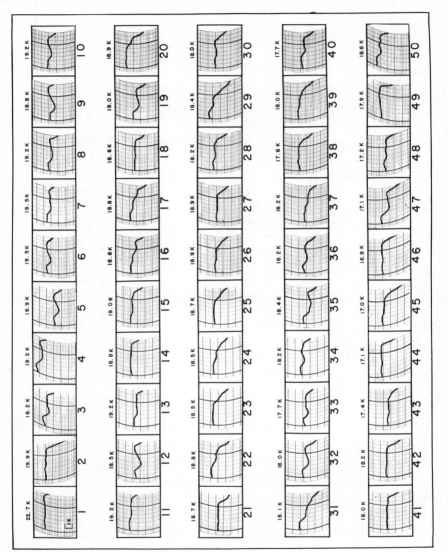

Fig. 8-6. Trial-by-trial GSR record of individual S (see text).

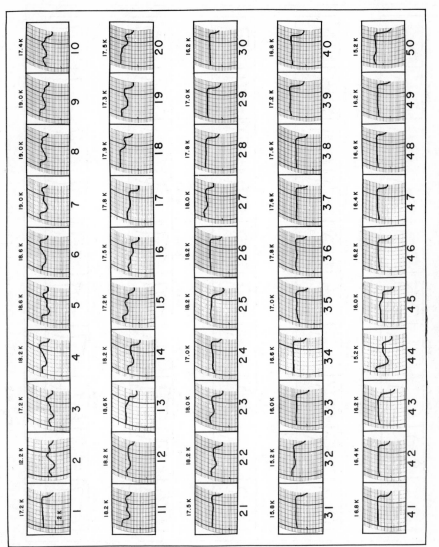

Fig. 8-7. Trial-by-trial GSR record of individual S (see text).

159

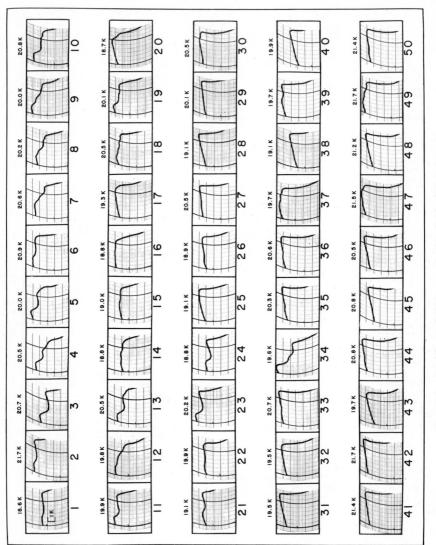

Fig. 8-8. Trial-by-trial GSR record of individual S (see text).

160

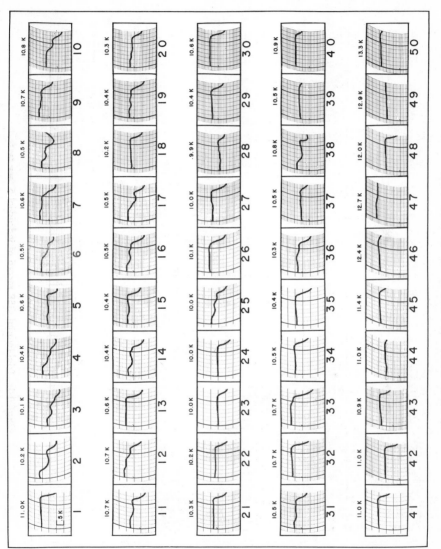

Fig. 8-9. Trial-by-trial GSR record of individual S (see text).

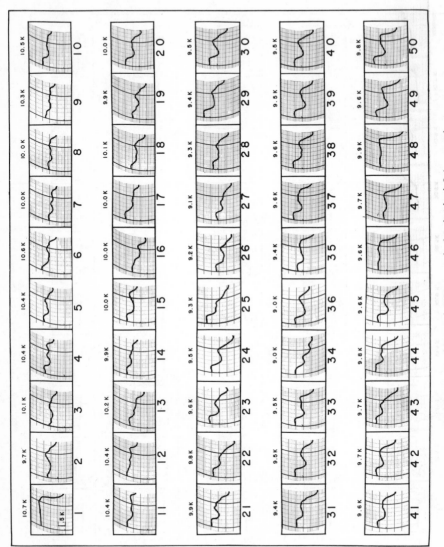

Fig. 8-10. Trial-by-trial GSR record of individual S (see text).

shown even more dramatically on Trial No. 11, when the CR appears to have started at the moment of delivery of the UCS. Several additional instances of this type of late CR can be found in later trials in this figure. Beginning on Trial No. 20, one can find instances of CRs that blend into the UCR and, finally, e.g., Trial No. 32, UCRs that occur too early to be genuine UCRs, but must be completely blended CR-UCRs.

Figure 8-6 shows the record of a S who made almost no CR following the first reinforcement but responded with a CR on the third trial and on most trials thereafter. In the record of this S there is a much more gradual appearance of very late CRs, the first clear instance being on Trial No. 20. Notice that from Trial No. 20 on there is an increasing frequency of occurrence of late CRs and, when there is almost no CR at all, early UCRs. The best examples occur on Trials No. 23, 25, 26, 27, 38, 39. Only once in the last ten trials did this S make a substantial CR (Trial No. 47), and this appears to resemble a "regression" to a very early type of response. This "regression" type of response appears to occur occasionally late in training.

Notice, in Figure 8-7, how the GSR pattern changed gradually between Trial No. 2 and Trial No. 13. This record is another good illustration of the underlying continuousness of this change in amplitude pattern. Notice also that this record contains another example of a "regression" (Trial No. 44) to a short latency CR.

Figure 8-8 shows the early buildup of CR amplitude (Trials No. 2 and 3), gradual shift in pattern as the peak moves toward the UCS, and finally, almost complete inhibition in the last ten trials. Figure 8-9 shows variations on the same theme, perhaps not as clearly demonstrated. Figure 8-10 is not unlike the others, but especially useful in demonstrating that no *one* of the deflections in the response record deserves to be singled out as the "true" CR (as Stewart, Stern, Winokur, & Fredman, 1961, tried to do). The entire pattern of deflections is the CR, and it changes from trial to trial.

DISINHIBITION

Following 0, 1, 2, 10, 25, or 50 conditioning trials the CS was presented and the disinhibitor was delivered at one of five different temporal points while the CS was on, after 0, 25, 50, 75, or 100 percent of its duration. Attention is directed first to the magnitude and latency of the GSR to the disinhibitor, averaged over all times of its delivery, as a function of the number of reinforcements given prior to the disinhibition test. Figure 8-11 shows this relationship for both magnitude and latency, each point in the Figure representing the mean of 50 Ss. As is indicated in Figure 8-11 the trend in the GSR magnitude means over number of reinforcements was essentially negatively accelerated, as

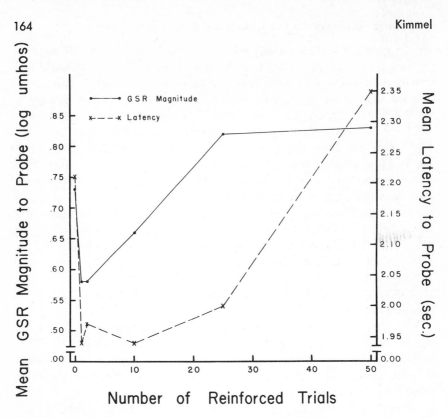

Fig. 8-11. Average GSR magnitude and latency (initial deflection) in response to disinhibitor (averaged across all 5 times of test). (Kimmel, 1964)

would be expected under the assumption that a *conditioned* inhibitory process underlay the strength of the response to the disinhibitor. Surprisingly, the latency data indicated that the longest latency occurred when the disinhibitor was delivered after 50 reinforcements, there being little variation among the latency means otherwise. Since it is conventional to associate longer latencies with weaker responses, it was unusual that in this situation the longest latency was associated with the largest response. While we can by no means be sure of an *ad hoc* interpretation of this paradoxical finding, it may be that it resulted from the fact that disinhibition involves inhibition of inhibition, a complication which may alter conventional temporal-magnitude relationships.

The present viewpoint assumes that conditioning with a noxious UCS involves two distinct stages. In the first stage there is an almost immediate association of conditioned excitation (fear?) to the *onset* of the CS. Then, after a few trials, the number being inversely related to the CS-UCS interval, inhibition of delay begins to develop in the early portion of the CS-UCS interval and the conditioned excitation appears

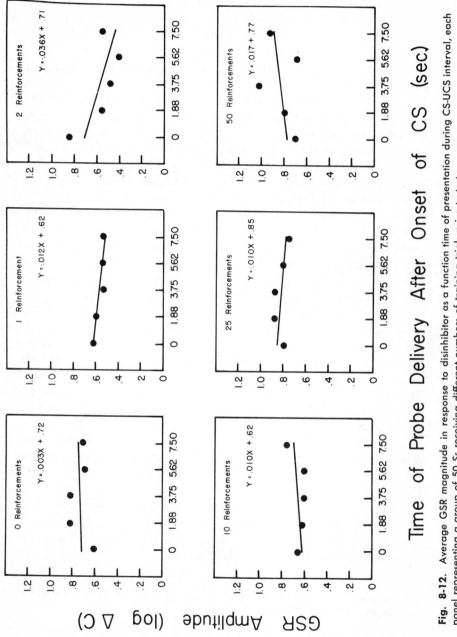

Fig. 8-12. Average GSR magnitude in response to disinhibitor as a function time of presentation during CS-UCS interval, each panel representing a group of 50 Ss receiving different numbers of training trials prior to test.

to be distributed more or less equally throughout the period of application of the CS. In a later stage of the development of inhibition of delay in conditioning with a noxious UCS, inhibition becomes sufficiently strong in the early part of the CS-UCS interval so that excitation is concentrated at a later point, a point which moves closer and closer to the approaching time of delivery of the UCS. Ultimately, it may occur that inhibition has completely taken over the CS-UCS interval, except perhaps for its very end.

Figure 8-12 shows the GSR magnitude means in response to the disinhibitor as a function of the time of its delivery during the interstimulus interval, each reinforcement group being represented in a separate panel. In this figure each point is based on the mean of 10 Ss. The first panel shows that following zero reinforcements (i.e., in the group that received the disinhibitor immediately after the adaptation series) it mattered little at which point in the interval the disinhibitor was delivered. The trend across times of delivery was essentially horizontal. After the first reinforcement (2nd panel), a slight downward trend appears in the means. This trend has become decidedly more negative following the second reinforcement (3rd panel). This early focusing of excitation in the beginning portion of the CS-UCS interval reveals the first stage of conditioning mentioned above.

After 10 reinforcements (4th panel), inhibition of delay has developed sufficiently in the early part of the CS-UCS interval to overcome the excitation that was present and to produce, again, a flat function. So it remains after 25 reinforcements (5th panel), although the whole curve is somewhat elevated. The last panel shows what happens when the disinhibitor is delivered after 50 reinforcements. A noticeable shift toward positive trend now appears in the means, as was expected from the present viewpoint. Since the changes in the trends of the magnitude means shown in this figure do not pass an eyeball test of reliability, it must be noted that a significant interaction was obtained between panels and time of test in the analysis of variance of these data (zero reinforcements group omitted).

The results of this experiment, in the main, confirmed the interpretation of inhibition of delay which led to its inception. For this reason, we turned our attention back to the UCR-diminution and increment phenomenon in our next experiment.

Experiment No. 2: Diminution and Recovery of the UCR in Classical and Avoidance GSR Conditioning

We have assumed that UCR-diminution is a consequence of the development of inhibition of delay in classical conditioning. CS-controlled inhibition, thus, is part of the adaptive machinery of the classically conditioned S, since its presence may serve to reduce the noxiousness of the UCS, if we can infer noxiousness from the size of the UCR.[5] But, such inhibition may be thought of as adaptive only in the light of the inevitability of the UCS. What would we expect in a situation in which the initially conditioned CR were made instrumental (i.e., led to shock-avoidance)? If our previous reasoning has been correct we would have to predict that UCR-diminution and recovery when the CS is omitted would not develop appreciably in such a situation, *since it would not be as adaptive to develop inhibition of delay (and to receive the shock) as it would to make the CR and avoid the shock.*[6]

Method.[7] Forty-six undergraduate students at the University of Florida served as Ss. They were run in 23 *yoked* pairs, one member of each pair receiving an avoidance procedure while the other received what may best be termed a partial-reinforcement classical procedure (Moore & Gormezano, 1962). In addition, 11 pairs were run under a delayed conditioning paradigm and the remaining 12 pairs under a trace conditioning paradigm. Assignment of Ss to conditions was essentially random except that the members of each pair were always of the same sex.

The CS was the same as in Experiment No. 1. In the delayed paradigm its duration was 5 seconds and in the trace paradigm 1 second. The UCS was an electric shock to the index and middle fingertips of the left hand. Its duration was 0.1 second. The interval between the onset of the CS and the UCS was 5 seconds for all Ss. Timing was controlled by Tektronix wave-form and impulse generators.

Within yoked pairs of Ss the intensity of the UCS was equated by means of special circuits that delivered a constant current regardless of change in S's resistance. Differences between pairs resulted from the fact that the shock intensity was increased occasionally during the training (see below).

The GSR was picked up as a DC resistance change from the palm and back of the right hand (zinc-zinc sulphate-NaCl-skin junction), amplified and recorded on a Texas Instruments Company Recti-Riter with a paper speed of 12 inches per minute. The response of the avoidance member of each pair was also led to a special unit which determined automatically which responses to reinforce. GSR amplitude, slope, or both could be used, depending upon gain settings chosen by E before each trial.

Data were collected in a ventilated dual-chamber, double-walled

---

[5] A recent study of perceived noxiousness of shock (Kimmel & Schultz, 1964) lends only partial support to this assumption.

[6] The similarity between this reasoning and that employed by Sheffield, our opposite preconceptions notwithstanding, is noteworthy.

[7] This study was conducted by William A. Greene.

IAC soundproof room, illuminated by a 100 watt bulb. The members of each pair were run simultaneously in adjoining chambers, having entered from completely separated doors to the main hall of the building. None of the Ss indicated any suspicion that another S might be involved at the same time. After the electrodes were attached to the two Ss and the doors to their chambers closed, noninformative instructions were read by E to both Ss via an intercom system.

Both Ss then received 3 trials of the UCS only, in intensity increments up to 1.5 milliamperes which was used as the UCS intensity at the beginning of training for all pairs of Ss. This was followed by either 10 presentations of the CS alone or as many as were needed to reach an adaptation criterion of two successive zero response trials. Then 16 conditioning trials were run. Ss in the delayed paradigm received a 5-second CS followed immediately by the UCS. Ss in the trace paradigm received a 1-second CS, a 4-second interval of no stimulation, and then the UCS. From Trial No. 3 on, when the avoidance S of a pair made a GSR during the last 4 seconds of the CS-UCS interval that equalled or exceeded the reinforcement criteria determined on the 2nd paired trial, no shock was delivered and, in the delayed condition, the CSs for both Ss were terminated. Following two successive avoidances, the reinforcement criteria were made slightly more demanding, to ensure that Ss would not avoid all subsequent UCSs. When the avoidance S failed to meet the reinforcement criteria and, as a result, both Ss were shocked, the intensity of the UCS was increased for both Ss on subsequent trials, to increase the likelihood of future avoidances. Once the reinforcement criteria and shock intensities had been elevated, they were never again reduced (except for 3 preliminary pairs of Ss). After the 16 conditioning trials, all Ss received the UCS alone. The intertrial interval throughout the whole experiment was varied unsystematically between 20 and 40 seconds.

Results and Discussion

The dependent variable was what will be referred to as the UCR-increment score. It was obtained as follows: The GSR immediately following the UCS (in log micromhos) was obtained on the last 2 acquisition trials containing a UCS. Within yoked pairs, of course, these were the same trials. The average of these two GSRs was determined for each S. This average acquisition UCR was subtracted from the UCR (in log micromhos) on the UCS-only trial following training to produce the UCR-increment score.

Table 8-1 shows the means and SDs of the UCR-increment scores for the avoidance and classical members of the delayed and trace paradigm pairs.

Table 8-1———UCR-increment means and SDs of avoidance and classical members of delayed and trace pairs

PARADIGM		AVOIDANCE	CLASSICAL
	$\overline{X}$	0.06	0.19
Delayed	SD	0.18	0.24
	n	11	11
	$\overline{X}$	−0.07	0.08
Trace	SD	0.36	0.28
	n	12	2

Examination of the means in Table 8-1 reveals that the avoidance Ss showed essentially zero UCR-increment when the CS was omitted, while the classical Ss' UCRs increased as in previous experiments of this type. It will be recalled that this is the outcome that was predicted. Statistical analysis of these results was complicated somewhat by the marked heterogeneity of variance indicated by the SDs in the table. A comparison of the within-pair variances of the delayed and trace paradigms showed that the within-pair variance in the trace paradigm was significantly greater than its counter-part in the delayed paradigm. For this reason, separate analyses of variance were done within the delayed and trace paradigms. These showed that a significantly greater amount of UCR-increment occurred in the delayed-classical group than in the delayed-avoidance group, $F(1/10) = 6.25$ but the avoidance-classical difference was not significant in the trace paradigm.

The results of this study showed that UCR-increment does not occur when the CS is omitted following an avoidance training procedure. Also, a significant difference in UCR-increment was associated with the avoidance-classical variable when a delayed training procedure was used. The lack of a significant difference in the trace paradigm data may be understood in the light of the fact that the delayed paradigm provided a longer CS to initiate inhibition in the classical condition and it also provided reinforcement via CS-termination as well as shock omission in the instrumental condition. It was necessary, as was explained in the procedure section above, to ensure that the avoidance S not be able to avoid almost all of the UCSs, otherwise there would not be available UCR data with which to examine the UCR-increment effect and, in addition, the classical control S would probably not get conditioned at all. Even under these limitations the predicted absence of UCR-increment in the instrumental condition occurred, and, in addition, UCR-increment was present to a sufficient degree in the classical Ss to be reliably different from the avoidance UCR-increment.

CONCLUDING REMARKS

The results of these experiments are taken by us to mean that a new view of classical conditioning deserves serious consideration. Rather than an automatic, purposeless ritual in which a "passive" S has things happen to him but can contribute little of an instrumental nature himself, classical conditioning may turn out to be just as "active" and "dynamic" as even the most elaborate kinds of human adaptive behavior. Our view can be summarized in a few sentences, albeit prematurely. First the S quickly learns to relate the onset of the CS to an impending event of adaptive significance (food, trauma, etc.). This may take only one trial in some Ss. It is manifested in a short-latency CR. Then, as the inevitability of the CS-UCS temporal relation begins to be experienced repetitively by the S, a change in the CR pattern gradually occurs, in which the early portion of the CS-UCS interval is a time of inhibition of responding and the peak of the CR shifts out toward the time of occurrence of the UCS. This is the change that Pavlov called inhibition of delay. Its consequence, in noxious UCS situations, is a reduction of the UCR. Whether this is its cause cannot be definitively asserted, but the evidence of the second experiment suggests this possibility. When the CR itself is made instrumental, UCR-increment produced by omitting the CS no longer occurs. The further possibility, that even the initial association may depend upon the instrumental aspects of UCR-reduction, cannot be rejected at this time, although it is mentioned here only because it is a "logical" possibility. Obviously, additional research on these matters is needed.

References

KIMBLE, G. A., & DUFORT, R. H. The associative factor in eyelid conditioning. *J. exp. Psychol.*, 1956, *52,* 386-391.

KIMBLE, G. A., & OST, J. W. P. A conditioned inhibitory process in eyelid conditioning. *J. exp. Psychol.*, 1961, *61,* 150-156.

KIMMEL, H. D. Management of conditioned fear. *Psychol. Rep.*, 1963, *12,* 313-314.

KIMMEL, H. D. Further analysis of GSR conditioning: A reply to Stewart, Stern, Winokur, and Fredman. *Psychol. rev.*, 1964, *71,* 160-166.

KIMMEL, H. D., & PENNYPACKER, H. S. Conditioned diminution of the unconditioned response as a function of the number of reinforcements. *J. exp. Psychol.*, 1962, *64*, 20-23.

KIMMEL, H. D., & SCHULTZ, C. A., JR. GSR magnitude and judgments of shock intensity as a function of physical intensity of shock. *Psychon. Sci.*, 1964, in press.

MOORE, J. W., & GORMEZANO, I. Yoked comparisons of instrumental and classical eyelid conditioning. *J. exp. Psychol.*, 1961, *62*, 552-559.

PAVLOV, I. P. *Conditioned reflexes*. London: Oxford University Press, 1927, (Transl.).

PENNYPACKER, H. S. External inhibition of the conditioned eyelid reflex. *J. exp. Psychol.*, 1964, in press.

SOLOMON, R. L., & BRUSH, ELINOR S. Experimentally derived conceptions of anxiety and aversion. In M. R. JONES (Ed.), *Nebraska symposium on motivation*. Lincoln, Neb.: University of Nebraska Press, 1956.

STEWART, M. A., STERN, J. A., WINOKUR, G., & FREDMAN, S. An analysis of GSR conditioning. *Psychol. Rev.*, 1961, *68*, 60-67.

WALLACE R. McALLISTER

DOROTHY E. McALLISTER

Syracuse University

9

Variables Influencing the Conditioning and the Measurement of Acquired Fear [1]

This paper will deal primarily with a series of fear conditioning experiments from this laboratory in which the learning of a hurdle-jumping response was used as the index of classically conditioned fear. The major concern will be with the elucidation of the role of the temporal interval between conditioning and the learning of the hurdle-jumping response and with the nature of the conditioned stimulus for the fear response. A brief discussion of some problems involved in measuring fear will precede the presentation of the research findings.

SOME METHODOLOGICAL CONSIDERATIONS

It is generally held that the appropriate pairing of a neutral stimulus (CS) with a noxious stimulus (UCS) results in the conditioning to the CS of an unobservable response, usually called fear or anxiety. Because this conditioned fear response is not observable, it is studied through a change in other behavior, which is taken as an index of fear. Several typical procedures can be mentioned. One uses responses such as the GSR or heart rate which, presumably, are conditioned concomitantly with fear. Other methods measure fear through its effect on the performance of an on-going response (e.g., conditioned suppression), on the magnitude of an unlearned response such as startle, or on the learning of another response. The underlying assumption for these indirect methods of measurement is, of course, that a correlation exists

[1] The research reported in this paper was supported in part by a research grant, M-2064, from the National Institute of Mental Health, Public Health Service.

between the magnitude of these measurable responses and of fear. There is no assurance, however, that this relationship is linear.

A theoretical rationale for the relationship between fear and some of the response measures has been provided by Mowrer (1939) and N. E. Miller (1951). They assume that fear has motivational properties; that is, it energizes behavior and its reduction serves as a reinforcer. These two properties explain the relationship between fear and the learning of a new response, while the energizing role accounts for the covariation between fear and an unlearned response (Brown, Kalish, & Farber, 1951). The use of conditioned suppression as a measure of fear can be fitted into this rationale if it is assumed that associated to the stimuli produced by the fear response is a learned, or innate, response which interferes with the on-going behavior. It could also be assumed that the fear response itself is the interfering agent (Kamin, 1961). Employing a response such as the GSR as a measure of fear is apparently based either on the assumption that since the two responses are conditioned simultaneously, the presence of one insures the presence of the other, or on the assumption that such a measurable response is one component of the fear response.

It is obvious that the responses used as indices of fear are not related exclusively to fear. That is, they occur on occasions when fear would not be assumed to be present. For example, the GSR can be conditioned when pictures of pin-up girls are used as the UCS,[2] and changes in the GSR, heart rate, respiration, etc. are known to occur in numerous non-fearful situations. Likewise, such responses as hurdle jumping and bar pressing occur under a wide variety of circumstances in the absence of fear. Thus, it seems unwarranted to define fear in terms of any particular response measure. In the final analysis, it appears that the concept of fear is only introduced after the occurrence of classical conditioning procedures employing a noxious UCS. Defining fear in terms of this antecedent condition would seem to answer the question raised by Solomon and Brush (1956, p. 281) concerning how the concept of fear can be defined objectively. Any response which is correlated with this antecedent condition can be used as a measure of fear.

Because fear is unobservable and its measurement indirect, complications may arise in the interpretation of experimental results. If no evidence for fear is obtained, it may be due to the failure of it to be conditioned because of the use of inadequate procedures. However, even if fear is conditioned, it may fail to be indicated because of inadequate methods of measurement. That is, other factors may interfere either with the response used as an index of fear or with the elicitation of fear. An example of the failure of fear to be evidenced, even though con-

[2] Dean, S. J. Personal communication.

ditioned, is contained in the research to be reported. The converse situation, in which fear is indicated by the response measure used but in which the results are due to processes such as pseudoconditioning or sensitization rather than to conditioning, can be handled adequately with appropriate control groups and, therefore, offers little problem in interpretation.

POSTCONDITIONING DELAY INTERVAL

Background. The original purpose of this research program was to study the second-order conditioning of fear. Although some evidence had been obtained indicating that second-order conditioning did occur, it was not found possible to replicate the finding.[3] The first step taken in attempting to determine the reason for this failure was to ascertain whether optimal conditions for obtaining first-order conditioning were being utilized. To this end, a study of first-order conditioning varying the level of shock parametrically was conducted. For this study, as well as for most of the studies from this laboratory to be discussed, the general method used was that first developed by N. E. Miller (1948) and later refined by Brown and Jacobs (1949) and Kalish (1954). Specifically, two conditioning boxes and one hurdle-jumping apparatus were used. Two subjects (rats) were conditioned simultaneously in the separate conditioning boxes and were then run alternately in the hurdle-jumping apparatus. The two conditioning boxes and the start box of the hurdle-jumping apparatus were painted white, had grid floors, and otherwise were constructed so as to be highly similar. The safe box of the hurdle apparatus was painted gray and had a wooden floor. The basic conditioning procedure used a six-second increase in illumination (from 7 to 115 foot candles) as the CS[4] and a two-second shock as the UCS. The CS-UCS interval was four seconds; the intertrial interval, two minutes. Following conditioning, the subject was placed in the start box of the hurdle-jumping apparatus, the CS was presented with the opening of a guillotine door, and the subject was allowed to escape into the safe box by jumping the hurdle and thereby terminating the CS. No shock was ever presented during the hurdle-jumping phase of the experiment. A more detailed description of the apparatus and general procedures can be found in McAllister and McAllister (1962a).

It was assumed that fear as a response would be classically conditioned to the light as a result of its pairing with shock. Subsequent presentation of the light in the start box of the hurdle apparatus would

3 Subsequent to the preparation of this report, evidence for the second-order conditioning of fear was obtained (McAllister & McAllister, 1964).

4 It will be demonstrated later that the effective CS is a compound consisting of the discrete CS and the static cues of the apparatus.

elicit fear which, in turn, would serve as motivation for the learning of the hurdle-jumping response. Reinforcement for such learning would be contingent upon the reduction of fear resulting from the escape from the CS.

In the parametric shock study, 25 hurdle-jumping trials were begun approximately two minutes following conditioning. On the next day 25 additional trials were given. Regardless of the level of shock used during conditioning (30, 40, 50, 60, or 100 volts), no evidence for the learning of hurdle jumping was obtained on the first day of training. However, on the second day of training, learning did occur for the groups with the higher shock levels. This finding suggested that fear had been conditioned but that some factor interfered with its measurement on the first day.

A subsequent experiment (McAllister & McAllister, 1962a) tested the hypothesis that the time intervening between conditioning and hurdle jumping was critical in determining whether hurdle jumping would be learned on the initial training trials. For this experiment, the shock level for conditioning was 70 volts. The results supported the hypothesis by showing that learning occurred during the first 25 trials of hurdle-jumping training when a postconditioning delay of one day was used but not when training occurred immediately following conditioning.

Interpretation of effect of variable. While the results of these experiments demonstrate the importance of the postconditioning delay interval, they give no indication as to its underlying mechanism. Since conditioning took place in boxes different from, although similar to, the start box of the hurdle apparatus, the finding of Perkins and Weyant (1958), that the amount of stimulus generalization increases with time, might apply to the present situation. On the basis of their results, it would be expected that little fear would be elicited by the generalized stimuli in the hurdle apparatus immediately following conditioning while an increased amount would be expected following a delay. Since fear, presumably, provides the source of motivation and its reduction the reinforcement for the learning of hurdle jumping, little or no learning would be expected until after a delay period. This hypotheis was tested by comparing the hurdle-jumping performance of two groups conditioned in the start box of the hurdle apparatus with two conditioned in the separate conditioning boxes (McAllister & McAllister, 1963). Of each pair, one was trained in hurdle jumping with a postconditioning delay of 3 minutes and the other with 24 hours. Fig. 9-1 presents the results as stimulus generalization gradients. The label on the abscissa indicates whether the hurdle-jumping training was administered in the same box in which fear was conditioned or in a different one.

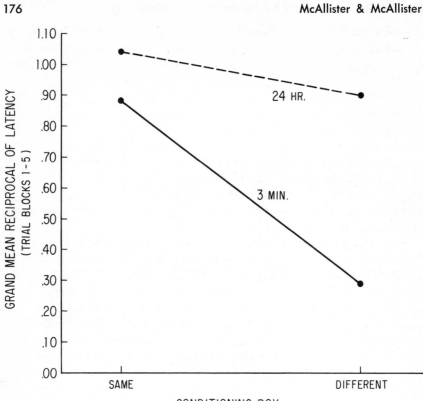

Fig. 9-1. Stimulus generalization gradients obtained with postconditioning delays of 3 min. and 24 hr. (McAllister & McAllister, 1963)

Statistical analysis of the data revealed that the slopes of the curves were significantly different. The 3-minute groups differed significantly while the 24-hour groups did not, and a significant difference due to delay was obtained only for the different conditioning box groups. These results clearly support the hypothesis. They also illustrate the importance of distinguishing between the conditioning of fear and the measurement of fear. That is, fear was conditioned in the 3-minute group with the different conditioning box although it failed to be evidenced under the measuring conditions which used an inadequate postconditioning delay.

Many explanations of the results which might be offered are ruled out by the differential effect of postconditioning delay along the stimulus dimension. A simple incubation of fear notion does not seem warranted since it would predict an equal increase in performance with delay regardless of the conditioning box used. Although it is possible that a ceiling on performance may have prevented a sizable improvement in the same conditioning box treatment, the high level of performance for the

3-minute group suggests that fear does not have to incubate. Also, a competing response notion seems unsupported by the data. This position might hold, for instance, that the performance of the 3-minute group with the different conditioning box was depressed because of a competing response (e.g., crouching) elicited during hurdle jumping either by the stimuli of the situation, by the stimuli produced by the fear response, or by the aftereffects of shock. Its dissipation with time would account for the increase in performance for the 24-hour delay group. Since such a competing response would be expected, however, to be elicited maximally in the original stimulus situation, it would be necessary to predict that the performance of the 3-minute group with the same conditioning box would be depressed at least as much as the other 3-minute group. The results are obviously contrary to this prediction.

An interpretation which is consonant with the results assumes that the subjects are responding to a psychophysical dimension. Basically, it assumes that if, in the scaling of a physical stimulus dimension, the stimuli are presented in close temporal proximity, a greater number of jnd's will separate them than when a longer time interval intervenes. The stimulus dimension of concern is that along which the conditioning box and the start box of the hurdle apparatus lie. The psychophysical scaling of this dimension with three minutes separating the presentations of the stimuli would, presumably, result in a greater number of jnd's than a similar scaling with 24 hours intervening between presentations. As applied to the present study, it would be expected that the start box of the hurdle-jumping apparatus and the different conditioning box would be more unlike (separated by more jnd's) for the 3-minute group than for the 24-hour group. Therefore, a greater stimulus generalization decrement would be expected in the former group than in the latter. No difference in performance between the two groups with the same conditioning box would be expected since the conditioning and hurdle-jumping phases of the experiment involve the same stimuli.

The generality of such a mechanism was tested with human subjects using a procedure described in Woodworth and Schlosberg (1954, p. 210). Each subject was shown a black line on a white cardboard (standard stimulus) and $\frac{1}{2}$ minute or 8 minutes later was shown the same line or one longer by 4, 8, or 12 millimeters (comparison stimulus).[5] After presentation of the second line, the subject judged whether it was equal or longer in length than the first. Separate groups of subjects were used for each of the four comparisons at each of the two time intervals. The results are shown in Fig. 9-2. With the longer interval between the presentation of the standard and the comparison stimulus, the subjects were significantly more likely to judge lines physically differing in length to be equal

5 These data were collected and analyzed by Joseph J. Franchina.

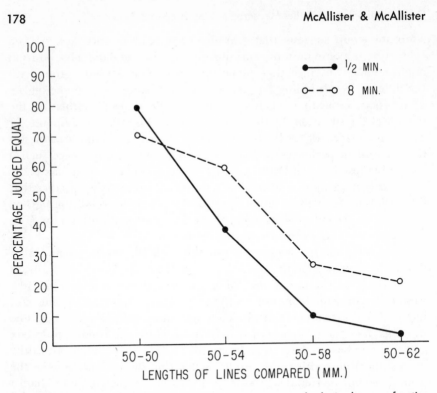

Fig. 9-2. Percentage equal judgments of comparison to standard stimulus as a function of length of comparison stimulus for two judgment intervals.

in length. Also, the larger differences were judged equal significantly less often than the smaller differences regardless of the time interval. Thus, the longer the interval between presentations of the stimuli, the greater the difference had to be between the stimuli to be noticed. Similar results have been obtained by Lipsitt and Engen (1961) using somewhat different procedures and much shorter intervals. These findings lend credence to the interpretation that the effect of the postconditioning delay variable can, at least in part, be accounted for in terms of stimulus generalization along psychophysical stimulus dimensions which differ for the two delay conditions. However, some experimenters, for theoretical or practical reasons, still might choose to interpret the results as due to stimulus generalization along a physical dimension plus an effect of time on the generalization gradient. The choice in alternatives would be between incorporating the time variable in the definition of the stimulus dimension, as in the psychophysical procedure, or considering that the temporal variable directly affects performance. For the remainder of this paper, the second alternative will be adopted.

A temporal function of stimulus generalization. The data presented thus far, although indicating the importance of the postcondi-

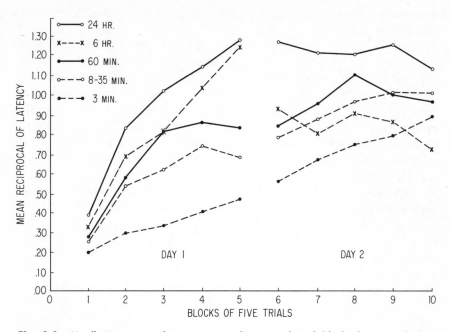

Fig. 9-3. Hurdle-jumping performance as a function of trial blocks for several post-conditioning delay intervals following conditioning in a box different from the start box of the hurdle apparatus.

tioning delay variable, do not provide evidence concerning its critical length. In order to determine the functional relationship between hurdle-jumping performance and length of postconditioning delay and, thus, to obtain a function describing the change in stimulus generalization with time, seven groups of subjects were conditioned in the separate conditioning boxes using a high level of shock (125 volts). They were then given 25 hurdle-jumping trials either 3, 8, 15, 35, 60 minutes, 6 or 24 hours later. On the following day 25 additional trials were given. These temporal intervals were chosen on the basis of preliminary work which had suggested that much of the effect of delay occurred within the first hour.

A trend analysis of the initial 25 trials yielded a significant interaction between Trials and Delay Interval indicating that the learning curves for the several groups differed. The means of the groups also differed significantly on the last block of trials of the first day. Further analyses showed that the performances of the 6- and 24-hour groups did not differ significantly but that each was significantly superior to each of the other groups, except the 35-minute group. In this last instance, the differences just fell short of the 5 percent level of significance. The difference between any pair of the 3-, 8-, 15-, 35-, or 60-minute groups was not significant. Also, there were several inversions in the order of performance of these groups, although the performance of the 3-minute group was consistently inferior.

To obtain the most stable estimate of the manner in which performance changes with postconditioning delay, data of groups from other experiments run under exactly the same conditions as the 3-minute, 60-minute, and 24-hour groups were combined with the comparable data from this experiment. In addition, the data from the 8-, 15-, and 35-minute groups were pooled. After these procedures had been carried out, there were five delay intervals represented: 3 minutes, 8-35 minutes, 60 minutes, 6 hours, and 24 hours. The number of subjects in each group was 47, 48, 31, 16, and 47, respectively.

The results are shown in Fig. 9-3. As may be seen, improvement in performance on Day 1 of hurdle jumping was directly related to the delay interval. Performance on Day 2 continued to improve for all except the 6- and 24-hour groups. For the latter group, performance tended to remain at the level reached at the end of Day 1 while, for the former group, it was much lower. The fact that the Day 2 performance of all of the other groups started at about the same level as at the end of the first

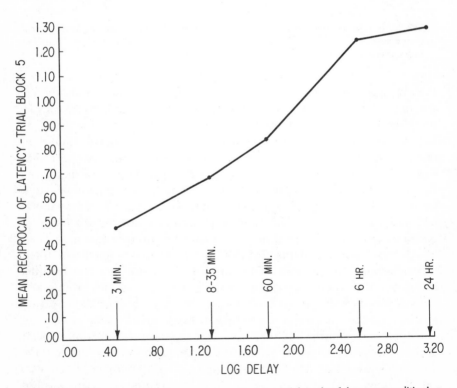

Fig. 9-4. Hurdle-jumping performance as a function of length of log postconditioning delay.

day suggests that the performance of the 6-hour group is artificially high on Day 1 or artificially low on Day 2. There is the possibility, of course, that this finding is intrinsic to the delay interval.

Fig. 9-4 presents the mean reciprocal of latency of hurdle jumping on Trial Block 5 as a function of log delay. The effect of postconditioning delay begins immediately after conditioning and continues progressively throughout the range of temporal intervals studied. This function may be interpreted as indicating that the amount of fear elicited by generalized stimuli increases monotonically with time, at least up to 24 hours.

Relation to temporal variable in avoidance conditioning. The question may arise as to whether or not the postconditioning delay variable, as studied in this series of experiments, is related to the temporal variable reported by Kamin (1957). In his experiment animals were given 25 avoidance conditioning trials and then, following either 0, .5, 1, 6, 24 hours or 19 days, were retrained in the avoidance procedure for 25 trials. Using number of avoidance responses on the relearning trials as the response measure, he found that no group performed as well as the zero delay group; that amount of retention decreased significantly from 0 to 1 hour, then increased significantly from 1 hour to 19 days; and that there was no significant difference between the 0- and 24-hour groups.

At first glance the results reported in the parametric study illustrated in Fig. 9-4 appear to be contrary to Kamin's findings. However, the data in that figure are based upon the performance of subjects who were given hurdle-jumping training in a different apparatus from the one in which they were conditioned, while Kamin used the same apparatus for both phases of his experiment. The most comparable data are those for the 3-minute and 24-hour groups with the same conditioning box treatment shown in Fig. 9-1. These groups did not differ in performance nor did Kamin's similar groups, 0 and 24 hours. To determine whether the depression in performance found by Kamin at one hour would occur in the present situation, three groups were conditioned in the start box of the hurdle-jumping apparatus. They were then given hurdle-jumping training after either 3 minutes, 1 hour, or 24 hours. The results are shown in Fig. 9-5. The findings for the 3-minute and 24-hour groups parallel those obtained previously. It is clear that there was no depression in performance for the one-hour group on either day of training.[6]

[6] A trend analysis revealed no significant differences among the groups on Day 1. The Day 2 data, although not pertinent to this discussion, were also analyzed. On this day, a Trials x Delay interaction, just significant at the 5 percent level, was found. Further analyses indicated a significant Trials effect for the 3-minute and for the 24-hour groups but not for the 1-hour group. However, no significant differences among the groups were obtained from analyses of the effects of delay on each trial block.

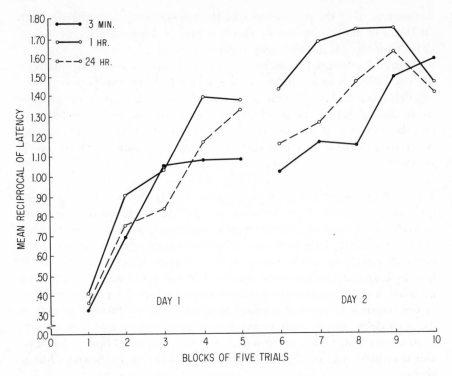

Fig. 9-5. Hurdle-jumping performance as a function of trial blocks for several post-conditioning delay intervals following conditioning in the start box of the hurdle apparatus.

A possible reason for these discrepant results may lie in the different procedures used. Kamin introduced a delay period following the partial acquisition of the instrumental response. In the present case, the delay occurred prior to the learning of the instrumental response. As a check on the effect of this procedural difference, a group of subjects was treated exactly as the 3-minute group above except that a one-hour delay was introduced after the second block of hurdle-jumping trials. It was found that there was an improvement, rather than a depression in performance, on the trial blocks following the delay. Thus, it may be that the effect of the temporal variable observed by Kamin is dependent upon some feature of the avoidance conditioning procedure, as yet unidentified.

Further implications. There is some evidence that the increase in stimulus generalization with time is a general phenomenon. The studies of Perkins and Weyant (1958), Saltz and Asdourian (1963), Thomas and Lopez (1962), and the present experiments each demonstrates this temporal effect on stimulus generalization even though the responses, species of subjects, and sources of motivation varied among the studies. In all of these investigations the experimental situation was such that this temporal variable led to an improvement in performance. There are situations, however, in which it would be expected to have a deleterious effect. For example, consider a hurdle-jumping situation in which fear is classically conditioned in the start box and in which the start and safe boxes of the apparatus are highly similar. Here it would be expected that, to the extent that fear generalized from the stimuli of the start box to those of the safe box, the learning of hurdle jumping would be interfered with because of the relatively small amount of fear reduction possible. With time, the increase in the stimulus generalization of fear should then result in a progressively greater interference with the learning of hurdle jumping. Further, it would be expected that as the possibility of stimulus generalization was decreased, by increasing the difference between the start and safe boxes, the effect of the temporal variable would also decrease.

This reasoning concerning the temporal effect on stimulus generalization is currently being applied to account for a series of studies, as yet incomplete, from this laboratory. A class experiment, and a later replication under more controlled conditions, provided the initial impetus for the development of this analysis. In these studies, which also used a hurdle-jumping apparatus, it was found that, after classical conditioning of fear in the start box, performance of hurdle jumping following a post-conditioning delay of 2-3 minutes was significantly superior to that following a one-day delay. This finding is, of course, inconsistent with that reported previously as may be seen by referring to Fig. 9-5 and to the groups with the same conditioning box in Fig. 9-1. In these instances, there was no difference between groups with 3-minute and 24-hour post-conditioning delays. Apparatus differences appeared to be a likely source of the disparity in results. In the second apparatus the start and safe boxes were larger, highly similar (both gray with grid floors), and one side of both the start and safe box was constructed of glass instead of wood. In addition, a buzzer instead of a light was used as the CS. Following the reasoning above, the potentially most important differences would be the similarity of the start and safe boxes and the glass sides which would permit extra-apparatus cues to become part of the stimulus complex to which fear was conditioned. The obtained results could, in fact, be predicted on the basis of these apparatus characteristics plus the operation of the postconditioning delay variable on stimulus generalization. That is, if fear were conditioned to a complex consisting of the CS, the static stimuli of the start box, and the extra-apparatus cues, the stimulus generalization gradient of fear might extend to the similar complex of stimuli in the safe box to a greater degree after one day, because of the increase in stimulus generalization with time, than after a few minutes. Thus, the learning of hurdle jumping should be superior, because of the greater fear reduction, the shorter the postconditioning delay.

A further experiment tested the implication that a decrease in the similarity of the start and safe boxes would reduce the effect of the temporal variable by lessening the opportunity for stimulus generalization of fear to occur. Four groups of subjects were used, two with a 3-minute and two with a 23-hour postconditioning delay. All groups received two days of hurdle-jumping training. One group at each delay interval was trained with the highly similar start and safe boxes and, hence, replicated the conditions of the previous studies. For the other group at each delay interval, the safe box was modified to make it dissimilar to the start box by the use of a white cover and a plywood insert which provided a white wooden floor and white walls on all but the glass side. Fig. 9-6 presents the results. It is apparent that, with a 3-minute postconditioning delay, performance was the same whether the start and safe boxes were similar or dissimilar. Although, as predicted, the 23-hour group with the dissimilar start and safe boxes performed better

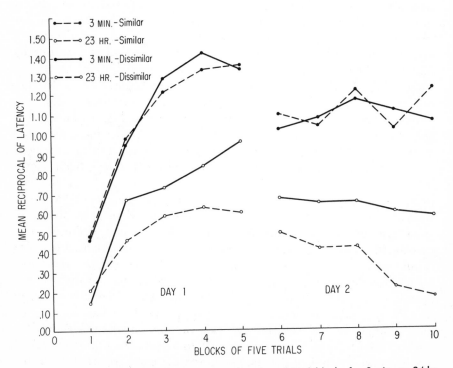

Fig. 9-6. Hurdle-jumping performance as a function of trial blocks for 3-min. or 24-hr. postconditioning delay intervals with similar or dissimilar start and safe boxes. Extra-apparatus cues were visible for all groups.

than the group in which the boxes were similar, the difference was not significant. The failure to demonstrate statistically the expected effect of the similarity variable can be accounted for by assuming that the extra-apparatus cues visible through the glass sides of the boxes constituted the major stimulus difference between the start and safe box situations. Thus, it might not be expected that the use of a dissimilar safe box would be highly effective in preventing the generalization of fear from the start box following the longer postconditioning delay.

This interpretation of the results was tested with an experiment designed to study the role of extra-apparatus cues. Two groups were given a postconditioning delay of three minutes, and two others, of 23 hours. For one group under each delay condition the extra-apparatus cues were eliminated by covering the glass sides of both the start and the safe boxes with wood. For the remaining two groups, the extra-apparatus cues were visible as before. The apparatus for all groups was the same as that employed for the dissimilar condition of the previous experiment except that the size of both the start and safe boxes was reduced by the use of wooden inserts, and a light source was provided in each.

The results on Day 1, as shown in Fig. 9-7, are consistent with expectations. A trend analysis of variance yielded a significant triple inter-

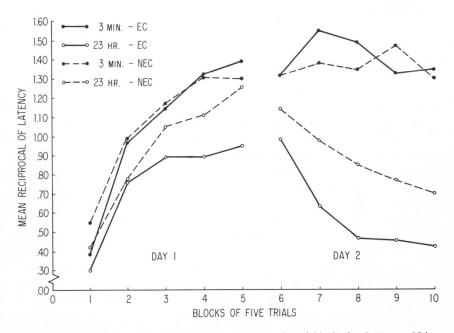

Fig. 9-7. Hurdle-jumping performance as a function of trial blocks for 3-min. or 23-hr. postconditioning delay intervals with (EC) or without (NEC) extra-apparatus cues: The start and safe boxes were dissimilar for all groups.

action (3 min. vs. 23 hrs. x EC vs. NEC x Trial Blocks). Therefore, the data from Trial Block 5 were analyzed. In this case, a significant double interaction (3 min. vs. 23 hrs. x EC vs. NEC) was obtained. Tests of the simple effects indicated a significant difference between EC and NEC for the 23-hour groups but not for the 3-minute groups. There also was a significant difference between the 3-minute and 23-hour groups for the EC condition but not for the NEC condition. Thus, the removal of the extra-apparatus cues eliminated the effect of a long postconditioning delay. As will be noted, this conclusion does not apply to the Day 2 results. Here, there was again a triple interaction, but the performance of the 23 hour-NEC group was much lower than that of the two 3-minute groups. The basis for this finding is as yet unknown, but a current preliminary investigation suggests that it might be due to a forgetting process.

In summary, the data of the above two experiments imply that as the opportunity for the stimulus generalization of fear to occur is decreased by making the start and safe boxes dissimilar (Fig. 9-6) or by eliminating the extra-apparatus cues (Fig. 9-7) the effect of a long postconditioning delay is decreased. These results give added support to the notion that the stimulus generalization of fear increases with time. Also, they would seem to rule out completely incubation and competing responses as explanations for the effect of postconditioning delay.

NATURE OF THE CONDITIONED STIMULUS

The conditioning of fear can be inferred from hurdle-jumping performance only when that performance cannot be attributed to other factors such as pseudoconditioning, sensitization, or the operation of an exploratory or activity motive. Normally, a group-administered backward conditioning procedure is considered to control for these factors adequately since the subjects in such a group experience all the stimuli but not in the order in which conditioning of fear is likely to occur. The study mentioned above, in which the level of shock used during conditioning was varied parametrically, employed such a control group for each level of shock (McAllister & McAllister, 1962a). It was found that the backward conditioning group with the highest level of shock learned the hurdle-jumping response while groups with the lower shock levels did not. Goldstein (1960) has also reported learning of hurdle jumping following backward fear conditioning. The most likely explanation is that fear is conditioned to the static cues of the situation when backward conditioning procedures are used and that with high levels of shock this fear is not extinguished in the intertrial intervals during conditioning. Two studies (McAllister & McAllister, 1962b) were conducted to ascertain the correctness of this interpretation. In addition, the design of the studies permitted a determination of the effective CS with forward conditioning.

In the first experiment there were four groups. Two groups were conditioned with the forward conditioning (FC) procedures described for the parametric shock study. The other two groups were administered backward conditioning (BC) procedures in which the UCS was followed 15 seconds later by the CS. On the day following conditioning, hurdle-jumping training was begun for all groups. For one FC and one BC group (FC-CS and BC-CS), the usual procedures were employed, while the CS was omitted for the remaining two groups (FC-NCS and BC-NCS).

If the assumption is correct that, during backward conditioning, fear is conditioned only to the static stimuli of the apparatus, it would be expected that the BC-CS and BC-NCS groups would perform equally. If, with FC, fear is conditioned to both the CS and the static cues of the apparatus, performance of the FC-CS group should be superior to that of the FC-NCS group. It would also be predicted that the latter group would perform at the same level as the BC groups. The results of the experiment, presented in Fig. 9-8, are in keeping with the expectations. Hurdle-jumping performance for the FC-CS group was significantly better than for each of the other groups, which did not differ from one another.

A second related experiment with two FC and two BC groups used

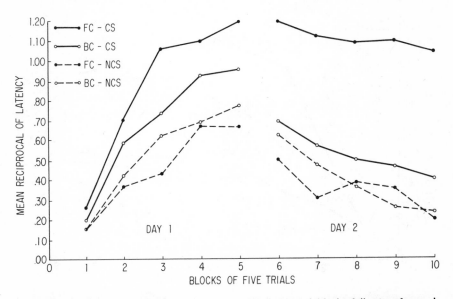

Fig. 9-8. Hurdle-jumping performance as a function of trial blocks following forward conditioning (FC) and backward conditioning (BC) with the conditioned stimulus (CS) or with no conditioned stimulus (NCS) presented during hurdle jumping. (McAllister & McAllister, 1962b)

the same conditioning and hurdle-jumping sequence as the previous study. However, in this case, the CS was presented during hurdle jumping for all groups, but fear conditioned to the static stimuli was extinguished in one FC and one BC group by placing the subjects in the conditioning box for one hour just prior to hurdle jumping (FC-E and BC-E). Subjects in the other two groups were given no extinction treatment (FC-NE and BC-NE) but instead were placed in a cage in the laboratory for the one-hour period. It was predicted that the use of the extinction procedure would depress the performance of the FC group and would result in no learning for the BC group due to the elimination of one source of fear in the former case and the only source of fear in the latter. Fig. 9-9 shows that the results supported the prediction. For both FC and BC, the NE group was significantly superior to the E group. For both the NE and the E conditions, FC was significantly superior to BC. In addition, all groups learned except the BC-E group.

The results of these studies indicate clearly that the effective CS for eliciting fear following FC procedures consists of two components: the discrete CS and the static cues of the apparatus. With BC procedures, fear is conditioned only to one of these components, the static cues. Further, because the extinction of fear to the static apparatus cues following BC eliminated the learning of hurdle jumping, it may safely be

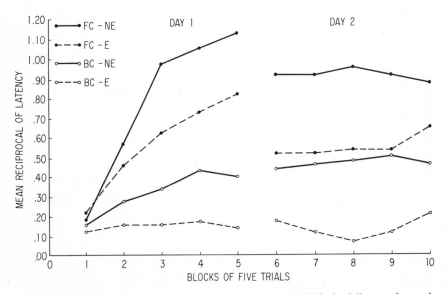

Fig. 9-9. Hurdle-jumping performance as a function of trial blocks following forward conditioning (FC) and backward conditioning (BC) with extinction (E) or with no extinction (NE) of fear to the static apparatus cues. (McAllister & McAllister, 1962b)

concluded that such learning in the present situation is not the result of pseudoconditioning, sensitization, activity, or exploratory tendencies.[7] It is evident from these results that the potential importance of static stimuli cannot be ignored in interpreting the results of experiments involving fear conditioning.

An implication of these findings is that a compound CS leads to better conditioning than a unitary CS. The basis for this conclusion lies in the demonstration that the CS for the FC groups had two components, that the CS for the BC groups had only one of these two, and that the FC groups showed a greater amount of conditioned fear as indicated by their better learning of hurdle jumping. Although these experiments provide ample evidence that fear was conditioned separately to the two components of the effective CS, it remains unclear whether fear was also conditioned to the compound *per se;* that is, whether patterning occurred.

Although the present evidence with respect to the augmentation of performance with a compound CS is consistent with that of other investigators (e.g., Pavlov, 1927; J. Miller, 1939), discrepant results have been obtained in a master's thesis recently conducted by Lawrence C. Perlmuter. In this research, each of three groups of subjects was given 80 eyelid conditioning trials. The CS, of 600 milliseconds duration, differed for the groups, being either auditory, visual, or compound (auditory plus visual). The UCS, a puff of air of two pounds per square inch of 100 milliseconds duration, followed the CS by 540 milliseconds. While the trends of the performance curves indicated that the compound group conditioned better than the auditory group which, in turn, was better than the visual group, the differences were small and not significant. A fourth group was conditioned with a CS which, from trial to trial, was either auditory or visual, the order varying in a fixed, irregular manner so that on half the trials the CS was auditory and on half, visual. Interestingly, the performance of this fourth group was not found to differ from that of the other three groups. The failure for any depression in performance to be observed with a varied CS indicates the possible importance in eyelid conditioning of either the static situational cues or mediational processes or both.

[7] Additional evidence that activity or exploratory tendencies play no role in accounting for the learning of hurdle jumping is provided by a control study which also ruled out the possibility that learning was based upon escape from a noxious CS. This study, which used the usual conditioning and hurdle-jumping procedures except for the omission of shock, showed that no learning occurred regardless of the postconditioning delay interval (3 minutes or 23 hours), or whether the "conditioning" box was the same or different from the start box of the hurdle-jumping apparatus. Another study ruled out the possibility that a preference for the safe box could account for the learning of hurdle jumping. Here it was shown that naive subjects, allowed to explore the hurdle-jumping apparatus freely, spent more than 80 percent of the time in the start box. Campbell and Campbell (1962) found a similar preference in their subjects.

SUMMARY

This paper was concerned with (a) the role of the temporal interval between the conditioning of fear and its measurement through the learning of a hurdle-jumping response and (b) the nature of the conditioned stimulus for the fear response. Fear was defined as an unobservable response classically conditioned to a neutral stimulus through the appropriate pairing of it with a noxious stimulus. It was assumed that fear motivated and its diminution reinforced the learning of hurdle jumping.

Evidence was reported to indicate that, when the conditioning box and the start box of the hurdle-jumping apparatus were highly similar but not identical, performance was much inferior with a short than with a long postconditioning delay. With the longer delay interval, performance was comparable to that obtained for all delay intervals when conditioning and hurdle jumping took place in an identical apparatus. The improvement in hurdle-jumping performance under the generalized stimulus condition increased monotonically up to 24 hours indicating that the stimulus-generalization of fear increased with time. Data obtained in a psychophysical experiment with human subjects suggested the feasibility of interpreting this change in the generalization gradient as being due to changes in the underlying psychophysical stimulus dimension.

Other studies were reported which demonstrated that under certain experimental conditions the lengthening of the postconditioning delay interval was detrimental to performance. In these experiments the similarity between the start and safe box situations in the hurdle-jumping apparatus coupled with the increase in the generalization of fear with time led to poorer performance with the longer delay interval.

Data relating to the nature of the conditioned stimulus for the fear response were reported. It was shown that with forward conditioning procedures fear was conditioned to the static cues of the apparatus as well as to the discrete CS; with backward conditioning procedures, only to the static cues.

References

BROWN, J. S., & JACOBS, A. The role of fear in the motivation and acquisition of responses. *J. exp. Psychol.*, 1949, *39*, 747-759.

BROWN, J. S., KALISH, H. I., & FARBER, I. E. Conditioned fear as revealed by magnitude of startle response to an auditory stimulus. *J. exp. Psychol.*, 1951, *41*, 317-328.

CAMPBELL, B. A., & CAMPBELL, E. H. Retention and extinction of learned fear in infant and adult rats. *J. comp. physiol. Psychol.*, 1962, *55*, 1-8.

GOLDSTEIN, M. L. Acquired drive strength as a joint function of shock intensity and number of acquisition trials. *J. exp. Psychol.*, 1960, *60*, 349-358.

KALISH, H. I. Strength of fear as a function of the number of acquisition and extinction trials. *J. exp. Psychol.*, 1954, *47*, 1-9.

KAMIN, L. J. The retention of an incompletely learned avoidance response. *J. comp. physiol. Psychol.*, 1957, *50*, 457-460.

KAMIN, L. J. Trace conditioning of the conditioned emotional response. *J. comp. physiol. Psychol.*, 1961, *54*, 149-153.

LIPSITT, L. P., & ENGEN, T. Effects of presentation of paired and single-stimulus on discrimination of length. *Amer. J. Psychol.*, 1961, *74*, 274-277.

McALLISTER, D. E., & McALLISTER, W. R. Second-order conditioning of fear. *Psychon. Sci.*, 1964, *1*, 383-384.

McALLISTER, W. R., & McALLISTER, D. E. Postconditioning delay and intensity of shock as factors in the measurement of acquired fear. *J. exp. Psychol.*, 1962, *64*, 110-116. (a)

McALLISTER, W. R., & McALLISTER, D. E. Role of the CS and of apparatus cues in the measurement of acquired fear. *Psychol. Rep.*, 1962, *11*, 749-756. (b)

McALLISTER, W. R., & McALLISTER, D. E. Increase over time in the stimulus generalization of acquired fear. *J. exp. Psychol.*, 1963, *65*, 576-582.

MILLER, J. The rate of conditioning of human subjects to single and multiple conditioned stimuli. *J. gen. Psychol.*, 1939, *20*, 399-408.

MILLER, N. E. Studies of fear as an acquirable drive: I. Fear as motivation and fear-reduction as reinforcement in the learning of new responses. *J. exp. Psychol.*, 1948, *38*, 89-101.

MILLER, N. E. Learnable drives and rewards. In S. S. STEVENS (Ed.), *Handbook of experimental psychology.* New York: John Wiley & Sons, 1951. Pp. 435-472.

MOWRER, O. H. A stimulus-response analysis of anxiety and its role as a reinforcing agent. *Psychol. Rev.*, 1939, *46*, 553-565.

PAVLOV, I. P. *Conditioned reflexes.* London: Oxford University Press, 1927.

PERKINS, C. C., JR., & WEYANT, R. G. The interval between training and test trials as a determiner of the slope of generalization gradients. *J. comp. physiol. Psychol.*, 1958, *51*, 596-600.

SALTZ, E., & ASDOURIAN, D. Incubation of anxiety as a function of cognitive differentiation. *J. exp. Psychol.*, 1963, *66*, 17-22.

SOLOMON, R. L., & BRUSH, E. S. Experimentally derived conceptions of anxiety and aversion. In M. R. JONES (Ed.), *Nebraska symposium on motivation.* Lincoln, Neb.: University of Nebraska Press, 1956. Pp. 212-305.

THOMAS, D. R., & LOPEZ, L. J. The effects of delayed testing on generalization slope. *J. comp. physiol. Psychol.*, 1962, *55*, 541-544.

WOODWORTH, R. S., & SCHLOSBERG, H. *Experimental psychology.* New York: Holt, Rinehart & Winston, 1954.

JOHN W. P. OST
DONALD W. LAUER
Indiana University

10

Some Investigations of Classical Salivary Conditioning in the Dog [1]

Our purpose in this paper is to summarize our experiences using the salivary response in the dog as a method for the investigation of classical conditioning problems. Certain matters pertaining to procedure will be discussed, and some results from the initial stages of a parametric analysis of intensity and temporal variables will be presented.

The choice of method was determined by certain advantages and opportunities offered by the Pavlovian techniques. First, salivary secretions may be elicited in the dog both by stimuli which the animal normally approaches—milk, food powders—and by stimuli from which the animal normally withdraws—acid or alkaline solutions. Therefore, one is able conveniently to explore "reward" as well as "defense" conditioning, and to make rather direct comparisons between the two. Though at present one can but speculate on this question because of the paucity of quantitative studies of "reward" classical conditioning, one must recognize the possibility of important differences between these two forms.

Second, the salivary response minimizes potential problems related to antagonistic action at the effector level. For example, the leg flexion response represents a resultant of flexor and extensor activity, an admixture which is at least difficult to resolve into its components. Though it seems not to have commanded appreciable attention, the same problem exists potentially with the eyelid response.

[1] The work here described was financed in part from the United States Public Health Service Grants #MPD-10237, HD-00951, and M-928; the Indiana University Graduate School; and the National Science Foundation Research Participation Program. We wish to express particular gratitude for the enthusiastic assistance of F. B. Colavita, M. D. Suboski, H. E. Warstler, and Mrs. A. Radell.

Third, there are certain important experimental uses for a response with the general characteristics possessed by salivary gland activity, i.e., a graded, glandular response, mediated by the autonomic nervous system, and integrally associated with the biologically significant complex of ingestive behaviors. As a representative of the class of autonomic responses it may be useful in the study of their properties, such as their susceptibility to modification by response-contingent scheduling of unconditioned stimulus presentations. As a conditionable component of the ingestive sequence it may be studied as a manifestation of fractional anticipatory goal activity by those using this concept in theoretical treatments of instrumental conditioning.

Fourth, these procedures provide the most direct link to the investigations on classical conditioning problems carried out by East European psychophysiologists, past and present. Virtually all conditioning phenomena were originally defined by Pavlov or his students in terms of the salivary response, and some of those phenomena which are most central to their thinking have never been systematically studied using other methods. American psychologists continually draw upon this rich body of information for its heuristic value, but in the main they tend to reject it as a source of evidence for the support of general conclusions. This attitude, if we may presume to speak for American psychologists, is rooted in the belief that these investigations do not meet current standards of acceptable research practice. They are considered deficient with respect to control conditions necessary for the support of generalized conclusions, statistical evaluations of the reliability of treatment effects, and description of important procedural details. Moreover, the language barrier stands in the way of those who would attempt to acquaint themselves with the details. This barrier is slowly disappearing, but the effect of the ensuing increase in communication will be felt primarily in future research.

We turn now to consideration of method. The procedures evolved out of the combined contributions of several workers during the past six years, building upon the efforts of predecessors too numerous to list. We will treat here only the surgical preparation employed, and matters relating to response measurement. More complete descriptions of early forms may be found in Shapiro (1959) or Fitzgerald (1963).

SURGICAL PREPARATION

The preparation involves the insertion of a polyethylene tube into the parotid duct. This technique has the advantage of an uncomplicated surgical procedure, a relatively short period of recovery, and a simple method of attachment to the recording device.

Two features are of particular importance. The first is the method of retaining the polyethylene tubing in the subject. This is accomplished by preparing a small shoulder on the tubing (Clay-Adams PE60) which is inserted into the duct, and by suturing into place a small piece of large tubing (Clay-Adams PE205) which has been slipped over the PE60 up to the shoulder. The second is the method of sealing the PE60 into the duct to prevent leakage. Failure to effect a long-lasting seal is the most common cause of breakdown of the preparation. Our recent experience indicates that some ninety percent of the preparations last two weeks; perhaps fifty percent last longer than three weeks; some as long as two months. Presently the seal is accomplished by placing a small piece of PE190, which has been slit longitudinally, around the duct and the tubing which is inside, and tying a No. 2 silk suture around the PE190.

The PE60 which has been secured in this manner can be brought to virtually any point of emergence. In the preparation typically used in classical conditioning the point of emergence is on the side of the dog's muzzle, the 3 cm.-long exposed end of the tube extending forward approximately as far as the nose itself. On the other hand, in the preparation used in an operant conditioning situation, the tube emerges at the nape of the neck (cf. Shapiro, 1962; Kintsch & Witte, 1962).

More complete details may be found in Lauer, Shapiro, and Radell (1961).

RESPONSE MEASUREMENT

In the research reported below, as in the case of most previous investigations using this response, the effects upon the organism of the sequence of events in conditioning are indexed by variations in the magnitude of salivary secretions through time. The central element in such measurements is the device whereby variations in volume of fluid secreted are transduced into a form more conveniently recorded permanently. In our case, the device used is a drop-former, which transforms volume secreted, a continuous variable, into a succession of drops, a discrete variable. More specifically, a long section of polyethylene tube (PE190), filled with a fluid medium, is connected to the end of the PE60 tube previously implanted in the duct. The other end of the PE190 leads to an unbevelled hypodermic needle located some fixed distance below the gland. The saliva produced by the gland displaces this column of fluid forward, and a drop forms at the needle orifice. When the drop achieves a certain size (which depends upon such parameters as density, surface tension, surface on which drop forms, orifice size), it falls, striking two stainless steel needles separated by a one-millimeter gap, thereby completing an electrical circuit. The circuit closure is indicated by a brief deflection of a Brush recording oscillo-graph.

Before moving to the technical problems inherent in this system, it should be noted that there are several other methods of transduction which might be used. For example, in recent years electromagnetic and ultrasonic flow meters have become available. At present, however, the drop-former is the least expensive, gives the best resolution, and appears the least disturbed by environmental changes.

There are certain requirements for the transducer. In the case of the drop-former these reduce to the following: The function relating volume secreted to the number of drops formed must be stable through time, and, since it would be vastly more convenient, linear. Moreover there should be no damping of the time-volume output function of the gland. Some recent checks of the drop-former have uncovered certain departures from the ideal.

First, it was found that the linear relationship between volume se-creted and drop size holds only under certain specified conditions. In pursuing this matter mean drop size was determined as follows: Exactly one milliliter of fluid in an open container was allowed to drain through the drop-former, and the number of drops into which it was divided was counted. Therefore, though we have no indication of the variability among individual drops, their average size may be obtained by dividing one milliliter by the number of drops registered.

One of the critical factors governing mean drop size was found to be the fluid medium employed. Empirical tests were conducted on several easily obtained fluids. Among these fluids were saline (2×10^{-5}m con-centration), which we had used until the time of these tests, and ethyl alcohol (95 percent) which was selected because it is eighty percent the density of water and has a surface tension only thirty percent that of water. Figure 10-1 shows, for these two fluids, the function relating mean drop size and flow rate. Note that there is a marked decrease in mean drop size with higher flow rates in the case of the saline. In contrast, the alcohol, when employed with the #24 hypodermic needle orifice, results in a reasonably constant mean drop size across considerable variations in flow rate. However, the same fluid medium in combination with the smaller orifice of a #27 hypodermic needle again results in a distorted function. Until the physics of such systems becomes more clear, it is suggested that those using drop-formers make careful empirical tests to check for possible distortions of this sort.

A second problem stems from the fact that a satisfactory degree of resolution is obtained only when mean drop size is about .005 ml, a size achieved only by use of a very small needle orifice. On the other hand, as the size of the orifice decreases, the back-pressure increases, against which the gland must operate. And since the gland's function depends in part on pressure gradients by which the glandular cells move water out of the vascular system and into the saliva, it was thought that increased back-pressure would result in decreased gland secretions, especially at high rates. The relationship was further complicated by a standing negative hydrostatic pressure on the gland produced in our apparatus by a sixty-centimeter head differential between the gland and the needle orifice.

An examination of the consequences of these facts revealed that, to a uniform standard stimulus, the amount secreted through a small needle orifice was less than through a large needle. Three different animals, surgically prepared as above, were each given an extended

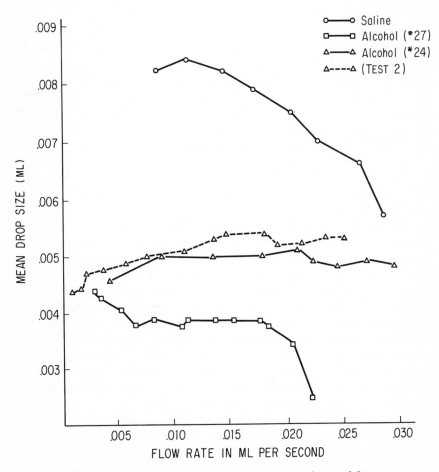

Fig. 10-1. Variations in drop size as a function of rate of flow.

series of 1.5 [2] dilute acetic acid presentations, spaced at three-minute intervals. A small needle (#24) was used in the drop-former on half the trials, and a large needle (#13) on the other half, one trial with each needle being given in each successive pair of trials. All other conditions were as in normal operation. Table 1 shows the mean volume of alcohol medium collected during the first thirty seconds following acid presentation for these two needle sizes. There clearly was less secretion during the period of observation when the small orifice was placed in the system, the error being in the order of twelve percent.

It appears, then, that the estimate of secretory rate varies with the size of the orifice in the system, possibly because of the detrimental effects of increased back-pressure upon the secretory mechanisms, or conceivably in part due to leakage around the point of intubation under conditions of high back-pressure. Yet another mechanism which could account for the results is the storage of saliva in distended gland tubules until such a time as the pressure is reduced. The effect of the orifice, then, would be to damp the true time-volume output function, distributing high volume responses over longer periods of time. We have no evidence as yet which would allow one to decide among these alternatives.

One final, more general, point should be made in regard to response measurement. Our breadth of observation during conditioning is quite limited, being restricted to recording the rate of saliva flow from the left parotid gland. First, it might be fruitful to investigate some of the other dimensions along which salivation varies. It is well known that the concentrations of various inorganic chemical constituents of saliva vary considerably depending upon the properties of the substance in the buccal cavity (Baxter, 1933).

Second, there are many other organismic activities "concomitant" to salivation which may be observed during our conditioning sessions. Pavlov (1927, p. 17), of course, recognized this fact, but chose to limit himself to measurement of salivation partly for reasons of technical convenience. Zener (1937) several years later emphasized the significance of these "concomitant" responses when describing the nature of the alterations in behavior produced by Pavlovian conditioning procedures. Moreover, certain of these behaviors may reflect the contribution of other processes such as the "orienting" reaction which appear to be of central importance in conditioning. In summary, by restricting the range of effector activities which we observe, we risk missing indications of significant events, and we risk prejudging the empirical questions concerning the nature of conditioning when deciding upon the component of response for observation. We should at some point attempt to specify

[2] This designation refers to the milliliters of glacial acetic acid added to 100 milliliters of distilled water in making the solution.

Table 10-1————Volume secreted (milliliters) in the first 30 seconds after US, as a function of the size of needle orifice used

DOG #	X̄ LARGE ORIFICE	X̄ SMALL ORIFICE
78	.493	.436
84	.474	.424
87	.393	.336
87 (test #2)	.381	.344

the rules we commonly employ in choosing a particular effector activity as our index of strength of conditioning. We might ask further if the alterations produced by imposing the sequence of conditioned and unconditioned stimuli upon the subject may not be as meaningfully indexed by changes in the reinforcing or behavior-suppressing properties of the conditioned stimulus as by changes in the behavior-cueing properties of that stimulus. Indeed, we might prepare ourselves for the possibili that certain manipulations may modify some of these properties a؟ not others.

We shall now summarize some investigations conducted at the Indiana University laboratories. Three studies will be reported, exploring the effects upon conditioned anticipatory salivary secretions of partial reinforcement, interstimulus interval length, and unconditioned stimulus intensity.

PARTIAL REINFORCEMENT

Fitzgerald (1963) recently reported research in which three groups of six mongrel dogs each were conditioned, each group using one of three proportions of reinforced trials: 100 percent, 50 percent, and 25 percent. Following four sessions in which they were progressively habituated to the restraining harness, the dogs were surgically prepared as described above. On the first post-operative day, the Ss received the first of ten consecutive daily acquisition training periods. Each of these daily periods consisted of twenty-four trials, given in six sessions of four trials each. A three-hour pause was given between sessions three and four, and a five-minute pause between each of the other sessions. The S remained in the harness during the short pauses, but was returned to his home cage for the long one. Within sessions, the intertrial interval length was varied randomly between 100 and 110 seconds.

Each conditioning trial consisted in a fifteen-second presentation of a 400 cps tone CS delivered through a speaker located above the S's head. On reinforced trials this was followed immediately by a 5 cc portion of .3 dilute acetic acid solution delivered over one second directly into the S's mouth. The 100 percent group received the US on all trials, while the other two groups received the US on 50 percent, or 25 percent, of the trials selected randomly. Immediately following acquisition, the animals were given extinction training for ten days, or until the S showed twenty-four consecutive trials without response. Extinction trials were identical in all respects to those in acquisition except that the US was never given.

During experimentation, the S stood on a table, his head held by an adjustable wooden yoke, and his lateral movements restricted by a cloth band which passed under his belly. The subject was shielded from the noise of stimulus control and response recording apparatus in the adjacent room by virtue of a double concrete block wall. The response recording system was as described above, using the #27 needle and the aforementioned saline solution. The rate of salivary secretions was recorded on each trial by counting the number of drops registered during each of the following periods: 1) fifteen seconds before CS onset, 2) the fifteen seconds during the CS-US interval, and 3) fifteen seconds after the US onset. Conditioned response magnitude was defined as the number of drops secreted during the CS-US interval minus the drops secreted in the pre-interval period. Unconditioned response rate was defined as the number of drops during the fifteen seconds following US onset.

When not in the harness, the Ss were housed indoors in individual wiremesh cages, about 135 cm. wide, 117 cm. deep, and 213 cm. high. The temperature was a constant 72 degrees, F., throughout the entire laboratory. Artificial lighting was maintained twenty-four hours a day in the animal quarters. Immediately upon arrival, the Ss were cleaned and, if ill, were restored to good health. They fed *ad libitum* on a balanced dry ration and water.

Figure 10-2, which is reproduced from the dissertation (Fitzgerald, 1962) upon which the above report was based, shows the changes in difference score with successive days of acquisition, and across successive trials within the twelve sessions in a two-day block of trials. Inspection of the figure suggests that there was an overall effect of increased acquisition training, which differed according to the percentage of reinforced trials used. Specifically, while the 100 percent group increased throughout all 240 trials, never reaching an asymptote, the 50 percent and 25 percent groups showed little increase with training, were consistently inferior to the 100 percent group, and did not differ from each other. An analysis of variance on these data confirms these findings. There was a significant overall effect of training ($F = 8.88$; $df = 4/60$; $p<.01$), and a significant interaction of training and proportion of reinforced trials ($F = 3.05$; $df = 8/60$; $p<.01$). The overall effect of proportion of reinforced trials was also significant ($F = 5.49$; $df = 2/72$; $p < 0.5$). A separate

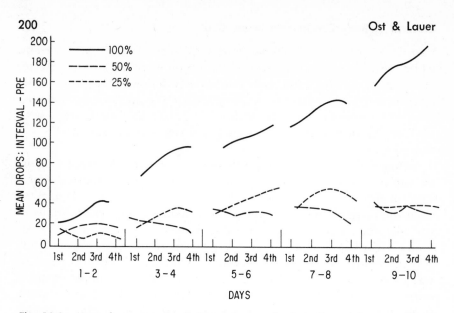

Fig. 10-2. Mean drops given by each group on each of the four trials, summed over the twelve sessions in a two-day block.

analysis of the 50 percent and 25 percent group performances indicates that there was a significant increase with training, but the effect of proportion of reinforced trials and the interaction of this treatment with training trials was not significant.

Fitzgerald noted a second interesting finding, having to do with the distribution of responding within the interval. In spite of the large differences in total interval responding among the three groups, the relative responding in successive thirds of the interval took very much the same form in all groups. During the first two acquisition days there was a tendency for responding to decrease with successive thirds in the interval. By days 5-6, the relative response rate was roughly equal in all three thirds, and by the last two days of acquisition, response strength was increasing with successive thirds of the interval.

With respect to unconditioned response strength, statistically significant ($F = 10.01$; $df = 4/60$; $p < .01$) increases were observed with increased days of training. The groups did not differ among themselves in this regard.

During extinction, the anticipated "partial reinforcement effect" was present, but not in unambiguous form. The decrease in performance with extinction, where this performance is expressed as a proportion of terminal acquisition response strength, was greater for the 100 percent Ss than for either the 50 percent or 25 percent Ss. These latter two groups did not differ among themselves. The drop in performance with extinction training was quite rapid.

CS-US INTERVAL LENGTH

A second investigation, accomplished at approximately the same time as Fitzgerald's, concerned itself with the differences in the distribution of responding during the CS-US interval as a function of four different interval lengths: 2, 5, 10, and 15 seconds. Four groups of five subjects each, were conditioned using procedures which were identical to those described for the Fitzgerald study, except for the following details. Each group received training with one of the above interval lengths. Acquisition training was begun on the second post-operative day, and continued for fifteen consecutive days. The first post-operative day was devoted to the assessment of baseline performance, each animal being tested with six CS and three US presentations. The daily acquisition trials were administered in two sessions of ten trials each. Between the two sessions, the animal was returned to his home cage for forty minutes. The intertrial interval, which varied randomly from trial to trial, was permitted to take any of the sixty values between 90 and 149 seconds, reckoning from the end of the previous CS-US interval. The CS duration was one second for all groups, i.e., the procedure would be considered trace conditioning. Only 80 percent of the CS presentations, randomly selected, were followed by the US.

Salivary secretions were observed on each trial and the number of drops registered were counted according to the following plan: 1) in successive five-second time periods for the fifteen seconds before the interval, 2) in successive one-second time periods for the duration of the CS-US interval, and 3) in successive one-second time periods for the thirty seconds following the interval, and in five-second time periods following that.

Figure 10-3 depicts the changes in response strength which occurred during successive three-day blocks in acquisition. Each of the five figures shows, for each of the four groups, the mean frequency of drops (above pre-interval frequency) as a function of successive seconds in the CS-US interval. Each point in the figure was obtained by summing, over all trials in a three-day period, the number of drops observed for a subject during the indicated one-second time period. This sum was then divided by the number of trials during those days. The subject's mean pre-interval rate for those days was subtracted from each of these mean values. The resulting difference scores were averaged across all Ss in the group, yielding a mean responsivity function for that group for the days in question.

Inspection of these functions for days 1-3 reveals that all four groups were responding very nearly at their mean pre-interval rate at all points in the CS-US interval. By days 4-6 the groups had begun to respond

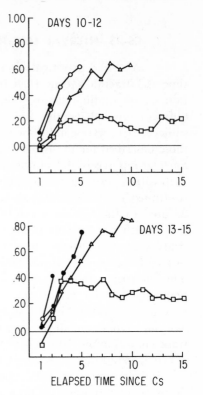

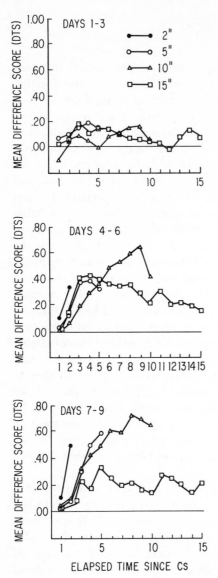

Fig. 10-3. Mean difference scores (DTS) as a function of elapsed time in the CS-US interval for the four CS-US interval groups.

well above their baseline rate, and furthermore there was a tendency for responsivity to increase at least for the first three seconds after the CS. By days 7-9 the responsivity functions for the four groups were clearly beginning to diverge, assuming the relative order of form which characterizes them during days 10-12 and 13-15. Specifically, the ascending limb common to all groups in the first part of the interval rose less sharply for the longer CS-US intervals. Moreover, in contrast to the five- and ten-second groups, the fifteen-second group showed a decline in responsivity around the fourth or fifth second.

These results, however, must be treated with caution. The smooth group functions, and their orderly relationships one to another during the later stages of training, cover an important troublesome fact. Each group contains two animals, three in the case of the ten-second group, for which there was little evidence of conditioning at any point in training. Those in each group that did show reliable increases over their respective baseline secretion rates, also showed quite similar individual responsivity functions. It is the data from these latter animals which is reflected primarily in the group functions. Statistical analyses of the group functions indicate that the apparent differences among them are not reliable. Though it seems reasonable to suppose that the lack of statistical reliability is due to the overlap among groups resulting from the animals which did not condition, these data permit no confident conclusions by themselves. Analyses on just those Ss that did condition yielded non-significant results, which is not surprising considering the low power of tests based on such a limited number of subjects. The experiment will be redone, taking advantage of recent technical improvements.

One may raise here the classic question concerning the relative efficacy of various CS-US interval lengths. Though the experiment was not designed for the purpose of detecting these differences, there is little in these data to suggest that conditioning is difficult with intervals longer than a second or two. In fact the highest response rates appear in the 5- and 10-second groups. Moreover, the four groups are markedly different in regard to the number of days required to develop the asymptotic responsivity function characteristic of particular interval lengths in this experiment.

UNCONDITIONED STIMULUS INTENSITY

This experiment concerned itself with the differences in the acquisition of conditioned salivary responses as a function of three different acid concentrations: .3, 1.5, and 7.5.

Three groups of six subjects each were conditioned using one of these concentrations as the unconditioned stimulus. Following three habituation sessions, the dogs were surgically prepared as above. The first post-operative day was given over to a fourth habituation session. This change was instituted since it was suspected that the dehydration aftereffects of the sodium pentobarbital used as anesthetic during surgery lasted more than twenty-four hours. If this were the case, the animals' secretion rate might be depressed during the critical first stage of training. The first of ten consecutive days of acquisition training was begun on the second post-operative day. The daily trials were given in one session of ten reinforced trials, except during extinction. This latter procedure began on the day following the last day of acquisition and consisted of a single session of thirty CS-alone presentations. When not being trained the Ss were confined in their home cage with the general environment the same as outlined above.

During training, the Ss were restrained in an enclosed, sound-resistant chamber, 46 cm. x 145 cm. x 137 cm. The S lay with his weight supported by a canvas sling, his legs extending below the sling and secured by four leg straps, and his head held in a loose-fitting yoke. A fan, which aided in maintaining constant chamber temperature, also provided noise to help mask laboratory sounds. A speaker, through which the CS was delivered, was mounted 30 cm. below the S's head.

The CS was a 400 cps tone of ten-second duration with an intensity of 9 dB. above an ambient noise level of 84 dB., SPL. The US was a 5 cc. portion of dilute acetic acid of the appropriate concentration for the condition in which the S was to be run. CS-US interval length was ten seconds. The mean intertrial interval was 3.5 minutes, with intervals varied from trial to trial, and ranging in length from three to four minutes.

Salivary secretions were observed on each trial and the number of drops registered were counted according to the following plan: 1) in successive one-second periods during the fifteen seconds before the trial, 2) in successive one-second periods during the ten seconds of the CS-US interval, and 3) in successive seconds during the forty-five seconds after the end of the CS-US interval.

The mean unconditioned response rate during the 45 seconds after the US averaged over all trials, for the .3, 1.5, and 7.5 acid concentrations was .29, .65, and 1.04 drops per trial per second, respectively. The differences between groups are statistically significant ($F = 10.81$; $df = 2/12$; $p < .01$). There were no significant differences in UR magnitude as a function of successive trials within daily sessions. In sharp contrast to Fitzgerald's findings, no significant differences in UR magnitude as a function successive days of training were found. The reasons for this are not yet clear, but it does not seem that one can appeal to the progressive loading with acid in explaining the Fitzgerald result. Loading in the present study was much more severe, but no increase in US was observed.

Figure 10-4 shows, for each of the three groups of subjects, the changes in the mean difference score through the CS-US interval for each of the five successive two-day blocks of acquisition training. These difference scores, expressed in terms of drops-per-trial-per-second, were computed in comparable fashion to that described in the above CS-US interval investigation. These data were analyzed by a 10 x 10 x 3 (Days x Seconds in Interval x Concentrations) analysis of variance.

With increased training, there was a statistically reliable increase in the overall difference score in CS-US interval ($F = 31.87$; $df = 9/1388$;

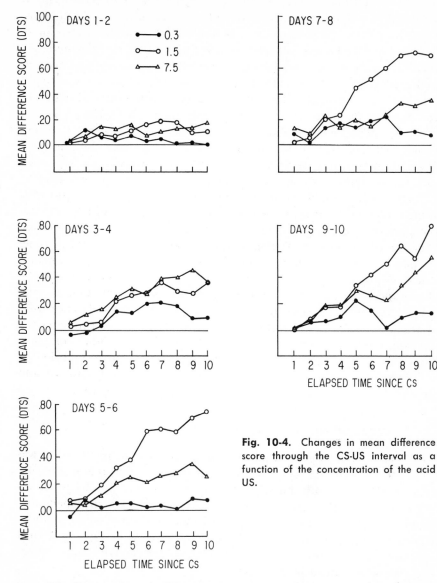

Fig. 10-4. Changes in mean difference score through the CS-US interval as a function of the concentration of the acid US.

p < .01). However, as indicated by a significant Days x Concentrations interaction (F = 7.87; df = 18/1388; p < .01), the increase was dependent upon the concentration of acid employed as US. Namely, the 7.5 Ss showed greater increase with training than did the .3 Ss, but showed less increase than did the 1.5 Ss. That is, acquisition seems to have been poorer with the 7.5 acid concentration as reinforcer than with a lower concentration, 1.5.

The increase in CS-US interval responding with increased training was not uniformly distributed throughout the CS-US interval. This is indicated in a significant Days x Seconds interaction (F = 1.30; df = 81/ 1388; p < .05). As may be seen in Figure 10-4, the increases were more marked for those portions of the interval closer to US onset. Furthermore, there was a significant interaction between Concentrations and Seconds in Interval (F = 8.66; df = 18/1388; p < .05). Specifically, it was found that the rise in response with successive seconds in the interval is steeper for the 7.5 Ss than for the .3 Ss, but less steep than that for the 1.5 Ss.

The difference scores obtained from extinction performance were also subjected to an analysis of variance. No significant contributions were found. However, since extinction was very rapid, this analysis was necessarily based upon very few observations, from progressively fewer Ss.

One final point to be made concerning these data has to do with using the pre-interval response rate as a baseline against which to evaluate performance in the presence of background stimulation plus the conditioned stimulus. Interpretation of this difference score can become complicated, as it is in this investigation. The relative performance differences between the 7.5 and the 1.5 groups was determined largely by the fact that the 7.5 Ss had a much higher pre-interval rate than did the 1.5 Ss. At present it seems reasonable to argue that the difference score is an appropriate index of the degree to which the S discriminates the CS from the background stimulation. Though involving other complications, the use of discrimination procedures in which relative conditioning is indexed by differences in secretion rate between the reinforced and non-reinforced stimulus might be of some help in this regard.

CONCLUDING STATEMENT

Our general goal in proceeding on this line of investigation was to provide a more firm empirical base for the increasing role of the concept of classical conditioning in some recent theoretical formulations (e.g., Mowrer, 1960). It was felt it would be desirable to expand the number of effective methods upon which one may draw for the study of issues of classical conditioning. The salivary response in the dog seemed one of the more promising of several methods not receiving much attention among American psychologists.

In this paper we have summarized our rather modest progress in implementing salivary conditioning as a convenient source of reliable information on significant problems. For a method with such a long history there are still a surprising number of technical details to be cleaned up.

Our empirical results are meager in contrast to the voluminous literature from past users of the method, here and abroad, and in contrast to the available literature using other methods. We feel that we have at a minimum shown that the technique yields orderly results more or less, though not entirely, consonant with results from the more commonly employed methods of eyelid and GSR conditioning. This encourages efforts at continued systematic parametric analysis using salivary conditioning techniques, attempts to reappraise the generality of some of the less frequently studied phenomena discovered by Pavlovian psychophysiologists, and the extension of application of the technique to new problems.

References

BAXTER, H. Variations in the inorganic constituents of mixed and parotid gland saliva activated by reflex stimulation in the dog. *J. biol. Chem.*, 1933, *102*, 203.

FITZGERALD, R. F. The effects of partial reinforcement on the classically conditioned salivary response in dogs. PhD thesis, Indiana University, 1962.

FITZGERALD, R. F. Effects of partial reinforcement with acid on the classically conditioned salivary response in dogs. *J. comp. physiol. Psychol.*, 1963, *56*, 1056-1060.

KINTSCH, W., & WITTE, R. S. Concurrent conditioning of bar press and salivation responses. *J. comp. physiol. Psychol.*, 1962, *55*, 963-968.

LAUER, D. W., SHAPIRO, M. M., & RADELL, A. A chronic preparation for salivary conditioning. *Bull. Acad. Polon. Sci.*, 1961, *9*, 121-123.

MOWRER, O. H. *Learning theory and behavior.* New York: John Wiley & Sons, 1960.

PAVLOV, I. P. *Conditioned reflexes.* London: Oxford University Press, 1927. (Transl. by G. V. ANREP.)

SHAPIRO, M. M. Classical salivary conditioning in dogs. PhD Thesis, Indiana University, 1959.

SHAPIRO, M. M. Temporal relationship between salivation and lever pressing with differential reinforcement of low rate. *J. comp. physiol. Psychol.*, 1962, *55*, 567-571.

ZENER, K. The significance of behavior accompanying conditioned salivary secretion for theories of the conditioned reflexes. *Amer. J. Psychol.*, 1937, *50*, 384-403.

WILLIAM F. PROKASY

The Pennsylvania State University

11

Classical Eyelid Conditioning: Experimenter Operations, Task Demands, and Response Shaping [1]

The label "classical conditioning" has suffered the fate of all commonly employed labels in becoming the source of extensive ambiguity. If one asserts that a subject is "classically conditioned," he may mean any number of things. For example, he may mean that there is evidence that an organism has associated two temporally-related external events; that a response has been acquired to a CS (conditioned stimulus) which in no way interferes with, or alters, the reception of the UCS (unconditioned stimulus); that a response has been acquired without any evidence of having been rewarded; that a response to a neutral cue has been acquired which is essentially indistinguishable from the UCR (unconditioned response); or that one aspect of an observed behavioral change is similar to an attribute of the UCR.

Such ambiguities arise in large measure from a failure to distinguish between experimenter-operations, speculations about the kinds of effects that CS and UCS events may have on the subject, and theories, or hypotheses, intended to account for behavior changes contingent upon the pairing of CS and UCS. This is well illustrated by the paradigm of classical conditioning frequently encountered in elementary textbooks (e.g., Munn, 1961; Wickens & Meyer, 1961; Kendler, 1963). According to this paradigm, the modification which occurs as a result of pairing is an association between an otherwise neutral stimulus and a UCR: the

[1] This paper is, in part, an outgrowth of research supported by grants from the National Science Foundation. The final manuscript was written while on a National Science Foundation Senior Postdoctoral Fellowship at Indiana in 1963-64. I would like to acknowledge the helpful comments made by John Ost and James Allison on an earlier version.

emphasis is not only on the operation of pairing but is also on an assumption of similarity, if not identity, between a CR (conditioned response) and the UCR.

The purpose of this paper is to describe some factors which appear to be an integral part of the acquisition of the classically conditioned eyelid response. To this end, the remainder of the paper will be divided into three major headings. The first, Experimenter Operations, emphasizes classical conditioning as a set of experimenter operations and provides a discussion of some commonly-employed control techniques. The second, Task Demands, is oriented toward the situational demands made on the subject. The final section, Response Shaping, describes response shaping as a major contributor to the acquisition of the conditioned eyelid response.

EXPERIMENTER OPERATIONS

An experimental session can be treated as a series of time units of arbitrary length. The only restriction on the length of a time unit for present purposes is that it be at least as long as the longest duration of a stimulus event. The experimenter can present any number of stimulus events as an arbitrary function of time. For simplicity, it will be assumed that (a) there are only two events, E_1 and E_2, (b) E_1 and E_2 can occur at most only once in any time interval, (c) if E_1 and E_2 both occur in the same time interval, E_1 will occur a constant amount of time ahead of E_2, and (d) the likelihoods of E_1 and E_2, c_1 and c_2, are constant across the N time intervals of a session. Assumptions (c) and (d) will be examined below. Beginning with

$$\Pr(E_{1 \cdot j}) = c_1 \text{ for } j = 1, N$$
$$\Pr(E_{2 \cdot j}) = c_2 \text{ for } j = 1, N$$

as statements for the independent presentation rates of E_1 and E_2, it is apparent that

$$\Pr(E_{1 \cdot j} E_{2 \cdot j}) = c_1 c_2.$$

What this means is that if an experimenter begins with two independent presentation rates, the events will be paired on some occasions, the frequency being a monotonic function of each independent rate. The usual conditioning and selected control procedures can be described as a relaxation of event independence, as shown in Table 11-1. The four controls involve "CS Only," "US Only," and "Mixed," the last being a randomly ordered presentation of the two events (CS and UCS).

Table 11-1————Event likelihoods per time unit for a conditioning group and for three "control" conditions

TREATMENTS

Event	CS-Only	US-Only	Mixed	Conditioning
E_1	c_1	0.0	c_1	c_1
E_2	0.0	c_2	c_2	c_2*
$E_1 E_2$	0.0	0.0	0.0	c_2

* If events are always paired $c_1 = c_2$.

Assumption (d), concerning a constant rate of event occurrence across all time intervals, can be relaxed to generate various event distributions. For example, assume that there are only $E_1 E_2$ joint occurrences (i.e., a typical 100 percent reinforcement situation). A specific time function since a pairing on the jth interval might be:

$$Pr(E_{1,j+k} E_{2,j+k}) = 0.0, k = 1, 2, 3 \qquad (1)$$
$$Pr(E_{1,j+k} E_{2,j+k}) = 0.33, k = 4, 5, 6. \qquad (2)$$

If the duration of the arbitrary time interval is five seconds, then the above describes an average intertrial interval of 25 seconds, with values of 20, 25, and 30 seconds.

Assumption (c) specified that E_1 always precedes E_2 if both occur in the same interval. Not only can this certainty be relaxed, the very distribution of E_1 in time with respect to E_2 must be defined once it is relaxed. It is to be noted that Pavlov (1927) varied the time between E_1 and E_2 within single experimental sessions in order to restore responding which had been observed but which had merged with the UCR via an increase in CR latency.

It would be possible to refine and extend the above statements as a description of classical conditioning (e.g., variations in number of events, functions expressing event detectabilities, etc.), but for present purposes it is more appropriate to pursue some immediate implications.

First, the typical classical conditioning situation is treated as a special case of signal transmission. Two signals are generated over time with any contingencies between them being expressed as departures from the product of their independent rates of occurrence. Nothing is known about the extent to which a random overlap of two independent events (assuming E_1 to precede E_2 when both occur in the same time interval) will produce systematic behavior change. In view of the number of attempts to contrast the effect of the joint event $E_1 E_2$ from the effects of the stimuli without pairing (see, e.g., Kimble, 1961, pp. 59-65) this lack of information is somewhat surprising.

Second, our conception of a control group, or groups, is quite limited. As was summarized in Table 11-1, "controls" are usually limited to groups which receive either "CS Only," "US Only," or "Mixed" treatments. Actually, these three groups represent arbitrary, discrete points on several continua. Referring to Table 11-1, varying c_1 and c_2 can produce a variety of mixed conditions which have not been investigated. With c_1 or c_2 equal to zero, then the extremes of "CS Only" and "US Only," respectively, are achieved. Note, further, from Table 11-1 that the "Mixed" case is hardly an unbiased control. Since the likelihood of a joint occurrence of two events is zero, the occurrence of either event provides the subject with information that the other will not occur within a particular time interval. If E_2 is a noxious event, then the occurrence of E_1 becomes, effectively, a kind of "safe" period.

The "Conditioning" group in Table 11-1 is, in a sense, the complement of the "Mixed" group: in the former, overlap of the two events is forced and in the latter is prohibited. By permitting c_2 to vary from zero to c_1 we progress from "CS Only" to intermittent reinforcement to 100 percent reinforcement. As c_2 increases in value from c_1 to unity, then the likelihood of a joint occurrence can be no more than c_1 and "interpolated US trials" are obtained (see, e.g., Ross & Hunter, 1959). Then, as c_1 is decreased, the "US Only" condition is achieved. Little is known about these interrelationships in the acquisition of any systematic behavior change resulting from event pairing.

Third, beyond the usual massed vs. spaced effects, there is now sufficient evidence to show that how a subject responds is determined in part by the specific time functions adopted by the experimenter. When using a variable ITI (intertrial interval) it is possible to determine the likelihood of a response following each of the values employed. After giving subjects extensive training, Prokasy and Whaley (1963) and Krauss and Prokasy (1963) have shown that response probability increases slightly as time between the paired events increases. Unpublished data from the Pennsylvania State University laboratory not only confirm those observations, but show that the very form of the response changes as a function of this within-subject variable. In general, we find that the longer the ITI (within the range of selected ITI values for a session), the shorter the latency, the smaller the SD of latency and the more shallow the slope of the response. For reasons, one of which will be evident below, that do not require elaboration here, it is doubtful that this effect can be attributed to some form of decay function, such as reactive inhibition. There does exist, however, a correlation between the likelihood of event occurrence and time since the last paired event occurred. Equations (1) and (2) above illustrate the correlation: after 15 seconds have gone by, the likelihood that a trial will occur is .33. If the trial doesn't occur then, the likelihood of occurrence in the next time unit is .5. If the trial doesn't occur then, the likelihood is unity that it will occur in the following five seconds. It does not appear unreasonable that the subject extracts these contingencies over protracted training sessions, and that this, in turn, affects his response probability.

Such an interpretation is all the more plausible in the light of more recent unpublished data from our laboratory. Subjects were run in two groups: either a fixed ITI of two seconds or a fixed ITI of eight seconds. After 105 trials, the two-second group was given an eight-second ITI, and the eight-second group was given a two-second ITI. In both instances response probability dropped significantly. It is evident that the subjects in both groups had been "temporally conditioned" and that departure from the training rate was sufficient to remove the CR. A reactive-inhibition formulation is inadequate as an explanation since the drop occurred when a two-second group (highly massed) was given an eight-second (relatively spaced) interval.

The evidence for temporal conditioning cited above is *not* reflected in overall average response probability. Studies by Grant, McFarling and Gormezano (1960) and by Prokasy and Chambliss (1960) show that, for average ITIs of 15 and 25 seconds, respectively, whether the ITI is fixed or varied is immaterial in the acquisition of the conditioned eyelid response. Unpublished research from our laboratory yielded the same result for average ITIs as short as four seconds.

A routine "control" in classical conditioning is the use of a variable ITI, ostensibly to control for temporal conditioning, with the implication that to use a fixed ITI would somehow be either a flaw in design or would contaminate the results. The data make clear, however, that, whether fixed or varied, the time functions adopted can influence behavior (i.e., can produce some form of temporal conditioning) and are worthy of analysis in their own right. The concept of "control" for temporal conditioning, therefore, is meaningful only as an experimenter-operation where time intervals are so spaced that the subject cannot abstract any contingent information about time between paired events. Such an operation cannot be perfectly obtained, and is rarely approximated; time functions of the form of equations (1) and (2) above are the rule.

TASK DEMANDS

When classical conditioning is viewed as a set of experimenter operations, a laboratory vehicle through which inquiry about behavior can be made, the more general question "what does the subject do?" can be asked in contrast to the more common, but limited, "is a CR which approximates the UCR acquired?" Such an inquiry can best begin with the demands made upon the subject during the experimental session.

In marked contrast to other laboratory paradigms, the behavior of the subject in classical conditioning is not specifically determined by the experimenter. The experimenter decides ahead of time what he is going to measure, but he does his best to communicate to the subject nothing about this. In most other experimental settings, the subject, if human, is told what alternatives are open to him and, if animal, is shaped through reinforcement contingencies to perform responses of pre-defined classes.

There are restrictions placed on the subject, but these are of the "do not," rather than the "do," variety. For example, in classical conditioning of the eyelid response, the subject is generally prohibited from removing the headgear, or from doing anything with his hands which would mitigate the effects of a puff to the cornea. With both cats and humans, considerable gentling is required to insure that the subject does not remove shock electrodes during GSR conditioning. In both leg flexion and salivary conditioning, dogs are harnessed to minimize the likelihood of any behavior which could be construed as "leaving the field."

Within the imposed constraints, then, the subject can "select" his own response strategy: the task demands are quite limited. This fact of the conditioning situation means that when a subject is exposed to paired events the experimenter measures either that which has been successfully measured in a similar context or that which occurs to him on the basis of a hunch. There exists no generally successful way to determine, a priori, what kinds of systematic behavior change will occur as a function of event pairing.

The most successful tactic in selecting a response is to measure a behavioral attribute of the organism which is effected by E_2, the unconditioned stimulus. This procedure, inherited from Pavlov and encouraged by its convenience, has several limitations. One is that it is well known that a high proportion of the learned responding in the conditioning situation is simply unlike the unconditioned response (e.g., Culler, 1938; Konorski, 1948; Liddell, 1942; Warner, 1932; Zener, 1937). Not only are many other kinds of responses acquired, the CR which resembles the UCR is usually characterized by a number of topographical differences from the UCR. A particular example of the latter from eyelid conditioning is that the measured CR differs from the UCR in latency, slope and duration. The net effect is that we can specify whether or not a particular response attribute modifies with event pairing, but that we know little about how various response attributes change with respect to each other.

Related limitations are the instances when such measures are completely unsuccessful in revealing any behavioral change. One such instance is the startle response to shock in rats. If the startle reaction is taken as the measured unit of behavior, for all intents and purposes there is no conditioning, since this response does not appear to be "conditionable." If, on the other hand, the experimenter wants to know whether a rat can associate E_1, a light or tone, with E_2, a shock, nowhere is this more clearly shown than with the conditioned emotional response, a response which appears to have little in common with the rat's typical reaction to shock.

A further limitation is the effect of this measurement tactic on theorizing. When conditioning was described as the acquisition of "an old response to a new stimulus," and the old response as a form of the UCR, a stimulus substitution view of conditioning was particularly attractive. A related view formed the basis for the application of statistical learning theory to conditioning (Estes, 1959). That the ways in which a subject modifies his behavior in the presence of paired events does not necessarily include the addition of a UCR-like response does not rule out the S-R contiguity theory, but there has been little attempt to account for departures from the "an old response to a new stimulus" dictum.

Regardless of its precise nature, however, if there is to be any kind of systematic behavior change as a function of event pairing, the task demand is that at least one of two kinds of association must be made: either an association between E_1 and E_2 or an association between E_1 and the response to E_2. Once a behavioral change occurs, two additional associations become possible: between the change and E_2 and between the change and the response to E_2.

The working hypothesis of this paper is that there is formed an association between E_1 and E_2 with consecutive event pairings, at least insofar as conditioning with adult humans is concerned. To begin with, the experimental setting is one with an extremely high signal-to-noise ratio. Two events occur in temporal contiguity within milliseconds of each other, but with time intervals between pairings ranging from a common minimum of ten or fifteen seconds up to minutes. Human adults, particularly, have had extensive past experience with stimulus relations in their environment. It would strain the imagination to assume that the fact that events were paired was not somehow abstracted and stored rather quickly during an experimental session.

Strengthening of this working hypothesis comes from research which indicates (1) that direct elicitation of the UCR fails to produce conditioning (Loucks, 1935) and (2) evidence for association as a result of pairing exists even when the UCR is absent (Solomon & Turner, 1962). This suggests that systematic change is possible without the UCR, and does not necessarily occur without some sensory effect eliciting it. If, then, change can occur without the presence of the UCR, the plausible alternative is that an association of E_1 and E_2 has been made.

There exists indirect evidence to support the belief that the association, regardless of its precise nature, is formed early in the conditioning series and before some indicators reveal its formation. The acquisition of conditioned eyelid responses in humans begins to occur within five or ten trials, but many subjects require substantially more trials. On the other hand, human GSR conditioning performance can be completed within a very few (under ten) trials (Prokasy & Ebel, 1964). Unless it is argued (implausibly, in my opinion) that the difference in acquisition rate is due solely to the possibility that shock leads to faster association than does a strong puff of air to the cornea, one interpretation of the difference is that the subjects form an association early in eyelid conditioning, but require several trials before they (or, at least, their eyelids) do anything about it. A similar effect is observed in albino rabbits. It typically requires many trials before the conditioned eyelid response is observed (Gormezano, Schneiderman, Deaux, & Fuentes, 1962), but unpublished data gathered in the Indiana laboratory by Neil Schneiderman, Marius Smith, and Abby Cohen indicates that a conditioned EKG response is observed in fewer than ten tone-shock pairings.

If further research sustains the position that an S-S association is formed early in the session, regardless of how many trials are required before a pre-selected response attribute reveals it, then it is clear that any particular measure can do no more than indicate the existence of a stored association: it provides little information on when the storage occurred.

RESPONSE SHAPING

One of the things that most subjects do after an E_1E_2 association is made in classical eyelid conditioning is blink their eyes prior to the occurrence of a puff. It is the purpose of this section to discuss some of the characteristics of the acquisition of this response. By no means is it intended, however, to convey the impression that this is the only behavioral change that occurs. The very fact that temporal conditioning exists illustrates that the subject abstracts information about temporal relationships over and above event pairing. Furthermore, we know (Champion, 1962) that the GSR is also conditioned during eyelid conditioning. Selection of the eyelid response as an indicator of stored information is particularly convenient primarily because so much is known about its characteristics. This asset notwithstanding, it does remain a selected attribute of what are probably numerous response changes contingent on event pairing, and, eventually, must be interpreted in the light of these other changes.

Reinforcement

Reinforcement in classical eyelid conditioning is interpreted along lines suggested by Perkins (1955) and Logan (1956). Perkins describes three ways to classify how reinforcement may operate:

1. all-or-none, with the same class of response reinforced throughout;
2. all-or-none, with gradual restriction of the response class;
3. varied, where the degree of reinforcement depends upon the nature of the response.

He proposes that behavior acquired via classical conditioning is acquired through varied reinforcement, where the reinforcing stimulus is an internal, rather than an external, event.

The effects of varied reinforcement can be manifest in highly molecular ways, such as those described by Logan (1956) for instrumental conditioning. Essentially, Logan has utilized the construct of response differentiation (Ferster, 1953) and employed Hullian theory as a framework from which to illustrate how a quantitative theory based upon reinforcement of specific aspects of a response can be developed. He treats different levels of amplitude, speed and latency all as distinct responses which can be differentially reinforced. For example, fast running or slow running may be reinforced, and these are analyzed as two distinct micromolar responses rather than as gradations of the same molar dimension. The shaping of, not only a molar response, but of molecular attributes of that response through varied reinforcement is assumed to characterize the acquisition of the conditioned eyelid response.

The second of the two paired events, usually a puff of air to the cornea, plays a dual role. It is first the motivating event: that is, it is sufficiently aversive to be annoying. It may become, in conjunction with what the organism does, a reinforcement in variable degree. In this second role, it is important to emphasize that E_2, the puff of air, is not, in and of itself, a reinforcer. The set of responses made by the subject on a particular trial, together with the resulting effect of the puff determines whether, and to what degree, there is reinforcement. This has meaning only relative to what has occurred on previous trials. Thus, the tensing of facial musculature when E_1 occurs as a kind of "set" for the puff would very likely be reinforced relative to no such set at all. The combination of a pre-laboratory behavioral history and variability of behavior leads most subjects eventually to respond with an eyelid movement prior to puff onset, and the extent to which both classes of response would occur together would depend jointly upon such factors as the facility with which they could be made together and the overall motivating properties of the puff.

We know by experimental precedent that humans and animals learn to blink their eyelids at E_1 onset, but we know little about what other systematic changes in behavior might occur in this situation. Since the experimenter does not specifically denote the response class for the subject, if varied reinforcement such as that described does operate, many unmeasured behavioral changes could occur unnoticed by the experimenter. Not only does this contrast sharply with what is done in instrumental conditioning where the reinforcement contingencies are designed to limit severely what changes might occur, but from this point of view it makes little sense to speak of "high" conditioners or "low" conditioners. A subject who gives few conditioned blinks can have abstracted as much information about event pairing as one who gives many blinks, but he may have evolved a totally different response strategy.

Although response shaping plays a prominent role in my interpretation of classical eyelid conditioning, it would be premature to reduce eyelid conditioning phenomena to another instance of instrumental shaping observed with lever pressing and key-pecking in a modified picnic box. First, in the latter instances the experimenter sets a criterion for delivery of an experimenter event (reinforcement) which can be met only by pre-selected behavior classes. In classical conditioning, the experimenter sets no behavioral criterion for the delivery of E_2, and whether or not there is reinforcement, even when E_2 is delivered, depends upon what the subject does. Second, in the instrumental model, the subject, even if he meets the behavioral criterion, can "reject" the reinforcing event (e.g., he can retrace a maze even after reaching the goal box), while in classical conditioning, with few exceptions (e.g., Kantrow, 1937), such a rejection is not possible. Third, if the subject is strongly controlled by the reinforcement schedule in the instrumental case, the experimenter can manipulate quite precisely the relationship between the character of the response (onset time, duration, rate, etc.) and the presentation of the reinforcing event. In the classical model, the subject is not only "free" to select his own response, he, and not the experimenter, controls the relationship between the response and the puff stimulation. This means that response differentiation (i.e., shaping) in classical conditioning is not under the control of the experimenter.

Initial CR Acquisition

While response shaping is assumed to underlie the modification of the eyelid CR, additional factors operate to result in its initial occurrence. One factor has to do with the restrictions imposed on the subject. To begin with, the instructions prohibit the subject from removing the puff jet and the situation is not sufficiently noxious to force him to remove it contrary to instructions. Thus, such a rather obvious response does not occur. Suffice it to say, however, the "neutral" instructions typically provided to the subject do not prevent alternative responses from developing. An inventory of some of these reported by the subjects is illuminating. We have found them doing the following: putting a finger over the puff jet; leaning back in the chair so that the light (E_1)

can be seen with the eyes nearly closed at all times; developing time estimation (by counting) with fixed intertrial intervals; and pushing the puff jet in a position where the puff strikes the upper lid rather than the cornea.

In addition, there are the "cooperative" subjects who have heard about conditioning and know they "should" close their eyes before the puff hits; and there are others who close their eyes consistently to E_1 after the first trial because they "don't want the puff hitting them in the eye." Some subjects go to the other extreme by doing their best *not* to blink.

Contributing to the occurrence of the initial responses are the specific instructions employed. It is evident (e.g., Norris & Grant, 1948) that when instructions are manipulated from punishments for responding to encouragement to respond they constitute one of the most powerful variables uncovered in classical eyelid conditioning. Furthermore, the "neutral" instructions routinely include references to the stimulation the subject will receive, including the puff, and follow the placement of the only recording pickup on the subject's eyelid.

Over and above the situational factors, subjects come into the conditioning session with a considerable amount of past experience using the eyelid response to mitigate the effects of stimulation, or prospective stimulation, of the cornea. It is plausible that such past experience affects acquisition performance during conditioning.

Apparatus, instructional, and past experience constraints converge to emphasize the role of the eyelid response during conditioning and, as a result, it is not surprising, first, that it occurs and, second, that the most dominant change observed is one which resembles the UCR. In effect, we design a situation which prevents the occurrence of what would be more obvious, molar responses (e.g., leaving the situation), and measure what is left at a more molecular level. Furthermore, the constraints which lead to the eyelid response will, similarly, limit the effects of subsequent response shaping to, e.g., molecular topographic shifts in the eyelid response itself.

The evidence for shaping in the acquisition of the conditioned eyelid response is revealed in both amplitude and latency shifts. Hilgard (1931) and Spence (1956) show that the size of the eyelid response increases during the early trials. It does not usually appear as a fully-developed either-or type of response. Since closure of the eye prevents the puff of air from reaching the cornea, this response, as it increases in size, reduces the extent to which it stimulates the cornea. The substantially more rapid acquisition with increases in puff intensity (e.g., Passey, 1948; Spence, 1953; Prokasy, Grant & Myers, 1958) is also consistent with the shaping interpretation.

Boneau (1958) reported that during acquisition the responses tended more and more to overlap the puff. Thus, either the latency or the duration modified in such a way that the response influences the reception of the puff, regardless of the level of amplitude. According to the data of Spence (1956), the precise direction that the latency changes is related to the initial rate of acquisition. This particular interaction may be related to how amplitude varies with the level ("high" or "low") of conditioning observed during the early trials.

CR Development and Maintenance

Latency is a very sensitive indicator in eyelid conditioning, reflecting independent variable manipulation, as well as topographic shifts with extended training. Boneau (1958) found that shifting subjects from a training ISI (interstimulus interval) of 500 msec. to 1000 and 1500 msec. resulted in a marked increase in response latency. Ebel and Prokasy (1963) found that shifting subjects from a training ISI of either 200, 500, or 800 msec. to one of the other two and then back to the original interval produced the same general effect: increasing the ISI increased latency and decreasing the ISI decreased latency.

More recently, Prokasy, Ebel and Thompson (1963) illustrated the shaping of response latency in a way which suggests its role in determining what level of responding is achieved at long ISI values. They ran three groups of subjects in an eyelid conditioning situation: one group (Group 6-25) received an ISI of 630 msec. for 300 trials and was then switched to an ISI of 2497 msec. for 60 trials; another (Group 25) received an ISI of 2497 msec. for 360 trials; and the third group (Group E) received ISIs of 630 msec. for 40 trials, 791 for 40 trials, 996 for 50 trials, 1246 for 50 trials, 1570 for 60 trials, 1977 for 60 trials and 2497 for the final 60 trials. Group E maintained a high level of responding throughout the increases in ISI, illustrating that a CR can be acquired with a "long" (i.e., substantially longer than 500 msec.) ISI. Group 25 responded on an average of just under 30 percent of the trials for the last 300 trials, while Group 6-25 dropped from a high performance level to one just above that of Group 25 upon the ISI shift to 2497 msec. The response latency for Group E was a linear function of ISI, but the slope of the function was less than unity. A CR was defined as any response which began 160 msec. after CS onset and which *also overlapped the UCS*. With a latency slope less than unity, the CR was beginning earlier with respect to puff onset and was, therefore, lasting longer as a function of ISI. Since the instructional set is for the subject to let his reactions take care of themselves, it may be that the usual procedure with long ISIs simply results in poor (or infrequent attempts at) time estimation, reduced reinforcement and, consequently, a low frequency of responding.

The average latency of Group 6-25 was 1866 msec., while that of Group 25 was 2212 msec. "Shaping" the subject, that is, starting him with a short interval where virtually any response that occurs will overlap the UCS to some extent, and then increasing the ISI may simply teach the subject that a permissible response is to close the eye and keep it closed long enough to overlap the puff. These results also make clear that whether or not CR latency asymptotes independently of past training is no longer an experimental issue: latencies for any particular set of conditions are a function of past training experience.

When subjects are given extended training, the evidence (Ebel and Prokasy, 1963) is that response latency gradually decreases, even though response frequency is nearly asymptotic. Both outer eyelid and nictitating membrane conditioning in albino rabbits exhibit the same characteristic, but in a far more pronounced fashion (Gormezano, Schneiderman, Deaux, & Fuentes, 1962).

Further evidence for how the form of the eyelid response is determined by the particular experimental circumstances comes from the data of Moore and Gormezano (1961). Subjects in Group A avoided the puff by giving a CR with CS onset, while subjects in Group AD delayed the puff for 2500 msec. by giving a CR. Since a response eliminated the puff in Group A, there is no particular reinforcement for keeping the eye closed once it occurs; but for Group AD, a response of longer duration would also partially avoid the puff at the delayed interval. Response durations for the second-last and last acquisition trials were measured for these two groups,[2] and the mean durations, in msec., are provided in Table 11-2. The results are biased against the expectation of longer-duration responses for Group AD simply because six responders on the second-last trial and seven on the last trial had response durations that were not completed when the paper drive was stopped. This did not occur once in Group A. Nonetheless, response durations were significantly longer in Group AD than in Group A on both the second-last ($F = 7.15$; df $= 1, 41$) and last ($F = 8.32$; df $= 1, 41$) trials.

Another attribute of the conditioned eyelid response which is susceptible to shaping is the slope (rate of closure). For example, when Ss are given the instruction to blink to avoid the puff (Hartman, Grant, &

Table 11-2——Mean response duration (msec.) in group A and group AD on second-last and last acquisition trials

	SECOND LAST	LAST
GROUP A	522	542
GROUP AD	1188	1191

[2] The original records were provided by Professor Gormezano.

Ross, 1960; Gormezano & Moore, 1962) response slope is sharper than that obtained without such instruction.

Instructional set is not the only experimenter-operation which leads to modified slope. Group E of the study by Prokasy, Ebel and Thompson (1963) yielded a steady decrease in slope as a function of ISI. That this shift in response was a function of within-subject shift over ISI and not of training trials is illustrated in Table 11-3 where mean slope (in mm. units) is given as a function of the ISI level for Group E and of trials for Group 6-25. No decrement exists in Group 6-25 across trials (F = 1.004; df = 5, 125), but does for Group E (F = 8.2; df = 6, 165).

Table 11-3————Mean slope (mm) of group E as a function of ISI and group 6-25 as a function of trials ISI (msec.) and trial block

GROUP	N	630	791	996	1246	1570	1977	2497
		1	*2*	*3*	*4*	*5*	*6*	*7*
E	27	10.02	9.31	8.81	7.77	7.01	7.59	6.96
6-25	26	8.87	9.64	8.43	8.57	8.97	8.31	*

* Switched to 2497 msec. in last block of trials, and the N making at least four responses dropped to 21.

An interesting illustration of how response topography can modify with extended training is shown by some unpublished data gathered in our laboratory. A single subject was run for 26,880 trials,[3] and two of the measures taken on the sampled trials were the slope and the standard deviation of slope. Trials sampled from the last 16,128 trials were divided into three blocks each representing samples from 5,366 trials. Both mean slope and the SD of slope decreased significantly across the three blocks, indicating that the rate of closure became slower and more homogeneous across trials. Whether or not all subjects would exhibit this characteristic is immaterial; it is doubtful that such refinements on a molecular scale could occur without the continued operation of feedback from the response and its effect on the puff of air to the cornea. In this respect, the results parallel the refined response characteristics of a highly developed motor skill, and constitute an unusual example of response shaping in classical conditioning.

While refinements of latency, response duration, slope and SD of slope strongly suggest response shaping, the most direct evidence we have that the relationship between the CR and E_2 controls at least some response variance comes from a study by Moore and Gormezano (1961). In

[3] The paid subject, David Schraer, was run under a variety of interstimulus interval conditions over forty sessions of 668 trials each. Probability, latency, latency SD, slope, and SD slope were assessed on trials sampled from the last 16,128. Dittoed copies of the results and analyses are available from the author.

this study, a CR to E_1 resulted in avoidance of E_2 in one group of subjects. A second group constituted yoked controls: they received the same pattern of E_2 presentations as that in the avoidance group, but the pattern was unrelated to their responses. The avoidance group yielded a greater number of CRs. Since the only operational difference between the groups was the correlation between response and E_2 absence in the avoidance group and no such contingency in the yoked groups, it is apparent that how the response affects the reception of E_2 contributes to performance. Not clear, however, is why a group which received continued E_1E_2 pairings (i.e., 100 percent reinforcement) responded to an even higher level. It may be that the high frequency of E_2 instances can account for the difference, although it would appear that the avoidance group should reach a higher performance level since the effects of a CR are greater in that group.

The response to E_2 (in this instance, the eyelid reflex to a puff) reflects the operation of learned response sets not directly measured in eyelid conditioning. For example, our unpublished data indicate that with over 100 E_2 presentations the size, slope and probability of the UCR decrease significantly. That this is a product of more than simple adaptation comes from two sources. First, if the puffs are presented at fixed intertrial intervals, and then a change is made in the intertrial interval, there is an increase in the size, slope and probability of response. This would appear to reflect the acquisition of sets for a specific rate of puff presentation: the introduction of a temporal disparity prevents these sets from being operative.

Second, Kimble and Ost (1961) have shown that the size of the UCR is smaller when it is preceded by E_1 than when it is not, and that this is a function of stage of training. The authors interpret their results in terms of the acquisition of conditioned inhibition under the control of E_1. Alternatively, it is possible that responses other than the eyelid response are acquired, and that these, in turn, result in a UCR of diminished vigor. This might be tested, for example, by shifting the ISI and then measuring the UCR. This should provide a disruption of alternative response sets and a consequent return to a larger UCR, as occurred with the time disparity tests summarized above.

CONCLUDING COMMENTS

The combination of methodology, theory and precedent has had a peculiar result in classical conditioning. Somehow, it is viewed as a kind of "thing" to be explained by a single set of rules or to be a basic working unit in the explanation of other behavior. The result has been an unnecessarily esoteric set of data which stands largely unintegrated with other forms of behavioral inquiry.

The emphasis of this paper has been on classical conditioning as a label for, and only for, a set of experimenter operations. The operations are defined as instances of event transmission, where the typical conditioning situation becomes a special case of the correlation between two stimulus events distributed in time. What event-contingencies a subject abstracts (or superstitiously invents) from the situation, whether related only to the event pairing or to other correlations inherent in the procedure, is a matter for experimental inquiry. It is doubtful that all, or even most, of the systematic behavioral changes produced in the conditioning setting can be discovered or appropriately analyzed by relying on precedents which confine measurement tactics to extremely limited features of special event combinations (e.g., looking ·for the behavioral change which approximates, however crudely, an aspect of the UCR).

If a subject is to make a systematic behavioral change which is contingent specifically on the pairing of events, minimal association demands must be met. The position of this paper is that an S-S association is frequently made very early in the conditioning session, and that the result of this association may show up in many ways and, often, not for many trials.

Depending upon species, quality of stimulation, distribution of events, and situational constraints, a variety of behavioral changes may occur. Of particular interest in this paper was a class of changes appearing to result from response shaping which, in this instance, is largely under the control of the subject. The manner in which the eyelid response is acquired, formed, and changed over trials strongly suggests that one reinforcing mechanism is the relationship between the eyelid CR and the puff stimulation. That response shaping controls all of the response variance is not to be implied; it appears to be a dominant factor in this instance, and it remains to be analyzed more fully in other situations which conform to the set of experimenter-operations which define classical conditioning.

References

BONEAU, C. A. The interstimulus interval and the latency of the conditioned eyelid response. *J. exp. Psychol.*, 1958, *56*, 464-471.

CHAMPION, R. A. Stimulus-response contiguity in classical aversive conditioning. *J. exp. Psychol.*, 1962, *64*, 35-39.

CULLER, E. A. Recent advances in some concept of conditioning. *Psychol. Rev.*, 1938, *45*, 134-153.

EBEL, H. C., & PROKASY, W. F. Classical eyelid conditioning as a function of sustained and shifted interstimulus intervals. *J. exp. Psychol.*, 1963, *65*, 52-58.

Estes, W. K. The statistical approach to learning theory. In S. Koch, *Psychology: A study of a science*. Vol. 11. New York: McGraw-Hill, 1959.

Ferster, C. B. The use of the free operant in the analysis of behavior. *Psychol. Bull.*, 1953, *50*, 263-274.

Gormezano, I., & Moore, J. Effects of instructional set and UCS intensity on the latency, percentage, and form of the eyelid response. *J. exp. Psychol.*, 1962, *63*, 487-494.

Gormezano, I., Schneiderman, N., Deaux, E., & Fuentes, I. Nictitating membrane: classical conditioning and extinction in the albino rabbit. *Science*, 1962, *138*, 33-34.

Grant, D. A., McFarling, C., & Gormezano, I. Temporal conditioning and the effect of interpolated UCS presentations in eyelid conditioning. *J. gen. Psychol.*, 1960, *63*, 249-257.

Hartman, T. F., Grant, D. A., & Ross, L. E. An investigation of the latency of "instructed voluntary" eyelid responses. *Psychol. rep.*, 1960, *7*, 305-311.

Hilgard, E. R. Conditioned eyelid reactions to a light stimulus based on the wink reflex to sound. *Psychol. Monogr.*, 1931, *41*, No. 184, 50 pp.

Kantrow, R. W. An investigation of conditioned feeding responses and concomitant adaptive behavior in young infants. *Univ. Ia. stud. child welf.*, 1937, *13*, No. 337, 1-64.

Kendler, H. H. *Basic Psychology*. New York: Appleton-Century-Crofts, 1963.

Kimble, G. A. *Hilgard and Marquis' conditioning and learning*, 2nd ed. New York: Appleton-Century-Crofts, 1961.

Kimble, G. A., & Ost, J. P. A conditioned inhibitory process in eyelid conditioning. *J. exp. Psychol.*, 1961, *61*, 150-157.

Konorski, J. *Conditioned reflexes and neuron organization*. New York: Cambridge University Press, 1948.

Krauss, H. H., & Prokasy, W. F. On intertrial interval discrimination in classical conditioning. *Psychol. rep.*, 1963, *12*, 138.

Liddell, H. S. The conditioned reflex. In F. A. Moss (Ed.), *Comparative psychology*. Englewood Cliffs, N.J.: Prentice-Hall, 1942.

Logan, F. A. A micromolar approach to behavior theory. *Psychol. rev.*, 1956, *63*, 63-73.

Loucks, R. B. The experimenter delimitation of neural structures essential for learning: the attempt to condition striped muscle responses with faradization of the sigmoid gyri. *J. Psychol.*, 1935, *1*, 5-44.

Moore, J., & Gormezano, I. Yoked comparisons of instrumental and classical eyelid conditioning. *J. exp. Psychol.*, 1961, *62*, 552-559.

Munn, N. L. *Psychology*. Boston: Houghton Mifflin, 1961.

Norris, E., & Grant, D. A. Eyelid conditioning as affected by verbally induced inhibitory set and counter reinforcement. *Amer. J. Psychol.*, 1948, *61*, 37-49.

Passey, G. E. The influence of intensity of unconditioned stimulus upon acquisition of a conditioned response. *J. exp. Psychol.*, 1948, *38*, 420-428.

Pavlov, I. P. *Conditioned reflexes*. London: Oxford University Press, 1927. (Transl. by G. V. Anrep.)

Perkins, C. C., Jr. The stimulus conditions which follow learned responses. *Psychol. Rev.*, 1955, *62*, 341-348.

PROKASY, W. F., & CHAMBLISS, D. J. Temporal conditioning: negative results. *Psychol. rep.*, 1960, *7*, 539-542.

PROKASY, W. F., & EBEL, H. C. GSR conditioning and sensitization as a function of intertrial interval. *J. exp. Psychol.*, 1964, *67*, 113-119.

PROKASY, W. F., EBEL, H. C., & THOMPSON, D. D. Responses shaping at long interstimulus interval in classical eyelid conditioning. *J. exp. Psychol.*, 1963, *66*, 138-141.

PROKASY, W. F., GRANT, D. A., & MYERS, N. A. Eyelid conditioning as a function of UCS intensity and intertrial interval. *J. exp. Psychol.*, 1958, *55*, 242-246.

PROKASY, W. F., & WHALEY, F. L. Intertrial interval range shift in classical eyelid conditioning. *Psychol. rep.*, 1963, *12*, 55-58.

ROSS, L. E., & HUNTER, J. J. Habit strength parameters in eyelid conditioning as a function of UCS intensity. *Psychol. rec.*, *9*, 103-107.

SOLOMON, R. L., & TURNER, L. H. Discriminative classical conditioning in dogs paralyzed by curare can later control discriminative avoidance responses in the normal state. *Psychol. rev.*, 1962, *69*, 202-219.

SPENCE, K. W. Learning and performance in eyelid conditioning as a function of the intensity of the UCS. *J. exp. Psychol.*, 1953, *45*, 57-63.

SPENCE, K. W. *Behavior theory and conditioning*. New Haven: Yale University Press, 1956.

WARNER, L. H. An experimental search for the "conditioned response." *J. genet. Psychol.*, 1932, *41*, 91-115.

WICKENS, D. D., & MEYER, D. R. *Psychology*. New York: Holt, Rinehart & Winston, 1961.

ZENER, K. The significance of behavior accompanying conditioned salivary secretion for theories of the conditioned response. *Amer. J. Psychol.*, 1937, *50*, 384-403.

GREGORY RAZRAN

Queens College of The City University of New York

12

Empirical Codifications and Specific Theoretical Implications of Compound-Stimulus Conditioning: Perception [1]

An empirical codification of principles of compound-stimulus conditioning is confronted with a very wide East-West differential in available experimental data. There are extant, to date, approximately 650 individual Russian experiments in the area and a dozen American. Animal subjects were used in at least 600 of the Russian studies but in only two of the American. Thus, the present undertaking must needs be concerned predominantly with Russian evidence.

An analysis of Russian CR experimentation is, as is known, fraught with a host of difficulties. Obtained data are seldom subjected to statistical treatments; often, only a portion of the data is presented; not uncommonly, experimental designs lack controls and fail to isolate differing parameters; and, at times, reports contain contradictory statements. Yet, on the other side of the ledger, even a cursory perusal of the Russian contributions, their nature and role, discloses very significant positive counterweighing aspects of which sheer bulk of replicative evidence is only one. There is the clear fact that the Russians' basic findings—the mere existence of, for example, extinction, generalization, spontaneous recovery, disinhibition, compound-without-component conditioning, and the like— are qualitative yes-or-no events demonstrable as such in a few trials and little in need of elaborate controls, statistics, and inferences. And there is the other fact that even their quantitative parametric findings such as gradients of generalization and specific intensive and temporal CR factors

[1] This report is one of a series on Soviet psychology and psychophysiology, on which research has, since 1957, been supported by Grant MH 02196(6) from the National Institute of Mental Health, National Institutes of Health, Public Health Service, Department of Health, Education, and Welfare.

which surely call for sound methodological and inferential treatments have more than once been verified in American laboratories. And surely there is no need to stress the general consideration that Pavlov's work and views are focal determinants in most American research and thought in learning and related areas. To cite an example pertinent to the topic under discussion, Hull has used Woodbury's (1943) reported verification of a Pavlov-reported finding as the basis of a whole chapter on Patterning of Stimulus Compounds. No one, it seems, suggests throwing out the modern Russian baby along with its indigenous methodological bath.

More than that, at least in the area of salivary conditioning in dogs, reported Russian findings are at times strikingly consistent within experiments and from experiment to experiment. Three sets of data on conditioning of two dogs reported by two experimenters in the same issue of a periodical will serve as examples. Prior to developing a salivary CR to a compound CS of the sight of whirligig plus the sound of rattle in dog "Pincher," Dolin (1940) tested the animal's stable positive CRs to a bell, a light (25 c.p.), a metronome of 120 beats per minute, the bubbling of water, and a negative differentiated CR to a metronome of 60 beats per minute. The CSs were in all cases continued for 30 sec at interstimulus intervals of 4.5 min, from 11:10 to 11:50 A.M. The respective results of nine consecutive tests, in salivary scale units, were: bell, 125; light, 84; bubbling, 119; metronome of 120 beats, 112; metronome of 60 beats, 10; metronome of 120, 110; bubbling, 120; light, 78; bell, 122—that is, replicative CS-CR magnitudes of: Bell, 125, 122; metronome, 112, 110; bubbling, 119, 120; light, 84, 78.

Nine months later, the dog was tested twice each with the bell, the metronome of 120 beats, and the new whirligig plus rattle compound CS, and once with the differentiated metronome of 60 beats—using identical interstimulus and CS durations. The CR magnitudes in the testing sequence were now: bell, 115; compound, 83; positive metronome, 95; differentiated metronome, 8; positive metronome, 96; compound, 82; bell, 108—replications of 115, 108 for the bell; 83, 82 for the compound; 95, 96 for the metronome. Moreover, in the nine months in which the CRs to the bell and to the metronome were each reinforced only a few times, their respective magnitudes were reduced only from means of 123.5 and 111 to 111.5 and 95.5 units, while the differentiated CR changed from 10 to 8.

In another experiment (Usiyevich, 1940), dog "Smirny" 's positive CRs to a light, a bell, and a metronome of 120 beats were tested three times each in one session, with one test of the animal's negative CR to a metronome of 60 beats. The interstimulus intervals were the same as in the preceding experiment but the CSs lasted for only 20 sec. The results were: metronome of 60 beats, 2 units; light, 34; bell, 58; metronome of 120 beats, 65; light, 26; bell, 50; metronome of 120, 63; light, 20; bell,

64; metronome, 62—respective CR magnitude replications of 34, 26, and 20 units for the light; 58, 50, and 64 for the bell; and 65, 63, and 62 for the metronome.

To be sure, not all dogs are so "strong and balanced"—to use Russian typological terms—as "Pincher" and "Smirny," nor are strong-and-balanced dogs always at their best. Yet the three examples illustrate well the rationale of what might be called the basic methodological philosophy of the Russian CR enterprise—adherence to a view that CS-CR norms are relatively invariant and hence that significant variance is in essence a neurobehavioral deviance calling for special causal accounts: improper training, "type" of conditioned animal, special pathological states, and other "dynamics" of higher nervous activity. "Experimental Psychology and Psychopathology in Animals" was the title of Pavlov's first (1903) article on conditioned reflexes. Or, in other words, notwithstanding the highly quantitative nature of the Russians' CR data, their methodology has essentially been non-statistical, single-animal, case-history, and clinical in character, reminiscent of the approaches of Skinner on the one hand, and of Freud and Lewin on the other—much more like the former than the latter two, though.

VARIETIES OF COMPOUND-STIMULUS CONDITIONING

In past experiments, three varieties of compound-stimulus conditioning have been used: (a) simultaneous, (b) successive, and (c) what has been called "dynamic stereotypes." In the simultaneous variety, two or more CSs, typically two to four, are applied at the same time prior—in Pavlovian food-conditioning, typically, 10 to 30 sec, prior—to US activation. In the successive variety, the several CSs—again, typically, no more than four—are presented in succession (successions of 3 to 10 sec in Pavlovian food-conditioning) before the US is administered. Dynamic stereotypes are a special kind of successive compounds in which the number of applied CSs is usually 5 to 8, all but one—occasionally, but two—CSs are separately reinforced, and there are fixed intervals of several minutes between CS administrations. As a rule, the CSs in the compounds are unrelated, commonly are of different sense modalities; even if in a limited number of experiments, chords, melodic tone successions, and light flashes in geometric patterns have been used. A special subvariety of simultaneous CR compounding is differential situational conditioning, in which subjects become conditioned differentially to the same stimulus in different experimental rooms, different times of the day, and in the presence of different experimenters. And a special subvariety of both simultaneous and successive compounding ensues when components are first conditioned separately and then trained in compounds.

Experiments using the simultaneous and successive varieties of compound-stimulus conditioning have been concerned with four types of problems: (*a*) the quantitative specificity of compound conditioning with respect to established CS-CR relations in simple conditioning; (*b*) its qualitative specificity, the discovery that subjects could be conditioned differentially to compounds and components and to different sequences of the same compounds; (*c*) the relation of compound conditioning to the conditioning of its constituent component, combinations of components, and nontrained sequences; and (*d*) the relation of this conditioning to various organismic and extraneous factors such as age and phyletic position of subjects and effects of ablations, some drugs, and the like. It is clear, also, that the compound successive variety comprises many more CR differentiations than does the simultaneous one. A simultaneous three-component compound involves six differentiations: compound vs. three single components and vs. three combinations of two components; whereas a like successive compound includes eight extra differentiations: compound vs. its five differing sequences and compound vs. three additional sequences of combinations of two components. Moreover, successive CR compounds permit *some* observation of component conditioning during compound training, which, of course, simultaneous compounds do not.

Dynamic stereotype problems have, on the other hand, stirred a different course of investigation. In Russian views, this variety of conditioning represents the highest type of neurobehavioral synthesis or systematization of separate CR units into fixed or stereotyped patterns of habit, a synthesis that they assume is primarily effected through replacement of external environment-produced CSs by internal response-produced ones. Hence, the main experimental task has been to study the pattern of CR magnitude and the mosaic of alternation of positive and negative CRs in CR stereotypes when, after long training, the sequential positions of individual CSs are changed. The hypothesis has been strikingly confirmed. After long training, CR patterns and alternations normally remain the same despite these changes. However, basic changes of sequences, particularly in early stages of stereotype training, have proven too difficult and conflict-producing for many subjects and organisms, so that this variety of compound-stimulus conditioning has also become another means of producing and studying experimental neurosis. The variety itself is a late development in the Russian CR discipline. Pavlov reported on it first in 1932. Yet by now it is in common use; indeed it is used also when no sequential changes are attempted.

EARLY STUDIES: 1906-1912

Data on compound-stimulus conditioning became available in Pavlov's laboratory almost from its very inception. In 1906, Palladin reported a study entitled "Artificial [laboratory-formed] Conditioned Reflexes to Sums of Stimuli." (It must be remembered that, in general, CRs to laboratory stimuli were uncovered only in 1905 by Boldyrev, earlier studies being of "natural" CSs—sights and odors of food.) Palladin found that when a thermal stimulus—previously demonstrated to be condition-able by Boldyrev and by Voskoboynikova-Granstren—had been added to a fairly well established tactile CS and the two reinforced simultaneously, isolated applications of the thermal stimulus did not come to evoke a CR even after 156 reinforcements of the thermal-tactile combination. More-over, when the CR to the isolated administration of the tactile CS had been completely extinguished, the tactile-thermal combination continued to elicit a lively CR. Two inactive CSs produced an active CR. Their "togetherness" did something special.

Palladin's results brought out two new CR findings; (a) that a stim-ulus may fail to acquire CR effectiveness when it is reinforced in a com-pound yet may well be conditioned when it is reinforced separately; and (b) that a compound may manifest conditioning even when its constitu-ent components are wholly ineffective. Interestingly, the two findings illustrate also the two *types* of Russian CR findings, quantitative and qualitative, discussed at the beginning of this article. For, obviously, with-out adequate controls and statistical inference, the failure of thermal stimulus to acquire CR characteristics in one dog after 156 reinforcements in a compound cannot be attributed with full confidence to the effect of the compound, even if it is known that in three other dogs the stimulus became effective after 30-60 separate, component reinforcements. On the other hand, the second finding—that the constituent components of a compound CR of considerable magnitude were by themselves wholly in-effective—is just as obviously a matter of existence authenticity and not of controls and statistical confidence.

Palladin's first finding was tested in four extensive studies made in the same year and in the following two years: Zeliony, 1906, 1907; Pereltsvayg, 1907; Kasherininova, 1908; Elyasson, 1908. In these studies, the CR compound was trained first and both compound and component CR action were tried at different stages of training. Pereltsvayg used the same stimuli as Palladin, a tactile and a thermal; but Zeliony worked with a light plus a sound and with two sounds of differing intensity, Kasherin-inova with two tactile stimulations of unlike intensity, and Elyasson with a musical chord $(G + c^1 + f^2)$, each tone of which was presumably of the same intensity. The Palladin finding was basically corroborated in the sense that some stimuli known to be conditionable through separate rein-forcements failed to acquire CR effectiveness when they were reinforced in compounds. However, while in the tactile-thermal compound, the thermal stimulus failed just as in Palladin's study, in the tactile and in the auditory compounds, the physically weaker of the two stimuli mani-fested the failure, and there was no CR failure in the musical chord experiment in which the tested individual tones merely evoked smaller—and relatively equal—CR magnitudes than the compound chord. Accordingly, a specific parametric generalization regarding Palladin's first finding was soon formulated in Pavlov's laboratory—namely, that the extent of compound suppression or inhibition of component conditioning is inversely proportional to the intensities of the component CSs and that only relatively weak CSs are fully affected. The generalization was later confirmed by Rikman (1928) using compounds of tactile and auditory CSs, by Kupalov and Gantt (1928) experimenting with combinations of auditory and visual and of auditory and thermal stimuli, and by a number of other students in the field.

Early confirmation of Palladin's 1906 second finding that compound CSs may manifest full-grown and wholly stable CR effectiveness while all their constituent components are totally ineffective—what I called in 1939 "configural conditioning"—was reported by Zeliony in 1910 using a CS combination of a light and a sound, by Nikolayev in 1911 using a tone plus a light plus a whirligig in one dog and a tone plus a light plus a metronome in another, and indirectly also by Babkin in 1910. Babkin was the first to study successive compounds, which, as indicated earlier, are more complex than the simultaneous variety involving an additional dimension of sequential configuring yet possessing certain methodological advantages. His specific experiment consisted of training a dog to salivate at the sound of a sequence of tones of 290, 325, 370, and 413 cy and not to react with salivation to the sound of several permutations of the tone sequence.

Babkin, like Zeliony and Nikolayev, and most other Pavlov students who followed them (Bykov, 1925; Ivanov-Smolensky, 1927; Kunstman, 1923; Stroganov, 1923—to name only a few) used differential CR contrasting, that is, alternation of repeated reinforcements of the compound or its particular sequence with repeated nonreinforcements of the components or to-be-differentiated sequences. There is of course no doubt that in practice such contrasting is an effective aid to the production of conditioned configuring. Yet a moment's thought will convince one that the contrasting—or discrimination—could not possibly be the chief pre-condition or mechanism of the configuring. For, obviously, mere extinction of a CR to CS components a, b, and c through nonreinforcement will not by itself generate conditioning to a compound a + b + c. There must be developed something in a + b + c which is not in a, b, or c, and for such development repeated combined applications of, and presumed cumulative interactions among, a, b, and c must surely be a *sine qua non*.

Or, in other words, simple logic dictates the view that the primary precondition for configuring in compound stimulus conditioning is the positive training of the CS compound, the differential negative training of its components being no more than ancillary in contribution. Full empirical support for the simple, hardly assailable logic of this view was slow in coming. However, indications of it were already discernible in Platonov's 1912 study in Bekhterev's laboratory with avoidable shock-conditioning of human subjects in which long series of tests of compound vs. component CR action were made when shock reinforcement had been discontinued and differential reinforcement was presumably no longer operative.

Table 12-1 presents the pertinent results of four of the six subjects in Platonov's study (one of the two remaining subjects failed to complete his experiment and the data of the other are incomplete [2] in the report). The UR was the plantar reflex (see Bekhterev, 1913 and 1933 for specific technique of conditioning), the CS a simultaneous compound of an electric bell and a light of 20 c.p., and 100-200 trials were made each training and testing session. Shock reinforcement was discontinued after 140 compound training trials in Subject A, 1220 in Subject B, 710 in Subject C, and 360 in Subject D—the shock itself being of course applied in only a portion of the training trials, at the beginning of each session and when the CR failed to appear.

Platonov's data no doubt disclose evidence that compound-without-component, or configural, conditioning may develop without differential reinforcement-nonreinforcement—solely through overtraining. Indeed, the data offer also a suggestive account of the entire developmental dynamics of compound-stimulus conditioning—namely, that it involves three stages: an initial stage in which the CR action of components is only weaker than that of the compound; an intermediary stage in which only the weaker components totally lose effectiveness; and a final stage when all components drop out. Interestingly, this finding, too, is vested in the general logic and knowledge of conditioning, for weaker CRs are admittedly more extinguishable (or inhibitable, or suppressible, of integrable). Or, to generalize, the quantitative differential of lesser component conditioning—a glaring finding in hundreds of Russian studies—must in course of equal CR training eventually lead to a qualitative differential, that is, to total disappearance or extinction of component conditioning. Yet, as stressed earlier, extinction of component CR action does not in itself constitute configural conditioning: there must be developed a *configure* or datum to bear this conditioning.

On the other hand, it should also be emphasized that Platonov's

---

[2] Early Russian conditioning experiments from Pavlov's and Bekhterev's laboratories were as a rule doctoral theses, in fulfillment of the requirements for the M.D. degree at the St. Petersburg Military Medical Academy, published as long monographs containing trial-by-trial protocols of data. In later years, however, the published theses became shorter and less detailed even as most experiments came to be performed by regular members of the various Russian laboratories and published in various periodicals. Hence, while Russian techniques and even methodologies have improved over the years, the data of only the early studies may be fully checked.

Table 12-1———Percent of occurrence of compound and component plantar conditioning in four adult human subjects with a simultaneous compound of an electric bell and a light as the CS and avoidable electric shock as the US, when the shock reinforcement was discontinued; approximately 40 compound and individual component tests were made each session (after Platonov)

SESSION	SUBJECT A			SUBJECT B			SUBJECT C			SUBJECT D		
	Compound	Bell	Light	Compound	Bell	Light	Compound	Bell	Light	Compound	Bell	Light
1	77	66	35	95	20	17	65	58	6	100[a]	100	100
2	67	50	32	95	15	10	76	61	00	100	100	85
3	89	80	25	100	00	00	90	47	3	98	92	55
4	90	21	13				86	59	3	100	76	28
5	95	20	13				96	46	0	100	67	36
6	95	15	10				95	39	0	100	68	31
7	100	0	0				92[b]	25	0	100	37	17
8										83[b]	2	0

[a] For this subject, data are means of 3 sessions.
[b] Continued overtraining produced total loss of CR, even in response to compound CS.

empirical evidence provided only indications but not full-fledged definitive insight into the relation of overtraining to the development of configural conditioning. For one thing, conditioning data of such consciously
—or verbally—controllable reactions as shock-withdrawal in human subjects are in general by themselves inadequately definitive in settling CR
basics. For another, even in animal subjects results of avoidable conditioning are replete with interpretative pitfalls. A possible—although, in
my view, not a plausible—argument could, for instance, be made that,
while there was no actual compound-component shock-reinforcement
differential in the Platonov overtraining testing series, a substitute type
of differential, established in the training series, persisted and was operative. Moreover, the fact that in two subjects, continued overtraining resulted in the total loss of the CR might also arouse querying disputes.
For although the general phenomenon of "extinction through overtraining" has long been known in classical conditioning (Hovland, 1936;
Razran, 1934, 1955) and was recently uncovered in the instrumental
variety (North and Stimmel, 1960; Clayton, 1963), its specific operation in
the avoidable conditioning is of course, with apologies for the word play,
wholly unavoidable. In fine, basic configural conditioning evidence with
animal subjects and with less controversial forms of conditioning was
needed, and, as will be seen in the followig section, has been forthcoming
and cumulating since 1912.

LATER AND RECENT DEVELOPMENTS: THE BERITOV LABORATORY

Aside from growing interest in dynamic stereotypes which will
be analyzed in the following section, later and recent studies in compound-
stimulus conditioning differ from the early ones mainly in (a) involvement of URs other than salivation and shock withdrawal—notably runways and instrumental food-fetching, the specific techniques of which have
been described elsewhere (Razran, 1961); (b) dominant concern with the
relation of compound CR specificities to overtraining (as discussed in preceding paragraph) in animals and with comparisons of overtraining and
differential-reinforcement methods of producing the specificities; (c) investigation of the correlations of the specificities with phylogeny and
ontogeny and with such "devolutionary" factors as cerebral ablations and
some drugs. Since no significant specification of all the studies could be
attempted here, two groups of studies have been selected for consideration: (a) those under the direction of I. S. Beritashvili (Beritov) of the
Beritashvili Institute of Physiology of the Georgian Academy of Sciences
in Tbilisi, in which, first shock-withdrawal and then runways were used;
and (b) those under the direction of L. G. Voronin of the University of
Moscow and the Laboratory of Comparative Physiology of the Pavlov

Institute of Physiology of the USSR Academy of Sciences, in which salivation and later instrumental food-fetching were employed. The Beritashvili experiments were first performed in 1918 but first reported in 1932; the Voronin studies were begun in 1940 and were first published in 1948.

Beritov's 1918 study was first reported by him in his 1932 text "Individually-Acquired Activity of the Central Nervous System" (Tbilisi, GIZ), in which 75 pages (pp. 357-431) under the heading of "Unifying (Integrated) Action of the Cerebral Cortex" were wholly taken up with an analysis of the evidence on compound CR action available at the time —the first extensive discussion of the topic (Pavlov's two books devote only several pages to it). Two dogs, *Bely* and *Besukh,* were used. The US was an unavoidable electric shock delivered to the left forepaw in one animal and to the right forepaw in the other; the CS was a successive compound of a tactile stimulus and a tone of 290 cy in one, and of a 300 cy tone and a tactile stimulus in the other. The results of 20 days of experimentation showed that the conditioning of both dogs proceeded in three discernible successive stages: (*a*) when CR reactions to only the second CS component, whether it was a sound or a tactile stimulus, were evident; (*b*) when CR reactions to the first component differed qualitatively from those to the second; that is, general preparatory orienting head movements and barking, but no precise flexion of stimulated paw; (*c*) when reactions to both CS components were specific and equal, but reactions to the second component were much facilitated by the application of the first component. Beritov's conclusions were: (*a*) *"When an individual reflex is formed to a successive compound of conditioned stimuli, separate temporary connections are established between the neural centers of each component conditioned stimulus and the neural center of the unconditioned stimulus"* (1932, p. 386; his italics); (*b*) *"Direct temporary connections are also established between the cortical foci of the component conditioned stimuli of the successive compound, but only after the establishment of connections between the foci of each component conditioned stimulus and the neural focus of the unconditioned stimulus"* (*ibid.*, p. 387; his italics). His second conclusion which he bases on his third stage of empirical findings that the "first CS component facilitates the action of the second" is of course like Wickens' formulation that "one element component acquires a capacity to evoke the 'sensory effects' of the other element" (1959, p. 86).

In 1927, Usnadze, a psychologist working in Beritov's physiological laboratory, trained a dog to form a shock-withdrawal CR to a stronger of two successive tones and to differentiate the reaction from that to a succession of two weak tones, two strong ones, and a weak tone following a strong. The differentiation was, however, only partial and no significant observations were made of its development. The experiment was then repeated, in 1929, by Beritov and Topurin who brought the "stronger than" CR to complete differentiation, and noted that its existence is preceded by a stage named intercomponental, in which the CR to the second CS was facilitated by the activation of the first CS, and by a still earlier, pure-componental, stage in which each CS evoked a CR but the first did not affect the second (cp. preceding paragraph). The final developmental stage of a wholly differentiated "stronger than" CR reaction must, the authors argue, be mediated by a "new extra [or supplementary; Russian: *dopolnitel'ny*] neural center" coming into being in the course of the conditioning. On the other hand, since their data have shown that the "stronger than" CR manifested little generalization when the pitch of the two tones was substantially changed, the authors argue further that learned or conditioned intensity relations in dogs must be specific rather than general CR acquisitions.

The concept of an "extra neural center" pervades the main series of compound CR experiments in the Beritov laboratory (Beritov, 1932, 1937; Beritov & Bregadze, 1929a, 1929b, 1930; Beritov, Bregadze, & Wolinsky—unpublished, cited by Beritov—1932; Beritov & Topurin, 1929; Bregadze, 1930, 1937; Bregadze & Tarugov, 1937) in which seven dogs and two rabbits were used. The CR in the series was running to the feeding box and the CSs a variety of musical triads; sequences of three or four tones; a simultaneous compound of two tones and two bells differing in intensity and timbre; and a screen that could be illuminated in differing portions, shapes, and locations. The objective was to study fully the development of differential compound-component and sequence-sequence conditioning through both differential reinforcement and overtraining as well as note the stages preceding the development. Besides tests of conditioning in several consecutive training stages, there were also made in a number of cases consecutive tests of generalization of extinction from one CS situation to another.

The results of the main series corroborated and extended the preliminary findings in both Beritov's own and other Russian laboratories. Only the two rabbits, *Maya* and *Rita,* failed some of the configural tasks. The dogs mastered all of them. They were able not only to retain full CRs to simultaneous compounds and to particular sequences of successive compounds while all components and combinations of components and differing sequences became ineffective, but could also be trained to form CRs to components when their compounds became inactive, as well as to form differing CRs such as running to different feeding boxes when compounds and constituent components or compounds and differing sequences were administered. In most instances, differential reinforcement was the means of training. Yet in some, CR compound overtraining sufficed, and Beritov stated as early as 1932 that: *"Differentiation of individual components of a compound is effected by itself through training of the compound, but the differentiation of constituent combinations of components requires several nonreinforced trials" (ibid., p. 365; his italics).* As we shall see in forthcoming paragraphs, Baru and his associates of Voronin's laboratory later demonstrated than even combinations of components may become wholly ineffective through CR compound overtraining without any nonreinforcement.

More than that, the 1929-1937 studies from the Beritov laboratory reaffirmed and further delineated the developmental stages of compound-stimulus conditioning through generalization of extinction tests. In these tests, it became quite evident that in the early componental stage of compound-CR training, extinction of CRs to components reduced considerably the CR to the compound even as the conditioning to the compound generalized to the conditioning of the components; but that in the later intercomponental stage, the extinction of only some components (presumably the stronger ones) produced compound effects so that the total generalization of extinction to compound was smaller; while in the final configural state there was but little interaction between the conditioning and extinction of the compound and the components. This finding may, interestingly, account for the developmental course of compound-without-component conditioning in Woodbury's (1943) experiment in which, too, three successive periods are evident: first 100 trials, when compound CR action is decreased; next 300 trials, when both compound and component CRs are increased; and final 1000 trials, when a gradual and eventually complete compound-component differentiation comes into being. The initial compound decrease might arguably be ascribed to a generalization of extinction from the nonreinforced trials of its constituent components, the later increase of both compound and component CR to a preponderance of the generalization of conditioning from the reinforced compound trials since generalization of extinction weakens in this stage, while the gradual development of the configural differentiation itself in Woodbury's main training period needs of course no special explanation following as it fully does Russian reports since the days of Zeliony and Babkin. And the finding is also generally in line with the results of Grings and his associates (1956, 1957, 1959) on the interaction of compound and component conditioning with human subjects.

On the other hand, it should be mentioned that Beritov and Topurin's data that a dog could be conditioned to a "stronger than" tone only after long training may well not hold for other stimulus relations. Kleshchov (1933) showed, for instance, that dogs condition initially to musical intervals, that is, specifically, that they generalize CRs from a conditioned fifth much more to other fifths than to thirds, even if the thirds are much closer to the conditioned fifth in absolute pitch; and my results (Razran, 1938) with 12 different musical intervals and four human subjects are quite similar.

Finally, it would seem instructive to juxtaposit Beritov's concept of an "extra neural center" for configural conditioning with a recent statement on the topic by Konorski (1959, pp. 195-196). Konorski writes:

There is much evidence collected both by Pavlov's school and in our laboratory showing that the cortical representation of the compound of conditioned stimuli cannot be simply considered as composed from the particular centres representing each element of the compound. First, the possibility of differentiation in which the compound plays a role of the positive conditioned stimulus while its elements are inhibitory speaks in favor of this conclusion. If the representation of this compound were nothing else than the sum of the centres of its elements such a differentiation would be of course impossible, because the sum of two inhibitory reflexes cannot result in the excitatory reflex. . . . All these data go to show that the compound stimulus must be considered as a stimulus different from its component stimuli. Of course it may be, and most often it is, similar to its elements, as judged by the high level of generalization between them. But it can be differentiated from its elements in exactly the same way as are differentiated simple stimuli when they are similar to one another.

THE VORONIN LABORATORY

Voronin's studies of compound salivary conditioning are reported in his 264-page 1948 monograph named "Analysis and Synthesis of Complex Stimuli in Normal and in Brain-Damaged Dogs: An Experimental Study" (Moscow, Akad. Med. Nauk.). The monograph contains significant evidence also on training dogs to execute various motor acts—jumping on a table, on a chair, over a barrier; lying down; and the like—in response to verbal, auditory, and gestural CSs, consideration of which is, however, beyond the scope of the present article. Eight dogs were experimented with in the normal state and each animal underwent moderate occipital, temporal, or occipital-temporal-parietal lesions. The CS was in all cases a successive three-component compound, two or all three components of which were of different sense modalities: e.g., metronome, noise, tactile stimulus; tone, sight of whirligig, noise; illuminated square, passive flexion of paw, rattling. The time sequence was: 10 sec during which the first component was applied; another 10 sec for the second component; and 25 sec for the application of the third component, 10 sec before and 15 together with feeding. The animals were permitted to finish their 18-20 g of meat powder, and the intertrial intervals were as a rule 5 min.

All CRs appeared after a few trials and in the course of their further training a variety of problems were investigated of which the following should be mentioned: (a) differentiation and overtraining-inactivation of compounds with one different component; (b) differentiation and overtraining of sequences other than the trained sequence; (c) differentiation and overtraining-inactivation of each constituent component of the compound; (d) the effects of the extinction of each component CR on the compound CR, and the general relative CR effectiveness of each component; (e) the effects of the omission of each of the components—to which must of course be added (f) the effects of the various brain lesions on the animals' CR action and CR characteristics during their normal state. There are so many parameters in the study and so much interaction between them that a large portion of the results is masked. Yet the indications are quite clear that (a) the cortical lesions affected mostly the differential and overtraining effects of the compound CR (what was called here configural conditioning and what Voronin classes as "synthesizing activity"); (b) the overtraining inactivated more readily differing sequences than constituent components; and (c) CR effectiveness of components correlated positively with their temporal closeness to the US of feeding although the intensity of the CSs was also a factor. Voronin emphasizes that his results differ from those of Beritov in that he found that CR compound overtraining had not wholly inactivated all component CR action, even if it did reduce such action very considerably. However, as he himself admits, the overtraining in his study was very moderate. Only one test of components is reported to have been made during 292-310 trials of compound training, one test during 361-426 trials, and one during 670-680 trials. (Nine tests of components during 5-73 compound training trials yielded mean component-compound CR magnitude ratios of .21, .53 and .81 for the first, second and third components, compared to mean respective ratios of .02, .43, and .62 of four component tests during 114-176 compounds trials.)

What Voronin was unable to show in salivary conditioning in dogs total inactivation of component conditioning through compound CR training, was fully demonstrated by his students with food-fetching conditioning in rabbits, dogs, and baboons. Their main results, as summarized recently (1959) by Baru, Malinovsky, Ovchinnikova, Prazdnikova, and Chernomordikov, are presented in Table 12-2. Six goldfish, 5 Greek turtles, 6 crows, 6 chickens, 3 pigeons, 8 rabbits, 2 dogs, and 2 baboons were used. The CS was in all cases a successive 3-component compound and the specific food-fetching CRs were: pulling a bead in the fish, biting a ring in the turtles and rabbits, pecking at a pedal in the birds, and pressing a lever in the dogs and baboons.

The data in Table 12-2 would seem to warrant six suggestive conclusions. (a) Overtraining of a CR compound may in itself wholly inactivate earlier-training conditioning of its constituent components and of nontrained sequences in birds, rabbits, dogs, and baboons, but not in fish and turtles; (b) The ease of obtaining the inactivation correlates positively with phyletic ascent of the experimental animals, being easiest in baboons, and hardest in birds and rabbits, and occupying an intermediate position in dogs. (c) Differing untrained sequences are more readily inactivated through compound overtraining than are constituent com-

Table 12-2————Configural conditioning in several classes and orders of vertebrates; total inactivation of constituent components and untrained sequences through overtraining of a successive 3-component compound: trials needed for inactivation (after Baru, Malinovsky, Ovchinnikova, Prazdnikova, and Chernomordikov)

KIND OF ANIMAL	NUMBER OF SUBJECTS	INACTIVATION OF SEQUENCES		INACTIVATION OF SEQUENCES	
		Number success-ful subjects	*Compound trials*	*Number success-ful subjects*	*Compound trials*
Goldfish	6	Not studied	—	2	780,[a] 1282 [b]
Greek turtles	5	No total success		No total success	
Birds	15	12	247-543	12	334-420
Rabbits	8	2 [c]	420, 650	2	678, 1200
Dogs	2	2	264, 270	2	399,[d] 410 [d]
Baboons	2	2	30, 60	2	30, 60

[a] 63 nonreinforced trials of components used.
[b] 144 nonreinforced trials of components used.
[c] When 28 nonreinforced trials of components were used, two rabbits were successful after 143 and 188 compound trials.
[d] CR to first component disappeared after 74 and 86 compound trials; to second, after 291 and 299 trials.

ponents. (*d*) The inactivation of the components correlates negatively with their temporal closeness to reinforcement. (*e*) Differential reinforcement produces inactivation more readily than does mere compound overtraining. (*f*) Total compound-component CR differentiation may be developed through differential reinforcement in fish, but in turtles such differentiation is only partial.

DYNAMIC STEREOTYPES

A portion of a pioneer experiment in the area by Asratyan (1938) and a succeeding study by Petrov (1940) will serve as illustrations. Asratyan's dog "Arch" possessed a well developed and overtrained CR stereotype of five positive and one negative component CSs, each *CS* applied for 20 sec at fixed intervals of 5 min. The order of application of the CSs and their normal relative magnitudes were as follows: bell, highest magnitude; metronome of 60 beats per minute, somewhat smaller; hissing sound, still smaller; negative metronome of 120 beats, CR either wholly absent or very small; light, smallest CR; tactile CS, CR on par with that of the hissing sound. Tests of the interiorization of the stereotyped pattern were made with four of the five positive CSs in trials—or rather experimental sessions since each trial lasted 32 min—205-211. That is, in each of these trials one particular CS was applied six times for 20 sec at intervals of 5 min—specifically, the metronome of 60 beats in Trials 205, 209, and 211; the hissing sound in Trials 206 and 210; the light CS in Trial 207; and the tactile CS in Trial 208.

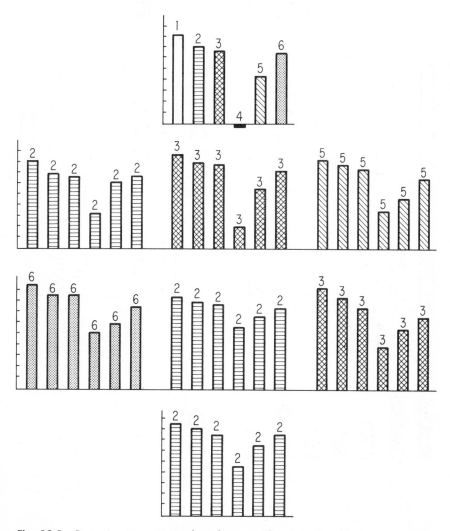

Fig. 12-1. Dynamic stereotypes in the salivary conditioning of a dog to one negative and 5 positive CSs (after Asratyan). Top bars—trained sequential pattern of CR magnitudes to individual CSs. Other bars—pattern of magnitudes when only one CS was applied throughout. 1—electric bell; 2—metronome of 160 beats per minute; 3—hissing sound; 4—differentiated metronome of 120 beats; 5—light; 6—tactile stimulus.

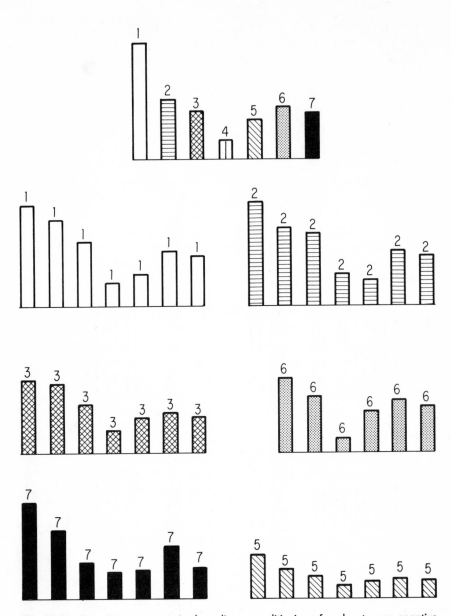

Fig. 12-2. Dynamic stereotypes in the salivary conditioning of a dog to one negative and 6 positive CSs (after Petrov). Top bars—trained sequential pattern of CR magnitudes to individual CSs. Other bars—pattern of magnitude when only one CS was used throughout. 1—metronome of 60 beats per minute; 2—noise; 3—crackling sound; 4—differentiated metronome of 75 beats; 5—light; 6—electric bell; 7—bubbling water.

The results of Test Trials 205-211 as well as of Training Trial 203 (for some reason, Trial 204 is not mentioned in the report) are presented in Figure 12-1, the bars of which have been copied from Asratyan's report. Clearly: (*a*) the exact pattern of descending and ascending values of CR magnitudes has been preserved in all seven trials; (*b*) hardly any changes occurred in the absolute magnitudes of the 35 CRs to the positive CS; and (*c*) the fourth position in the sequence, where during training the negative CS was administered, produced in all cases the smallest CR. Through overtraining, the dog learned to interiorize his CRs—to make them relatively independent of the specific nature of his environment-supplied CSs.

The main data in Petrov's study are quite similar. His dog "Krepysh" was trained for 17 months with a CR stereotype of one negative and six positive CSs: metronome of 150 beats per minute, noise, crackle, negative metronome of 75 beats, light, bell, and bubbling of water. Interstimulus intervals were, again, 5 min but each CS was applied for only 15 sec. The means of the CR magnitudes for each of the seven CSs in the last nine training sessions, November 17 through December 1, 1933, were, in salivary scale units (8 units in a drop): metronome, 70; noise, 42; crackle, 37; negative metronome, 16; light, 23; bell, 34; bubbling, 32. Testing sessions with only one CS were performed December 2, 4, 5, 7, 8, and 9—respectively with metronome, noise, crackle, bell, bubbling, light. The results of the six testing as well as the mean of the nine last training sessions are given in Figure 12-2. As may be seen in Figure 12-2, these results are equally clear-cut. In only one of the six tests was there a slight change in one of the seven positions in the patterned stereotype—noise test, position 4 and 5. And a significant reduction in absolute CR magnitudes occurred only in the last test with the light as the CS, which might be attributed either to some effect of extinction or to the fact that the light was the weakest CS in the stereotype—the latter being most likely.

Results of scores of other studies could be cited in support of the mentioned Asratyan and Petrov findings which, as far as I am aware, are almost *terra incognita* to CR experimenters outside the Soviet Union. And it should also be mentioned that, as discussed at the beginning of this article, these findings are in the main of a qualitative "mere-existence" type, little in need of special variance and design treatments.

THEORETICAL IMPLICATIONS

Only several summary theoretical statements will, for lack of space, be offered here. It is, for instance, quite evident that the data presented in this article strongly suggest that the disclosed specificities of compound-stimulus conditioning relate much more to mechanisms of integration and patternization in what is known as perception than to those of replacement and strengthening of reactions in conventional conditioning. Or, to put it differently, compound conditioning tells us more about compounding (or configuring) than about conditioning. True, compounding, like conditioning, is a learned modification coming into being through reaction-interactions; yet its resultant is quite different: concrescent novelty and supra-summation synthesis rather than additive and substractive shifts and concatenations. Moreover, compounding involves afferent-afferent reaction-interactions, whereas conditioning may well be largely a matter of interaction of afferent-efferent and efferent-efferent (chaining) reactions. And, again, unlike the efficacy of conditioning, that of compounding: (a) correlates highly with evolutionary ascent (most likely, totally absent in lower animals); (b) is much affected by moderate cortical lesions; and (c) at least in animals, is largely a function of considerable overtraining which brings it in line with recent American experimental findings and theoretical discussion on the effect of overlearning on transfer and habit reversal (Harlow, 1949, 1959; Mandler, 1962). Lastly —and of very special significance—adduced Russian studies on dynamic stereotypes lend empirical support to the tempting view that the mechanism of perceptual patternization inheres in the organism's interiorization or recoding of environment-supplied information in term of its own response-produced events—a view that expands old "motor-theories of consciousness" and is not unrelated to, although by no means identical with, sensory-tonic and (on the other hand) *aktualgenese* or microgenetic formulations of perception (Werner & Wapner, 1952; Undeutsch, 1942).

In short and at any rate, I am tempted, in view of all that has been said so far, to express a somewhat optimistic hope that just as simple conditioning has supplied a physical-behavioral body to the phenomenal mind-data of traditional Associationism, compound conditioning will do equally for the phenomenal mind-data of traditional Perceptionism, the mental chemistry and creative synthesis of which have troubled psychology since the days of John Stuart Mill and Wilhelm Wundt—and even earlier.[3]

[3] All cited—and uncited—studies do not, however, by themselves warrant, in my opinion, Hull's (1943, p. 379) thesis that "the response of organisms to stimulus configurations is logically secondary . . . the result of a rather complex process of learning" in the sense that it is invariably so. Some configures may well be phyletic acquisitions and immediate data of conditioning (cp. Kleshchov's aforementioned finding of a dog's immediate conditioning to a musical interval). What seems more warranted is the view that, inasmuch as configures are formed and deformed through learning, their role is much more a function of the organism's conditioned past than of its sensory present, and, moreover, that their learning reveals the dynamic essence of their "becoming" if not also of their "being." Discussing several of my experimental findings on configural conditioning in adult human subjects, I stated in 1939 that "the patternization of conditioned behavior—and possibly of all behavior—of adult human subjects is more affected by the habits, attitudes, sets, and interests of the subjects than by the sensory fields of the stimuli, their adjudged forces and organization" (Razran, 1939b, p. 104). I would tend now to substitute "higher organisms" for "adult human subjects" and surely to replace "more" by "very much more."

References

ASRATYAN, E. A. Systematicity in the work of the cerebral cortex. *Trud. fiziol. Lab. Pavlova,* 1938 *8,* 1-15.

BABKIN, B. P. Contributions to the study of the acoustic analyzer. *Trans. St. Petersburg Russ. Soc. Physicians,* 1910, *77,* 197-230.

BARU, A. V., MALINOVSKY, O. V., OVCHINNIKOVA, N. P., PRAZDNIKOVA, N. V., & CHERNOMORDIKOV, V. V. Conditioned motor food reflexes to chains of stimuli in some vertebrates. *Trud. Instit. Fiziol. I. P. Pavlova,* 1959, *8,* 107-113.

BECHTEREFF, V. M. *La psychologie objective.* Paris: Alcan, 1913.

BECHTEREW, W. M. *Objektive Psychologie oder Psycho-reflexologie. Die Lehre von den Assoziations-reflexen.* Leipzig-Berlin: Teubner, 1913.

BEKHTEREV, V. M. *General principles of human reflexology.* London: Jarrolds, 1933.

BERITOV, I. S. *Individually-acquired activity of the central nervous system.* Tbilisi: GIZ, 1932.

BERITOV, I. S., & BREGADZE, A. Physiology of behavior to complex stimuli: II. Individual reflex reactions of animals to complex sound stimuli. *Med. Biol. Zh.,* 1929, No. 3, 131-150. (a)

BERITOV, I. S., & BREGADZE, A. Physiology of behavior to complex stimuli: III. Role of special experimental settings and conditions. *Med. Biol. Zh.,* 1929, No. 4, 83-100. (b)

BERITOV, I. S., & BREGADZE, A. Physiology of behavior to complex stimuli: IV. Further studies on roles of component and complex reflexes. *Med. Biol. Zh.,* 1930, Nos. 1-2, 104-105.

BERITOV, I. S., & BREGADZE, A. Physiology of behavior to complex stimuli. *Trans. Soc. Russ. Physiologists,* 1931, No. 5, 45-46.

BERITOV, I. S., & TOPURIN, S. Physiology of behavior to complex stimuli: I. Individual reflexes to two successive stimuli. *Russ. Fiziol. Zh.,* 1929, *12,* 545-569.

BOLDYREV, V. N. The formation of conditioned (psychic) artificial [laboratory-trained] reflexes and their characteristics. (The transformation of auditory, olfactory, and visual stimuli into artificial stimulators of salivation.) *Trans. St. Petersburg Russ. Soc. Physicians,* 1905, *72,* 321-347.

BOLDYREV, V. N. The formation of conditioned (psychic) artificial [laboratory-trained] reflexes and their characteristics. (The transformation of local cooling of the skin into a stimulator of salivation.) *Trans. St. Petersburg Russ. Soc. Physicians,* 1906, *73,* 446-456.

BREGADZE, A. Physiology of behavior to complex stimuli: Food motor behavior to a complex visual figure. *Med. Biol. Zh.,* 1930, No. 6, 483-496.

BREGADZE, A. Study of individual reflexes to a complex figure. *Trans. Soc. Russ. Physiologists,* 1931, No. 5, 48-49.

BREGADZE, A. The formation of individual reactions to a complex of musical tones in dogs. *Trud. Instit. Beritashvili,* 1937, *3,* 415-430.

BREGADZE, A. Physiology of differentiation of successive tonal complexes. In *Materialy, 5th All-Union Congress Physiologists, Biochemists and Pharmacologists.* Moscow: Medgiz, 1943, P. 74.

BREGADZE, A., & TARUGOV, S. Individual reactions of rabbits to complex sound stimuli. *Trud. Instit. Beritashvili,* 1937, *3,* 431-447.

BYKOV, K. M. Characteristics of individual components of a complex (synthetic) stimulus. *Trud. fiziol. Lab. Pavlova,* 1925, *1,* 161-165.

CLAYTON, K. V. Reversal performance by rats following overlearning with and without irrelevant stimuli. *J. exp. Psychol.,* 1963, *66,* 254-259.

DOLIN, A. O. The synthetic reflex and physiological interrelations of its components. *Trud. fiziol. Lab. Pavlova,* 1940, *9,* 23-36.

GRINGS, W. W. *Stimulus patterning in learning.* Los Angeles: University of Southern California, 1957. (Dittoed manuscript.)

GRINGS, W. W., & O'DONNELL, D. E. Magnitude of response to compounds of discriminated stimuli. *J. exp. Psychol.,* 1956, *52,* 354-359.

GRINGS, W. W., & SHMELEV, V. N. Changes in GSR to a single stimulus as a result of training on a compound stimulus. *J. exp. Psychol.,* 1959, *58,* 129-133.

HARLOW, H. F. The formation of learning sets. *Psychol. Rev.,* 1949, *56,* 51-65.

HARLOW, H. F. Learning set and error factor theory. In S. KOCH (Ed.), *Psychology: A study of a science.* Vol. 2, New York: McGraw-Hill, 1959.

HOVLAND, C. I. Inhibition of reinforcement and phenomena of experimental extinctions. *Proc. Natl. Acad. Sci.,* 1936, *22,* 430-433.

HULL, C. L. *Principles of behavoir: An introduction to behavior theory.* New York: Appleton-Century-Crofts, 1943.

HUMPHREY, G. The effect of sequences of indifferent stimuli on a reaction of the conditioned response type. *J. Abn. & Soc. Psychol.,* 1928, *22,* 194-212.

IVANOV-SMOLENSKY, A. G. The analysis of a sequence of four conditioned stimuli. *Trud. fiziol. Lab. Pavlova,* 1927, *2,* 47-91.

KASHERININOVA, N. A. *Contributions to the study of salivary conditioned reflexes to tactile stimuli in dogs.* St. Petersburg: Military Medical Academy, 1908. (Thesis.)

KLESHCHOV, S. V. The relations of tones as conditioned stimuli. *Trud. fiziol. Lab. Pavlova,* 1933, *5,* 213-218.

KONORSKI, J., & LAWICKA, W. Physiological mechanisms of delayed reactions: I. The analysis and classification of delayed reactions. *Acta Biol. Exp.,* 1959, *19,* 175-196. Appendix 3.

KUNSTMAN, K. I. Conditioned reflexes to chains of stimuli. *Izv. Instit. Lesgafta,* 1923, *7,* 57-84.

KUPALOV, P. S., & GANTT, W. H. The relations between intensities of conditioned stimuli and magnitudes of conditioned reflexes. *Trud. fiziol. Lab. Pavlova,* 1928, *2,* 1-12.

MANDLER, G. From association to cognition. *Psychol. Rev.,* 1962, *69,* 415-427.

NIKOLAEFF, P. N. Contribution a l'analyse des reflexes conditionnels complexes. *Arch. Sci. Biol. St. Petersburg,* 1911, *16,* 411-444.

NORTH, A. J., & STIMMEL, D. T. Extinction of an instrumental response following a large number of reinforcements. *Psychol. Rep.,* 1960, *6,* 227-234.

PALLADIN, A. Formation of laboratory conditioned reflexes to sums of stimuli. *Trans. St. Petersburg Russ. Soc. Physicians,* 1906, *73,* 393-401.

PAVLOV, I. P. Psychologie et psychopathologie animale experimentale. In *C. R. Cong. Intern. Med.* Madrid, 1903. Pp. 9-25. Also, *Izv. Imper. voy.-med. Akad.* St. Petersburg, 1903, *7,* 109-114.

PERELTSVAYG, I. *Materials to the study of conditioned reflexes.* St. Petersburg: Military Medical Academy, 1907. (Thesis.)

PETROV, S. A. Dynamic stereotype effects on individual stimuli in different sequential positions. *Trud. fiziol. Lab. Pavlova,* 1941, *8,* 332-336.

PLATONOV, K. I. *The formation of associated motor reflexes to simultaneous auditory and visual stimuli in human subjects.* St. Petersburg: Military Medical Academy, 1912. (Thesis.)

RAZRAN, G. Conditioned responses in animals other than dogs. A behavioral and quantitative critical review of experimental studies. *Psychol. Bull.,* 1933, *30,* 261-324.

RAZRAN, G. Studies in configural conditioning: VII. Ratios and elements in salivary conditioning to various musical intervals. *Psychol. Rev.,* 1938, *2,* 370-376.

RAZRAN, G. Studies in configural conditioning: I. Historical and preliminary experimentation. *J. gen. Psychol.,* 1939, *21,* 307-330. (a)

RAZRAN, G. Studies in configural conditioning: II. The effect of subjects' attitudes and of task-sets upon configural conditioning. *J. exp. Psychol.,* 1939, *24,* 95-105. (b)

RAZRAN, G. Studies in configural conditioning: III. The factors of similarity, proximity, and continuity in configural conditioning. *J. exp. Psychol.,* 1939, *24,* 202-210. (c)

RAZRAN, G. Studies in configural conditioning: IV. Gestalt organization and configural conditioning. *J. of Psychol.,* 1939, *7,* 3-16. (d)

RAZRAN, G. Studies in configural conditioning: VI. Comparative extinction and forgetting of pattern and of single-stimulus conditioning. *J. exp. Psychol.,* 1939, *24,* 432-438. (e)

RAZRAN, G. Studies in configural conditioning: V. Generalization and transposition. *J. gen. Psychol.,* 1940, *56,* 3-11.

RAZRAN, G. Partial reinforcement of salivary CRs in adult human subjects: preliminary study. *Psychol. Rep.,* 1955, *1,* 409-416.

RAZRAN, G. Recent Soviet phyletic comparisons of classical and of operant conditioning: experimental designs. *J. comp. Physiol. Psychol.,* 1961, *54,* 357-365.

RICKMAN, V. The problem of the intensity of conditioned reflexes. *Trud. fiziol. Lab. Pavlova,* 1928, *2,* 13-20.

SIEGEL, S., & WAGNER, A. R. Extended acquisition training and resistance to extinction. *J. exp. Psychol.,* 1963, *66,* 308-310.

STROGANOV, V. V. Development of a conditioned reflex to and differentiation from compound stimuli. *Pavlov 75th Jub. Vol.,* 1925, *369-377.

UNDEUTSCH, U. Die Aktualgenese in ihrer allgemeinpsychologischen und ihrer charakterlogischen Bedeutung. *Scientia,* 1942, *72,* 37-42.

USIYEVICH, M. A. A new functional method to overcome developing hypnotic states in dogs. *Trud. fiziol. Lab. Pavlova,* 1940, *9,* 137-147.

USNADZE, D. Zum Problem der Relationserfassung beim Tier. *Arch. ges. Psychol.,* 1927, *60,* 361-390.

VORONIN, L. G. *Analysis and synthesis of complex stimuli in normal and in brain-damaged dogs: an experimental study.* Moscow: Akad. Med. Nauk, 1948.

VORONIN, L. G. *Analysis and synthesis of complex stimuli in higher animals.* Leningrad: Medgiz, 1952.

Voronin, L. G. *Comparative physiology of higher nervous activity.* Moscow: Moscow University, 1957.

Voronin, L. G. Some results of comparative-physiological investigations of higher nervous activity. *Psychol. Bull.,* 1962, *59,* 161-195.

Voskoboynikova-Granstren, E. E. 50°C warmth as a new artificial [laboratory-trained] conditioned stimulus of the salivary gland. *Trans. St. Petersburg Russ. Soc. Physicians,* 1906, *73,* 381-384.

Werner, H., & Wapner, S. Toward a general theory of perception. *Psychol. Rev.,* 1952, *59,* 324-338.

Wickens, D. D. Conditioning to complex stimuli. *Amer. Psychologist,* 1959, *7,* 180-188.

Wickens, D. D., Born, D. G., & Wickens, C. D. Response strength to a compound conditioned stimulus and its elements as a function of the element interstimulus interval. *J. comp. physiol. Psychol.,* 1963, *56,* 727-731.

Wickens, D. D., Gehman, R. S., & Sullivan, S. N. The effect of differential on set time in the conditioned response strength to elements of a stimulus complex. *J. exp. Psychol.,* 1959, *58,* 85-93.

Woodbury, C. B. The learning of stimulus patterns by dogs. *J. comp. Psychol.,* 1943, *35,* 29-40.

Zeliony, G. P. The reactions of dogs to auditory stimuli. St. Petersburg: Military Medical Academy, 1907. (Theses); preliminary communication *Trans. Soc. Physic. St. Petersburg,* 1906, *73,* 337-357.

Zeliony, G. P. Contribution a l'analyse des excitants complexes des reflexes conditionnels. *Arch. des Sci. St. Petersburg,* 1910, *15,* 437-453.

LEONARD E. ROSS

University of Wisconsin

13

Eyelid Conditioning as a Tool in Psychological Research: Some Problems and Prospects [1]

Much of this paper is derived from a review of the eyelid conditioning literature recently completed by Tom Hartman and myself (Ross & Hartman, in press). In the course of trying to integrate and summarize recent eyelid conditioning studies, several previously vague impressions emerged in rather clear cut form. The two principal ones that I want to discuss are in a sense contradictory: the relative neglect of some very important methodological problems, and the failure to use eyelid conditioning as a tool in several areas of psychological research where it appears to have considerable potential.

Eyelid conditioning is often characterized as a relatively well developed experimental procedure. Impressions of the simple, well controlled, nature of the eyelid conditioning situation probably result from a classical conditioning halo effect, since classical conditioning has generally been considered to have these desirable features. Furthermore, in comparison to other learning situations, the techniques employed in eyelid conditioning seem to be well developed since there have been a relatively large number of methodological studies that hopefully have resulted in carefully controlled, well understood, procedures.

Those working in the area recognize that while eyelid conditioning may be simple compared to some other experimental techniques used to investigate learning, it is still a very complicated technique. It is only

[1] This paper was made possible by support from National Science Foundation Grant GB-765, and Grant MH 06333-02 from the National Institute of Mental Health. The author expresses his thanks to Judy Yeager for her help in the preparation of the manuscript. The final draft was prepared while the author was a Kennedy Foundation Fellow at Peabody College.

very recently, however, that some of the complexities resulting from the active involvement of the S in the experimental situation have become so obvious that they can no longer be ignored. I believe the recognition of these problems is due to three developments: (1) the methodological difficulties that have arisen concerning the identification of different kinds of responses; (2) the presence of data that are difficult to interpret without recognizing the S as something more than a passive appendage of a conditionable eyelid; and (3) the controversies that have grown from failures to replicate certain phenomena from laboratory to laboratory.

In the first section of this paper I will discuss some methodological problems that will, I believe, seriously limit the usefulness of eyelid conditioning until they are resolved. Despite these problems, it seems quite apparent that eyelid conditioning has not been utilized as a research tool in several areas of research where it might be expected to be very useful. The second section will survey these possible applications.

METHODOLOGY: PROBLEMS

"Voluntary" Responding

One of the first topics to be considered when discussing the methodology of eyelid conditioning is the modification of the definition of the conditioned eyelid response that has taken place since the early conditioning studies. The procedure of removing the short latency "alpha" response and the longer latency "beta" response from data has been adopted by a great majority of laboratories. Somewhat more controversial, and of more interest for the present discussion, is the removal of the type of responses generally called "voluntary." Investigators have gone from an early interest in voluntary responding (e.g., Hilgard & Marquis, 1940), through a phase where some laboratories routinely removed the data of Ss who met certain "voluntary" response criteria and now, since it appears that there are many problems that remain to be solved, into a new phase of interest and concern with voluntary responses and the variables that produce them.

The analysis of eyelid conditioning data for the removal of voluntary responses started with Spence and Taylor's (1951) observation that some Ss gave a high incidence of responses characterized by a sharp closure of the eyelid with the eye remaining closed until after the air puff was received. They further noted that these responses were similar in form to those given by subjects instructed to blink to avoid the air puff, and by subjects who reported they had been voluntarily blinking to avoid the air puff. In an attempt to avoid the complications posed by this kind of response, which apparently followed different laws than did irregular responses of longer latency, these authors suggested a criterion for the removal of voluntary responses from the data. This was a latency criterion since, with the experimental conditions employed, the majority of responses showing voluntary response characteristics occurred during the 200-300 msec. interval following the onset of the CS, and latency provided a more objective criterion than judgments of form. The CRs of Ss not showing this response pattern seemed to occur predominantly between 300 and 500 msec. In a later study (Spence & Ross, 1959), Ss were given conditioning trials with quite a strong air puff in order to elicit a large number of voluntary form responses. The latency distribution of these responses was plotted and various criteria tried in order to most efficiently eliminate them from the data, while simultaneously eliminating a minimum number of nonvoluntary form responses. The results of this study confirmed the appropriateness of the previously used latency criterion. Since then two further studies have examined latency criteria. The first found clear indications that latency criteria are not as appropriate as a derivative (slope of response) measure when a ready signal is not given prior to each trial (Hartman & Ross, 1961). In a second study Hartman, Grant, and Ross (1960) found a correspondence between latency distributions of responses judged voluntary by various criteria and those elicited by instructions to the subject to blink to avoid the air puff. Finally, Goodrich (1963) recently has presented both ready and no-ready signal trials to the same Ss and found that with a ready signal the voluntary responses were of a shorter latency than in the absence of the signal, and that the distribution of "nonvoluntary" responses was unaffected by presence or absence of the ready signal.

Rather than elaborate on these results and the results of other studies that have analyzed data with an interest in voluntary responders, I would like to briefly discuss the rationale that led to the use of voluntary response criteria, and the implications of voluntary responding for the use of eyelid conditioning in psychological research. Concern here is with the fact that the response measure in eyelid conditioning is susceptible to volitional control by the S. This has been generally understood, but it poses certain problems that as yet have not been fully faced. Let me first state the position with which I am in accord and then go on to present objections that have been made to voluntary responder classification procedures.

It seems to me that voluntary response analyses are only a way of taking a more molecular look at the data. Currently a trend in this same direction is apparent in other learning areas, e.g., the micromolar work of Logan in instrumental alley situations, and the examination of several properties of the free operant response. As stated by Spence and Ross (1959), the rationale behind the procedure of eliminating Ss whose responses are primarily of the short latency, voluntary form is that such responses are:

> ...governed by different laws than those obtaining in the case of the longer latency class of responses. Thus our studies have indicated that the conditioning performance levels of Ss who fall into the voluntary group are not related either to level of a Manifest Anxiety score or to intensity of the UCS as is the case with the nonvoluntary group...Moreover, performance curves of conditioning obtained with such Ss differ markedly from those of Ss whose responses are predominantly nonvoluntary in form. Not only do they start at a much higher level, but they also tend to reach their asymptotes at a much earlier stage of training. (p. 377)

Vigorous objections to the voluntary response criteria approach have been presented by Gormezano and Moore (1962), and Moore and Gormezano (1963). According to these authors, Ss should not be eliminated unless their voluntary response characteristics are not a function of independent variables employed in the conditioning procedure:

> Unless it has been empirically determined that the response characteristics attributed to voluntary responders, and employed as criteria in their selection, are not a function of independent variables employed in the conditioning procedure, the equally valid assumption can be made that Ss will be rejected as voluntary responders for behavior lawfully related to different independent variables and/or different values of the independent variables...the basic difficulty is that one is forced into the logically difficult position of having to employ criteria in the selection of these Ss which have been shown to be invariant, not only for a restricted set of conditioning parameters, but for the infinite population of parameters. In the absence of such cross validation of these criteria, one is confronted with the possibility of erroneously classifying (or failing to classify) different numbers of Ss as voluntary responders for behavior functionally related to the conditioning parameters employed. (Gormezano & Moore, 1962, p. 493)

They further suggest that, "Ss classified as voluntary responders on the basis of response latency are simply those with higher learning rate parameters" (Moore & Gormezano, 1963, p. 257). I would like to examine their argument since it appears to be quite basic to the methodological problems posed by the volitional involvement of the S. Its acceptance would, I believe, have quite serious consequences for the further methodological development of eyelid conditioning.

In considering this position one must recognize, of course, that the most appropriate, i.e., most useful, degree of "molecularity" in an experimental situation is always an empirical question. It is possible that in some situations, with certain kinds of relationships being investigated, the involvement of a different kind of response in the data is not of great importance. However in many cases the failure to recognize the interaction of voluntary responding with experimental variables could be misleading. While Gormezano and Moore argue that we should not analyze for these different types of responses, I would argue that in fact it is extremely important to recognize situations where the effect of an experimental variable is due to a different mode of responding on the part of the S. Surely if differential effects of our experimental variables are in some cases due to a qualitatively different kind of responding we should know about it. Similarly, if at some value of a variable the S shifts to a different mode of responding we would want to identify that value. I would further point out that one does not "violate" the data by such an analysis, nor is one in some way destroying data. It would obviously be ridiculous to include "alpha" and "beta" responses just because they occur; and while it is possible that voluntary responses are more complicated, in the sense of being a function of more experimental parameters and of some S variables that are apparently more difficult to control, the rationale for their identification and evaluation remains the same.

There are a number of independent variables that have been demonstrated to increase greatly the frequency of voluntary form responses. It was recognized quite early in conditioning work that instructions could result in Ss adopting this form of response and, as one might expect, the frequency of such responses increase as the strength, and therefore the noxiousness, of the UCS is increased. In fact it might be expected that any feature of the experimental situation that explicitly or implicitly encourages the S to violate his instructions, which typically are inhibitory to a greater or lesser degree, would increase the number of voluntary responses. Our lack of knowledge about these factors is of course very unfortunate, and it is hoped that these variables may eventually be brought under experimental control. It does, however, seem reasonable to look now for those situations where the experimental conditions might encourage voluntary responding and to work toward a better understanding of their occurrence.

The impossibility of relying upon common sense prediction when these undefined S "set" variables are involved is illustrated by considering one situation which surely would be suspect in terms of the involvement of voluntary responses: classical avoidance eyelid conditioning, where complete omission of the air puff is contingent upon the occurrence of a response preceding the air puff. We might expect many Ss to adopt voluntary responding, since escaping the puff entirely should be more rewarding than in the case of the "defense" response in the classical situation, where the air puff falls on the closed eyelid. On the other hand, it has been observed that some Ss react to an omitted puff in quite a different manner. For example, Ss who have received partial reinforcement have reported that they felt the E was trying to make them feel silly since they blinked and then there was no puff! Furthermore there are undoubtedly S personality factors that interact with the experimental conditions to determine whether avoidance conditions are more, or less, apt to result in voluntary responses than the usual classical conditions. Clearly at our present stage of knowledge it is useless to engage in such speculation. Despite the fact that we need studies investigating functional relationships that hold between different modes of responding and experimental, situational, and individual difference variables, we can at the present time look at the data to see if we have qualitatively different kinds of responses and then decide if we want to consider the different types separately.

There have been a few studies which have compared the differential conditioning performance of Ss classified as voluntary and nonvoluntary. Hartman and Grant (1962a) found that degree of discrimination increased progressively as CS-UCS interval increased for voluntary Ss, while nonvoluntary Ss showed optimal differential conditioning at an intermediate (800 msec.) value. The authors conclude that "the differences between the CS-UCS interval functions for the Vs and Cs indicate that in the differential conditioning situation as in the simple conditioning situation . . . the Vs follow different behavioral laws in the eyelid conditioning situation than do the Cs" (p. 133). Goodrich, Markowitz and Wall (1963) have recently compared the differential conditioning performance of voluntary and nonvoluntary Ss with a 500 msec. CS-UCS interval. After giving their Ss 60 trials of continuous reinforcement followed by 90 trials of differential reinforcement, they found no difference in the differential responding to the positive and negative stimuli on the part of the voluntary and nonvoluntary Ss. Hartman and Grant have also failed to find such a difference at approximately the same CS-UCS value.

Goodrich, Markowitz and Wall speculate that in their experiment there was "insufficient time following CS onset for S to identify which CS it was and control his responding appropriately," since the Hartman and Grant data indicate the difference should occur at longer CS-UCS intervals. Goodrich, Markowitz and Wall ". . . wonder whether the outcome of experiments . . . may not depend on the degree to which S 'trusts' the source of information." They suggest that if a voluntary S is one who is especially annoyed by the air puff, he might require greater certainty with "no UCS" information than a nonvoluntary S before ceasing to respond. This seems quite a reasonable hypothesis that would fit with the present data, as well as with the continued responding of voluntary Ss in extinction reported by Hartman and Grant (1962b).

Finally Goodrich, Markowitz and Wall report that the voluntary Ss began at a higher response level and maintained their superiority throughout training which is consistent with data discussed by Spence and Ross (1959). Special caution is necessary in interpreting such averaged voluntary responder curves, since individual voluntary S curves show jump type "acquisition" functions much more frequently than is the case with nonvoluntary Ss. There is, however, considerable variability in the speed with which voluntary responding is adopted, and it may be necessary to include some index of this in future refinements of voluntary criteria.

In concluding this discussion of voluntary responding I would like to discuss two examples of situations where the involvement of voluntary responders is of considerable importance. The first is the previously mentioned study by Moore and Gormezano (1963), which was designed to compare two nonreinforcement techniques used in partial reinforcement: UCS omission and UCS delay. After comparing the final performance levels of Ss given various reinforcement percentages under either puff omitted or puff delayed conditions, they concluded that the "decremental effects attributable to nonreinforcement alone can be spuriously overestimated by using a UCS delay procedure" (p. 256). Let us consider this statement. Looking at their 50 percent partial reinforcement data, the puff omitted group appears to asymptote at something over 80 percent, the puff delay group at approximately 60 percent. If we compare these performance levels with those of previous studies involving partial reinforcement (Table 13-1), it is very obvious that the puff omitted performance level in this study is a great deal higher than has been previously found. Furthermore, the response latency distributions of the omission and delay groups are quite different, with the omission group showing a distribution that is very similar to that of Ss judged voluntary by form criteria (Hartman & Ross, 1961), or for Ss instructed to blink to avoid the puff (Hartman, Grant, & Ross, 1960). When we consider the high level of responding and the latency distribution, it appears quite plausible that the omitted-delayed difference reflects the adoption of voluntary responding on the part of the omitted puff Ss. This is supported by the fact that a 350 msec. latency criterion resulted in 12 of the 20 puff omission Ss being classified as voluntary. as compared to 5 of the 20 in the puff delay group. Certainly the author's conclusions need to be qualified since the lower levels of performance found by other investigators may simply reflect procedures less likely to result in voluntary responses.

The argument that voluntary Ss are simply conditioners with high rate parameters is similar to the recent use of eyelid conditioning data by Estes in developing his all-or-none formulation of the learning process. For example Estes (1960) has taken the data of the first few acquisition trials from a large number of Ss and computed the probability of a conditioned response for Ss who had previously failed to give a condi-

Table 13-1————Approximate performance levels of *S*s receiving partial reinforcement

	INVESTIGATOR	PUFF STRENGTH lb/in ^{2}	# OF TRIALS	# *S*s	PERFORM. LEVEL	VOL. RS.
	Moore & Gormezano (1963)	3.09	80	15	54%	out
	Moore & Gormezano (1963)	3.09	80	20	60%	in
DELAYED UCS	Reynolds (1958 Reinf. 60%)	2.0	100	36	51%	out
	Ross (1959)	2.0	220	20	48%	out
	Ross & Spence (1960)	.33, .6, 1.0, 4.0	140	30, 14 9, 18	38%	out
	Spence & Trapold (1961)	2.0	100	20	47%	out
	Froseth & Grant (1961)	2.90	80	20	33%	in
	Grant & Hake (1951 day 1)	—	48	20	48%	in
	Grant & Schipper (1952 day 1)	adequate	60	14	45%	in
OMITTED UCS	Grant, Schipper, & Ross (1952 day 1)	adequate	60	18	30%	in
	Gynther (1957)	1.74	100	14	38%	in
	Hartman & Grant (1960)	2.90	80	20	65%	in
	Moore & Gormezano (1963)	3.09	80	8	77%	out
	Moore & Gormezano (1963)	3.09	80	20	86%	in

tioned response on one, two, or three consecutive trials. The finding that the sequence of probabilities was practically constant was interpreted as supporting the all-or-none position with respect to the learning process. Here obviously the adoption of voluntary responding would be an important factor to consider before drawing conclusions regarding the speed of the learning process. Voluntary *S*s certainly are fast in starting to respond before the puff, but whether we want to consider them fast conditioners is another question. One could insure sudden, fast acquisition by increasing the strength of the puff to an extremely noxious level, or, to go to another kind of extreme, by instructing the *S* to blink when the CS occurs. It is doubtful whether those involved in the all-or-none vs. gradual learning controversy are referring to this sort of situation, and it certainly would be a matter of interest to know whether or not data interpreted as supporting the all-or-none position contains a large number of voluntary responders. We might well have a gradation from gradual to all-or-none kinds of learning as a function of experimental variables in the situation that result in more and more voluntary responding. Of course it may be that *Ss* are in fact conditioned "underneath" their voluntary responding. The point is that if this is the case we do not know how gradual the acquisition process is, or what its final level would have been, if voluntary responding had not been adopted. Here then is another situation where a voluntary response analysis would be very helpful.

Set Factors with Inhibitory Effects

I now want to consider factors that produce an opposite effect; that is, the notion that subjects may adopt, under certain experimental conditions, some kind of "set" or "cognitive" behavior that has the effect of depressing performance. It has often been noted by experimenters that some *Ss* appear to be "actively" resisting conditioning, in the sense of trying to keep from closing the eye during the conditioning trial. This is often apparent in the eyelid record as a slight opening of the eye prior to the receipt of the UCS. Occasionally such subjects report that they were trying to keep from blinking during the experimental session. Athletes, for example, sometimes say that they felt blinking to that little air puff would be a sign of weakness. There has been very little investigation of such inhibiting *Ss* although this characteristic is very probably related to personality factors of the *S* as well as to features of the experimental situation.

In addition to the complete inhibitor, there are two further lines of evidence which indicate the potent effect of inhibitory set factors in eyelid conditioning. The first of these is the well-known fact that partial reinforcement schedules produce considerably lower levels of performance than we find with continuous reinforcement. This is quite in contrast to the results found in some other learning situations; e.g., in instrumental work with animals where performance with intermittent reinforcement schedules often equals or exceeds that found with continuous reinforcement. While it is quite possible that this represents some fundamental difference in the learning processes involved, it would also seem reasonable that the decrement in eyelid conditioning in part represents some sort of inhibitory set adopted by the *S*. This notion is supported by the results obtained in studies where reinforcement schedules have suddenly been changed from 100 percent to 50 percent (Ross, 1959; Spence & Trapold, 1961; Runquist, 1963). The objective in my study (Ross, 1959) was to investigate the gradual growth of inhibition following a switch from continuous to intermittent reinforcement and a gradual increasing decrement with nonreinforced trials was expected. As it turned out, the continuous-to-partial group dropped immediately, within one or two trials, to the performance level of the partial group and remained there for the remaining trials. This sudden drop in performance obviously did not support the notion of the gradual growth of an inhibitory factor over a number of nonreinforced trials, and I suggested that the suddeness of the performance decrement indicated that set variables, i.e., variables related to some degree of inhibitory control, might be acting in the situation. Runquist (1963), and Spence and Trapold (1961), have presented data which replicates this sudden performance decrement. Runquist used quite different experimental conditions of no-ready signal, omission rather than delay of the UCS on nonreinforced trials, a longer CS-UCS interval, a longer UCS duration, and two separate UCS intensities, but still found the same general effect. In other studies Spence (1963) has presented data which indicate that the rate of extinction is closely related to the degree to which the subject recognizes a procedural change at the start of the extinction period, and Hartman and Grant (1962b) report that information as to whether or not a trial will be reinforced seems to result in "generalized inhibition," i.e., a reduced responsiveness rather than assistance in responding.

Assuming then that inhibitory set factors do operate in many of our experimental situations, we might well investigate those variables which influence Ss' perceptions of and reactions to the experimental situation. Here we find three obvious factors, instructions to the S, knowledge of the experiment, and the presence or absence of a ready signal preceding each trial. It has been demonstrated that variations of these factors may facilitate or depress conditioning performance, but as yet little is known about how they operate or how we may control their effects. As we pointed out in the Ross and Hartman paper (1963), these variables, as well as the relative sophistication of S, may represent considerable sources of variation in comparing conditioning data from laboratory to laboratory, or even in the case of intra-laboratory comparisons. We further suggested that procedures involving the assessment of the sophistication of the S, the standardization of procedures informing S of the nature of the experiment, and the specification of when the Ss were used relative to classroom discussions of classical conditioning might well be desirable.

In view of the relative lack of control of such variables it is not so surprising, but yet it is disturbing, that there have been several instances where investigators have been unable to replicate the results of other laboratories. Examples here include the different results found in studies where interpolated puff alone trials were given during conditioning (e.g., Dufort & Kimble, 1958; Goodrich, Ross, & Wagner, 1959), and the quite different conditioning performance levels found when Ss scoring high and low on the Taylor Manifest Anxiety Scale have been conditioned (e.g., King, Kimble, Gorman, & King, 1961; Spence, 1962). Spence has suggested that various factors such as the degree of emotionality produced in the S by the experimental situation, the interaction of S and E, the removal vs nonremoval of voluntary Ss, and the sophistication of S, may all be important in accounting for the differences found in the A scale studies. It is not very encouraging to note that the majority of these factors are typically uncontrolled and unreported in eyelid conditioning studies.

What then may we conclude after this brief survey of these methodological problems? We see that the S's involvement in the situation is a factor of critical importance for some kinds of experimental questions and a variable we should be concerned about, or aware of, in all studies. At the same time we do not yet know how to control these S factors since there has been a lack of studies investigating the effects of situational, procedural, and individual difference variables on the S's reaction to the conditioning situation. Just how far we have to go even in recognizing the influence of set or cognitive factors on eyelid performance is indicated by a recent study (Spence, 1963). In this experiment the introduction of a second learning task into the conditioning situation produced a markedly slower rate of extinction than was found without the distracting task. The group given the Estes-Straughan light-guessing procedure showed only a 14.4 percent drop across thirty extinction trials while a similar group without the added task dropped 45.2 percent. The author's statement that attempts to work with quantitative properties of intervening variables representing inhibition would have to "take account of these potent cognitive factors" would seem to be an understatement of the case. While we have carefully controlled the properties of, and time relations among, physical stimuli in the eyelid conditioning situation we have sadly neglected a large number of extremely important S variables.

There may be a bright side to these problems. In exploring these troublesome variables we may find valuable new research areas and, in addition, this type of research may lead to experimental controls that will allow some reduction in the relatively large variability now found in eyelid conditioning data. Both of these developments would be very welcome.

SOME NEGLECTED AREAS: PROSPECTS

It may seem inconsistent to argue that eyelid conditioning has been neglected as a research tool in various areas of psychology after having expressed these reservations about the methodological status of the technique. However, the fact that eyelid conditioning *has* been so neglected is the point I wish to make in this section of the paper. I believe there are several subject areas where eyelid conditioning work would be useful with the present state of our methodological knowledge. We obviously can't, and don't, wait to do research until all of the methodological problems in an area are solved. The realization that problems exist and the discovery of the extent to which they prove bothersome often comes only after a considerable amount of work.

Individual Difference Variables

As I mentioned before, the investigation of facilitating and inhibiting set factors pose interesting possibilities. Aside from obvious questions of what effects they have on the data, and how we may want to take this into account, there remains the possibility of an individual difference approach to these phenomena. Thus research relating various personality dimensions to eyelid conditioning and the adoption of voluntary or inhibitory sets may be feasible. For example, it may be possible to determine a kind of puff strength threshold at which Ss would adopt the voluntary form of response. Similarly by a combination of a weak puff and instructions we might obtain a large number of Ss meeting some inhibitory criterion. A comparison of the personality characteristics of inhibiting and voluntarily responding Ss would be of interest. Similar studies involving the personality characteristics of Ss who respond in certain ways in discrimination learning, partial reinforcement, and classical avoidance situations are possible. It may be that one of the most significant contributions of eyelid conditioning will come about through our growing ability to classify different modes of responses on a dimension from nonvoluntary to voluntary, and relate these both to personality factors and the traditional learning parameters.

A survey of eyelid conditioning experiments that might be considered to be oriented toward individual differences reveals a surprisingly meager effort. There has been little such research, aside from the extensive Taylor Manifest Anxiety scale literature and a few studies attempting to relate "physiological responsiveness" to conditioning, all of which is more properly considered to be concerned with the role of motivational factors in conditioning than with any kind of an individual difference analysis.

An example of the possibilities of a form of response analysis can be seen in considering an experiment by Warren and Grant (1955). These authors hypothesized that Ss who scored high on the psychopathic deviation (Pd) scale of the MMPI would

... tend to seek immediate gratification and avoid immediate annoyances, social pressure notwithstanding. It was predicted that these Ss having learned an avoidance response to an annoying stimulus (corneal airpuff), would fail to develop good conditioned discrimination because they would continue to respond to the negative stimulus, thus avoiding possible discomfort. This should occur in spite of instructions which lead to good discrimination in Ss with lower Pd scores. (p. 23)

This prediction was confirmed by the data, i.e., high Pds showed the least discrimination due to their high frequency of responding to the negative stimulus. Here a response form analysis would be quite appropriate. It might be expected that high Pd responses would be more voluntary in form, and a comparison of response form on positive and negative stimulus trials for the two groups could be quite useful. One also might expect noxiousness of air puff, or CS-UCS interval (see Hartman & Grant, 1962a), to be important parameters in such a situation.

Franks has been involved with a number of studies concerned with the conditionability of normal and neurotic Ss and the relationship of the introversion-extroversion dimension to eyelid conditioning (Franks, 1956, 1957; Franks & Leigh, 1959).[4] This is an extremely interesting and promising approach that is, however, disappointing due to the fact that so few conditioning parameters have been varied. That is, these studies have all involved 30 conditioning trials, interspersed with 18 nonreinforced test trials, followed by 10 extinction trials. While this is advantageous in allowing inter-study comparisons, it is unfortunate that conditioning and extinction were not carried out so that interactions of personality and learning variables could be investigated. Thirty trials is a very short conditioning period, especially since the 18 nonreinforced trials make it a 60 percent partial reinforcement situation. In view of the fact that some conditioning and extinction procedures increase the probability of voluntary responses, while others result in inhibitory tendencies, it would be reasonable to expect personality types to interact to a considerable extent with such factors. Some experimental procedures may be insensitive, some sensitive, in reflecting personality variables, but research involving the manipulation of a number of parameters is needed before we will know.

[4] For other studies comparing the eyelid conditioning performance of normal and neurotic or psychotic Ss, see Spence and Taylor, 1953; Taylor and Spence, 1954; Field and Brengelmann, 1961; and Sweetbaum, 1963. For a short discussion of Russian work with non-normal populations see Ross and Hartman, in press.

A similar restricted use of conditioning and extinction procedures is evident in work by Franks and Laverty (1955), which investigated the effect of sodium amytal on conditioning performance, and in an experiment by Das (1958) relating depth of hypnosis to the acquisition and extinction of the eyelid response. In these studies there is a pronounced contrast between the imaginative application of eyelid conditioning and the limited use of the technique. It might be hoped that those in personality areas will become more sophisticated in their application of eyelid conditioning to these problems, or those with a primary interest with eyelid conditioning will include more S variables in their future research.

Eyelid Conditioning with Children

The most surprising fact that comes to light when reviewing the eyelid conditioning literature is the almost total absence of studies dealing with eyelid conditioning in children. Aside from normal control groups run in a few experiments dealing with retarded children, the only study appears to be by Braun and Geiselhart (1959), where acquisition and extinction were compared in children (mean age 9.36 years), young adults (mean age 20.63 years), and old adults (mean age 70.5 years).[5]

While the Russians have made use of eyelid conditioning with children, their work has no counterpart in the United States. It is hard to understand why we do not have well controlled systematic developmental studies of learning utilizing eyelid conditioning. Even the development of verbal behavior could be profitably investigated, perhaps in a manner similar to that used in Hartman's study (1936), which involved conditioned response transfer from words to stimulus objects possessing characteristics of words. We can only hope that investigators will soon respond to these obvious opportunities for research.

[5] Three other studies, by Wenger (1936), Morgan and Morgan (1944), and Rendle-Short (1961), should be mentioned. Wenger used a tactile CS and light flash UCS with three neonates and reported unstable conditioning. The three sec. CS-UCS interval employed would not be expected to lead to conditioning. Morgan and Morgan reported no conditioning before 45 days. Rendle-Short found that children six months old and younger could not be conditioned but that conditioning became progressively easier until the "typical adult response of immediate conditioning" was reached at about four years of age. Retarded children were reported more difficult to condition than normal children of the same CA. It is difficult to evaluate these studies because of lack of control of stimuli and inter-stimuli intervals, and the fact that responses were only observed by the E. In the Morgan and Morgan study the E's hand was the CS and the CS-UCS interval was on E's count, estimated to average 1.8 sec. In the Rendle-Short experiment a puff gun held by the E was the CS with the CS-UCS interval a "moment" between presentation of the gun and its firing. E's control of the UCS intensity and location of impact must have been very poor. In both studies the responses were probably more of the voluntary type. Rendle-Short mentions that the Ss were either conditioned by 20 puffs or not at all.

There are undoubtedly many problems in working with children. Distracting tasks or games may be necessary to keep the child happy through the experimental session, especially in the case of younger children. Whether this will be as potent a factor with children as it appears to be with college sophomores remains to be seen. In most cases an auditory CS would seem necessary to eliminate the problem of receptor orientation, and considerable trouble may be encountered in trying to equate the effectiveness of the UCS for children of different ages. However, the experimental problems do not appear to be serious enough to preclude eyelid conditioning with children of all ages.

Retardation

Considering the current interest in learning processes in the retarded, the lack of research employing eyelid conditioning with mentally retarded Ss is regrettable. A relatively large amount of research has been carried out in instrumental selective learning situations with these Ss, yet a search of the literature shows only a handful of eyelid conditioning studies. Few in number, and limited to simple acquisition and extinction procedures, they still provide impressive examples of the possibility of the technique. Cromwell, Palk, and Foshee (1961) report a small but significant correlation between "conditioning rate" and MA, but no relationships between I.Q. or age and conditioning. Voluntary blinking was indicated "with fairly steady frequency through the 80 (acquisition) trials" but no analyses of voluntary responses by MA, I.Q. or chronological age were reported. Since MAs were quite low, ranging from 2-5 to 10-2 with a mean of 5-2, and the CS was an illumination of a 2" disk, "attention" to the CS could have played a role in the MA conditioning results. Systematic variation of the "obviousness" of CS stimuli with normal and retarded children would be interesting. Franks and Franks (1962a) found no difference in acquisition or extinction between "normal" Ss and "non-organic" mental defectives, but did find a large decrement on the part of "organic" defectives. Non-organic and organic were defined respectively as no demonstrable evidence of central nervous system deficit, and early damage of sufficient severity to be demonstrated as "unequivocally" having neurological impairment. As the authors point out, those in the non-brain-damaged retarded group probably did suffer from central nervous system impairment, but nevertheless the results are quite impressive in supporting the notion that conditioning is inversely related to degree of organic pathology. This study also failed to find a relationship between I.Q. and conditioning performance. Finally, Franks and Franks (1962b) report a relationship between the vocational adjustment of mental defectives and the acquisition of the conditioned eyelid response. Those with more effective work adjustment also showed more resistance to extinction. This is a surprising finding, especially since the authors report no indications of deliberate blinking or avoidance of blinking to any stimuli. Franks and Franks also suggest, optimistically, that with more research eyelid conditioning might turn out to be useful as a screening device for those with poor vocational adjustment prospects.

Eyelid conditioning appears to have several characteristics which particularly suit it for investigations of learning processes in the retarded. All of the "basic" learning phenomena can be studied, and eyelid procedures could be especially valuable in examining differences in, and comparing the inhibition processes utilized by, normals and the retarded. Consider, for example, the usual instrumental discrimination learning situation where the S's task is to respond to one stimulus or stimuli complex rather than another. It is quite obvious that in free choice situations the relative amounts of approach strength associated with the positive cue and inhibition developed to the negative cue are hopelessly confused in a choice or latency of response measure. As soon as the S's responses to the negative stimuli drop off in frequency we have lost our measure of response strength to that cue. A similar problem in evaluating the effects of reward and nonreward in reinforcement schedule switches or reversal learning is apparent. In attempting to avoid these problems, investigators have resorted to only moderately successful transfer and partial reversal paradigms in order to try to tease out the processes involved. Contrast this situation to that in differential eyelid conditioning, where the percent response curves give a clear picture of the relative response strengths to the positive and negative stimuli. When one considers the hypotheses that characterize the retarded child as one who suffers from an inability to inhibit responses, it is amazing that not a single differential eyelid conditioning study comparing retarded Ss with normal Ss can be found in the American psychological literature.

Very recently Charles Koski, Judy Yeager, and I have attempted to develop an eyelid conditioning procedure that could be used with all levels of retardates as well as with normal children (Ross, Koski, & Yeager, 1954). We decided to work with the severely retarded since we believed that a technique that proved successful with this population could also be used with other retardates and with normals.

The most serious problem in working with the retarded is obtaining their cooperation so that they will tolerate the eyelid apparatus, and keep their eyes open. The technique we employed was to show a silent movie during the conditioning session in order to distract the S. In addition we used a tone CS to eliminate problems of receptor orientation, and kept an experimenter by the S's side during the experimental session as a safety precaution and to make sure the S's eyes were open when the trial was initiated. Furthermore, fifty trials were the maximum given in any day.

This procedure was quite successful. Of 43 retardates taken from wards for the severely retarded, 40 completed three sessions successfully. All of these Ss were severely retarded, with no I.Q. above 30. In view of these results there appears to be no reason why systematic research cannot be carried out with retardates using this movie-distraction procedure.

Finally I would like to mention some planned research which I believe demonstrates the advantage of using eyelid conditioning to investigate the generality of behaviorial phenomena. Previous work with animals (Ross, 1962a, b, c) has indicated that the inhibition that develops to the nonrewarded cue in black-white discrimination learning persists, in terms of differential response speed, for a long period after both cues receive the same reinforcement schedule. As I have pointed out (Ross, 1962c), a similar phenomenon was reported by Pavlov, and there are indications from eyelid conditioning studies (primarily Spence & Trapold, 1961) that the same results would be found there. (A comparison of the performance of normal and retarded children in this type of inhibition situation will be of obvious interest). The point is that eyelid conditioning offers not only the opportunity to investigate the generality of the phenomenon but will also provide data that will allow a comparison of the effects of various parameters in the two situations. There is no reason why parallel programs of research on the same phenomena in instrumental animal and classical eyelid conditioning can not be carried out.

We already know that in some cases the effects of variables are different in these situations (e.g., partial vs continuous reinforcement in acquisition) but there has been little work comparing the two experimental situations in other ways. For example, the percent conditioned response curves in differential eyelid conditioning are quite similar to the running speed curves found in animal discrimination learning when trials are "forced" to the negative stimulus. Yet there are relatively few differential conditioning eyelid studies compared to the large literature in animal selective learning. Many of the phenomena investigated in the animal literature have not received attention from those doing eyelid conditioning. Contrast the extensive amount of animal work on reversal learning with the almost complete lack of such data involving eyelid conditioning. Presumably with research more and more "phenomena" centered, we may expect an increasing utilization of eyelid conditioning to investigate the generality of conditioning phenomena.

References

BRAUN, H. W., & GEISELHART, R. Age differences in the acquisition and extinction of the conditioned eyelid response. *J. exp. Psychol.,* 1959, *57,* 386-388.

CROMWELL, R. L., PALK, B. E., & FOSHEE, J. G. Studies in activity level: V. The relationships among eyelid conditioning, intelligence, activity level, and age. *Amer. J. ment. Def.,* 1961, *65,* 744-748.

DAS, J. P. Conditioning and hypnosis. *J. exp. Psychol.,* 1958, *56,* 110-113.

DUFORT, R. H., & KIMBLE, G. A. Ready signals and the effect of interpolated UCS presentations in eyelid conditioning. *J. exp. Psychol.,* 1958, *56,* 1-7.

ESTES, W. K. Learning theory and the new "mental chemistry." *Psychol. Rev.,* 1960, *67,* 207-223.

FIELD, J. G., & BRENGELMANN, J. C. Eyelid conditioning and three· personality parameters. *J. abnorm. soc. Psychol.,* 1961, *63,* 517-523.

FRANKS, C. M. Conditioning and personality: a study of normal and neurotic subjects. *J. abnorm. soc. Psychol.,* 1956, *52,* 143-150.

FRANKS, C. M. Personality factors and the rate of conditioning. *Brit. J. Psychol.,* 1957, *48,* 119-126.

FRANKS, C. M., & LAVERTY, S. G. Sodium amytal and eyelid conditioning. *J. ment. Sci.,* 1955, *101,* 654-663.

FRANKS, C. M., & LEIGH, D. A theoretical and experimental application of a conditioning model to a consideration of bronchial asthma in man. *J. psychosom. Res.,* 1959, *4,* 88-98.

FRANKS, V., & FRANKS, C. M. Conditionability in defectives and in normals as related to intelligence and organic deficit: the application of a learning theory model to a study of the learning process in the mental defective. In B. W. RICHARDS (Ed.), *Proc. London Conf. on the Scientific Study Ment. Def. 1960.* Dagenham, England: May & Baker, 1962. Pp. 557-583. (a)

FRANKS, V., & FRANKS, C. M. Classical conditioning procedures as an index of vocational adjustment among mental defectives. *Percept. Motor Skills,* 1962, *14,* 241-242. (b)

FROSETH, J. Z., & GRANT, D. A. Influence of intermittent reinforcement upon acquisition, extinction, and spontaneous recovery in eyelid conditioning with fixed acquisition series. *J. gen. Psychol.,* 1961, *64,* 225-232.

GOODRICH, K. P. Supplementary report: Effect of a ready signal on the latency of voluntary responses in eyelid conditioning. *J. exp. Psychol.,* 1964, *67,* 496-498.

GOODRICH, K. P., MARKOWITZ, J., & WALL, A. M. Differential.eyeblink conditioning in voluntary and nonvoluntary subjects. *Psychol. Rep.,* 1963, *13,* 723-730.

GOODRICH, K. P., ROSS, L. E., & WAGNER, A. R. Supplementary report: Effect of interpolated UCS trials in eyelid conditioning without a ready signal. *J. exp. Psychol.,* 1959, *38,* 319-320.

GORMEZANO, I., & MOORE, J. W. Effects of instructional set and UCS intensity on the latency, percentage, and form of the eyelid response. *J. exp. Psychol.,* 1962, *63,* 487-494.

GRANT, D. A., & HAKE, H. W. Dark adaptation and the Humphreys random reinforcement phenomenon in human eyelid conditioning. *J. exp. Psychol.* 1951, *42*, 417-423.

GRANT, D. A., & SCHIPPER, L. M. The acquisition and extinction of conditioned eyelid responses as a function of the percentage of fixed ratio random reinforcement. *J. exp. Psychol.*, 1952, *43*, 313-320.

GRANT, D. A., SCHIPPER, L. M., & ROSS, B. M. Effect of intertrial interval during acquisition on extinction of the conditioned eyelid response following partial reinforcement. *J. exp. Psychol.*, 1953, *44*, 203-210.

GYNTHER, M. D. Differential eyelid conditioning as a function of stimulus similarity and strength of response to the CS. *J. exp. Psychol.*, 1957, *53*, 408-416.

HARTMAN, T. F. Semantic transfer of the differential conditioned eyelid response from words to objects. *J. exp. Psychol.*, 1963, *65*, 194-200.

HARTMAN, T. F., & GRANT, D. A. Effect of intermittent reinforcement on acquisition, extinction, and spontaneous recovery of the conditioned eyelid response. *J. exp. Psychol.*, 1960, *60*, 89-96.

HARTMAN, T. F., & GRANT, D. A. Differential eyelid conditioning as a function of the CS-UCS interval. *J. exp. Psychol.*, 1962, *64*, 131-136. (a)

HARTMAN, T. F., & GRANT, D. A. Effects of pattern of reinforcement and verbal information on acquisition, extinction, and spontaneous recovery of the eyelid CR. *J. exp. Psychol.*, 1962, *63*, 217-226. (b)

HARTMAN, T. F., GRANT, D. A., & ROSS, L. E. An investigation of the latency of "instructed voluntary" eyelid responses. *Psychol. Rep.*, 1960, *7*, 305-311.

HARTMAN, T. F., & ROSS, L. E. An alternative criterion for the elimination of "voluntary" responses in eyelid conditioning. *J. exp. Psychol.*, 1961, *61*, 334-338.

HILGARD, E. R., & MARQUIS, O. G. *Conditioning and learning*, 1st ed. New York: Appleton-Century-Crofts, 1940.

KING, M. S., KIMBLE, G. A., GORMAN, J., & KING, R. A. Replication report: Two failures to reproduce effects of anxiety on eyelid conditioning. *J. exp. Psychol.*, 1961, *62*, 532-533.

MOORE, J. W., & GORMEZANO, I. Effects of omitted versus delayed UCS on classical eyelid conditioning under partial reinforcement. *J. exp. Psychol.*, 1963, *65*, 248-257.

MORGAN, J. J. B., & MORGAN, S. S. Infant learning as a developmental index. *J. genet. Psychol.*, 1944, *65*, 281-289.

RENDLE-SHORT, J. The puff test. *Arch. Dis. Childh.*, 1961, *36*, 50-57.

REYNOLDS, W. F. Acquisition and extinction of the conditioned eyelid response following partial and continuous reinforcement. *J. exp. Psychol.*, 1958, *55*, 335-341.

ROSS, L. E. The decremental effects of partial reinforcement during acquisition of the conditioned eyelid response. *J. exp. Psychol.*, 1959, *57*, 74-82.

ROSS, L. E. The effect of equal reinforcement of the positive and negative discriminanda of a learned discrimination. *J. comp. physiol. Psychol.*, 1962, *55*, 260-266. (a)

ROSS, L. E. Note: Persisting inhibitory effect found in both classical and instrumental learning situations. *Psychol. Reps.*, 1962, *11*, 691-692. (b)

Ross, L. E. The response to previous discriminanda during the learning of a new problem. *J. comp. physiol. Psychol.*, 1962, *55*, 944-946. (c)

Ross, L. E., & Hartman, T. F. Eyelid conditioning: The recent experimental literature. *Gen. psychol. Mong.*, in press.

Ross, L. E., Koski, C. H., & Yeager, J. Classical eyelid conditioning of the severly retarded: Partial reinforcement effects. *Psychon. Sci.*, 1964, *1*, 253-254.

Ross, L. E., & Spence, K. W. Eyelid conditioning performance under partial reinforcement as a function of UCS intensity. *J. exp. Psychol.*, 1960, *59*, 379-382.

Runquist, W. N. Performance in eyelid conditioning following changes in reinforcement schedule. *J. exp. Psychol.*, 1963, *65*, 617-618.

Spence, K. W. Anxiety (drive) level and performance in eyelid conditioning. *Psychol. Bull.*, 1964, *61*, 129-139.

Spence, K. W. Cognitive factors in the extinction of the conditioned eyelid response in humans. *Science*, 1963, *140*, 1224-1225.

Spence, K. W., & Ross, L. E. A methodological study of the form and latency of eyelid responses in conditioning. *J. exp. Psychol.*, 1959, *58*, 376-381.

Spence, K. W., & Taylor, J. A. Anxiety and strength of the UCS as determiners of the amount of eyelid conditioning. *J. exp. Psychol.*, 1951, *42*, 183-188.

Spence, K. W., & Taylor, J. A. The relation of conditioned response strength to anxiety in normal, neurotic, and psychotic subjects. *J. exp. Psychol.*, 1953, *45*, 265-272.

Spence, K. W., & Trapold, M. A. Performance in eyelid conditioning as a function of reinforcement schedules and changes in them. *Proc. National Acad. Sci.*, 1961, *47*, 1860-1868.

Sweetbaum, H. A. Comparison of the effects of introversion-extraversion and anxiety on conditioning. *J. abnorm. soc. Psychol.*, 1963, *66*, 249-254.

Taylor, J. A., & Spence, K. W. Conditioning level in the behavior disorders. *J. abnorm. soc. Psychol.*, 1954, *49*, 497-502.

Warren, A. B., & Grant, D. A. The relation of conditioned discrimination to the MMPI *Pd* personality variable. *J. exp. Psychol.*, 1955, *49*, 23-27.

Wenger, M. A. An investigation of conditioned responses in human infants. In M. A. Wenger, J. M. Smith, C. Hazard, & O. C. Irwin. Studies in infant behavior III. *Univ. Ia. Stud. Child Welf.*, 12, No. 1. Pp. 7-90.

MARTIN M. SHAPIRO
THOMAS M. MILLER
Emory University

14

On the Relationship Between Conditioned and Discriminative Stimuli and Between Instrumental and Consummatory Responses [1]

Most psychologists in the field of learning accept the convention of distinguishing between two types of conditioning, or, at least, between two types of experimental conditioning procedures. The validity or utility of such a classification system will not be discussed here. Rather, four particular points will be covered: (1) a technique which has been found to be useful, (2) data on the relationship between Pavlovian salivary conditioning and operant lever pressing, (3) the interpretations of these data, and (4) data pertaining to the relationship between Pavlovian conditioning and discriminative stimuli for operant responses.

In recent years, there have been numerous attempts (many of which appear to have been successful) to measure what commonly have been called consummatory responses. For example, many experimenters now record not only the frequency of lever pressing but also the frequency with which the animal licks the water mechanism that delivers the reinforcing stimulus, e.g., Premack (1961). Others not only record the panel-press responses of dogs in a shock avoidance situation, but also the cardiac responding that occurs concurrently (Black, 1959); and, to belabor the issue, still others record not only the instrumental response being conditioned, but also electro-encephalographic activity, e.g., Magoun (1961). However, it appears that the number of interpretations which have been made from the data far exceeds the number of different techniques employed. If sheer number were a measure of importance, a determination

[1] This research was supported by Grant No. MH-05713 from the National Institutes of Health, United States Public Health Service, and by the University of Houston. The authors express their appreciation to Miss Jean L. Bresnahan for her assistance during the various stages of this study.

of the relationship between instrumental and consummatory responses should be expected to have profound, theoretical significance.

Several years ago, Lauer, Shapiro, and Radell (1961) reported what they considered to be a greatly improved technique for measuring salivation in dogs during Pavlovian conditioning. A modification of this technique which permits the recording of salivation from a free moving dog has been reported only briefly (Shapiro, 1961b); the technique has been extended also to the preparation of the submaxillary duct in dogs.

A Preparation of the Parotid Salivary Duct

With as much asepsis as possible, a polyethylene tube is inserted into a parotid salivary duct (Stensen's duct), the only function of this tube being that it facilitates the later localization and identification of the duct (Figure 14-1a). The mouth of the dog then is closed; the dog is prepared, draped with sterile towels, and aseptic conditions are observed. An incision is made in the external labial tissue over the course of the duct. The duct is located and dissected free from the surrounding tissue (Figure 14-1b). A longitudinal incision is made in the wall of the duct and the polyethylene tube pulled from the distal end; at the same time, the proximal end of the duct and the polyethylene tube are clamped with a hemostat (Figure 14-1c). At this time the animal is ready for the permanent implantation of a specially prepared polyethylene tube (Figure 14-1d). The short end of the V-shaped tube is inserted into the duct and the duct then ligated. At this time the original tube is removed and that portion of the duct ligated to prevent any further communication with the mouth (Figure 14-1e). The suturing material tied to the tab at the crook of the "V" is then sewn into the surrounding tissue so that any subsequent pulling on the long end of the tube will result in pulling the surrounding tissue and not the duct itself (Figure 14-1f). A flexible metal probe is then used to pass the long end of the tube under the skin and out through a small incision on the external dorsal surface of the neck. The skin layer is then ready to be closed (Figure 14-1g). The end result is that the secretion of a parotid salivary gland now flows out the polyethylene tube instead of into the dog's mouth (Figure 14-1h). The surgical preparation takes thirty minutes to one hour.

A Preparation of the Submaxillary Salivary Duct

With a small alteration, the polyethylene tubing used in the parotid preparation can be modified to accommodate the submaxillary duct in the dog. A wire is inserted five inches into the tubing. Two ninety degree turns, approximately one-half inch apart, are made in the tubing by bending the wire within the tube; a polyethylene tab is then heat welded to

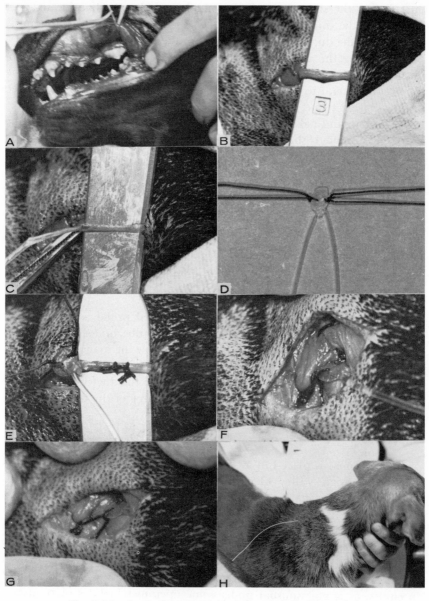

Fig. 14-1. Surgical preparation of the parotid salivary duct.

each corner. The wire is withdrawn. One end of the U-shaped tube is cut three inches from the nearest tab; the other end is cut approximately eighteen inches from the nearest tab.

As in the parotid preparation, a short piece of polyethylene tubing is inserted into the submaxillary duct in order to easily locate the duct during the subsequent dissection. One of the papillae located just anterior to the midventral septum, i.e., the frenulum, of the tongue is clipped and the duct's lumen is exposed in the resulting cross-section.

Following the insertion of the short piece of tubing into the sub-maxillary duct, an incision is made caudal to the duct opening into the mouth and lateral to the tongue. The submaxillary duct is dissected free of the adjacent tissue.

The longitudinal incision in the duct wall and the insertion of the short end of the U-shaped tube follows the same procedure as in the parotid preparation with the exception that this procedure occurs within the oral cavity. The duct is ligated anterior and posterior to the incision in the duct wall as in the parotid preparation.

Entering just below the incision in the duct wall, a rod is forced through the various muscle layers and the cutaneous tissue ventral to the mandible in such a way that when the rod is removed there will be a clear passageway from the oral cavity to the external cutaneous tissue through a hollow metal tube. The long end of the U-shaped polyethylene tube with the second tab is passed through this metal tube, out of the oral cavity.

As in the parotid preparation, a long metal probe is used to pull the long section of the U-shaped polyethylene tube under the skin and out the dorsal side of the neck. The incision below the mandible is closed, covering the second tab. The purpose of having two tabs in the prepared tube is to insure against its being dislodged from the duct by mandibular action, tongue movement, or slight external pulling of the tube.

Apparatus

The animal is placed in a commercially manufactured experimental chamber (Lehigh Valley Electronics) which has been slightly modified (Figure 14-2a). A length of cable hangs from the roof of the box and is connected at its lower end to a harness. A polyethylene tube passes through this cable and after the polyethylene tube is filled with water, it is slipped over the end of the tube emerging from the back of the dog's neck (Figure 14-2b). The entire cable and tube system is on an airtight swivel so that there is no raveling of the cable if the animal walks around in circles, as is not unusual under some operant schedules of reinforcement. The chamber contains two retractable levers, only one being available in the chamber at the time of this photograph. The polyethylene tube is passed through the wall, into the control room, and connected to a hypodermic needle. The contacts of a commercially available "Drink-ometer" (Grason-Stadler) are connected to this needle and another needle located directly below (Figure 14-2c). Thus, when the animal salivates, the column of liquid moves and a drop forms, momentarily connecting

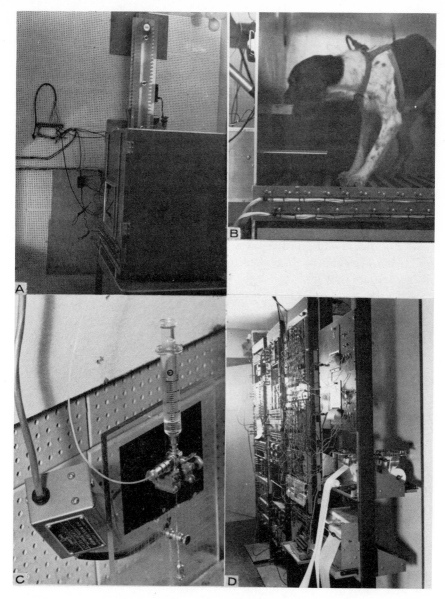

Fig. 14-2. (a) Outside view of experimental chamber. (b) Dog B-53 inside chamber with lever available. (c) Salivary drop counter. (d) Programming and recording equipment.

the two needles and, therefore, operating the "Drinkometer." It is worth noting that in classical conditioning experiments, using these methods, salivary response latencies less than $\frac{1}{2}$ second are regularly observed; latencies of $\frac{1}{2}$ second would appear to be considerably shorter than those reportedly obtained with older surgical and recording procedures. The

experiments are programmed and recorded with the customary operant
conditioning apparatus (Figure 14-2d).

DATA ON THE RELATIONSHIP BETWEEN PAVLOVIAN SALIVARY CONDITIONING AND OPERANT LEVER PRESSING, AND THE INTERPRETATION OF THESE DATA

1. *On the concept of mediation between concurrent responses.*
Recent work has investigated concurrent salivary and lever pressing conditioning (Shapiro, 1960, 1961b, 1962; Kintsch & Witte, 1962) during
different schedules of reinforcement. One of the purposes of this paper is
to discuss the theoretical significance and limitation of such experimental
results. Although these comments may be relevant for a larger class of
experimental results, this discussion, for purposes of clarity, will be restricted to the salivation-lever press investigations.

It has been shown that when food reinforcement is contingent upon
the occurrence of a lever press, the temporal relationship between the recorded salivation and the recorded lever press differs with the various
schedules of reinforcement (Shapiro, 1962; Kintsch & Witte, 1962). Given
a salivary response criterion and a lever press response criterion, the
temporal sequence of occurrences of the two responses can be measured,
and if the criteria are held constant, any alteration in the sequence of
responses corresponding to changes in the experimenter-programmed reinforcement schedules can be measured.

However, one may not be content with these observations. One may
be curious as to what is going on in this situation. Is salivation acting as
part of the complex of conditioned cues for lever pressing? Or, are the
preliminary movements leading up to a lever press serving as cues for
salivation? Or, are the two response systems independent? For example,
Konorski and Miller (1937) said some twenty-five years ago, that salivation "has for its stimulus the kinesthetic excitations raised by the movement." [This particular point of view is no longer supported by the data
at hand (Shapiro, 1961a, 1962; Kintsch & Witte, 1962).] These questions
are also possibly prompted by concepts such as the fractional anticipatory
goal response, r_g (Hull, 1943); however, there is some disagreement as to
whether such questions should arise from this formulation by Hull.
MacCorquodale and Meehl (1948) call r_g a hypothetical construct, "i.e.,
involve(s) the supposition of entities or processes not among the observed"; since salivation during lever pressing would seem to be a legiti-
mate component of r_g, the hypothetical construct, r_g, would now be
observable (at least in part) and the hypothesized entity or process would
now be open to direct empirical test. The aforementioned questions then
could have arisen possibly from Hull's formulation. However, taking the
position advanced by Logan (1959) that "r_g is an intervening variable

and not a response of the real organism" (p. 311), there would be no theoretical bases for such questions, since salivation, a response of the real organism, is not an observable component of r_g. Nevertheless, questions concerning one response generating stimuli for another response are often raised in the psychological literature and a discussion of them seems warranted, whatever their theoretical origin(s).

2. *Some attempted experimental solutions.* Let us consider how such questions might be investigated experimentally. Specifically, to answer the question "are preliminary movements leading up to a lever press serving as cues for salivation?" one could take an animal that had been trained on a fixed-interval (FI) two-minute reinforcement schedule contingent upon lever pressing and retract the lever from the experimental space. To do this, it would be necessary either to make the reinforcement contingent upon salivation or to present the reinforcement every two minutes noncontingently. In the particular case studies, the reinforcement was made contingent upon salivation during the entire session following the regular training on lever-press contingent food. The results are shown in Figure 14-3. [The decrease in lever pressing from the first half hour to the last half hour may be of interest also for a consideration of whether or not extinction is simply the acquisition of competing responses since in this situation lever pressing was displaying a reduction in rate although it had never been subjected to the usual lever press-nonreinforcement paradigm. Control data showing that lever pressing does not decrease during an experimental session of this length with food contingent upon pressing can be seen in Shapiro (1961b, Figure 14-2).] The animal was observed continuously through a one-way screen and he was not seen raising or lowering his paw during the second hour when the lever was retracted. As another possibility, a naive animal could be trained on a particular schedule with food reinforcement contingent upon salivation; since the lever would never have been available, preliminary movements leading up to a press would not exist. Three animals were run on FI two-minute food reinforcement contingent upon salivation; all three showed the same phenomenon and the data from one dog are shown in Figure 14-4. (These results may also be of interest for a consideration of whether or not salivation can be conditioned with contingent reinforcement.)

Consider the question, "is salivation acting as part of the complex of conditioned cues for lever pressing?" An animal that had been trained on the differential reinforcement of low rates (drl) for food contingent upon lever pressing and had been regularly observed to salivate before each lever press (using constant response criteria), was given, over a period of time, various doses of pilocarpine. As expected, the rate of salivation increased markedly, but the rate of lever pressing not only failed to

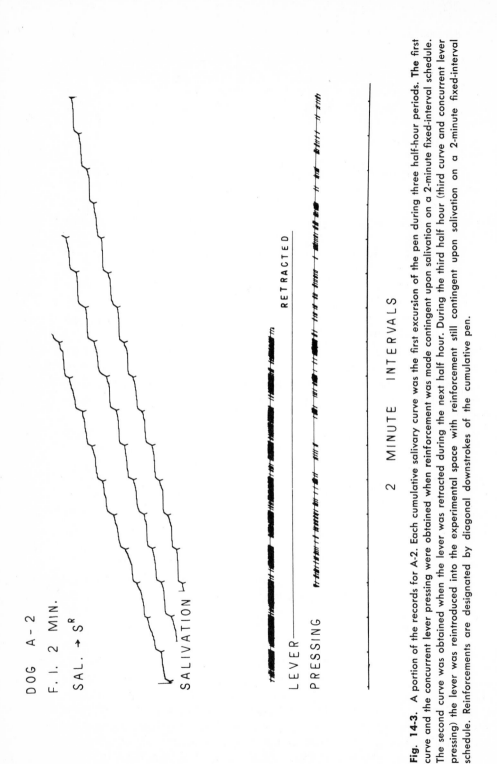

DOG A - 2

F.I. 2 MIN.

SAL. → S^R

SALIVATION

LEVER

RETRACTED

PRESSING

2 MINUTE INTERVALS

Fig. 14-3. A portion of the records for A-2. Each cumulative salivary curve was the first excursion of the pen during three half-hour periods. The first curve and the concurrent lever pressing were obtained when reinforcement was made contingent upon salivation on a 2-minute fixed-interval schedule. The second curve was obtained when the lever was retracted during the next half hour. During the third half hour (third curve and concurrent lever pressing) the lever was reintroduced into the experimental space with reinforcement still contingent upon salivation on a 2-minute fixed-interval schedule. Reinforcements are designated by diagonal downstrokes of the cumulative pen.

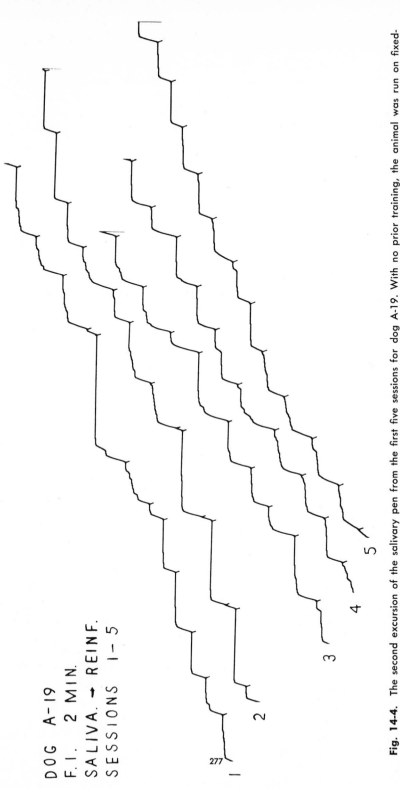

Fig. 14-4. The second excursion of the salivary pen from the first five sessions for dog A-19. With no prior training, the animal was run on fixed-interval 2-minute reinforcement contingent upon salivation. Each curve represents the salivary responding during a daily session of 2 hours. Reinforcements are designated by diagonal downstrokes of the pen.

increase, but became virtually zero. Observation through a one-way screen allowed the experimenter to witness the increase in rate of another response class which might be labeled nausea. [The work of Lewis, *et al.* (1958) and Lewis and Kent (1961) is of interest on this point.]

Whatever else these results may or may not tell us, they obviously shed no real light on the questions originally posed. In the first example, the removal of the lever precludes lever pressing but does not necessarily preclude the occurrence of more subtle component movements; therefore, it is still possible that movements leading up to a lever press provide the stimuli for salivation. In the second example, the fact that an animal can be conditioned to salivate when food is contingent upon salivation does not lead to the conclusion that lever pressing provides no stimuli for salivation when food is contingent upon lever pressing. In the third example, the fact that salivation increases and lever pressing decreases does not lead to the conclusion that salivation provides no stimuli for lever pressing since the administration of pilocarpine also drastically alters the other stimulus-response conditions; the animal defecates, vomits, and in general appears nauseous. Rather than consider the almost inexhaustible supply of such inconclusive and inadequate investigations, let us attempt to analyze the logical status of the problem and then consider whether more plausible experimental alternatives exist.

3. *An analysis of the problem's logical status.*   It should be kept clearly in mind that the following analysis is with respect to two responses (salivation and lever pressing) which are not necessarily mutually exclusive in time, i.e., there is no independent evidence that the two responses cannot occur in the same instant. The analysis is not intended to apply to such phenomena as verbal behavior in which it is possible to argue on quite different and independent grounds that the various responses of the vocal system are mutually exclusive in time; i.e., in any instant, this system makes one, albeit multidimensional, measurable response. The following argument, then, is with respect to two responses made by two different effectors and not with respect to two or more responses by the same effector.

To answer the question "which response provides the stimuli for the other?" requires that one determine which response occurs first; that is, to demonstrate that R_1-produced S_1 is a stimulus for R_2 requires, as a first step, a demonstration that R_1-S_1 precedes R_2 and that R_2 has a higher probability of occurrence after R_1-S_1 occurs than it does after R_1-S_1 does not occur. If response means the satisfaction of some criterion such as a lever press or a drop of saliva, the determination of the temporal sequence of responses is possible.

When criteria are specified, two binary systems result, time intervals being specified such that during an interval one or no lever press occurs and one or no salivation occurs; furthermore, the interval may be made sufficiently short so that it is very unlikely that one of each will occur in the same interval. However, the determination of the temporal sequence of criterion responses does not provide very convincing evidence for the existence of an R_1-S_1-R_2 chain. The temporal relationship which one observes is a function of the response criteria selected; in fact, it is easily shown empirically that the temporal sequence can be changed by altering the size of the salivary drop or the force of the required lever press. If one wishes to show the existence of an R_1-R_2 sequence (as the first step in demonstrating the existence of an R_1-S_1-R_2 chain), it is not enough to show that R_1-R_2 occur in that order given some selected response criteria; one would have to show that the criteria for the two responses are equivalent. Needless to say, no one has yet determined how much saliva is equal to how much lever press, and it would appear that no pair of criteria would equate them along all possible dimensions.

If the problem discussed above is not sufficiently discouraging, consider the added difficulty raised by such a phrase as "movements leading up to" a lever press. The manner in which the question is posed clearly implies that it is not sufficient to know the temporal sequence of R_1 and R_2; one must also be able to identify and measure the sequence of responding that "leads up to" R_1 and then R_2. To show that movements leading up to a press provide stimuli for salivation (for the sake of brevity, this shall henceforth be referred to as press *mediates* salivation), it would appear that one must be able to show that the movements leading up to a press begin before the sequence of events leading up to salivation. (Actually, why stop with movements? One could consider the events in the central nervous system, etc.) However, it is patently obvious that if we assume response component r_n to constitute the beginning of the sequence leading up to R, then it must be true that (if behavior is predictable) response component r_{n-1} leads up to r_n and must, therefore, be the beginning of the sequence leading up to R. This argument can be reiterated until we come to the previous occurrence in time of R or some experimenter-controlled stimulus.

An additional difficulty is created by phrases such as "serving as cues" and "part of the complex of conditioned cues." Some degree of ambiguity is apparent. To show that R_1 mediates R_2, must one demonstrate that R_1 produces the necessary cues for R_2, the sufficient cues for R_2, or just some of the possible cues for R_2?

4. *An analysis of the problem's empirical status.* In Section 2, some unsuccessful empirical attempts to determine the mediational relationships between the two responses were presented. In each attempt

the same difficulty of interpretation was encountered; that is, both response classes were measured as dependent variables and it was not possible to manipulate the occurrence of one response class and leave everything else constant. As responses of the organism they are under the control of the experimenter only through the manipulation of a separate experimental operation; to manipulate the occurrence of a response class, some environmental aspect must be manipulated also, thereby producing a confounding of variables. The only possible way to remove the confounding would be to find an experimental operation which could be proved to affect only one of the responses being studied and nothing else; however, this is not really very reasonable to expect since it would involve proving a single cause-single effect relationship which would involve a new set of logical and methodological difficulties. Furthermore, if R_1 were "caused" peripherally and R_2 did not occur subsequently, it could be argued that movements leading up to R_1 and not R_1 itself were mediating R_2; that is, a disproof of R_1-R_2 mediation would still be most unlikely.

It would appear that a test of salivation-lever press mediation is not available with any presently adoptable methods. An adequate test would involve the demonstration of the existence or nonexistence of a "causal chain" and such a demonstration would require considerably more information about the anatomy and functioning of the organism than is now available. [For a discussion of the nature of a "causal chain" see Hanson (1958).]

ON A POSSIBLE DIRECTION FOR RESEARCH CONCERNING THE RELATIONSHIP BETWEEN OPERANT AND RESPONDENT CONDITIONING

Assuming that a determination of possible mediational relationships between Pavlovian salivary and operant lever pressing conditioning is not, at least currently, plausible because of the confounding of variables, it is then apparent that one possible approach is to put the confounding to good use. There are possible experiments in which the confounding of an independent variable with the two dependent variables might be of particular interest. For example, if a lever press is reinforced by food, will an external stimulus which is correlated with salivation also be correlated with an increase in the probability of a lever press? Hull (1943, p. 100) had hypothesized that the ability of a stimulus to serve as a secondary reinforcing stimulus is proportional to its ability to elicit r_g. Furthermore, Dinsmoor (1950) showed, for positive reinforcement, that a stimulus could serve as either a secondary reinforcing stimulus or as a discriminative stimulus, after Estes (1943, 1948) had shown previously that a stimulus which had been paired with food according to a Pavlovian paradigm, when presented during extinction of a previously food reinforced lever press, resulted in an increased rate of pressing. The problem is still receiving considerable attention with Dinsmoor and Clayton (1963) extending the phenomenon to escape conditioning and Solomon and Turner (1962) studying transfer of training in an avoidance situation. However, the above studies do not carry the point to its logical conclusion: a stimulus will act as either a discriminative stimulus or a secondary reinforcing stimulus for an operant when and only when that stimulus also acts as a conditioned stimulus for a respondent appropriate to the reinforcing stimulus. Specifically, if lever presses are reinforced with food, a stimulus will act as a discriminative stimulus or a secondary reinforcing stimulus for lever pressing if and only if it also acts as a classically conditioned stimulus for salivation.

EMPIRICAL EVIDENCE ON THE RELATIONSHIPS AMONG DISCRIMINATIVE STIMULI, CONDITIONED STIMULI, LEVER PRESSING, AND SALIVATION

1. *Experimental design: abortive attempts.* Two experimental procedures were employed in the initial stages of this investigation. The first was as follows: in phase I, dogs were trained on a tone which was followed by food and on another frequency tone which was not followed by food. After several weeks in phase I, the tone was discontinued, a lever was introduced into the experimental chamber, and phase II was begun. The dogs were trained to lever press for food and by gradually changing the reinforcement schedule, lever pressing was finally established on a tandem variable-interval thirty-seconds differential reinforcement of low rates ninety seconds (tandem VI 30 drl. 90). After many weeks on this operant lever-pressing schedule, phase III was begun and tones were presented at unsystematic times during the operant lever pressing schedule. Subjectively, it appeared that the tone previously followed by food in phase I resulted in a lever press in phase III and the tone not previously followed by food in phase I, did not result in a lever press during phase III. However, there was no apparent way to demonstrate this possible effect quantitatively because of the rapid extinction of the conditioned salivary response to the food associated tone during an experimental session and because the interresponse times of the lever presses on this schedule are so variable that it is difficult to show that the lever press following a tone was or was not the result of the tone. Another added complication was that the total time required to run the experiment on any one animal was many months, due to the difficulty of adjusting to the tandem VI 30 drl 90 schedule; this meant that if the surgery were performed prior to phase II, there was a considerable risk that the prepa-

ration would not maintain itself for the duration of the experiment, and if the surgery were delayed until just prior to running phase III, there was always the danger that the conditioned salivary response to the food followed tone, unknown to the experimenter, had not really been acquired in phase I.

The second procedure employed was the same as the first except that a drl two-minute schedule was used instead of the tandem VI 30 drl 90. Although this schedule produced less variable interresponse times for the lever pressing, it of course did not completely solve the other problems. However, it became increasingly apparent that there existed a systematic relationship between tones that elicited salivation and the interresponse time of the next lever press, although no clear cut relationship seemed to exist when the tone did not elicit salivation. It was then decided that rather than run both food followed tones and non-food followed tones, that only one tone would be used and the data·would be analyzed in terms of whether or not the tone elicited salivation on any specific presentation. The drl schedule appeared desirable since it produces orderly distributions of lever press interresponse times and a two-minute interreinforcement interval is sufficiently long to allow the cessation of salivation to the food prior to the next reinforcement availability. [The analysis of several thousand consecutive lever-press interresponse times obtained in an earlier study (Shapiro, 1962) showed that the hypothesis of independence, between interresponse times of presses n and n + 1, could not be rejected; this also was considered a desirable feature.]

2. *Experimental design: second version.* In phase I, the animals were trained to eat a teaspoonful of Wayne Krumettes out of the food tray whenever the food was presented by a Gerbrands Universal feeder, following which the lever was introduced and lever presses were reinforced on increasingly long fixed-interval (FI) schedules up to FI two minutes. The schedule was then changed to conjunctive FI two minutes drl. The drl component was gradually increased until conj FI 2 minutes drl 2 minutes was reached, the schedule being identical with a simple drl 2 min. An Elmeg ZDG III 2/1 print out counter counted pulses at the rate of 115/2 min.; a lever press caused the counter to print and reset, thereby providing a record of the successive interresponse times of lever pressing. The lever was automatically retracted and the house lights turned off after sixty reinforcements. A session was run each day for several weeks or months until the distribution of lever press interresponse times appeared to have stabilized. (Animals were observed and required to press with their paws or legs and not allowed to press with their noses.) The animals were then surgically prepared.

In phase II, each trial consisted of a 1600 cps tone of 5-second duration followed by the presentation of a food reinforcement, i.e., simple delayed Pavlovian conditioning. The food reinforcement consisted of one teaspoonful of Wayne Krumettes presented by means of a Gerbrands Universal feeder.

The trials were programmed on a two-minute variable interval tape. The tape was automatically stopped and the house lights turned off after sixty trials. An experimental session was run every day for several weeks or until the classically conditioned salivary response was well established. The latencies and magnitudes of the salivary response during the 5-second period before the beginning of the trial, during the 5-second tone, and during the 5-second period after the tone (food), were automatically recorded and printed out after each trial. Latencies were measured by counting the number of time pulses (approximately one per 0.1 sec.) occurring between the onset of the period and the occurrence of the first recorded drop of saliva. Responses and stimuli were also recorded on a Gerbrands Polygraph ink writer.

In phase III, the lever was again introduced and food was presented contingent upon lever pressing on the same drl 2-min schedule used in phase I. However, a 1600 cps tone of 10-sec duration was presented 8 times during each experimental session, twice at 35/115 of 2 min., twice at 50/115 of 2 min., twice at 80/115 of 2 min., and twice at 95/115 of 2 min. after a reinforcement. A tone was never presented unless at least the two last consecutive lever presses had been reinforced. The tone presentation times were counterbalanced within days and between days. Four presentation time values were used, so that the tone would not become a cue for the next reinforcement availability period. A conditioned salivary response was said to have occurred to the tone if the number of drops recorded during the 10-sec. presentation of the tone and in the 10-sec. interval after the tone was at least two more than twice the number of drops in the 10-sec. interval before the tone. The data were analyzed as follows: The distribution of all nontest trial lever-press interresponse times in a given session was determined (those following a test tone being excluded). The observed interresponse time of a press following a tone was then compared to this distribution, and the proportion (probability) of nontest interresponse times shorter than or equal to the observed test value was calculated. For example, if the tone had been presented at 80 and the lever press occurred at 97, i.e., had a waiting time of 17, the number of nontest trial lever presses which occurred between 80 and 97 divided by the number of nontest trial presses which occurred at 80 or more was computed. This proportion is, therefore, the empirical probability of having a lever press occur after a waiting time of 17 or less following a tone at 80 if the tone was not present, that is, had no effect.

In the afternoon of each day the animal was given approximately 10 trials of tone-food as in phase II. The animal was then rerun on the drl

DOG B-53

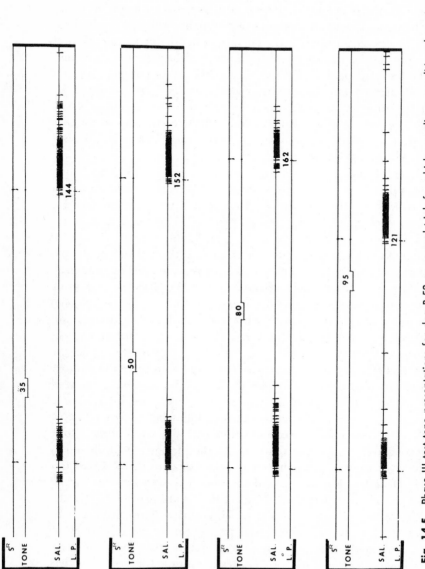

Fig. 14-5. Phase III test tone presentations for dog B-53 on several trials for which no salivary conditioned response was observed. The top line of each portion denotes the occurrence of food reinforcement. The second line shows the presentation of the tone and the time since the last response. The third line indicates salivary responses, and the fourth line lever-press responses, and lever press interresponse times.

schedule, with tones presented, on the following morning. This procedure was repeated for several days.

3. *Results.* Figure 14-5 shows some of the results for the first dog, B-53. The top line of each segment shows the presentation of food; the second line, the presentation of the tone; the third line, salivation; and the fourth line, lever press. The number over the tone mark signifies the time since the previous reinforcement and the number over the lever press signifies the interresponse time of the lever press. The examples shown in this figure are of test trials on which the dog did not salivate during or immediately after the tone presentation and it can be seen that the lever press interresponse times are fairly long, 115 counts being required to obtain a reinforcement.

Figure 14-6 shows test trials on which the dog did salivate during and/or after the tone and it can be seen that the lever presses have false alarmed; their interresponse times are too short to obtain the food reinforcement.

Figure 14-7 summarizes the lever press waiting time analysis results for dog B-53. The probability distribution for waiting times has been divided into fifths and the table shows the frequency of observed waiting times falling in each fifth. The top portion of the figure shows the frequency distribution for those lever presses following tones observed to elicit salivation; the bottom portion of the figure shows the distribution for lever presses after tones observed not to elicit salivation. It is evident from the top portion of the figure that if the animal salivated during the 10-sec tone or in the 10 seconds thereafter, the distribution of observed waiting times of the next lever press is significantly different from the distribution during nontest periods (p less than 0.02). The expectation is that, by definition, 7 of the 35 would fall in each of the five waiting time probability intervals; but, in fact, 15 of the 35 have waiting time probabilities less than 0.2, and actually 8 of these have probabilities less than 0.05. The lower portion shows that on test trials which had no salivation during or immediately after the tone, the subsequent lever presses apparently are distributed in the same manner as the nontest trial presses.

It is equally interesting to note that the amount of salivation elicited by the tone is a function of the "phase" of the reinforcement schedule at which the tone is presented. That is, tones presented soon after a previous reinforcement do not elicit as much salivation as those presented soon before the next reinforcement availability period. The result of this analysis was a correlation, $r = 0.358$, $t_{46} = 2.599$, significantly different from chance at the 0.02 level. It is for this reason that the first analysis of the data (lever press waiting time values) was done dichotomously in terms of salivation occurring or not occurring.

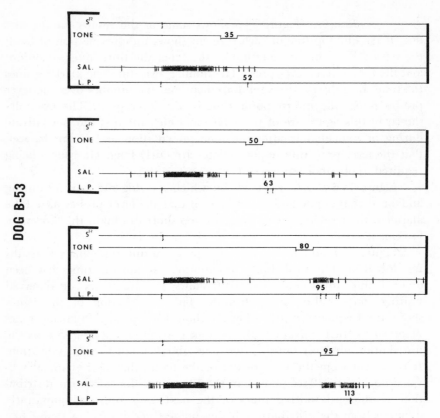

Fig. 14-6. Phase III test tone presentations for dog B-53 on several trials for which a salivary conditioned response was observed. The top line of each portion denotes the occurrence of food reinforcement. The second line shows the presentation of the tone and the time since the last response. The third line indicates salivary responses, and the fourth line lever-press responses, and lever-press interresponse times.

As a check on the validity of the waiting time analysis of lever pressing, the relationship between tone presentation time and lever-press waiting time probability was also investigated; if the method of analyzing waiting time probabilities was valid, there should not exist any significant relationship between tone presentation time and waiting time probability. The mean waiting time probability was calculated for each of the four presentation times occurring on each day, and these values were then ranked one to four. The result clearly does not differ significantly from chance, $\chi^2_{r\,3d.f.} = 1.40$, p ~ .75.

Another animal, B-65, was run in precisely the same manner, but

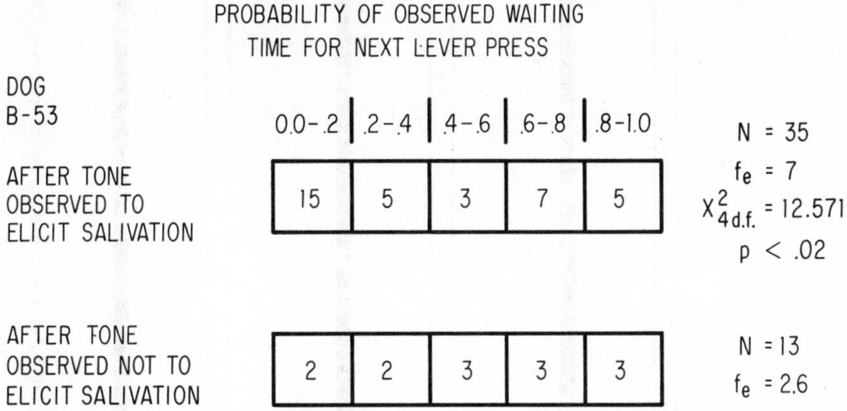

PROBABILITY OF OBSERVED WAITING
TIME FOR NEXT LEVER PRESS

DOG
B-53

0.0-.2 | .2-.4 | .4-.6 | .6-.8 | .8-1.0   N = 35

AFTER TONE
OBSERVED TO   15 | 5 | 3 | 7 | 5 $f_e = 7$
ELICIT SALIVATION $x^2_{4\,d.f.} = 12.571$
                                                       $p < .02$

AFTER TONE
OBSERVED NOT TO   2 | 2 | 3 | 3 | 3   N = 13
ELICIT SALIVATION $f_e = 2.6$

Fig. 14-7. Frequency of observed lever-press waiting time probabilities falling in each quintile for dog B-53. The top portion shows the frequency distribution for trials on which the tone was observed to elicit salivation; the bottom portion shows the frequency distribution for trials on which the tone was observed not to elicit salivation.

presented a much more difficult problem in terms of analyzing the data. To illustrate the difficulties, a sample of his phase II data is shown in Figure 14-8. The salivary responding to food continued for a relatively long time and, in spite of many weeks of training on the tone-food combination, the animal's response to the tone, as can be seen in Figure 14-8, was usually a cessation of salivation. Nevertheless, the animal was initiated on phase III with rather striking results; samples of the phase III data are shown in Figure 14-9. Out of 56 tone-presentation trials only 2 had a clearly discriminable conditioned salivary response. Figure 14-10 shows the waiting time probability results for this animal's lever presses following tone presentations. The result is significantly different from chance; however, for this dog, for whom the tone was "inhibitory," the significant effect is an increase in the probability of lever press waiting times. That is, the tone resulted in delaying the next lever press.

An analysis of the relationship between tone presentation time and magnitude of the conditioned salivary response could not, obviously, be carried out. The relationship between tone presentation time and lever-press probability was again insignificantly different from chance.

Another animal, B-67, very rapidly acquired a conditioned salivary response in phase II, and a sample of his results is shown in Figure 14-11. However, it can be seen that the response to food was relatively long lasting, thereby making it very difficult to determine whether a conditioned salivary response was occurring to the short tone presentation time values, after phase III was initiated. A sample of these phase III results is

DOG B-65
CLASSICAL

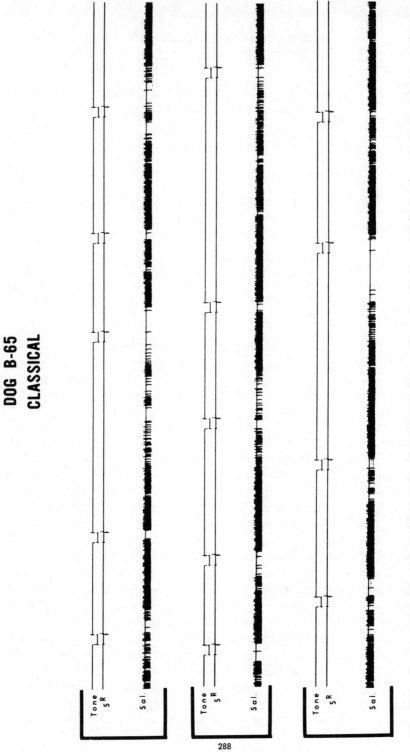

Fig. 14-8. A portion of the classical conditioning data for dog B-65. The top line of each segment indicates the presentation of a tone; the second line, reinforcement (food); and the third line, salivation.

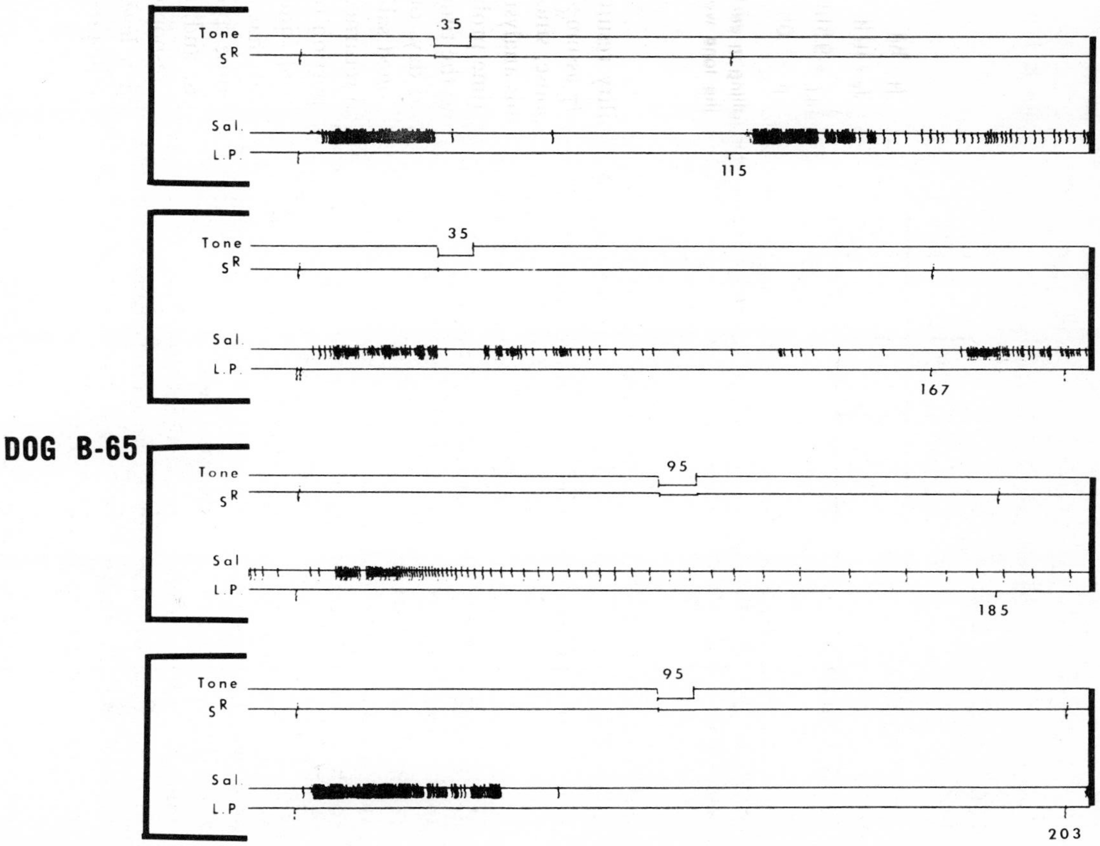

Fig. 14-9. Phase III tone presentations for dog B-65 on several trials for which no salivary conditioned response was observed. The top line of each portion shows the presentation of the tone and the time since the last response. The second line denotes the occurrence of food reinforcement. The third line indicates salivary responses; and the fourth line, lever-press responses and lever-press interresponse times.

289

DOG B-65

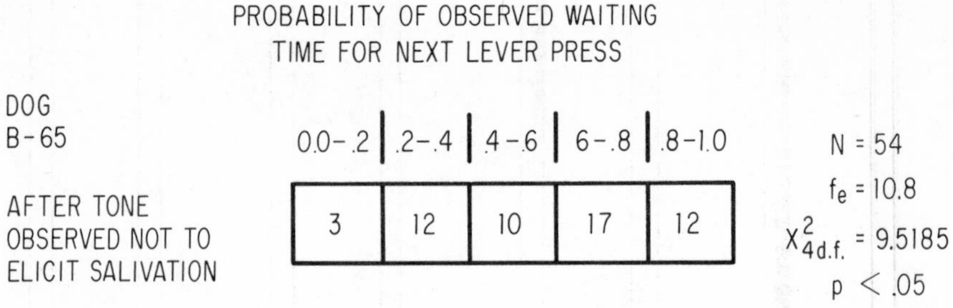

PROBABILITY OF OBSERVED WAITING
TIME FOR NEXT LEVER PRESS

DOG
B-65

0.0-.2	.2-.4	.4-.6	.6-.8	.8-1.0

N = 54

$f_e = 10.8$

AFTER TONE
OBSERVED NOT TO
ELICIT SALIVATION

3	12	10	17	12

$X^2_{4 d.f.} = 9.5185$

$p < .05$

Fig. 14-10. Frequency of observed lever-press waiting time probabilities falling in each quintile for dog B-65. The frequency distribution for those trials on which the tone was observed not to elicit salivation is shown.

shown in Figure 14-12. The lever-press waiting time probability results are shown in the top portion of Figure 14-13, where it is simply assumed that all tone presentations elicited a conditioned salivary response, since no trial had a clear failure to obtain a response. The result of this analysis is a significant difference from chance, the lever press waiting time probabilities being increased. That is, the tone resulted in decreasing the time to the next lever press. This animal was then rerun for several days on phase II, except that tone alone was presented, i.e., the conditioned salivary response to the tone was extinguished. The animal was then returned to the phase III procedure, and, as can be seen in the lower portion of Figure 14-13, the tone no longer had any effect upon the waiting time of the subsequent lever press. Therefore, for dog B-67, it is clear that a tone, which has been associated with food and has a salivary response conditioned to it, acts as a discriminative stimulus for a lever press; and, a tone which has not been associated with food and has a salivary response to it extinguished, does not act as a discriminative stimulus for a lever press. The relationship between waiting-time probability and tone-presentation time was again insignificant.

4. *Discussion.* A discussion of these results is somewhat difficult because of the many theoretical issues for which they have relevance. Taking an extraordinary tack, it would perhaps be worthwhile to discuss what the results do not demonstrate. It has been pointed out in a previous study (Shapiro, 1962) that salivation reliably precedes lever pressing when food reinforcements are presented on a drl schedule contingent upon lever pressing; furthermore, this previously reported finding could have been construed as evidence in support of the notion that the classically conditioned consummatory response is the *modus operandi* for instrumental conditioning (Hull, 1943, p. 100). The results of the present study reported in this paper could be taken as even stronger support for this hypothesis; they could be interpreted to mean that whenever the salivary

DOG B-67
CLASSICAL

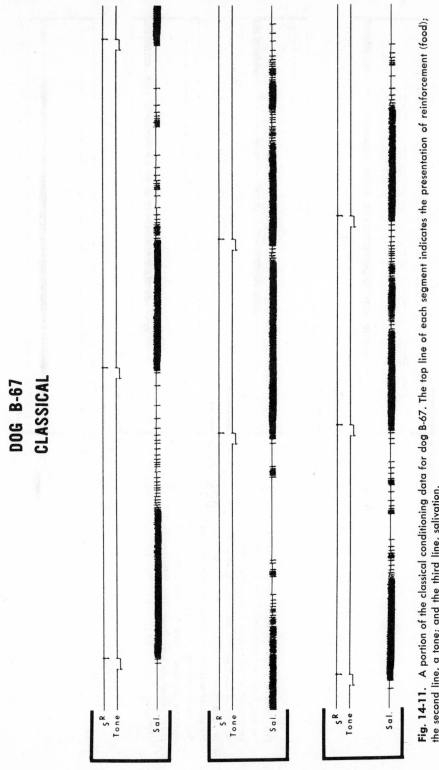

Fig. 14-11. A portion of the classical conditioning data for dog B-67. The top line of each segment indicates the presentation of reinforcement (food); the second line, a tone; and the third line, salivation.

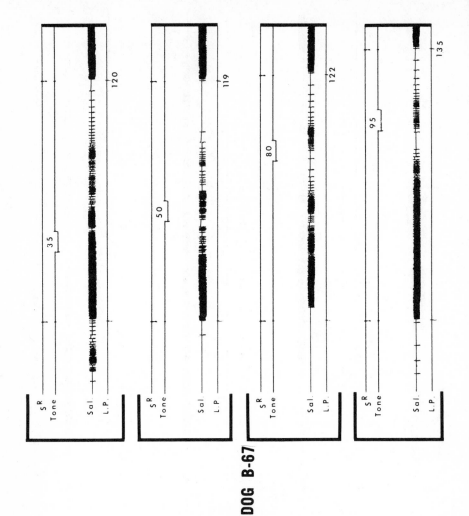

DOG B-67

Fig. 14-12. Phase III test tone presentations for dog B-67 on several trials for which a salivary conditioned response was observed. The top line of each portion denotes the occurrence of food reinforcement. The second line shows the presentation of the tone and the time since the last response. The third line indicates salivary responses; and the fourth line, lever-press responses and lever-press interresponse times.

292

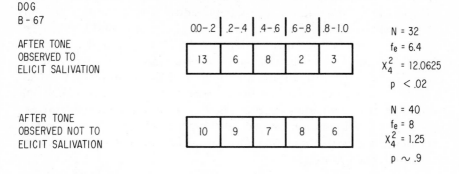

PROBABILITY OF OBSERVED WAITING
TIME FOR NEXT LEVER PRESS

DOG
B - 67

	0.0-.2	.2-.4	.4-.6	.6-.8	.8-1.0

AFTER TONE
OBSERVED TO
ELICIT SALIVATION

| 13 | 6 | 8 | 2 | 3 |

$N = 32$
$f_e = 6.4$
$x_4^2 = 12.0625$
$p < .02$

AFTER TONE
OBSERVED NOT TO
ELICIT SALIVATION

| 10 | 9 | 7 | 8 | 6 |

$N = 40$
$f_e = 8$
$x_4^2 = 1.25$
$p \sim .9$

Fig. 14-13. Frequency of observed lever-press waiting time probabilities falling in each quintile for dog B-67. The top portion shows the frequency distribution for trials on which the tone was observed to elicit salivation; the bottom portion shows the frequency distribution for trials on which the tone was observed not to elicit salivation.

response is "forced" by the presentation of a conditioned stimulus, it in turn results in an increase in the probability of a lever press, a decrease in waiting time (probability). This "forcing" of the "salivation-press chain" could be viewed as particularly convincing because under the drl schedule a "false alarm" of the lever press is highly unadaptive, resulting in a missed reinforcement. However, the drawing of such conclusions from these results is highly dangerous. First, it is clear that the occurrence of a salivary response cannot be a sufficient condition for the occurrence of a lever press, since the animal does not press a lever immediately after he finishes eating the food and is still salivating. Secondly, the preliminary results (dog B-53) on the relationship between the "phase" of the lever press schedule and the magnitude of the conditioned salivary response might indicate that the relationship between salivation and lever pressing is a two-way street. Thirdly, does the occurrence of the salivation "force" the lever press, or does the occurrence of the tone-salivation combination "force" the lever press? This difficulty of interpretation has been previously noted by Hull (1943, p. 98). That is, as discussed in a section of the introduction, results such as these provide no clear evidence, in and of themselves, for the existence of a mediational relationship.

From these results reported here, it would be reasonable to conclude that the ability of a stimulus to act as a stimulus for an instrumental response is a function of the ability of that stimulus to act as a stimulus for a classically conditioned consummatory response, or vice versa. The relationship would seem to be substantiated by the evidence both between and within subjects. However, two additional refinements would appear to be required at this stage: (1) the previous assumption that lever-press waiting times would be distributed equally over the probability value range is highly suspect because of the criterion employed for the presentation of a test tone, i.e., a tone was presented only if the two previous lever presses had been reinforced; (2) it would appear desirable to demonstrate that the observed relationship between salivation and lever pressing, following the presentation of a conditioned stimulus, required the prior pairing of that conditioned stimulus with the appropriate unconditioned stimulus, i.e., it has not been demonstrated that the classical conditioning procedure, phase II, was a necessary condition for the establishment of the relationship between the instrumental and consummatory responses. To clarify these two points, two animals were tested on an additionally refined procedure.

5. *Experimental design: final version.*   Phase I was identical to that of the second version of the experimental design. Following this drl schedule training, "test trials" were run in the same manner as the previous phase III except in one respect; the audio generator was disconnected, preventing the actual presentation of the tone. These "dummy" trials were analyzed in the same manner as ordinary test trials. Following this phase of training, the audio generator was connected again and tones were presented in the usual manner. However, unlike phase III of the second version the tone had not been paired previously, in the animal's training, with food. Following this phase of training the animal was presented with tone-food pairings utilizing the same procedure employed in phase II of the second version of the experimental design, the lever being retracted. Following this Pavlovian training the lever was reintroduced and phase III was conducted in the same manner as before. With this refinement it was possible to compare (a) the effect of a conditioned stimulus with the effect of a novel stimulus upon the relationship between the instrumental and consummatory responses, and (b) the effect of either external stimulus upon lever-press waiting times and salivation occurrences with the empirical control data obtained from the "dummy" trials. The results are shown in Figure 14-14. The top portion of the figure shows the relationship between salivation and lever-press waiting-time probability for all "dummy" trials for the two animals combined. It is apparent that the lever-press waiting-time probabilities are not equally distributed in the intervals, more specifically, large waiting time probabilities are relatively infrequent. This can be attributed to the criterion that was used for determining when a trial was presented. It is obvious that the null hypothesis, that a salivary conditioned response and a lever-press waiting-time probability are independent, cannot be rejected, $\chi^2_{4\,d.f.} = 5.381$, $p > 0.25$.

The middle portion of Figure 14-14 shows the results obtained during

<table>
<thead>
<tr><th colspan="2">PROBABILITY OF OBSERVED WAITING
TIME FOR NEXT LEVER PRESS</th><th>0.0-.2</th><th>.2-.4</th><th>.4-.6</th><th>.6-.8</th><th>.8-1.0</th><th></th></tr>
</thead>
<tbody>
<tr><td>AFTER DUMMY TONE</td><td>OBSERVED TO ELICIT SALIVATION</td><td>13</td><td>8</td><td>11</td><td>15</td><td>11</td><td>$x^2_4 = 5.381$</td></tr>
<tr><td></td><td>OBSERVED NOT TO ELICIT SALIVATION</td><td>28</td><td>34</td><td>33</td><td>34</td><td>15</td><td>$p > .25$</td></tr>
<tr><td>AFTER NOVEL TONE</td><td>OBSERVED TO ELICIT SALIVATION</td><td>24</td><td>11</td><td>8</td><td>15</td><td>11</td><td>$x^2_4 = 4.515$</td></tr>
<tr><td></td><td>OBSERVED NOT TO ELICIT SALIVATION</td><td>41</td><td>28</td><td>22</td><td>17</td><td>14</td><td>$p > .33$</td></tr>
<tr><td>AFTER CONDITIONED TONE</td><td>OBSERVED TO ELICIT SALIVATION</td><td>34</td><td>19</td><td>10</td><td>15</td><td>14</td><td>$x^2_4 = 10.359$</td></tr>
<tr><td></td><td>OBSERVED NOT TO ELICIT SALIVATION</td><td>17</td><td>17</td><td>22</td><td>16</td><td>16</td><td>$p \sim .035$</td></tr>
</tbody>
</table>

DOGS
B-76
B-78

Fig. 14-14. Frequency of observed lever-press waiting time probabilities falling in each quintile for dogs B-76 and B-78. The top portion shows the frequency distribution on "dummy tone" presentations, the middle portion on novel tone presentations, and the lower portion on conditioned tone presentations. Each portion is subdivided into those trials on which a salivary response was observed, and those trials on which no salivary response was observed.

the presentation of the novel tone. Again, the null hypothesis of independence between salivary conditioned response and lever-press waiting-time probability cannot be rejected, $x^2_{4\,d.f.} = 4.515$, $p > 0.33$. However, a comparison of these lever-press probabilities with those obtained on the "dummy" trials, collapsing across the variable of salivary conditioned response, shows that there are significantly more low waiting-time probabilities following the novel stimulus, $x^2_{4\,d.f.} = 11.483$, $p \sim 0.024$. The novel stimulus, therefore, does have the effect of reducing lever-press waiting times, but its ability to do this on any trial is not a function of its ability to elicit the consummatory response on that trial. (The total number of trials is not a multiple of eight because occasional trials were not amenable to analysis.)

The lower portion of Figure 14-14 shows the results obtained from the presentation of a trained conditioned tone. The total lever-press probabilities are not significantly lower than on the "dummy" trials, $x^2_{4\,d.f.} = 6.535$, $p \sim 0.16$, but in contrast to the results obtained with "dummy" and novel stimuli, the hypothesis of independence between the salivary response and lever-press response now must be rejected, $x^2_{4\,d.f.} = 10.359$, $p < 0.035$.

The analysis of the data in terms of 5 x 2 contingency tables tends to obscure the phenomenon. Inspection of the bottom portion of Figure 14-14 shows that the effect is substantially all in the first column, i.e., the

0.0-0.2 waiting-time probabilities. If the 5 x 2 tables are converted into 2 x 2 tables of salivation-no salivation and 0.0 to 0.2-0.2 to 1.0, the conclusions remain unchanged, but the results are more evident. The hypothesis of independence between lever-press waiting-time probability and salivary conditioned response is rejected in the case of the conditioned stimulus, $\chi^2_{1\,d.f.} = 6.890$, $p < 0.01$, but not in the case of either the "dummy" or novel stimulus, $\chi^2_{1d.f.} = 0.225$, $p > 0.5$, and $\chi^2_{1d.f.} = 0.027$, $p > 0.8$, respectively.

Reconsidering the three animals of the second version, and combining all three into one contingency table, with salivary conditioned response, no salivary conditioned response, and the lever-press probability intervals, one obtains a $\chi^2_{4d.f.} = 18.11$, $p < 0.0012$. Therefore, the final version of the experimental design also serves to replicate the results of the second version of the experiment.

6. *Conclusions.* The results of the study reported here show that, with these particular procedures, the ability of a conditioned (trained) stimulus to act as a discriminative stimulus for an instrumental response on a particular trial is a function of the ability of that stimulus to act as a conditioned stimulus for a classically conditioned consummatory response on that trial. This relationship does not exist with novel stimuli. This relationship does not exist with "dummy" stimuli.

Considerable further work will be required to test the generality of these findings. For example, suppose the stimulus and the instrumental reinforcer both elicit the same type of response (salivation) but the reinforcement for the tone (acid) and the instrumental reinforcer (food) are not the same; will the relationship still hold? Will the relationship hold for reinforcement schedules other than a drl, specifically, during schedules in which it is known that subjects may not salivate before completing a lever press? Does the result hold across different reinforcement modalities, as might be hypothesized from the results of Estes (1949)? One certainly would not expect the results to apply to instrumental avoidance responses (Black, 1959).

The suggestion, particularly from dog B-53, that the "phase" of the instrumental response and reinforcement sequence alters the magnitude of conditioned salivation to a conditioned stimulus, is equally interesting and deserving of further study. The fact that instrumental responses also become conditioned during classical salivary conditioning has been qualitatively observed by many investigators, e.g., Pavlov (1932), Zener (1937). The techniques reported here in this paper allow a quantitative study of a slightly different aspect of this problem; a known instrumental response and reinforcement sequence is established and conditioned stimuli can then be presented during quantitatively determined "phases" of this sequence.

EMPIRICAL EVIDENCE ON THE RELATIONSHIPS AMONG SEC-ONDARY REINFORCING STIMULI, CONDITIONED STIMULI, LEVER PRESSING AND SALIVATION

It has been shown that when a backward conditioning procedure is employed, and therefore no conditioned response is acquired to the conditioned stimulus, that the conditioned stimulus does not have the ability to function as a secondary reinforcing stimulus for an instrumental response (Schoenfeld, Antonitus, & Bersh, 1950). From the finding that a backward conditioned stimulus cannot serve as a secondary reinforcer, we were encouraged to pursue considerable pilot work on the possible relationship between effective conditioned and secondary reinforcing stimuli, and instrumental and classically conditioned responses; however, none of the techniques we have used to date have proved satisfactory. The most promising possibility is suggested by some results which show that when the lever press is put on an extinction schedule following the differential reinforcement of low rates (drl), the salivary response which follows each lever press gradually diminishes in magnitude in direct relation to the gradual increase in·the time between successive lever presses (interresponse time). An example of this result is shown in Figure 14-15. An attempt is now being made to investigate the effect, of following each lever press by a conditioned stimulus (tone) for salivation, upon the interresponse times of the lever presses. If it is found that, after some level of lever-press extinction is obtained, the presentation of a tone following each press results in a specific magnitude of salivation, and that the interresponse times of the presses return to the same values they had when the press itself formerly was followed by that specific magnitude of salivation, this will be taken as evidence that the ability of a stimulus to act as a secondary reinforcing stimulus is a function of its ability to elicit the consummatory response.

SUMMARY

1. A technique for the concurrent study of instrumental and classical conditioning is reviewed and new developments reported.

2. The difficulty of interpreting the results obtained from concurrent conditioning is discussed with relevant examples.

3. Data are presented in support of the hypothesis that the ability of a conditioned stimulus to act as a discriminative stimulus for an instrumental response is a function of the stimulus' ability to elicit the consummatory response on that particular trial.

4. An effect of the instrumental response and reinforcement sequence upon classically conditioned reflexes is suggested.

5. The possibility of extending the results to the secondary reinforcing functions of stimuli is shown and experimental techniques for further study suggested.

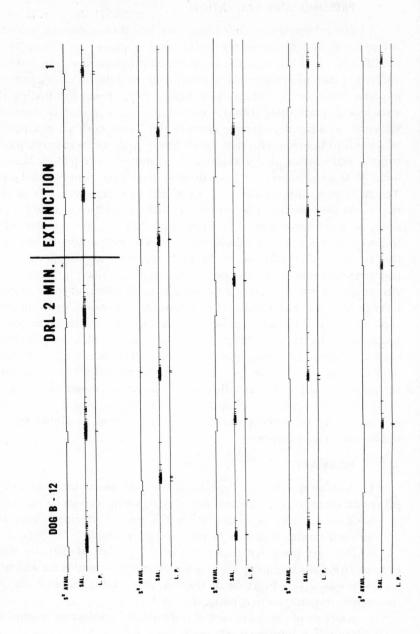

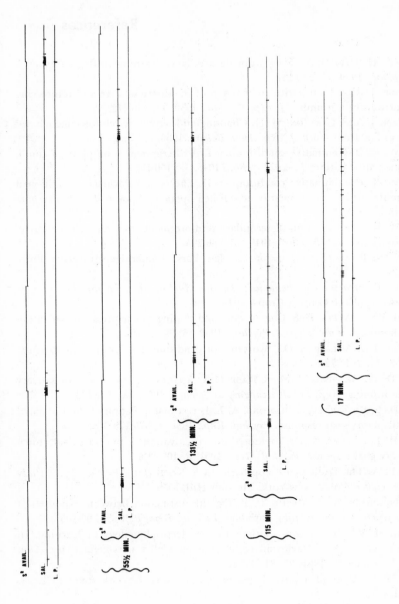

Fig. 14-15. Portions of the record for dog B-12 on extinction following drl 2-minute reinforcement. The top line shows reinforcement availability; the second line, salivation; and the third line of each segment, lever pressing. The length of each omitted portion of the record is indicated.

References

BLACK, A. H. Heart rate changes during avoidance learning in dogs. *Canad. J. Psychol.*, 1959, *13*, 229-242.

DINSMOOR, J. A. A quantitative comparison of the discriminative and reinforcing functions of a stimulus. *J. exp. Psychol.*, 1950, *41*, 458-472.

DINSMOOR, J. A., & CLAYTON, M. H. Chaining and secondary reinforcement based on escape from shock. *J. exp. Anal. Behav.*, 1963, *6*, 75-80.

ESTES, W. K. Discriminative conditioning. I. A discriminative property of conditioned anticipation. *J. exp. Psychol.*, 1943, *32*, 150-155.

ESTES, W. K. Discriminative conditioning. II. Effects of a Pavlovian conditioned stimulus upon a subsequently established operant response. *J. exp. Psychol.*, 1948, *38*, 173-177.

ESTES, W. K. Generalization of secondary reinforcement from the primary drive. *J. comp. physiol. Psychol.*, 1949, *42*, 286-295.

HANSON, N. R. *Patterns of discovery*. New York: Cambridge University Press, 1958.

HULL, C. L. *Principles of behavior: An introduction to behavior theory*. New York: Appleton-Century-Crofts, 1943.

KINTSCH, W., & WITTE, R. S. Concurrent conditioning of bar press and salivation responses. *J. comp. physiol. Psychol.*, 1962, *55*, 693-698.

KONORSKI, J., & MILLER, S. On two types of conditioned reflex. *J. gen. Psychol.*, 1937, *16*, 264-272.

LAUER, D. W., SHAPIRO, M. M., & RADELL, A. A chronic preparation for salivary conditioning. *Bull. Polish Academy of Science*, 1961, *IX*, 121-123.

LEWIS, D. J., BUTLER, D., & DIAMOND, A. L. Direct manipulation of the fractional anticipatory goal response. *Psychol. Rep.*, 1958, *4*, 575-578.

LEWIS, D. J., & KENT, N. D. Attempted direct activation of the fractional anticipatory goal response. *Psychol. Rep.*, 1961, *8*, 107-110.

LOGAN, F. A. The Hull-Spence approach. In S. KOCH (Ed.), *Psychology: a study of a science*, Vol. 2. New York: McGraw-Hill, 1959.

MACCORQUODALE, K., & MEEHL, P. E. On the distinction between hypothetical constructs and intervening variables. *Psychol. Rev.*, 1948, *55*, 97-105.

MAGOUN, H. W. Recent contributions to the electrophysiology of learning. In N. S. KLINE (Ed.), Pavlovian conference on higher nervous activity. *Ann. N. Y. Acad. Sci.*, 1961, *92*, 813-1198.

PAVLOV, I. P. Reply of a physiologist to psychologists. *Psychol. Rev.*, 1932, *39*, 91-127.

PREMACK, D. Predicting instrumental performance from the independent rate of the contingent response. *J. exp. Psychol.*, 1961, *61*, 163-171.

SCHOENFELD, W. N., ANTONITUS, J. J., & BERSH, P. J. A preliminary study of training conditions necessary for secondary reinforcement. *J. exp. Psychol.*, 1950, *40*, 40-45.

SHAPIRO, M. M. Respondent salivary conditioning during operant lever pressing in dogs. *Science,* 1960, *132,* 619-620.

SHAPIRO, M. M. Salivary and motor conditioning: A reply to Konorski. *Science,* 1961, *133,* 1286-1287. (a)

SHAPIRO, M. M. Salivary conditioning in dogs during fixed-interval reinforcement contingent upon lever pressing. *J. exp. Anal. Behav.,* 1961, *4,* 361-364. (b)

SHAPIRO, M. M. Temporal relationship between salivation and level pressing with differential reinforcement of low rates. *J. comp. phyisol. Psychol.,* 1962, *55,* 567-571.

SOLOMON, R. L., & TURNER, L. H. Discriminative classical conditioning in dogs paralyzed by curare can later control discriminative avoidance responses in the normal state. *Psychol. Rev.,* 1962, *69,* 202-219.

ZENER, K. The significance of behavior accompanying conditioned salivary secretion for theories of the conditioned reflex. *Amer. J. Psychol.,* 1937, *50,* 384-403.

FRED D. SHEFFIELD

Yale University

15

Relation Between Classical Condition-
ing and Instrumental Learning [1]

This paper is directed to the topic of how rewards function in
learning. Another way of describing the topic, in modern par-
lance, would be to call it "the nature of the reinforcement process," or to
say it is concerned with "theories of reinforcement." The modern usage
of the concept of "reinforcement," however, involves considerable dis-
tortion in the original Pavlovian (1927) meaning, and I would like to be
clear first on the sense in which the concept is used here. This is particularly appropriate because the kind of theory which I support would
be called by some a "non-reinforcement" theory.

In the original terminology of conditioning, "reinforcement" referred
to the specific operations of pairing US with CS in appropriate temporal
contiguity. These operations "reinforced" (i.e., strengthened) the CR, a
new functional connection between the "neutral" CS and the UR, the
latter being the reflex response to US. Probably unfortunately, the same
descriptive terms were borrowed when psychologists underwent a revival
of interest in a different set of operations which also strengthened a new
functional connection between a neutral stimulus and a response. I refer
here to the operations used by Thorndike (1898, 1911) in which a response
made for whatever reason in a particular stimulus complex is immediately followed by reward.

The stage was set for mixing terminology when Miller and Konorski
(1928), using a Thorndikian set of operations, referred to the outcome as
"a special type of conditioned reflex." The sharing of terms with different meanings was further extended by Skinner (1935, 1938), who kept

[1] The research work on which this report is based was supported by Yale University,
The American Philosophical Society, and The National Science Foundation.

the terms "conditioning," "reflex," and "reinforcement" even though the operational meanings were very different depending on whether he was speaking of Pavlovian (respondent) conditioning or Thorndikian (operant) learning. Multiple meanings were essentially made official in the influential book, *Conditioning and Learning,* by Hilgard and Marquis (1940). They used the term "conditioning" whether the operations were Pavlovian ("classical conditioning") or whether they were basically Thorndikian ("instrumental conditioning") and they followed Hilgard (1937) in using the term "reinforcement" whether a US elicited the response ("homogeneous reinforcement") or whether a reward followed the response ("heterogeneous reinforcement").

In addition, Hilgard and Marquis gave a new slant to the concept of "reinforcement" by treating it as a concept related to process theory. They essentially defined reinforcement as that which when present strengthens connections. This followed Skinner in applying the same term to more than one kind of operation. But they also organized their book around leading theories of the process involved—and thereby transformed the concept into one of "strengthening mechanism" rather than "strengthening operations." Since the strengthening mechanisms were all hypothetical this paved the way for confusion of theory and operations.

The chief effect of this latter confusion was that "reinforcement" essentially became identical with "reward" due to the ascendancy of the Hullian theoretical position as presented by Mowrer (1939), Miller and Dollard (1941), Hull (1943), and others in the group that subscribed to what Kendler (1951) called "S-R reinforcement" theory. They distinguished themselves from Tolman 1932) by the "S-R" and they distinguished themselves from Pavlov (1927) or Guthrie (1935, 1940) by the "reinforcement," which in their mechanics meant reward, need-reduction, drive-reduction, or in general what the animal gains by responding. They did not use "reinforcement" to stand for operations (as did Skinner, 1938) but rather as a theoretical construct, present even in Pavlovian conditioning in some hidden rewarding aspect of the US or the procedure.

Given this background of confusion of meanings, my preference is to use "conditioning" only when talking about a Pavlovian learning situation and "instrumental learning" when referring to a Thorndikian learning situation. My preference also is to distinguish between "reward" and "reinforcement" and use the latter term as little as possible and only in the sense of the *operations* which strengthen a functional connection between a stimulus complex and a response. In these terms "reinforcement theory" is concerned with the mechanics of the process or processes by which such strengthening operations achieve their effects.

It should be clear that this usage is different from Kimble's in his recent revision of Hilgard and Marquis. Kimble (1961, p. 203) identifies "reinforcement" with an *event,* such as giving food or water, turning a shock off or on, etc., and essentially commits everyone to a particular theoretical position by saying that some such event is necessary to *learning* and that there is no important dispute about the validity of this empirical principle of reinforcement. It is in this unfortunate frame of reference that my own position would be classed as a "non-reinforcement" theory since I am convinced that contiguity in time is the only essential of the learning process per se.

Turning now from "reinforcement" concepts to research, the problem which was responsible for my undertaking investigations in classical conditioning derived from the classical experiment in avoidance training by Brogden, Lipman, and Culler (1938). You will recall that in this experiment a two-second tone terminated in a brief, tenth-second shock in the Pavlovian procedure, whereas in the avoidance procedure the brief shock was omitted if the guinea pig moved his squirrel cage at least a minimal distance (one inch on the circumference). The results were a fairly rapid acquisition of consistent, conditioned forward movements with the avoidance procedure but poor performance, averaging about only 50 percent conditioning at best, with the 100 percent shock procedure. This experiment was widely interpreted as evidence that preventing an impending shock functioned as a reward which had a Thorndikian strengthening effect which more than offset the effects of Pavlovian extinction expected from the frequent omissions of US.

It may also be recalled that in a subsequent experiment Sheffield (1941, 1948), using the methods of Brogden, Lipman, and Culler, presented evidence (a) that omission of an impending shock led to extinction of the CR even during avoidance training and (b) that their alleged Pavlovian procedure involved incompatible UR's in that shock during an anticipatory run to CS was about as likely to stop the running response as to facilitate it. In later experiment, Sheffield and Temmer (1950) showed that if escape training is used to guarantee forward locomotion on every trial, performance is better during 100 percent shock training than during avoidance training, although resistance to extinction was greater after avoidance training. This latter feature was interpreted by Sheffield and Temmer in terms of a generalization decrement factor, which is greater during extinction after 100 percent shocks than during extinction following the relatively infrequent shocks involved toward the end of avoidance training.

This interpretation was not very well received by some colleagues. In particular, the greater resistance to extinction following avoidance training in the Sheffield and Temmer experiment could be interpreted as evidence for the rewarding effects of avoidance, which was not immediately stopped from the animal's standpoint when the experimenter disconnected the shocking device during extinction proper.

To get around this difficulty of interpretation it seemed appropriate to do an experiment with the same procedures as Brogden, Lipman, and Culler but with a benevolent US rather than a noxious one. Specifically it was proposed to present a tone CS which always terminates in food in the 100 percent Pavlovian procedure, the CR being conditioned salivation with dogs, but to omit food whenever the dog shows anticipatory salivation to the tone CS in the alternative procedure. Obviously it is not very appropriate to call this latter procedure an "avoidance training" procedure since the US (food) is something appetitive rather than something aversive, so I invented the name "omission training" to cover the general case in which the US is omitted on every trial on which the subject gives an anticipatory CR.[2]

It should be clear that "omission training," as here used, is a general case of a conditioning procedure of which classical avoidance training is only the special type in which the US is noxious. From classical conditioning principles we expect the type in which US is noxious to obey the same principles as the type in which US is "benevolent," as with food when hungry, or neutral, as when US is a click which elicits a PGR. What is expected is that both the 100 percent Pavlovian procedure and the omission procedure will start alike during acquisition but will diverge to a lesser CR amplitude for the omission procedure during training, especially with a low amplitude criterion of a CR. The lesser amplitude during omission training is expected because of the admixture of extinction from trials when US is omitted. From the standpoint of frequency rather than amplitude we might expect both acquisition curves to rise at about the same rate, especially if we plot in terms of a CR amplitude that is less than the value used as the criterion of omission of US. During extinction, on the other hand, we expect the curves to cross, performance after omission training extinguishing more slowly due to the smaller generalization decrement alluded to above.

The purpose of the proposed experiment thus was to see whether these expectations based on classical conditioning and confirmed with shock in the experiment by Sheffield and Temmer (1950), would also be found in the case of omission training using conditioned salivation and food as US.

An additional appeal of the experiment, however, was that it offered an indirect opportunity to test the single-principle law-of-effect interpretation of classical conditioning, which argues that hidden Thorn-

---

2 This meaning of "omission training" should be distinguished from Kimble's (1961) usage, which he attributes to the present writer. In Kimble's usage "omission training" is a mixture of reward and punishment, reward being withheld if an undesirable response occurs and presented if the response fails to occur. My intention was to apply the term only to classical conditioning procedures, "omission" referring only to omission of US, which is withheld if an anticipatory CS occurs and presented if an anticipatory CR fails to occur. Kimble's treatment differs in that it substitutes "reward" for "US."

dikian operations account for Pavlovian phenomena. Thus the omission procedure outlined above is one in which, from the standpoint of the law of effect, the dog is rewarded with food whenever he fails to salivate to tone. This should teach the dog to keep its mouth dry in order to get rewarded on every trial. Clearly the motivational setup is quite different for omission training with food versus omission training with shock, making the experiment quite relevant to law-of-effect interpretations of avoidance training. This aspect of the experiment was perhaps of more general interest than the initial purpose, the question of interest being: is reward a factor in classical conditioning of autonomically controlled respondents?

The experiment was formally simple, but it ran into a number of complications, which will be taken up in order.

The initial complication was concerned with the methodology of salivary conditioning with dogs. Whereas salivary conditioning has always played a large role in textbooks, and is fairly central to learning theory in America, very few American psychologists had ever either mastered or used the Russian methods. A detailed description of the fistula operation was provided by Roger Loucks (private communication) and elucidated by Karl Zener, who had learned the operation from Loucks and who demonstrated it to Byron Campbell, my collaborator in setting up a conditioning laboratory. We also learned from Zener about the discouraging aspects of the Pavlovian techniques, which no doubt accounted for the dearth of American research in this area.

These difficulties, and the outlines of alternative procedures, were mentioned in an earlier report (Sheffield, 1957); the details of the procedures currently in use are also available (Sheffield, Williams, & Ellison, 1964). Briefly, the method is to make an "artificial fistula" by means of a chronic cannula in the normal parotid duct, the cannula being held in place by attachment to a chronic "cheek-piece," which is a structure consisting of two plates, one inside and one outside the cheek, these being held together by two rods which pierce the cheek. The cannula terminates in a metal spigot on the outside plate used for attaching the recording equipment. Recording is by means of a rigid closed-water system which lets small drops out of a hypodermic needle at the same rate as saliva is put into the system by the dog. Drop size is approximately .004 cc and the flow of drops is electrically transmitted to an Esterline Angus polygraph also used for recording stimuli and counting drop rate per second.

With the major methodological difficulties out of the way the subsequent complications in the original experimental plan were concerned with the phenomena observed.

The first attempt was carried out in collaboration with David R. Williams. We had two dogs, and the design called for training them first on 100 percent Pavlovian reinforcement, then extinguishing, then shifting to omission training, and finally extinguishing after omission training. This was an unbalanced design but the research was primarily exploratory; also we assumed that, other things constant, a second extinction should go faster, so that the imbalance would work against expected greater resistance after omission training, which was to come second in the sequence.

Under this regime one of the dogs (Vicki) attained a level of 100 percent anticipation (20 trials per day) for three successive days, at which point we gave extinction trials and found extinction to be very rapid (only 4 CRs). We then shifted to omission training, the criterion of a CR being at least one anticipatory drop of saliva in the 4 sec. of tone preceding the onset of the feeder motor (the tone continued through the sound of the feeder, terminating with the presentation of food 5½ sec. after onset of tone). Under these omission conditions she quickly reached a level of about 50 percent anticipation, varying little above or below this value over a period of 40 successive days, a total of 800 trials. We had already abandoned the original design of this pilot study, for reasons to be discussed later in connection with the performance of the other dog, and were mainly concerned with whether this dog (Vicki) would learn to inhibit saliva because a dry mouth always brought food.

We regarded the fact that she maintained a fairly stable level of 50 percent responding during 800 trials as strong evidence against the operation of the law of effect in the case of the salivary response. Also, when we did extinguish after 800 trials the number of CR's was much larger than after the prior 100 percent Pavlovian reinforcement. This appeared to substantiate the expectation, from generalization decrement, that resistance to extinction would be greater after omission training.

Long before this, however, we had a different view of the experiment as a whole due to the performance of the other dog (Belle). She gave her first anticipatory CR on the 8th trial and was close to 100 percent anticipation immediately thereafter in the first condition (100 percent Pavlovian). Within a day or so of training, however, she showed a lengthening of CR latency until her CR began about the time US was presented. The existence of the CR, and its delayed character, could be readily demonstrated by test trials on which food was omitted. On such trials she always salivated about the time food normally arrived.

The implications of this outcome for the omission-training experiment are fairly obvious. This dog could not be carried to the omission phase of the experiment for the simple reason that she had learned to keep her mouth dry to tone even under 100 percent Pavlovian reinforcement. Thus, in order to program the omission conditions it is necessary to get *anticipatory* salivation as the basis for preventing US if a CR is given. If the normal conditioned salivation to food is delayed until the food delivery device is already activated it is impossible to program the omission training.

It should be clear that this dog's behavior was not in support of the law of effect. She was fed no matter what she did, in a strictly Pavlovian classical conditioning procedure. But she nevertheless adopted a lagging CR despite the fact that onset of CS (tone) invariably signaled that food would be delivered in 5½ seconds.

In formal Pavlovian terms this phenomenon could be called "inhibition of delay." Williams and I did not think of it in these terms at first because "inhibition of delay," as portrayed by Pavlov, was a phenomenon associated with a relatively long delayed CS, such as from about 30 seconds up to about 2 or 3 minutes' duration. He does not describe a comparable phenomenon with a short CS, such as 4 to 8 seconds, which would be included in his range of "simultaneous" conditioning. We were more inclined to think in terms of the dog's forming a discrimination between the onset of the tone CS, which is never accompanied by food, and the compound of feeder noise and termination of tone, which always overlapped with the sudden appearance of food in the food bowl. Our feeder mechanism was inside the soundproof room with the dog, and made a noise for about 1½ seconds leading to the arrival of food. (It will be recalled that there were 4 seconds of tone, followed by 1½ seconds of tone plus feeder noise, culmination in food itself.) It should also be mentioned that the dogs had numerous adaptation trials of magazine training with feeder followed by food prior to conditioning proper; this might be expected to help the dogs discriminate the tone from tone plus feeder.

I am now inclined, however, to discount the idea that our particular feeder and magazine-training procedures accounted for our finding "inhibition of delay" even with a short CS. For one thing the dog can always use the final sight of food in the food bowl as the equivalent of the sound of the feeder. That is, he can discriminate the CS alone from the compound of CS plus sight of food, and learn to salivate only when the food is present. Furthermore he can make a temporal discrimination between the initiation of CS and the point in time at which US arrives, even if there is no specific extra signal, such as sight of food, which immediately precedes US. This kind of procedure might tax the sensory capacities of a dog to their limits, but the mechanism would be the same, namely, a conditioned discrimination between onset of CS, which is never reinforced, and time of presenting US, which is always reinforced.

With this discrimination mechanism in mind the concept of "inhibition of delay" seems unwarranted except as a description of the particular case in which the cues are primarily temporal. The basic mechanism is that of generalization and discrimination. At the outset of training the dog responds to the onset of CS because it is similar to the cues present at the time US is presented. Later the dog discriminates the onset pattern from the cue-pattern present when US is presented. With a long CS, or a trace CS, the difference is primarily temporal, and "discrimination of delay" (as contrasted with "inhibition of delay") might be an appropriate concept. But with either a short or a long CS the dog can still learn to discriminate any cue (e.g., sight of food) which signals the immediate imminence of US.

It should be pointed out that this interpretation makes the assumption that something very close to simultaneity of CS and US is the optimum timing for conditioning. We cannot speak of a temporal discrimination between onset and termination of CS without the hypothesis that onset of a delayed CS, even though always followed later by US, is nevertheless non-reinforced from the standpoint of precise temporal contiguity. By making the assumption that conditioning is optimal with precise simultaneity, we expect the peak of the CR to coincide with the point in time at which UR is normally elicited.

Support for this interpretation comes from a recent study by Gaylord Ellison (1963, 1964). Ellison was concerned with trace conditioning of the salivary response but one of his controls involved an 8-sec. delayed CS, and he included test trials in which US (food) was omitted in order to plot the form of the CR without the complication of the UR. Relevant data from his study are shown in Figure 15-1, in which it can be seen that with continued training the peak of the CR coincides fairly well with the time UR normally begins, while at the same time the relative proportion of CR that is anticipatory declines. Ellison's experiment was not complicated by a feeder sound; the feeder was pre-loaded between trials and the only "feeder" sound was the noise of the food dropping into the food bowl.

The above interpretation in terms of a temporal discrimination also fits very well the phenomena described by Pavlov under a different heading from "inhibition of delay." This is covered in Pavlov's Lecture XIV (1927) and can be paraphrased as "the disappearance of conditioned reflexes" under conditions of 100 percent reinforcement. Pavlov here refers to instances in which, for example, a 30 second CS is used over extended periods. As he says:

As time goes on the latent period lengthens out and finally during the 30 seconds of isolated action of the conditioned stimulus no trace of salivary conditioning is produced. (Pavlov, 1927, p. 235)

He also points out that if the CS is lengthened by 5-10 seconds the CR reappears, but further says that:

Finally a stage is reached when no conditioned salivation can be obtained during any length of isolated action of the conditioned stimulus. (Pavlov, 1927, p. 235)

In this context Pavlov does not describe any results found with test trials in which US is omitted in order to find out whether the CR is present with a latent period corresponding to the usual time of presenting US. The expectation offered here is that such test trials would reveal a CR, timed at about the usual temporal location of the UR.

All this digression into the topic of so-called "inhibition of delay" has taken me rather far off the basic topic of the role of rewards in learning. It is an essential digression, however, in understanding the dif-

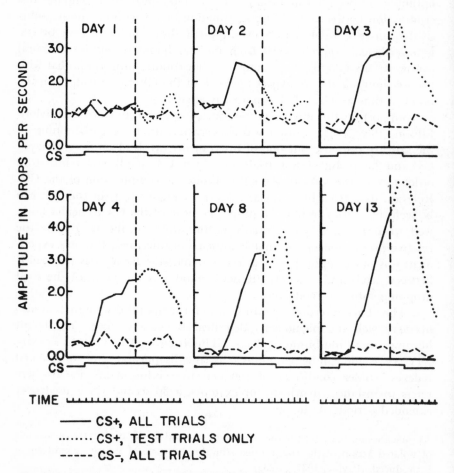

Fig. 15-1. Progressive changes in the proportion of CR that anticipates US. The vertical dashed line is the point at which food delivery was initiated. The solid-line curve reflects trials on which the reinforced tone CS was presented; the dashed-line curve reflects trials on which a control tone (non-reinforced) of a different pitch was presented; the dotted-line curve reveals the course of CR to reinforced CS on test trials (food reinforcement omitted so that UR does not mask CR). Results are averages of 4 dogs, 26 trials per day, of which 12 each are CS tone and control tone and 2 are test trials. (Ellison, 1964)

ficulties encountered in attempting to carry out the omission-training experiment. Even the 100 percent dogs are capable of learning to "keep their mouths dry" in response to tone, regardless of the fact that this is not at all instrumental in obtaining reward.

Despite these difficulties we have come to the conclusion that omission training does not produce results that conform to the law of effect. I have already referred to the results with Vicki, in which she never learned to control salivation during 800 omission-training trials. This was a lucky result in the sense that she also did not develop "inhibition of delay" during this period; if she had, she would have dropped to 0 percent anticipation and 100 percent reward. This would have simulated the law-of-effect result even though the real process was discrimination learning. Fortunately for our pilot experiment, Vicki did not achieve the discrimination even after prolonged omission training whereas Belle achieved it early in 100 percent Pavlovian training.

In subsequent work using the omission-training procedure (with Williams and Ellison), we have uniformly obtained the result that acquisition proceeds faster with 100 percent conditioning than with omission training. We have not, however, found that dogs with omission training learn to keep their mouths dry any sooner than dogs with 100 percent Pavlovian conditioning. At one point we thought they would, on the grounds that any form of partial reinforcement should teach the dog that the only dependable evidence that eating is imminent is sight of food itself, since part of the time CS is not followed by food. We thought this might facilitate discrimination between CS proper and that part of the total CS sequence which includes seeing the food fall into the food bowl. So far this expectation, which would simulate the law of effect if verified, has not been confirmed in any obvious fashion. The major factor appears to be the tendency for CR to become more and more coincident with presentation of US, and this process goes on whether the conditions are those of omission training or those of 100 percent reinforcement. The process also appears to proceed at grossly different rates for different dogs, which makes it difficult to demonstrate any small differential trends due to training procedure.

In an attempt to circumvent this aspect of omission training and give the law of effect a better chance to reveal its operation, Ellison and I tried a different program designed to use reward as a means of preventing "inhibition of delay," assuming reward is relevant to salivary conditioning. In this program, if the dog gives an anticipatory response it is immediately rewarded. Specifically, a 7-sec. tone overlapped with the presentation of food, which came 6-sec. after onset of tone. If the dog gave at least one anticipatory drop of saliva after tone onset the food was immediately presented; if it failed to anticipate, food came at the end of 6 sec. of tone. This is a 100 percent reinforcement procedure but is calculated to reward anticipatory salivation and prevent "inhibition of delay."

The data did not support the expectation from the law-of-effect conception. Short latency responses were not more in evidence than with the usual 100 percent reinforcement procedure, and the peak CR rate tended to converge toward the limiting time of presenting US. This might be regarded as a weak test of the law of effect because it makes the assumption that the hungry dog would prefer to get fed as soon as possible rather than waiting out the six seconds before inevitable reward. The results so far at least indicate, however, that the timing of reward is a less important factor than the timing of dependable events in the environment, the most dependable feature being that no matter what else happened, the food was never delayed more than six seconds after onset of CS.

In a very recent attempt to investigate the possible role of the law of effect in salivary conditioning we used omission training with acid rather than food as the US. This omission procedure would classify as "avoidance training" on the assumption that a sour solution of 1.5 percent (by volume) acetic acid is a noxious or aversive stimulus for dogs. This is a good assumption in terms of the increase in struggling in the conditioning stand seen when the prior adaptation sessions are shifted to conditioning sessions. In this research, with Gaylord Ellison and Edward Zamble, we used a 5-sec. tone CS which overlapped with 3 cc of the acid solution, delivered at the end of the 4th second in one sudden gravity-controlled squirt through a hollow rod in the cheek-piece. In the 100 percent reinforcement procedure acid was delivered on each of 10 daily trials spaced an average of 3 minutes apart. In the omission procedure the acid delivery device was intercepted if the dog showed sufficient anticipatory salivation.

From the standpoint of the law of effect the use of acid should work against the "inhibition of delay" factor since anticipatory saliva is rewarding because it helps dilute the acid. Also from the standpoint of the most general form of the law of effect (animals learn the adaptive response) this omission-training procedure should foster anticipatory salivation since a CR that meets the criterion prevents acid entirely.

The results so far do not support the idea that prevention of acid under omission training strengthens the anticipatory salivary CR. Dogs trained with this procedure apparently go through cycles of acquisition and extinction, the CR showing a steady increase in frequency but a lengthening of latency and a decline in amplitude toward the limit set by the criterion for preventing acid. In general the acid used was a more effective US than food in the sense that it gives a larger amplitude of UR and CR, faster conditioning, and a higher CR frequency under omission training. It has the disadvantage of producing more "spontaneous" bursts of salivation between trials. Otherwise it is comparable to food US in that 100 percent conditioning produces more anticipatory responding than omission training. Also under 100 percent conditioning the latency tends to lengthen and the peak rate of CR tends to move in the direction of the time of occurrence of US, as if an "inhibition of delay" factor were present rather than a tendency for strong early salivation which would dilute the acid in line with the law of effect.

In general, in all of our results with omission training and salivary conditioning we have seen no evidence of the operation of a reward factor which strengthens connections by a different process from those covered under the heading of classical conditioning.

The findings on resistance to extinction of salivary conditioning after omission training are less secure. We have not found a striking difference in this respect, as was originally predicted from the generalization decrement factor. A difficulty in testing this expectation is that omission training tends to create a CR that is weak in amplitude compared to the 100 percent conditioning procedure. The question of whether the extinction curves will cross or whether they will converge at zero amplitude is therefore partly determined by the criterion chosen for an anticipatory CR. If the criterion is small enough, omission training tends to produce a fair frequency of CRs, but CRs that are close to zero in amplitude. If the criterion is large enough omission training becomes essentially identical with 100 percent conditioning, there being only a few anticipatory CRs during training that are large enough to produce omission of US. Our data have not revealed any particularly "happy median," and although they favor slightly more resistance to extinction after omission training, the difference has not been particularly noticeable.

A conclusion which might be drawn from our results to date is that the law of effect does not apply to involuntary responses, or what Skinner (1938) has called "respondents." I am inclined to agree with this conclusion, especially if "respondents" are defined as responses which are executed with essentially no sensory feedback to inform the animal that the response has occurred. An inherent feature of Thorndike's (1911) law of effect is that the effect of a response determines whether it is learned. This equally inherently implies that the effect of the response must somehow be detected by the animal or recorded in its nervous system, that is, it means that the animal's nervous system must detect the temporal contiguity of the response and its consequences. If a response has little or no sensory feedback it is difficult to understand how the nervous system could take account of the fact that it was executed, let alone rewarded.

There is, of course, some feedback from salivation: it produces fluid in the mouth which is detectable and may even be enough to stimulate swallowing. Also apparently there are both afferent and efferent fibers to the salivary gland, so the nervous system could have information both that the salivary gland had been stimulated and that saliva had been produced. My argument is mainly that salivary feedback is relatively weak and non-distinctive compared to feedback from skeletal responses, which commonly have cutaneous, visual, and auditory consequences as well as being felt. Thus salivation and many other autonomic responses would be low in the scale of feedback and therefore low in the scale of susceptibility to influence by any process which depends on the effect of the response on the environment. These considerations are mentioned in passing at this time; they will be taken up again in connection with a general theory of the operation of rewards.

Before discussing this general theory I would like to discuss some phenomena which, like the observations concerning "inhibition of delay," were incidental to the general attempt to carry out the originally planned omission-training study.

One of these observations is concerned with the salivary behavior of the dogs between trials. My original expectation was that there would be a certain amount of generalized salivation to being in the conditioning stand, once the dog had been exposed to the US during preliminary training, but that this would extinguish, in the course of discrimination, so that the dog would salivate only when CS is present. My conception was that this early generalized salivation would be a sort of random dribble between trials, which might fluctuate in magnitude but would be spread fairly evenly through the interval between trials. Instead, the observation was that the between-trial salivation came in bursts, each of which looked like the kind of burst characteristic of a CR. Moreover, such bursts are never completely eliminated, although their frequency and magnitude may go down somewhat in the course of training.

These bursts are such an ever-present nuisance that the experimenter, who is watching the dog, the polygraph, and the tape that programs trials, is kept in a continual state of anxiety lest a burst start just ahead of CS, spoiling the record of what otherwise might be a clearcut CR. Also it is often difficult to tell whether a "CR" was actually a response to the CS or whether it was a lucky burst, accidentally timed with the CS. Moreover, the bursts between trials look so much like the response to CS that one is obliged to raise the question of whether the bursts also have a "CS" and, if so, what the nature of this unobserved CS is.

A relevant further observation has been that these bursts tend to be accompanied by motor responses that indicate orientation toward the food bowl in the case of conditioning based on food as US. For example, the dog might be looking away from the food bowl between trials, then show signs of impatience, and finally put its head down to the food bowl. Such a response is commonly timed with a burst of saliva.

One interpretation of this correlation between motor and salivary behavior is that the motor response provides proprioceptive cues which have been conditioned to the salivary response. We can think of the motor behavior of approaching the food bowl as a response whose operant level has been increased by presenting food, and explain the salivary bursts as respondent conditioning to the response-produced cues. In line with this idea, in a pilot experiment, Williams and I arranged a program in which our dog, Vicki, after all her prior experience with both 100 percent conditioning and omission training, was required to press a panel in order to set up a regular Pavlovian trial. We had a separate "time in" stimulus, a buzzer, to indicate when the press would be effective; when the buzzer was on, a panel press turned on the tone CS, which overlapped with the presentation of food at the end of about 5½ seconds.

The findings which are immediately relevant are those based on false presses when the buzzer was not sounding. Eventually, of course, the dog learned to press only if the buzzer was operating, but during the initial phases she often falsely pressed in the absence of this time-in signal. Such occasions were invariably accompanied by a salivary response. The most important fact, however, was that whereas salivary secretion usually either accompanied or followed the panel press, it also frequently *preceded* the panel press. From this I concluded that between-trial bursts in salivary conditioning cannot be explained simply as CRs to the proprioceptive cues of food-orientation responses, and that some central cue must account for both the salivary and the motor behavior.

I would make a similar interpretation of the results reported by Ellison and Williams (1962) in which both salivary and instrumental behavior were recorded simultaneously in a study in which dogs bar-pressed for food either on a fixed ratio or fixed-interval schedule. With fixed interval they found a high correlation between the temporal onset of pressing and the onset of salivation. They also found that sometimes salivation preceded pressing, although it usually followed slightly. In its crudest subjective form, my conception of the mechanism involved is that when their time-in stimulus, which functioned as a delayed CS, had been on sufficiently long, the dogs started "thinking" about food, which set off both pressing and salivation.

Essentially the same interpretation can be made of the temporal correlation in salivary and motor behavior of dogs conditioned with acid as US. Here there is nothing comparable to orienting to the food bowl since acid is squirted directly into the dog's mouth. There is nevertheless concomitant motor behavior which can be described best as "mouthing," which is a mixture of tongue movements, jaw movements, and swallowing. This motor response is a distinct part of the UR, is almost always present in the CR, and is equally prominent in bursts of saliva between trials. We do not have any data on the precise temporal relations between salivation and "mouthing" with acids, but there is an obvious correlation between the two when the dogs are observed between trials during conditioning.

Since such bursts cannot be distinguished, in response form, from a CR, an important question is raised both about the nature of the "hidden CS" for bursts and the nature of the "true CS" for a CR that is identified by the fact that it was tripped off by the controlled CS. Again my interpretation is inclined in the direction of thinking of the "true CS" as some form of central representation of US.

Most of the foregoing observations and interpretations have been consistent with the assumption that rewards are irrelevant in classical conditioning. They are directed to the question of whether the law of effect is applicable to classical conditioning and have not been directed to the phenomena to which the law of effect was originally applied. I apologize for the fact that most of the findings referred to are not published results, but I should emphasize that the ones mentioned are sufficiently recurrent to be a good basis for conjecture.

I would now like to change the subject to situations in which rewards are relevant. The typical situation is one in which the animal executes a so-called "spontaneous" skeletal response and this is followed by a reward due to a cause-and-effect relation in the environment, making the reward contingent on the execution of the response. The phenomenon observed is that the successful response becomes more likely to occur in the stimulus complex in which it originally competed with a variety of other "spontaneous" responses.

Thorndike's (1911) wording, in calling his learning principle the "Law of effect," was well chosen; he clearly referred to the causal *effect* of the response on environmental events. Similarly the wording of Hilgard and Marquis (1940), in calling Thorndikian learning *instrumental,* was very appropriate since it equally recognized the contingency of reward on execution of the response.

As interpreted here, a key fact in understanding the mechanics of instrumental learning is the fact that such a cause-and-effect relation necessarily implies that something done by the animal is invariably followed by reward. If the instrumental response has sensory concomitants, and if the animal gives a uniform response to the reward, we have a perfect setup for classical conditioning of the response elicited by the reward, the CS being response-produced and the US being the reward stimulus. Thus if the environment is rigged so that a bar press immediately causes food to appear, we can take for granted, from the phenomena of classical conditioning, that the animal will learn to salivate whenever he presses the bar. The bar itself might become a temporary CS for salivation, and approaching the bar might also become a temporary CS for salivation, but these generalized stimuli will also be subject to discrimination, and the only stimulus complex that will be classically reinforced 100 percent of the time is the complex emanating from execution of the correct response.

I have phrased the above paragraph in terms of conditioned salivation in order to be specific; actually any and all consistent responses to US (reward) should also become classically conditioned. Salivation is only one aspect of the total UR to reward, which includes central as well as peripheral components. The important derivation is that every instrumental learning situation is a classical conditioning situation, with reward as US and response-produced cues as CS. More specifically, instrumental learning is a differential conditioning situation, in which cues from the general environment are only partially reinforced and cues specific to responses that are in any way incorrect are never reinforced. We can safely deduce that the relation between the correct-response feedback and the response to reward as a US will be exactly that of a classical CR.

This is a forward step in understanding the function of rewards in learning but it does not in itself explain why a functional connection is formed between the situation and the instrumental response. So far it only explains why the animal will anticipate reward if and when he starts to perform the correct response; it does not explain why this anticipation of reward causes the animal to select out the correct response as his habitual way of behaving in the situation.

To explain this I have made the hypothesis that anticipation of reward has an exciting effect which feeds into whatever behavior is underway at the time reward is anticipated. Using the example of food as the reward, the idea is that if the animal starts to execute the correct response he gives an anticipatory CR based on his UR to food. This CR carries an excitement component which immediately adds vigor to the behavior underway, namely correct responding, and makes it prepotent over other possible responses in the situation. If we keep the hypothesis at this simple level it is easy to see why the animal acquires the correct response. *Only correct responding can initiate anticipation of reward,* and if anticipation of reward is exciting, and if this excitement feeds into the response underway, then the correct response is the only one that will be favored by the exciting effects of reward. Given this mechanism for prepotency of the rewarded response it will not only be more likely to occur than others after a single reward but will also become the dominant habit in the situation through sheer frequency of practice.

In point of fact my basic hypotheses are somewhat more reductive than the simple assumption that anticipation of a reward is exciting.

At a more molecular level my assumption is that the UR to a reward stimulus inherently carries a component of relaxation rather than excitement but that any stimulus which tends to elicit the UR under circumstances in which it cannot occur is a source of excitement. The conception is that the US itself, in the case of rewards, is a dominant stimulus which takes precedence over all others and which channels all of the activity into the UR. Thus, the hungry animal exposed to food starts eating, and in the typical environment there are few stimuli which would interfere with this response. Also the skeletal musculature as a whole is relaxed while eating and all of the "excitement" is channeled into the eating response. If the same hungry animal is exposed to familiar food out of reach, however, he necessarily is stimulated to eat under circumstances in which eating is not possible. The hypothesis is that these are the circumstances which produce general excitement which feeds into whatever behavior is underway. This hypothesis I have called the "drive-induction" hypothesis (Sheffield, Roby, & Campbell, 1954) because it implies a special sort of excitement induced, not by the animal's deprivation state, but rather by the stimulation of a consummatory response under circumstances in which the consummatory response cannot occur. This is not to say that the drive state is irrelevant, but drive is conceived not as a stimulus but rather as an internal state affecting the vigor of the UR to the consummatory stimulus. Thus if hunger drive is low, eating cannot even be elicited; if hunger drive is high, eating in response to food is vigorous and food out of reach is the occasion for general excitement.

It should be clear that the most common type of stimulus which can arouse the consummatory response without allowing it to occur in the driven animal is a *conditioned* stimulus for the consummatory response. We can find a few exceptions, as when a hungry neonate is stimulated with a dry nipple or when a mother rat is stimulated to retrieve a stray that has been made inaccessible by covering it with a wire mesh cone. In general, however, the important stimuli in the life of the organism which stimulate a consummatory response when it cannot occur are conditioned stimuli which have regularly preceded the rewarding US. This includes the case of the hungry animal that can see and smell food that is out of reach as well as the case of the hungry rat who is halfway down a runway that has food in the goal box. In either case the driven animal is exposed to a CS for the response to food, and the expectation is that it will show excitement due to the unconsummated stimulation of the consummatory response.

Stated in general terms, the proposed mechanism for Thorndikian learning is that early in training the animal is obliged to follow the courses of action which maximize anticipation of the reward. Later in training the animal responds partly in terms of motor conditioning, which reduces the response to an habitual form as contrasted with the earlier phase involving response selection.

With this mechanism in view there are a number of questions still to answer in testing it or in understanding the differences between classical conditioning and instrumental learning.

One such question has already been alluded to, namely the question of whether a response requires some form of feedback in order to be subject to instrumental learning. The proposed mechanism requires this since the response-produced cues serve as the CS for the critical excitement involved. Our findings tend to discredit the idea that salivation can become instrumental, and on the assumption that salivation is a low feedback response the results accordingly tend to confirm the expectation from the proposed mechanism.

Another question is whether the "excitement" from unconsummated consummatory arousal feeds into any and all ongoing responses or whether it energizes only skeletal behavior. If such excitement affected all behavior, we might expect, for example, that a hungry rat would not only run faster and faster in the runway, in proportion to the extent to which he has learned to anticipate food in the goal box, but would also salivate more and more in the runway as training progressed. He might even be expected to salivate more in anticipation than he does to food itself, just as he runs to food with more energetic behavior than his eating when he gets to food. The present findings are against this idea. The "inhibition of delay" phenomena are quite the opposite in implication since they show that as training progresses dogs at least are more and more inclined to delay their salivation until the moment of arrival of food. This is obviously different from what happens in the case of an instrumental sequence. Thus if "inhibition of delay" applied to the running behavior of a rat in a maze or in a runway he would eventually be immobilized at the outset instead of showing (as is typically found) faster and faster running in all sections, and a decreasing latency of getting started.

An implication seems to be that the consummatory arousal feeds primarily into skeletal behavior rather than energizing all response mechanisms indiscriminately. If true, this would give two reasons for thinking there might be a real dichotomy between autonomic and skeletal behavior, in line with the distinction made by Skinner (1938) between involuntary (autonomic) and voluntary (skeletal) responses. The first reason is that autonomic responses tend to have little feedback; the second reason would be that excitement from consummatory arousal affects primarily the skeletal system. From the standpoint of the present proposed mechanism for instrumental learning both of these differences would imply that instrumental learning is primarily confined to skeletal behavior and is quite unlikely in the case of autonomic responses.

I do not consider the proposed mechanism to be the final answer and have already made several revisions since it was first presented at a Brown University colloquium (Sheffield, 1954). I once thought, for example, that consummatory arousal could be identified with "frustration," the increased excitement being an innate "anger" response to *preventing* the consummatory response under circumstances in which it was stimulated but could not be performed. I gave this up for several reasons, including the fact that excited activity in a stabilimeter fell off rapidly if a food signal continued past the using time for presenting food, no food being presented. I also once thought that vigor of consummatory behavior was the best index of reward value in instrumental learning. I have since been obliged to shift to strength of consummatory *stimulation* on the basis of an experiment by Kraeling (1961) in which the concentration of a sucrose reward in hungry rats was found to be a better predictor of instrumental vigor than the asymptotic level of consummatory vigor. Rats apparently tend to reach toward a maximum of consummatory response vigor in drinking sucrose if training is continued long enough and concentration is high enough. They nevertheless continue to show wide variation in speed of running depending on the sweetness of the solution. This result suggests that consummatory excitement is more closely related to central events based on consummatory stimulation than on peripheral events such as vigor of responding.

There are also numerous things still to be learned within the framework of the drive induction approach. For example, it would be interesting to know whether an autonomically controlled response can become subject to instrumental learning if artificial feedback is provided, as would be the case if our dogs were allowed to hear the drop-counter relays and the polygraph clicking off every .004 cc of saliva. We were careful to shield these sounds from the dogs, but the question remains whether operant control of salivation would be possible with instantaneous artificial sensory feedback. It would also be interesting to know whether skeletal excitement in response to anticipated food when hungry, as reflected in a stabilimeter activity device (Sheffield & Campbell, 1954), is subject to an "inhibition of delay" type of phenomenon as contrasted with moving forward—and staying forward—to the point of onset of CS. In a maze the running vigor moves all the way forward to the start box—and stays there as long as the animal is rewarded in the goal box. Would the same be true if only non-instrumental skeletal excitement were measured in a situation in which a signal indicated that food would soon arrive but in which the behavior of the animal had no influence on whether or not food came or how soon it came?

In all such questions it should be emphasized that the present approach is one in which the learning process per se is better reflected by classical conditioning phenomena than it is by instrumental learning phenomena. My best guess is that so-called "instrumental learning" and all forms of "learning" that obey the law of effect, are more closely related to motivational principles than to principles about the learning process. The latter process appears to be based entirely on temporal contiguity and to have classical conditioning as its behavioral prototype. I mention this only in case it was not noticed that all of the hypotheses I used in connection with the drive-induction interpretation of instrumental learning were consistent with the idea that learning itself is merely a question of temporal contiguity of stimulus and response.

References

BROGDEN, W. J., LIPMAN, E. A., & CULLER, E. The role of incentive in conditioning and extinction. *Amer. J. Psychol.*, 1938, *51*, 109-117.

ELLISON, G. D. Differential salivary conditioning to traces. PhD dissertation, Yale University Library, 1963.

ELLISON, G. D. Differential salivary conditioning to traces. *J. comp. physiol. Psychol.*, 1964, *57*, 373-380.

ELLISON, G. D., & WILLIAMS, D. R. Conditioned salivation during FI and FR bar-pressing for food. Paper read at EPA meetings, 1962.

GUTHRIE, E. R. *The psychology of learning.* New York: Harper, 1935.

GUTHRIE, E. R. Association and the Law of Effect. *Psychol. Rev.*, 1940, *47*, 127-148.

HILGARD, E. R. The relationship between the conditioned response and conventional learning experiments. *Psychol. Bull.*, 1937, *34*, 61-102.

HILGARD, E. R., & MARQUIS, D. G. *Conditioning and learning*, 1st ed. New York: Appleton-Century-Crofts, 1940.

HULL, C. L. *Principles of behavior: An introduction to behavior theory.* New York: Appleton-Century-Crofts, 1943.

KENDLER, H. H. Reflections and confessions of a reinforcement theorist. *Psychol. Rev.*, 1951, *58*, 368-374.

KIMBLE, G. A. *Hilgard and Marquis' conditioning and learning*, 2nd ed. New York: Appleton-Century-Crofts, 1961.

KRAELING, DORIS. Analysis of amount of reward as a variable in learning. *J. comp. physiol. Psychol.*, 1961, *54*, 560-565.

MILLER, N. E., & DOLLARD, J. *Social learning and imitation.* New Haven: Yale University Press, 1941.

MILLER, S., & KONORSKI, J. Sur une forme particulière des reflexes conditionnels. *C. R. Soc. Biol.*, Paris, 1928, *99*, 1155-1157.

MOWRER, O. H. A stimulus-response analysis of anxiety and its role as a reinforcing agent. *Psychol. Rev.*, 1939, *46*, 553-565.

PAVLOV, I. P. *Conditioned reflexes.* London: Oxford University Press, 1927. (Transl. by G. V. ANREP.)

SHEFFIELD, F. D. A simple conditioning explanation of an avoidable vs. unavoidable shock training study. *Psychol. Bull.*, 1941, *38*, 569. (Abstract.)

SHEFFIELD, F. D. Avoidance training and the contiguity principle. *J. comp. physiol. Psychol.*, 1948, *41*, 165-177.

SHEFFIELD, F. D. A drive induction theory of reinforcement. New Haven: Yale University, 1954 (mimeographed manuscript).

SHEFFIELD, F. D. Salivary conditioning in dogs. *Yrbk. Amer. Philos. Soc.*, 1957, 284-287.

SHEFFIELD, F. D., & CAMPBELL, B. A. The role of experience in the "spontaneous" activity of hungry rats. *J. comp. physiol. Psychol.*, 1954, *47*, 97-100.

SHEFFIELD, F. D., ROBY, T. B., & CAMPBELL, B. A. Drive reduction versus consummatory responding as determinants of reinforcement. *J. comp. physiol. Psychol.*, 1954, *47*, 349-354.

SHEFFIELD, F. D., & TEMMER, HELENA W. Relative resistance to extinction of escape and avoidance training. *J. exp. Psychol.*, 1950, *40*, 287-298.

SHEFFIELD, F. D., WILLIAMS, D. R., & ELLISON, G. D. A simplified technique for the study of salivary conditioning in dogs. New Haven: Yale University, 1964 (mimeographed manuscript).

SKINNER, B. F. Two types of conditioned reflex and a pseudo type. *J. gen. Psychol.*, 1935, *12*, 66-77.

SKINNER, B. F. *The behavior of organisms: An experimental analysis.* New York: Appleton-Century-Crofts, 1938.

THORNDIKE, E. L. Animal intelligence. An experimental study of the associative processes in animals. *Psychol. Monogr.*, 1898, *2*, No. 4 (Whole No. 8).

THORNDIKE, E. L. *Animal intelligence.* New York: Macmillan, 1911.

TOLMAN, E. C. *Purposive behavior in animals and men.* New York: Appleton-Century, 1932.

DELOS D. WICKENS

The Ohio State University

16

Compound Conditioning in Humans and Cats [1]

The typical laboratory classical conditioning situation differs
from the environment of the real world not only because the two
contrast in degree of stimulus complexity which is present, but because
they also contrast in degree to which the stimulus dimensions of these
two environments are controllable. It is fairly traditional for the subjects
of classical conditioning experiments to be located in rooms which are
generally free from the extraneous introduction of ambient noises or
patterns of visual stimulation. Save for stimuli which may be introduced
by the subject himself, the experimenter, therefore, can readily prescribe
and accurately program the stimulus events and their interrelationship.

Working within the austere environment of this special laboratory
arrangement, psychologists have been highly successful in identifying
lawful relationships between CS and UCS manipulations and consequent
behavior. These relationships are the phenomena of conditioning and
they are statements about the factors which determine the strength of the
association between a relatively uncomplicated stimulus and a relatively
simple response.

In complex environments the behaving subject seems often to engage
in a process which functionally simplifies the environment for him, and
various terms such as perception, stimulus selection, attention or encod-
ing have been used to refer to this process. The consequence of this
activity is to simplify the complex stimulus environment so that only a
single aspect of the environment becomes the actual stimulus for the
response (Warren, 1953; Reynolds, 1961; Underwood, 1963). It is appar-

[1] This research was supported by a National Science Foundation Grant, G 6203 and
G 19606.

ent that knowledge of the laws of S-R connections will be of very limited value for behavior prediction if when the total complex environment has been modified, the functional stimulus for the response cannot be identified by the predictor.

The solution to this difficulty is to identify the principles governing stimulus selection, thus making it possible to predict what, in any given complex environment, the functional stimulus for the organism will be. The assumption behind this solution is, of course, that the process of stimulus selection is lawful and predictable by means of public data and not a purely idiosyncratic process, depending upon the whim of the particular subject at a particular time.

The classical conditioning situation offers an excellent vehicle for investigating this type of problem. It does so because it readily permits the introduction of controlled complications of the environment—in this case the CS—into a situation in which a great deal is known about methodology of research as well as the effects of variations of stimulus and temporal parameters upon the behavior. It is in this manner that I have used the classical conditioning situation in the studies on compound conditioning to be reported below. Thus, what I will have to say is concerned primarily with the problem of stimulus selection rather than with the characteristics of classical conditioning *qua* classical conditioning.

The essential strategy guiding the program has been to choose a variable which is known to affect the degree of conditioning when a single CS is used and then produce a compound CS in which the elements differ from each other with respect to this variable. After training to the compound, the elements alone are presented. The question which is asked is whether or not the individual elements will differ in their effectiveness and if so, could the direction of the difference be predicted from what we know of how this variable operates for a single conditioned stimulus. Differential responding to the elements is considered as evidence of stimulus selection.

The variable with which we have worked thus far is time under two conditions: (1) a differential in offset for elements of a compound which come on simultaneously, or (2) a differential in onset for elements which terminate simultaneously. It turns out that the conclusions insofar as prediction of stimulus selection from how a single stimulus operates are not the same for these two conditions.

ONSET SIMULTANEITY WITH DIFFERENTIAL IN OFFSET TIME

There is evidence that superior conditioning is obtained if, in an instrumental avoidance situation, the CS is made to terminate simultaneously with the escape or avoidance response rather than to continue for a brief time after that response had been made (Mowrer & Lamoreaux, 1942; Wickens & Platt, 1954). Using a finger withdrawal situation, with simultaneous recording of the GSR, Drs. Cross, Morgan and I investigated this variable as it operated on the elements of a compound (1959).

One CS was a 1000 cps tone of 40 db, and the other the illumination of a 2-w light. The UCS was a shock delivered by means of one electrode attached to S's palm and another on a microswitch upon which S's finger rested. The microswitch served the dual purpose of making possible a measurement of the latency of S's response and of terminating a CS element when the response occurred.

Four group of Ss were run, two with single stimulus CS and two with complex stimulus CS. The single stimulus groups were conditioned to a tone which came on 450 msec. before the UCS. For one of these groups the tone was terminated by the finger withdrawal response, and for the other it was terminated by the timer 450 msec. after shock onset. Its total duration was, in other words, 900 msec. The complex groups were conditioned to the complex of light and tone. These stimuli came on simultaneously 450 msec. before the UCS, but one was terminated by the response and the other continued until it was cut off by the timer 450 msec. after shock onset. One experimental group was tested on Trial 8 and during extinction to the component which was terminated by the response, while the other group was tested to the delayed termination component. Training was counterbalanced so that the test component was always the tone.

The results for the finger withdrawal frequency are presented in Figures 16-1 and 16-2. The data in Figure 16-1 are for the controls and they simply demonstrate the operation of the variable when a single stimulus is used. It should be added that the latency differences are significant, and also that there was a significant tendency for the GSR magnitude to be greater for the Interrupted CS group than for the Delayed group. Figure 16-2 contains the data for the groups trained to the compound and then tested to an element on Trials 8 and 14 through 18. It is apparent that the component of the CS which was interrupted at the time of the response is the more dominant one as inferred from the greater frequency of CR's on Trial 8 in particular, but also during the extinction session. For the GSR data the trends are once again in the direction of greater responses being evoked by the interrupted component but the differences do not reach the .05 level.

Although the differences in response to the continued as opposed to the interrupted stimulus are more reliable when investigated in the context of a single stimulus than in the context of an element of a compound stimulus, this variable does, nevertheless, operate for elements of a compound stimulus. The principle of termination time of an element of a compound stimulus may therefore be used to predict the element which will be the dominant one. Thus, in this particular instance a relationship

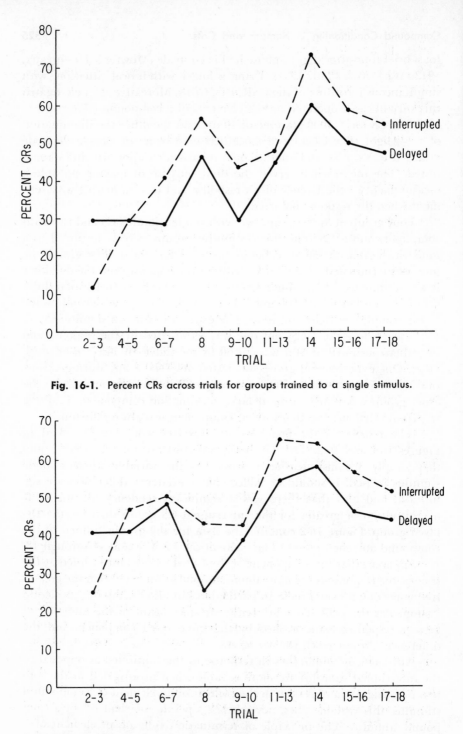

Fig. 16-1. Percent CRs across trials for groups trained to a single stimulus.

Fig. 16-2. Percent CRs for groups trained to a complex CS, with critical tests of the components on Trials 8, and 14 through 18.

which holds for individual stimuli holds also without modification for elements of a compound. No special problems involving Gestalt-like principles seem to arise. The story proves to be somewhat more complicated when we turn to the other end of the time dimension.

OFFSET SIMULTANEITY WITH DIFFERENTIAL IN ONSET TIME

The interstimulus interval and conditioning. There is a fairly large amount of evidence indicating that the relationship between effectiveness of conditioning and interstimulus interval over a range of zero to 2 or 3 sec. in GSR conditioning is curvilinear (Moeller, 1954; White & Schlosberg, 1952; Prokasy, Fawcett, & Hall, 1962). Although there is still some question concerning the exact form of this curve, and whether it is a function of other parameters, the evidence points toward a maximum in the neighborhood of 500 msec. In Figure 16-3 I have presented the theoretical curve fitting the magnitude data collected by Dr. Frank Vattano in a dissertation done in the laboratory at The Ohio State University. It was an ambitious study with groups every 50 msec. from 50 to 1650 msec., with two groups added, an 1800 msec. and a control for whom tone and shock were never paired. There were 25 Ss in each group and they were given 10 conditioning trials and then extinguished. The curve is the fit to data of extinction trials 2, 3, and 4. The horizontal dotted line is the level of the control. According to these data the maximum is at 600 msec. with little or no conditioning below 200 or above 2000 msec. As mentioned earlier, we do not know whether other parameters must be considered, so I will make no claims for the generality of this function.

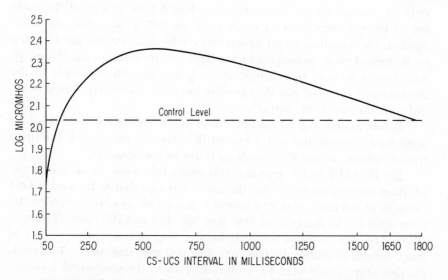

Fig. 16-3. The interstimulus interval function for GSR as obtained by Vattano.

However, because his procedure parallels closely that which we have employed in work on the compound CS, Dr. Vattano's time function is directly applicable to the compound research.

The strategy of this research is identical to that in the research on time of termination of the elements of a compound. A compound is formed of two elements—a light and a tone—which terminate simultaneously with the shock UCS but which have different onset times with respect to it. After conditioning trials to the compound, one or another element is presented alone for separate groups. The question asked, of course, is whether the response strength of an element can be predicted by its onset time with respect to the UCS. In all the human research the shorter stimulus of the compound has preceded the shock by 500 msec. (This work was begun long before Vattano's dissertation suggested that the optimum may be at 600, but it will be noted that his curve is very flat from about 400 to 600 msec. so 500 turned out to be an appropriate short stimulus.) The other stimulus of the compound had onset durations prior to the shock of from 600 to 4500 in the first study conducted, but later research has restricted the upper figure to approximately 1500 msec., and I shall restrict my discussion to events within this narrower range.

The first full scale research on this topic obtained data which indicated that the response strength produced by an element was a function of the temporal relations of the long and short stimulus, but in a manner which was not obviously predictable from the interstimulus interval function (Wickens, Gehman, & Sullivan, 1959). This experiment had included groups with a long stimulus value of 600, 700, 800, 920, 1040 and 1550 msec., the shorter stimulus being 500 msec. in all cases. Presumably the response evoked by the short stimulus should have remained the same for all groups since its onset in all cases was 500 msec. before the UCS. Instead, the statistical trend which was established was for the response to the long element to become increasingly greater through the 920 group and then to decline. Surprisingly, the response magnitude evoked by the short stimulus showed just the opposite trend, the two curves being essentially mirror images of each other.

Before attempting an interpretation of these data I wish to describe some further researches which essentially were concerned with the question of whether or not these findings could be corroborated.

Dr. Harold Fletcher repeated this study, following the design of the previous experiment in all essential characteristics; that is, he used a short stimulus of 500 msec. and long stimulus groups whose onset preceded the short stimulus by intervals of 100, 200, 300, 400 and 700 msec. (Fletcher, 1960). The interstimulus intervals for the long stimulus with respect to shock would, of course, be 600, 700, 800, 900 and 1200 msec. To review the procedure, there were 10 reinforced trials to the compound followed by extinction trials to the long element alone. His results, consisting of the data points together with the curve of best fit for the long stimulus alone, are presented in Figure 16-4. The time interval by which the long stimulus preceded the short is plotted on the X axis, while the magnitude of the response is plotted on the Y axis. Once again we find an increasing response strength with increased interstimulus interval out to about 900 msec. with respect to onset of the UCS or 500 msec. with respect to onset of the short stimulus.

I should add that the data with respect to the short stimulus did not form a clear pattern, and certainly did not produce a mirror image to the long stimulus curve. The data are not presented because of their ambiguity.

Another conceptual repetition of the original study was done with cats as the Ss (Wickens, Born, & Wickens, 1963). Again the GSR, recorded from the animal's right front paw, was the response measured. The UCS was a shock and the animal was suspended and lightly restrained in a sling during the experimental session. The short stimulus preceded the 50 msec. shock by 550 msec., and the long preceded the shock by 700, 1050, or 1250 msec. The elements consisted of a tone and a light, and as in the other experiments, they overlapped each other and terminated simultaneously with the shock. Six animals were employed and each animal served under each interval, the responses to the preceding session being extinguished before conditioning at a new interval was begun. Appropriate counterbalancing was employed for order of intervals and whether

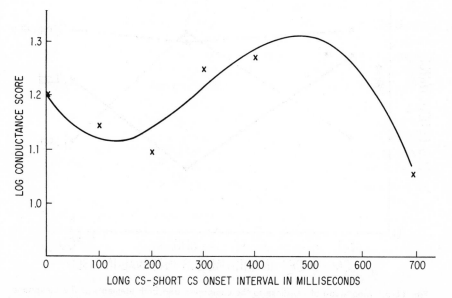

Fig. 16-4. Magnitude of response to the long element of a compound as a function of the interval between the long and short element.

the light or tone was used as the long or short stimulus. Data for a particular interval were collected over a period of a week, with three days for training to the compound and two days of extinction involving 4 presentations of each element and also of the compound on each day. The data are presented in Figure 16-5. The results may be summarized by stating that the lower element differed at the .05 level or less from the higher elements and the compound at each interval, but the higher element and the compound did not differ significantly from each other.

The three experiments are in general agreement, particularly with respect to the long stimulus. They sketch out a curve which shows the long stimulus to become more effective as an element as its interstimulus interval increases to approximately 1000 and then to decline. The opposite form seems to characterize the curve of the short element, although the evidence in support of this statement is less strong, since the trend was not obtained in the Fletcher study.

Interpretation. The cat study seems to represent a relatively complete picture of the phenomenon since it includes data on the compound itself as well as the elements and the interpretation will, therefore, concern itself primarily with this experiment. In doing so it will be assumed that the time parameters are essentially the same for the cat as for the human.

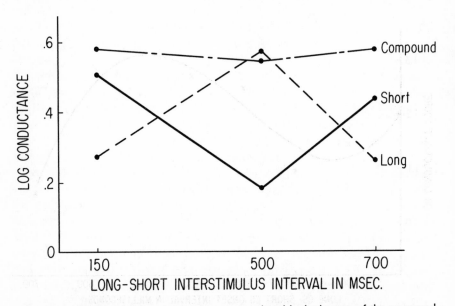

Fig. 16-5. Magnitude of response to the compound and both elements of the compound as a function of the interval between the long and short element. (Wickens, Born, & Wickens, 1963)

The interpretation assumes that the nature of the effective stimulus for the CR varies as a function of the interstimulus interval between the long and short CS. When the interval between the long and short stimulus is small, specifically less than 200 msec. or greater than about 600 msec., it will be assumed that these two elements do not interact in such a manner as to produce an integrated sensory compound. They do so, at least for the degree of training used in these studies, only when the interval is within the range of 200 to 600 msec. At the long-and short interstimulus intervals, therefore, each element is assumed to function independently of the other one and it is as if S were being conditioned to two different stimuli whose individual effectiveness would be a function of the interstimulus interval between it and the UCS.

Within the 200 to 600 msec. range it is assumed that the two elements interact with each other and it is this interaction which forms the actual CS. Simultaneously with the attachment of the responses to the CS another learning process occurs. This process consists of sensory conditioning among the elements of the compound. As a result of this sensory conditioning, an element can acquire the capacity when presented alone to evoke the sensory effect of the compound.

This sensory conditioning is assumed to obey the usual interstimulus interval function as found for a single stimulus and its UCS. This relationship predicts that the long stimulus will become increasingly capable of eliciting the effective cue for the response as the interstimulus interval increases to approximately 500 msec., while the short, as a result of being in a backward temporal relationship, does not acquire the capacity to redintegrate the compounded CS. When, then, the long stimulus is presented alone it will reinstate to a greater or lesser degree the sensory characteristics of the compound depending upon its previous interstimulus interval value with respect to the short stimulus. Through the mechanism of stimulus generalization, a GSR of greater or lesser magnitude will be evoked as a function of the degree of similarity of the reinstated sensory effects to that produced by the compound itself.

In the application of this interpretation to the experimental data, it should be recalled that the compound does not differ significantly from the higher of the two elements at any interval, but that it, as well as the higher element, is significantly greater than the lower element at each interval. At both the 150 and 700 intervals, the elements are assumed to function independently of each other and with respect to the US alone. Thus the short stimulus, being located at a more favorable interval with respect to the US, is predicted to acquire more response strength than does the long stimulus and the results conform with the prediction. If one were to assume—despite the lack of positive statistical evidence—that the compound is actually superior to the short element alone, its superiority could result from the summation of the independent habit strengths to the two elements (Hull, 1943). The assumption of independence would also imply that the magnitude of response to the short stimulus would be equal at the 150 and 700 long-short intervals. Actually, there is no significant difference in response to the short stimuli at these intervals. In view of the fact that this prediction involves acceptance of the null hypothesis, it is a weak one, and offers only background support for the interpretation.

At the 500 msec. interstimulus interval, independence is no longer the case. Here the effective stimulus for the CR has been the integrated sensory effects of the two elements. Because of favorable sensory conditioning, the long element is capable of redintegrating this pattern and so it evokes a GSR of a magnitude comparable to that of the compound itself. The short stimulus, ineffective as a sensory conditioned stimulus, is also ineffective in evoking the GSR.

Although this interpretation handles the rank order of the two points within each interval, its prediction for the overall magnitude of response differs somewhat from that which was obtained. The long stimulus at the 700-msec. interval might be expected to differ more from the long at 150 msec. than it does, since its onset time *prior to shock* is 1250 as opposed to 700 msec. as it is at the 150 msec. interval. This discrepancy might be handled by assuming that some sensory conditioning is occurring at the 700-msec. interval and the long stimulus profits thereby. Another embarrassment arises from the rather large difference between the long and short stimulus at 150 msec. The obtained difference seems to be greater than what would be found between 550 and 700 msec. on the usual interstimulus interval curve for a single stimulus.

In summary, the data are interpreted as resulting from two learning processes, an S-R hook-up process and an S-S association process. Furthermore it is held that the extent of learning for either of these relationships is determined by the same variable, the interstimulus interval. The point of origin for the interstimulus interval curve is the UCS for the S-R hook-up process and the second stimulus for the S-S association process.

A basic assumption which is made in this interpretation is that the response which is evoked by the elements results from the fact of its pairing in the complex with the GSR-producing UCS. In other words, a past history of association with the UCS is considered to be a necessary condition for the production of the varying response strength to the element.

The perceptual disparity reaction.   An alternate interpretation would imply that the element testing situation does not reflect response strength which was acquired during the training situation, but is a product of the *S*'s perceptual reaction to the change in stimulation inherent in the element testing situation. It is a notorious fact that the GSR is elicited by a wide variety of stimuli and recently Sokolov has used this response as a means of studying the orienting reflex (1959). Grings also

(1960) has demonstrated a similar phenomenon which he interprets to be the consequence of a perception of procedural changes.

In short, novelty of stimulation is a sufficient condition for the evocation of the GSR. It is apparent that the element testing procedure employed in the compound experiment introduces the necessary conditions for the evocation of the orienting reflex or perceptual disparity reaction and its associated GSR. It does so because the 10 pairings of light, tone, and shock are immediately followed by tests to a single element and this constitutes a disruption in the previous pattern of stimulation. If one assumes that the degree of perceptual disparateness generated by an element when presented alone is a function of its temporal relationship to the other stimuli in the complex, then it is possible to suppose that the curves generated by the elements are a measure of the orienting response and not the result of some association established between the two conditioned stimuli and the shock.

The effect of this variable was investigated by Allen, Hill, and Wickens (1963) in an experiment which essentially substituted for the shock UCS the innocuous illumination of a neon bulb. That is, it too employed three stimuli, presented in certain temporal relations, but the third did not have the consistent and powerful response-evoking characteristics of the shock. Three different intervals between onset of the long and short element—150, 450, and 700 msec.—were employed. After 10 pairings of the three stimuli the Ss were presented with either the short or long stimulus alone. The usual counterbalancing was employed so that the tone was always the test stimulus.

There was a significant heightening in GSR when the single stimulus was presented, and this response decreased regularly in successive tests to the element alone. Finally the magnitude of the GSR to the element proved to be a function of the interstimulus interval. This relationship is shown in Figure 16-6. The measure on the Y axis is the difference between the magnitude of the response for a S on the last two adaptation trials and the magnitude of the response during the element testing.

The results of the experiments clearly indicate that a GSR is generated by the shift in procedure involved in testing to an element of the compound stimulus, and that it persists with declining strength for at least five trials. In addition, the magnitude of this response proved to be an interacting function of order of presentation of the elements of the compound and their interstimulus interval in that the long and short elements differ significantly from each other at the interstimulus intervals of 150 and 450 msec. The long produced the larger response at 150 and the short, at 450 msec. Presumably these reflect the operation of a perceptual disparity reaction or the orienting reflex. If shock is used as the UCS, as in the compounding experiment, significant differences in response strength to the two elements at these interstimulus intervals are

also expected. Under those conditions, however, the magnitude relationships are reversed, with the long stimulus evoking the smaller response at
150 and the larger response at 450 msec.

Although the trend of the results of this experiment is the opposite
in direction to that obtained when a shock is employed, the interpretation
offered for the shock situation can be applied to these results as follows.

One or another element, as a function of the time interval, becomes
to a greater or lesser degree the dominant or salient element of the complex. This would be true of the short element at the 150 msec. interval
because it is located at a near optimal interval—500 msec.—with respect
to the light flash, whereas the long stimulus precedes it by the less effective time interval of 650 msec., but at a CS_1-CS_2 interstimulus interval too
short for effective sensory conditioning. At 450 msec. the long stimulus
dominates because it is located at a near optimal interval before the short
stimulus so far as sensory conditioning is concerned, and, therefore, evokes
the characteristics of the complex itself. The short stimulus, however, because of its backward relationship to the long stimulus is unable to elicit
the characteristics of the compound. At the 700 interval the long stimulus

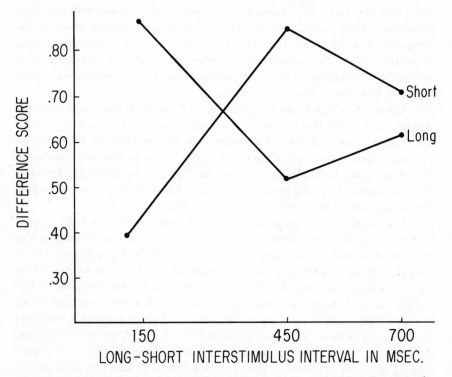

Fig. 16-6. Magnitude of the perceptual disparity response as a function of interstimulus
interval during training and the element to which the test was made. (Allen, Hill, &
Wickens, 1963)

is too distant in time to be a highly effective sensory conditioned stimulus for either the short stimulus or the light flash and thus the short stimulus—still 500 msec. from the light flash—begins to dominate the stimulus complex. In summary, the dominant stimulus of the complex is the short, the long, and possibly once again the short at the 150, 450, and 700 intervals, respectively.

If the dominant stimulus of the complex is presented alone, its occurrence—simply because it has dominated the complex—should not produce a marked disparity reaction. That is, this stimulus, by itself, has acquired the capacity to produce an effect quite similar to that of the compound. There is, then, for S no great disparity between this event and those which have occurred before, and hence, only a small perceptual disparity reaction or orienting reflex results. The converse would be true for the minor stimulus when presented alone. Its single occurrence is perceived as being markedly different from the prior stimulation and hence, a strong perceptual disparity response occurs. Essentially this is what the data show to be the case.

I should add that I have attempted to replicate this experiment either in its exact form, or using the same temporal relationship between the elements and omitting the shock surrogate. In neither of these experiments did we obtain a significant increase in response when the shift from multiple to single stimulation occurred. The minimal conclusion to be drawn from these replication experiments is that the shock as a UCS contributes to the results in the compounding experiments because it is an effective elicitor of the GSR and those experiments are dealing with something more than an alerting or orienting reflex.

Contiguity or secondary reinforcement. Another topic concerns the question as to whether or not the association found—or presumed to be found—between the two conditioned stimuli is formed because of contiguity alone or is dependent on some derived reinforcement. Thus, it is possible that the CR first becomes attached to the second CS, and through higher order conditioning becomes transferred to the second CS.

In order to evaluate this interpretation Dr. Henry Cross and I performed a sensory preconditioning experiment (1963). The long-short interstimulus intervals of 100, 400, and 600 msec. were chosen. The first part of the experiment consisted of ten paired presentations of the tone followed by light in the particular time relationship for the group in question. This was followed by 10 conditioning trials of light and shock, with a 500 msec. interstimulus interval and finally by a group of extinction trials to the tone which was never associated with shock. On the first trial the mean for all groups was essentially the same, a result which may be attributed to the orienting reflex. Under the assumption that the trials were highly contaminated by this effect, a single classification analysis of variance was done on trials 2, 3, and 4. The Fs proved to be significant for trials 2 and 3 but not in the case of trial 4, possibly because of the leveling effect of extinction. The data for the mean of trials 2 through 4 are presented in Figure 16-7. It is clear that the sensory preconditioning effect is a function of interstimulus interval, with values similar to those obtained in the typical interstimulus interval study as well as with the above mentioned work with elements of a compound.

In view of the similar effect of time in these experiments, one of which employed a sensory preconditioning design and the others in which the two conditioned stimuli were present at the time the UCS occurred, it would seem justifiable to conclude that the occurrence of a reinforcement is not a necessary condition for establishing the differential effectiveness of the individual components of a complex stimulus. This conclusion emphasizes the importance of the relationship of the two conditioned stimuli to each other rather than their individual relationships to reinforcement, a view which is certainly quite different from that which I suspected might be the case at the time I began these series of studies some time ago.

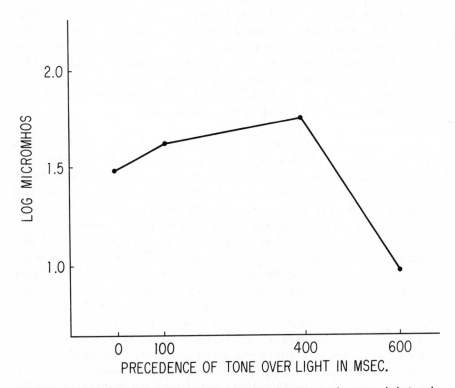

Fig. 16-7. Mean response magnitude as a function of interstimulus interval during the sensory preconditioning period. (Wickens & Cross, 1963)

An effort to investigate this compounding effect at the molecular level has led to somewhat ambiguous results. It is an investigation of the potential role of reticular stimulation in determination of the results. This explanation loosely uses the known effect of reticular activity on cortical activity (Moruzzi & Magoun, 1949); the influence of cortical activity on reticular activity (Adey, Segundo, & Livingston, 1957); and the influence of the reticular formation on the GSR (Wang, Stein, & Brown, 1956). These researches suggest that complex interaction relationships may be obtained as a consequence of slight temporal differences in the occurrence of stimulation.

Unipolar electrodes were placed by stereotaxic technique in the reticular mesencephalon of six cats, and our intent was to use stimulation in this area as one of the CS elements. Before working with the compound, we employed the reticular stimulation alone as a CS, the UCS being a shock. The interstimulus interval between CS and UCS was 50 msec. and also 550 msec., each cat being conditioned to each interval. Order was counterbalanced among cats. Conditioning to the 550 msec. interstimulus interval proved to be significantly superior to the 50, and this implied to us that the reticular stimulation (at every weak levels) may serve as a CS and it is not simply a UCS itself. We then went on from here and used the reticular stimulation as an element of a compound CS with a tone being the other element, the procedure paralleling the previously described experiment with light and tone as the elements of the compound. The reticular stimulation was always the second or shorter stimulus and it came on 550 msec. before the shock UCS, the tone preceded the reticular CS by 150, 500, or 700 msec. The results, as I mentioned earlier, were somewhat ambiguous; in the instance of two animals curves of the mirror image type were obtained, another animal showed the usual curve for the long stimulus, the curve for the short stimulus being essentially flat. The curves for the other animals generally differed from each other and certainly formed no clear pattern. In general, the three animals that produced the mirror image curves had lower electrode placements than the other three animals, but I would hesitate to engage in neurologizing on the basis of these data. In conclusion, this molecular digression simply indicates to me that the form of the curves obtained from the elements of the compound are not explained in any simple manner by reticular participation.

SUMMARY

I believe that these researches in compound conditioning have served to throw some light on the larger problem of stimulus selection. With respect to the validity of generalizing from principles applicable to a single stimulus to elements of a compound, these researches offer a complicated answer. Insofar as termination time is concerned, the principle derived from work with single stimuli seems to be directly applicable to compounded elements. In the instance of interstimulus interval, however, the answer is both yes and no. At certain interstimulus intervals it seems that data drawn from single stimulus studies are predictive of the results and the relative strength of an element can be predicted by its temporal relationship to the UCS. At other intervals the dominant variable seems to be the interrelationship between the elements of the compound, without much regard for the relationship of the elements to the UCS. Within this temporal range it appears, however, that the normal interstimulus function can be used for predictive purposes.

References

ADEY, W. R., SEGUNDO, J. P., & LIVINGSTON, R. B. Corticifugal influences on intrinsic brain stem conduction in cat and monkey. *J. Neurophysiol.*, 1957, *20*, 1-16.

ALLEN, C. K., HILL, F. A., & WICKENS, D. D. The orienting reflex as a function of the interstimulus interval of compound stimuli. *J. exp. Psychol.*, 1963, *65*, 309-316.

FLETCHER, H. J. A re-examination of conditioning to elements of a complex as a function of differential onset times. Unpublished dissertation, Ohio State University, 1960.

GRINGS, W. W. Preparatory set variables related to classical conditioning of autonomic responses. *Psychol. Rev.*, 1960, *67*, 243-252.

HULL, C. L. *Principles of behavior: An introduction to behavior theory.* New York: Appleton-Century-Crofts, 1943.

LAWRENCE, D. H. The nature of a stimulus: some relationships between learning and perception. In S. KOCH (Ed.), *Psychology: A study of a science,* Vol. 5. New York: McGraw-Hill, 1963.

MOELLER, G. The CS-UCS interval in GSR conditioning. *J. exp. Psychol.*, 1954, *48*, 162-166.

MORUZZI, G., & MAGOUN, H. W. Brain stem reticular formation and activation of the EEG. *EEG clin. Neurophysiol.*, 1949, *1*, 455-473.

MOWRER, O. H., & LAMOREAUX, R. R. Avoidance conditioning and signal duration: A study of secondary motivation and reward. *Psychol. Monogr.*, 1942, *54* (5), (Whole No. 247).

PROKASY, W. F., FAWCETT, J. T., & HALL, J. F. Recruitment, latency, magnitude, and amplitude of the GSR as a function of interstimulus interval. *J. exp. Psychol.*, 1962, *64*, 513-518.

REYNOLDS, G. S. Attention in the pigeon. *J. exp. anal. Beh.*, 1961, *4*, 203-208.

SOKOLOV, E. N. Neuronal models and the orienting reflex. In Mary A. B. BRAZIER (Ed.), *The central nervous system and behavior.* Madison, N.J.: Madison Printing, 1960.

UNDERWOOD, B. J. Stimulus selection in verbal learning. In C. N. COFER (Ed.), *Verbal behavior and learning.* New York: McGraw-Hill, 1963.

WANG, G. H., STEIN, P., & BROWN, V. W. Brainstem reticular system and galvanic skin reflex in acute decerebrate cats. *J. Neurophysiol.,* 1956, *19,* 350-355.

WARREN, J. M. Additivity of cues in visual pattern discriminations by monkeys. *J. comp. physiol. Psychol.,* 1953, *46,* 484-486.

WHITE, C. T., & SCHLOSBERG, H. Degree of conditioning of the GSR as a function of the period of delay. *J. exp. Psychol.,* 1952, *43,* 357-362.

WICKENS, D. D., BORN, D. G., & WICKENS, C. D. Response strength to a compound conditioned stimulus as a function of the element interstimulus interval. *J. comp. physiol. Psychol.,* 1963, *56,* 727-731.

WICKENS, D. D., & CROSS, H. A. Resistance to extinction as a function of temporal relations during sensory preconditioning. *J. exp. Psychol.,* 1963, *65,* 206-211.

WICKENS, D. D., CROSS, H. A., & MORGAN, R. M. CS termination and the response strength acquired by elements of a stimulus complex. *J. exp. Psychol.,* 1959, *58,* 363-368.

WICKENS, D. D., GEHMAN, R. S., & SULLIVAN, S. N. The effect of differential onset time on the conditioned response strength to elements of a stimulus complex. *J. exp. Psychol.,* 1959, *58,* 85-93.

WICKENS, D. D., & PLATT, C. E. Response termination of the cue stimulus in classical and instrumental conditioning. *J. exp. Psychol.,* 1954, *47,* 183-186.

DAVID R. WILLIAMS
University of Pennsylvania

17

Classical Conditioning and Incentive Motivation[1]

Reinforcers control behavior by proxy: it is not the reinforcer itself, but some derived effect of the reinforcer, which exerts immediate control over behavior. When a rat presses a lever for food reinforcement, it is not the pellet of food, but the stimulus conditions present at the time of the press, which directly control the response. The problem of incentive motivation is the problem of understanding the mechanism through which stimulus conditions motivate the performance of instrumental acts, and thus help establish the powerful, if indirect, control exerted by reinforcement.

This paper is concerned with the contribution that studies of classical conditioning can make to an understanding of incentive motivation. The assumption that stimuli motivate instrumental behavior to the extent that they elicit classically conditioned responses appears in the theories of Hull (1943), Sheffield (1954), and Spence (1956). Although the manner in which this assumption is introduced differs among these formulations, in all of them it is the actual occurrence of classically conditioned responses that provides motivation for instrumental performance. If this assumption is valid, the behavioral laws that describe the occurrence of classically conditioned behavior are identical to the laws of incentive motivation.

Evidence showing a close relationship between the occurrence of operant and respondent behavior provides strong support for this behavioristic approach (Konorski, 1948; Shapiro, 1961, 1962).[2] A detailed

---

[1] The writer is indebted to Francis Irwin and Fred Sheffield for their constructive criticisms of the manuscript. This work was supported primarily by a grant, G-23839, from the National Science Foundation.

[2] Throughout this paper, references to "classical conditioning" and "respondent behavior" are made principally with respect to the salivary response, and the discussion is directed at situations where positive reinforcement is used.

comparison of operant and respondent phenomena, however, raises the possibility that a close association of operant and respondent measures may be found only under limited conditions. One disturbing fact pointing to this possibility is the importance of CS-US overlap for the appearance of anticipatory responding, at least in the case of salivation. The importance of CS-US overlap is referred to by Pavlov (1927, p. 27) and was very clearly observed by the writer when assisting Professor Sheffield in some initial experiments on classical conditioning. One simple interpretation we considered was that nonoverlap served to facilitate discrimination of the delay-conditioning stimulus situation from the stimulus situation prevailing at the moment when the US was presented. This interpretation seemed in line with the observation that, as training under delay conditioning proceeds, the appearance of anticipatory salivation increasingly approximates the time of presentation of the US. Generalizing from considerations of this sort, Sheffield offered the suggestion that "any method which makes the cues for arrival of the unconditioned stimulus ambiguous favors anticipatory conditioned salivation" (1959). For convenience, this suggestion will be referred to as the "discrimination hypothesis": that anticipatory salivation weakens and disappears at moments that are distinctively different from the moment of reinforcement.

In considering operant rather than respondent behavior, the discrimination hypothesis is often incorrect. Abrupt and unambiguous change of stimuli at the moment of reinforcement favors the efficient learning of operants, although its respondent conditioning analog—nonoverlap of CS and US—retards the formation of anticipatory salivation. Further, there is ample evidence to show that operants are maintained in stimuli which are distinctively different from those present at the moment of reinforcement. Evidence that the remote stimulus is clearly discriminated is furnished by the differing patterns of operant responding in the component stimuli of the sequence. Thus, responding on a variable interval schedule may be reinforced by presentation of the opportunity to respond on a fixed interval schedule (Ferster, 1953). Only the latter is reinforced by food and the pattern of responding in each of the component schedules is appropriate to the schedule in force. Kelleher and Gollub (1962) review many studies of this kind.

These considerations suggest that the observed relationship between operant and respondent behavior can be manipulated by an appropriate choice of schedules of reinforcement. In any operant situation where chaining is an important factor, the stimulus conditions at the beginning of the chain are presumably discriminable from those at the end of the chain. In this case, operant behavior should begin well in advance of respondent behavior. This expectation is based on the assumption that the discrimination hypothesis may hold at least roughly for respondents, but is clearly inadequate when applied to operant behavior. If operant responses are emitted in the presence of stimuli which do *not* elicit classically conditioned responses, the possibility that the incentive motivation provided by a stimulus is intimately linked to its ability to elicit classically conditioned responses is called into serious question.

A study conducted by the writer in collaboration with Gaylord D. Ellison was directed at this point. Two operant schedules—fixed ratio and fixed interval—were chosen for comparison. A fixed ratio schedule has the characteristics which should provide a dissociation of operant and respondent behavior. The initial responses on a ratio schedule serve only to produce conditions under which reinforcement takes place; they are not immediately followed by a reinforcer. In the terminology of Ferster and Skinner (1957), early ratio responses change the controlling stimulus from "low count" to "high count." Accordingly, early responses in a ratio, under "low count" stimulus control, should not be accompanied by salivation. [It is interesting to note that Hull (1952) explicitly discussed fixed ratio schedules and "r_g," that is, anticipatory respondent behavior. In Theorem 27, Hull clearly states that r_g becomes attached to the traces of the individual responses in the ratio. The explicit expectation within Hull's system, therefore, is that on a ratio schedule bar pressing will be accompanied by salivation.]

Comparisons between operant and respondent behavior must be made with care, because there is no clear way to establish units of measurement that are comparable for the two responses. In the case of salivation, the precise time of occurrence as measured may even depend on the type of collection system and on the arbitrarily chosen "drop size." In the present study fixed interval schedules were used as a baseline control procedure to take account of this problem. Fixed interval schedules demand only a single response, rather than a chain of responses, as a condition for reinforcement. Performance under fixed interval reinforcement resembles performance under fixed ratio reinforcement in that a number of responses, and a period of time, both occur between "trial onset" and reinforcement. The surplus responses under fixed interval schedules, however, are probably the result of an imperfect discrimination of the moment at which reinforcement is made available. Thus fixed-interval responses are emitted under conditions similar to those which, according to the discrimination hypothesis, elicit salivation. Strictly, the expected outcome of this experiment was that pressing would occur further in advance of salivation under fixed ratio than under fixed interval schedules.

The operant schedules were FR 33 for one group of four dogs, and FI 16 seconds for a second group of three dogs. The value of the fixed interval was chosen to be roughly equal to the time that elapsed between the start of the trial and the presentation of reinforcement for the fixed ratio subjects. The reinforcer in this and subsequent studies was a single Hartz Mountain Dog Yummie. A constant time-out period of one minute was introduced after each reinforcement to allow the UR accompanying reinforcement to subside and to put the experiment on a "discrete trial" basis resembling, except for the requirement of instrumental behavior, the typical classical conditioning experiment.

Trials were signalled by dimming the general level of illumination and presenting a tone. With three dogs in the fixed interval group, and three of the four dogs in the fixed ratio group, operant trials alternated with standard classical conditioning trials of matched duration. The lever was withdrawn during the matched classical trials, and reinforcement was presented independent of S's behavior. One dog in the ratio group received only operant trials. This S was not experimentally naive; she had previously been used in a respondent conditioning experiment. She was included to provide an additional case in the ratio group because one S unavoidably received only a limited amount of training before termination of the experiment.

The main findings from both groups are presented in Fig. 17-1, which shows mean rate of lever pressing and mean rate of concomitant salivation from a representative day late in training for each dog. Because trial duration was partly controlled by S, certain conventions had to be adopted in order to exclude the salivary UR from these data. Curves from the fixed interval Ss include only the 16 second period before reinforcement became available. Even though some trials lasted longer than this time because S did not respond immediately after 16 seconds, the additional data are not included. Data for the fixed ratio group were also averaged in a way which precludes the inclusion of UR. The upper three fixed ratio curves (D-4, D-5, and D-6) were truncated on all trials at the time of reinforcement of the trial of shortest duration in the session. Thus the final responses on most trials were excluded, along with the UR on all trials. The period before reinforcement for all trials is included in the case of D-7, but trials were dropped from the analysis as soon as they terminated in reinforcement. On the graph for this dog, the last three points on the curve include data from only one trial.

Onset time of salivation and lever pressing was quite close for the dogs reinforced on fixed interval (D-1, D-2, and D-3). Salivation leads lever pressing for D-1, lags slightly for D-3, and the coincidence is nearly exact for D-2. An increase in response rate for both measures takes place throughout the interval. Although the averaging method used here could artifactually produce gradual changes in rate from different onset times of pressing at a constant rate, inspection of the raw data indicated that rates actually were increasing throughout the trial.

Quite a different relationship between the two measures is observed under the ratio schedule, except possibly in the case of D-5, the subject which received only limited training. D-4 and D-6 show remarkably close similarity: approximately half the presses are made before salivation

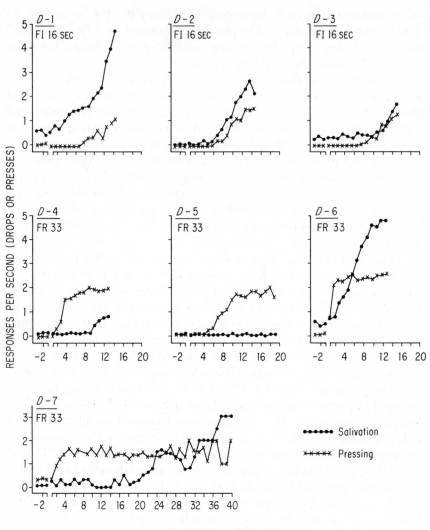

Fig. 17-1. Final performance of each dog under fixed interval or fixed ratio schedules of reinforcement. Mean rates of lever-pressing and salivation on a single day late in training are shown.

begins. D-5 showed no anticipatory salivation, although she gave a normal UR and showed some conditioned response in subsequent tests where no pellet was given when the trial terminated. The somewhat gradual increase in lever-pressing rate for these dogs is partly an artifact of the averaging procedure used; the gradual increase in salivation was a generally consistent feature of the unaveraged data.

The results under fixed ratio reinforcement, while typical of performance late in training, emerged only after repeated exposure to the schedules. In the first few sessions there was only a small tendency for lever pressing to precede salivation. The performance of D-6 reflects the characteristics of this period. Early in training under fixed interval reinforcement, both lever pressing and salivation took place at substantial levels after the start of the trial and tended to follow a parallel course.

These results clearly demonstrate that the relationship between an operant response and salivation can be manipulated by appropriate choice of schedules of reinforcement. They lend further support to the discrimination hypothesis for respondents, and confirm the suspicion that operant and respondent measures may become dissociated in situations involving operant chaining. Thus, they cast doubt upon the possibility that incentive motivation is directly linked to the actual occurrence of classically conditioned responses.

Fig. 17-2 compares salivation on operant trials with salivation on the alternate trials of equal duration, where the lever was not present. There

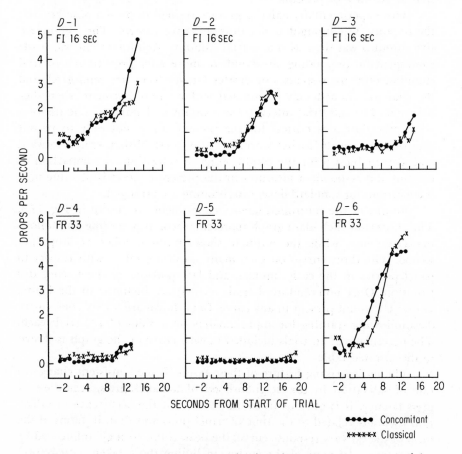

Fig. 17-2. Mean rate of salivation on trials where lever-pressing was required (concomitant), and on matched trials without lever-pressing (classical).

is no clear pattern to the differences on concomitant and yoked classical trials, suggesting that, at least with these procedures, the performance of an operant response does not markedly disturb the classical conditioning structure of the situation.

The relative lack of effect of operant schedules on the pattern of anticipatory salivation, and the dissociation produced by the fixed ratio procedure, raise the possibility that the two measures are entirely independent. Perhaps the close correspondence between salivation and pressing under fixed interval reinforcement is accidental, and does not reflect the operation of a common discriminative process. If the two measures are indeed independent, it should be possible to arrange a situation where salivation occurs in advance of pressing. Such a situation would be one in which the onset of pressing was delayed, relative to its normal time of onset under a fixed interval schedule. If salivation is unaffected by the operant manipulation, it should occur at the usual time, and thus begin well in advance of pressing.

Two experimentally naive dogs were trained to press a nose key and the response was brought under discriminative control. The discriminative stimulus was then used as a trial stimulus. Reinforcement was made contingent on responding 30 seconds or more after presentation of trial stimulus. Operant responses of shorter latency were not reinforced, and the trial was immediately terminated without reinforcement when they occurred. The intertrial interval was constant at 1 minute. The use of a trials procedure was critical for the present study, not only to permit comparison with the earlier work, but also to establish a straightforward and identifiable CS for the conditioning of salivation. A comparison of operant and respondent measures in the present context is of value only if conditions for standard delay conditioning are arranged.

Results of the controlled latency experiment are shown in Fig. 17-3. The abscissa of each main graph represents seconds preceding and following a response, while the ordinate shows mean number of drops per second. The three curves on each main graph are taken with respect to panel presses in the early, middle, and late portions of the latency distribution. Only non-reinforced trials (errors) are included in the figure, so that UR is not present in any curve. Data shown are for six consecutive days following training for approximately 60 sessions of 120 trials each. The percentage of all trials included in each curve of the graph is shown in the inserted table.

The most striking feature of these results is the consistent change in rate of salivation in the neighborhood of a panel press, regardless of press latency. It is obvious from the figure that the occurrence of salivation is closely related to the time of panel press and that, in terms of the form of the salivary response curve, the peak is not strongly influenced by press latency. In none of the curves, including those taken with respect to presses of long latency, is there strong tendency for salivation to take place well in advance of pressing. Were the two response measures independent, quite a different relationship would have been expected: certainly for the presses of long latency, salivation should have been near its peak amplitude before the response took place.

The close association between the two response measures in this experiment might reflect the influence of a common set of stimuli on both response measures. Alternatively, it is possible that stimuli from operant behavior elicited salivation. These two possibilities cannot be distinguished on the basis of the present data. Because salivation did not markedly lead pressing, however, the hypothesis that the two measures are independent may be rejected. Apparently then, some kind of relationship can be assumed between pressing and salivation. Related results, using a free operant drl procedure and no trial stimulus, have been obtained by Shapiro (1962). His data, like these, show a preponderance of salivary activity in the neighborhood of the operant response. In his experiment, salivary activity clearly began before the operant response. The actual peak of the response came after the operant in two of the three cases presented.

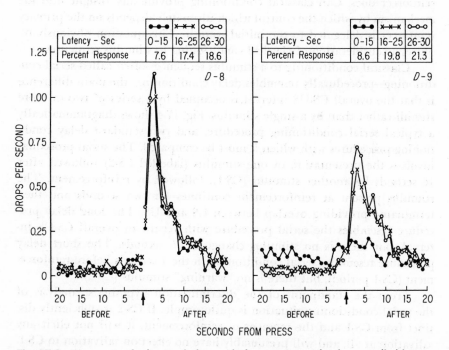

	●–●–●	x–x–x	o–o–o
Latency – Sec	0–15	16–25	26–30
Percent Response	7.6	17.4	18.6

D-8

	●–●–●	x–x–x	o–o–o
Latency – Sec	0–15	16–25	26–30
Percent Response	8.6	19.8	21.3

D-9

Fig. 17-3. Mean rate of salivation before and after pressing under the controlled latency procedure. The insert shows the relative frequency of panel-presses in each major latency category.

It seems apparent that, at a behavioral level, a simple relationship cannot be found between the occurrence of classically conditioned responses like salivation and operant behavior. To conclude that the two measures are entirely independent, however, also seems unwarranted. Perhaps the clearest inference that can be made from these results is that, where occurrence of the operant response depends primarily on discrimination of the moment of reinforcement, pressing and salivation are closely associated; when pressing is required in a stimulus situation which differs from that at the moment of reinforcement, pressing occurs in advance of salivation, and the two measures become dissociated.

SERIAL CONDITIONING

Procedures like fixed ratio, which involve response chains and a sequence of accompanying stimuli, raise the problem of incentive motivation in its most acute form. Operant responding in the presence of the initial stimuli is not immediately reinforced by a presentation of a primary reinforcer; indeed, the initial stimuli are negative discriminative stimuli for that event. An appeal to secondary reinforcement sidesteps the problem raised here, just as an appeal to "control" by the primary reinforcer does. Can classical conditioning provide any insight into the mechanism by which the control which ultimately depends on the primary reinforcer is delegated to the initial stimuli? This question obviously requires a consideration of classical conditioning to stimulus sequences.

Classical conditioning to a stimulus sequence—often called serial conditioning—procedurally resembles delay conditioning; the main difference is that the overall CS-US interval is occupied by a series of two or more stimuli rather than by a single stimulus. Fig. 17-4 shows diagrammatically a typical serial conditioning procedure, and two standard delay conditioning procedures with which it must be compared. The serial procedure involves the presentation of one stimulus (labelled CS-2) followed after 16 seconds by another stimulus (CS-1), followed by reinforcement. The stimulus present at reinforcement continues for two seconds and then terminates, providing overlap between CS and US. The long delay procedure resembles the serial procedure with regard to overall CS-US interval, but there is no stimulus change at 16 seconds. The short delay procedure resembles serial conditioning in the 4 seconds before reinforcement (CS-1 period), but there is no "warning" stimulus (CS-2).

From the standpoint of the discrimination hypothesis, analysis of the serial conditioning situation is quite simple. If CS-2 is sufficiently distinct from CS-1 and the moment of reinforcement, it will not elicit any salivation at all, and will presumably have no effect on salivation to CS-1. To the extent that generalization takes place between CS-2 and CS-1, anticipatory salivation during the serial stimulus should be similar to salivation at corresponding times in the long delay stimulus. From the standpoint of the discrimination hypothesis, then, serial conditioning is an intermediate case of long and short delay conditioning.

The conditional stimuli were a steady 1000 cps tone, an intermittent 1000 cps tone, and a clicker. The US was a single Hartz Mountain Dog Yummie delivered automatically into the food dish in the conditioning stand. Subjects were run daily for 30 trials, separated by an average intertrial interval of 90 seconds.

Several other aspects of the procedure should be noted. Because of quantitative differences in learning rate and magnitude of response between dogs, as well as a general long-term downward drift in response magnitude within dogs, pairs of the above conditions were tested together. A series of daily sessions included two of the three pairs of conditions with trials of both kinds occurring within the same daily sessions in a mixed order. Appropriate choice of stimuli allowed discrimination of the trial types. The particular stimulus qualities associated with the serial and delay procedures were varied between dogs; the only restriction was that CS-1 and the short delay stimulus were the same. No consistent effect attributable to stimulus quality has been noted. On occasional serial trials a "probe" was made: CS-2 was presented for a relatively brief period of

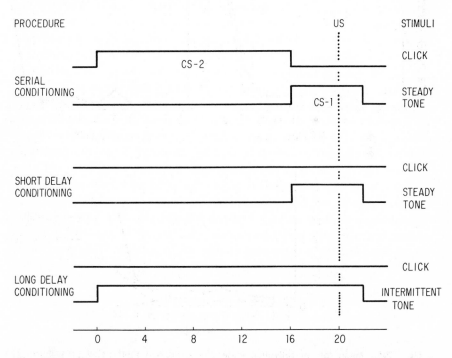

Fig. 17-4. Diagram of procedures in the serial conditioning experiment. The stimuli listed are given as an example of one arrangement used.

time—6 or 10 seconds—and was then followed by CS-1. The results from this probe procedure, although consistent with *S*s, did not reveal a consistent pattern between dogs and will not be considered here. Finally, it has proven feasible to use the same *S* in both pairs of conditions. Although this procedure was followed in the case of only one dog in the data presented here, subsequent work has shown that performance curves are readily reproduced after a series of intervening procedures.

Figure 17-5 presents a comparison of serial and short delay conditioning. Each graph includes data from four successive asymptotic days from an individual dog. Data from daily sessions and after those presented reveal a similar pattern of results. The point at which the stimulus changes in the serial condition is shown by the dotted vertical line at 16 seconds. This is also the point at which the CS is presented in short delay conditioning. With all three dogs, salivation during CS-2 was reliably greater than salivation when no stimulus was present, indicating that some conditioning had taken place to CS-2. During the final 4 seconds pre-

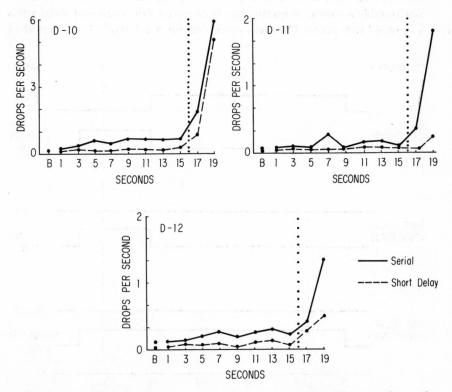

Fig. 17-5. Mean rate of salivation under the serial and short delay procedures. The isolated points show the baseline rate, obtained in the 10 seconds prior to the start of the recording period.

ceding reinforcement, salivation was greatest to CS-1 in the serial procedure. This difference cannot be attributed to the increased level of salivation present in CS-2. The increment in salivation between seconds 15 and
17 is reliably greater in the serial condition than in the short delay condition for D-10; and for D-11 and D-12, the increment between seconds 17
and 19 is reliably greater.

A clear interpretation of the enhancement effect obviously requires a
comparison between serial and long delay conditioning. Could the enhanced responding to CS-1 reasonably be attributed to a similarity in
response pattern between serial conditioning and long delay conditioning? The data in Fig. 17-6 are relevant to this question. It is apparent in
both cases that salivation in the final seconds of the CS-US interval is
greater in the serial condition. In the case of D-10, salivation at second 17
is reliably lower in the serial condition than in the long delay condition,
but salivation at second 19 is reliably greater in the serial condition. In
the case of D-13, salivation is not reliably different at second 17, but by
second 19 salivation to the serial stimulus is reliably greater. In both dogs,
salivation is reliably lower in the CS-2 period on serial trials even though
it exceeds the baseline rate. Although salivary rate is depressed during
most of the CS-US interval, relative to the level established by the long
delay procedure, at the end of the interval it rises rapidly and finally
exceeds the rate obtained with the long delay procedure.

The major implication of these results is that serial conditioning is
not a simple intermediate case of long or short delay conditioning. Near
the point of reinforcement, salivation in the serial condition is greater
than salivation in either of the comparable delay conditioning procedures.
Thus a straightforward analysis of stimulus sequences, using a hypothesis
of generalization, does not appear justifiable.

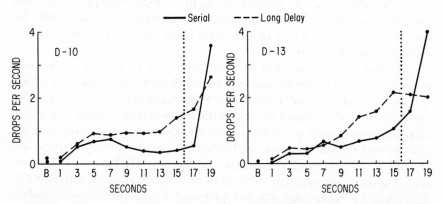

Fig. 17-6. Mean rate of salivation under the serial and long delay procedures. The
isolated points show the baseline rate, obtained in the 10 seconds prior to the start of
the recording period.

It is interesting to note that effects similar to those obtained in the serial conditioning experiment have been observed in operant conditioning situations. The most comparable experiments are those reported by Skinner (1953) on the effect of "clocks," that is, external stimuli correlated with various portions of the inter-reinforcement interval under fixed interval schedules. The use of clocks results in decreased responding early, and greatly enhanced responding late, in the fixed interval period.

In attempting to understand the phenomena of serial conditioning, it seems clear that the major analytical problem is presented by CS-2: on the one hand, it is highly correlated with the presentation of reinforcement, serves as a reliable predictor of eventual reinforcement, and thus resembles a positive CS; on the other hand, it is a negative stimulus with regard to the immediate presentation of the reinforcing event. It seems possible to develop Pavlov's notion of internal inhibition in a way that would encompass these results: such an attempt might begin with the assumption that opposing states of inhibition and excitation are both established by presentation of CS-2. Given that assumption, either of two mechanisms might be advanced to account for the results. One would focus on the inhibitory character of CS-2. If CS-2 were assumed to be inhibitory, then one would expect a positive induction effect upon its removal. Although it may be questionable to assume that the inhibition which opposes responding to a positive stimulus is so similar to the conditioned inhibition established to a negative CS, nonetheless a positive induction effect might suffice to account for these results. A second alternative account would focus on the excitation built up during application of CS-2. The removal of CS-2, and the corresponding removal of the inhibition to it, would result in a release of previously built up excitation. Performance in the short delay condition would, according to this interpretation, be weaker because at the start of the short delay stimulus less excitation would be present. In both of these interpretations, the greater salivation in CS-1 relative to the long delay procedure would be attributable to the fact that in long delay conditioning no sudden decline in inhibition takes place.

A Pavlovian orientation to these results has been taken for two reasons. One is that the Pavlovian framework provides a means by which the dual nature of serial stimuli is readily expressed. The second is the appearance, in the operant as well as the classical conditioning literature, of phenomena which point directly at the operation of interrelated excitatory and inhibitory processes. Perhaps the most dramatic of these are induction or "contrast" phenomena. In Lecture 11, Pavlov (1927) presented several experiments which showed augmentation of salivation to a positive CS when that CS was preceded by an inhibitory stimulus. Pavlov interpreted these induction phenomena as the result of "excitation leading to increased inhibition and inhibition leading to increased excitation." Processes of this sort have been extensively studied in several sensory systems, and direct measurement of the excitatory and inhibitory processes has in some instances been possible (see, for example, Hartline & Ratliffe, 1958). Pavlov clearly recognized the close analogy to sensory systems: "There can be no doubt that the phenomenon of mutual induction described above provides a physiological basis for the large group of contrast phenomena described in connection with the physiology of the sense organs."

INDUCTION EFFECTS IN AN OPERANT SITUATION

Recently Reynolds (1963) has demonstrated what appeared to be induction effects in an operant situation using pigeon subjects and food reinforcement. Because the phenomenon of induction points clearly to the operation of a Pavlovian mechanism, it complements the serial study, and strengthens the assumption that excitatory and inhibitory processes are involved in the performance of operant as well as respondent behavior.

A study by the writer, using central stimulation to reinforce the running response in rats, indicates that the operant induction effect bears a close resemblance to the induction effect reported by Pavlov. The study used a "multiple schedule procedure" in which rats were sometimes reinforced on a high density schedule of reinforcement (relatively positive), and sometimes on a low density of reinforcement (relatively negative) schedule. Each schedule was accompanied by a distinctive discriminative stimulus and was in force for 1.5 minutes or 4.5 minutes before being replaced by the other schedule and its associated stimulus. The reinforcer was positive brain stimulation (a 0.5 second train of 60 cps sine waves delivered through electrodes aimed at the lateral hypothalamus), and running was measured in a specially constructed running wheel. For both subjects, reinforcements were delivered according to a "time" schedule: whenever S ran at a speed at or above 1 inch per second at the circumference of the wheel, reinforcements were given at the rate of 1/1.5 seconds or 1/5 seconds for R-1 or 1/1 second or 1/4 seconds for R-2. If running ceased or speed fell below the minimum criterion, no reinforcement was given.

The final performance obtained after approximately 10 days of training, is shown in Fig. 17-7. The abscissa of each graph represents time since the last schedule change. The ordinate shows the mean number of seconds during which running actually occurred in each successive 30-day period after schedule change. The most noteworthy feature of the results is the marked drop in performance immediately after switching the subject to the low density schedule. It is this time-dependent de-

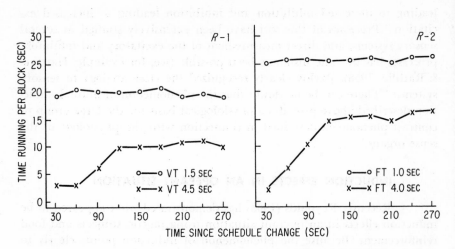

Fig. 17-7. Mean number of seconds running in each component of the multiple schedule, averaged over 4 sessions. The origin represents the moment of schedule change.

pression which is referred to here as an "induction" effect. It provides a striking similarity to the Pavlovian phenomenon, which is also time-dependent.

A 30-minute exposure to one of the two schedules followed each daily session. The schedule left in force for this period was alternated daily. During the 30-minute exposure, there was a small decline in running time under both schedules, but generally stable running was maintained by each. This result indicates that running in the low density schedule was not maintained by adventitious reinforcement arising from eventual presentation of the high density schedule, and further suggests that fatigue from running is not of major importance in this procedure.

Other results from one rat give further information about the contrast phenomenon. Fig. 17-8a shows the first training session of R-2. Following schedule change, the pattern of running was exactly in reverse of the pattern observed after training: the level of running under one component persisted into the other component. This persistence represents a failure to discriminate the change in schedule components and indicates that the contrast effect is not produced solely by the abrupt change in the density of reinforcement. The gradual emergence of the depression effect as training continued suggests that well developed stimulus control is an important condition for obtaining the phenomenon, and indicates that a mechanism of conditioning may be involved.

It seemed at least possible that the depression phenomenon might depend on fatigue resulting from running and that the rat learned to rest after an exposure to the high density component. To test this hypothesis, the wheel was locked during the high density schedule, so that

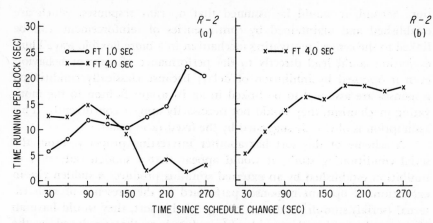

Fig. 17-8. (a) Mean number of seconds running in each component of the multiple schedule, on the first day of training. (b) Mean percentage of time running on the low density component, when the wheel was locked during the high density component.

running could not take place. Reinforcing stimulation was automatically delivered in much the same pattern that had occurred earlier in the experiment, but this time without a running requirement. The depression following the change to the low density schedule, when running was again required, persisted with this procedure, as shown in Fig. 17-8b. This result indicates that an interpretation of the depression effect in terms of fatigue is not appropriate. Observation of the ănimal while the wheel was locked gave no suggestion of vigorous activity of any sort taking place. By indicating that the contrast effect is not the result of fatigue, this observation helps justify the use of a Pavlovian concept of inhibition. Apparently, it is not responding per se, but rather a strong prior state of excitation, that produces the phenomenon.

Current experiments by the writer, using pigeons reinforced by food on a multiple schedule, have shown a similar time-dependent effect. It would appear that the phenomenon reported here is not unique to the reinforcement conditions used, and that the contrast effects found in operant behavior bear a close similarity to those demonstrated by Pavlov with respondent behavior. It is proposed that both arise as a result of the interaction of excitatory and inhibitory processes.

CONCLUSION

It is beyond the scope of this paper to propose a mechanism of immediate control based on the processes which have been posited. Such a mechanism might, however, include the following properties. First, it would be assumed that classically conditioned responses such as salivation bear a fixed (perhaps additive) relationship to excitation and inhibition. Second, it would be assumed that operant responses, which are established and maintained by contingencies of reinforcement, can be linked to the central motivating mechanism in a more flexible way. Thus, excitation could lead directly to the performance of operant behavior, even if opposed by inhibition of delay; because classically conditioned responses are assumed to be linked in an invariant fashion to the motivating mechanism, they would not necessarily appear concurrently. This assumption is obviously suggested by the fixed ratio result.

A scheme of this sort has another interesting property. From the serial conditioning study, it would appear that a sudden reduction in inhibition established by an external stimulus produces a sudden rise in excitation. If operant responses performed in the presence of such external (serial) stimuli produce a change of this sort, they would have an effect similar, although considerably reduced, to that produced by the presentation of a primary reinforce.

These *ad hoc* comments on possible relationships between Pavlovian concepts and incentive motivation are only intended to indicate a direction for future work. Further work is obviously required for the development of a specific and testable theory of incentive motivation. Even in its present form, this approach suggests the way in which studies of classical conditioning can contribute to an understanding of incentive motivation. First, it would appear that respondent behavior presents a simpler experimental problem than operant behavior; while the variables important in classical conditioning also play a role in operant behavior, operants appear to be subject to additional effects as well (particularly effects involving reinforcement contingencies). Second, if a central mechanism is to be inferred, the use of a variety of measures and techniques greatly strengthens the inferences that can be made about such a process. The problem of immediate control, then, may profitably be studied through classical conditioning. It is the theory of classical conditioning, however, and not the behavioral laws, which will ultimately lead to an understanding of the problem of immediate control.

References

FERSTER, C. B. Sustained behavior under delayed reinforcement. *J. exp. Psychol.*, 1953, *45*, 218-224.

FERSTER, C. B., & SKINNER, B. F. *Schedules of reinforcement.* New York: Appleton-Century-Crofts, 1957.

HARTLINE, H. K., & RATLIFFE, F. Spatial summation of inhibitory influences in the eye of *Limulus,* and the mutual interaction of receptor units. *J. gen. Physiol.*, 1958, *41*, 1049-1066.

HULL, C. L. *Principles of behavior: An introduction to behavior theory.* New York: Appleton-Century-Crofts, 1943.

HULL, C. L. *A behavior system.* New Haven: Yale University Press, 1962.

KELLEHER, R. T., & GOLLUB, L. R. A review of positive conditioned reinforcement. *J. exp. anal. Behav.,* 1962, supplement 13, Vol. 5, 543-597.

KINTSCH, W., & WITTE, R. S. Concurrent conditioning of bar press and salivation responses. *J. comp. physiol. Psychol.,* 1962, *55,* 963-968.

KONORSKI, J. *Conditioned reflexes and neuron organization.* Cambridge, England: Cambridge University Press, 1948.

PAVLOV, I. P. *Conditioned reflexes.* London: Oxford University Press, 1927. (Transl. by G. V. ANREP.)

REYNOLDS, G. S. Some limitations on behavioral contrast and induction during successive discrimination. *J. exp. anal. Behav.,* 1963, *6,* 131-139.

SHAPIRO, M. M. Salivary conditioning in dogs during fixed interval reinforcement contingent upon lever pressing. *J. exp. anal. Behav.,* 1961, *4,* 361-364.

SHAPIRO, M. M. Salivation and lever pressing relationships. *J. comp. physiol. Psychol.,* 1962, *55,* 567-571.

SHEFFIELD, F. D. A drive induction theory of learning. New Haven: Yale University, 1954 (mimeographed manuscript).

SHEFFIELD, F. D. A new look at Pavlovian conditioning. New Haven: Yale University, 1959 (mimeographed manuscript).

SHEFFIELD, F. D., ROBY, T. B., & CAMPBELL, B. A. Drive-reduction versus consummatory behavior as determinants of reinforcement. *J. comp. physiol. Psychol.,* 1954, *47,* 471-481.

SKINNER, B. F. Some contributions of an experimental analysis of behavior to psychology as a whole. *Amer. Psychol.,* 1953, *8,* 69-78.

SPENCE, K. P. *Behavior theory and conditioning.* New Haven: Yale University Press, 1956.

FRANCIS A. YOUNG
Washington State University

18

Classical Conditioning of Autonomic Functions

The subtitle of this paper might well be "What is conditioned
during the process of conditioning?" The paper seeks to answer
this question without restriction to type of conditioning for both skeletal
and autonomic behavior. This question is basic to Kendler's (1959) discussion of the attempts to condition pupillary dilation by Gerall, Sampson, and Boslow (1957) and by Young (1958). Kendler notes that the
source of the difference between the positive findings of Gerall *et al.* and
the negative findings of Young lies not in their empirical results but
instead in their *definition* of *conditioning*. Young insists that a positive
demonstration of pupillary conditioning occurs in the complete absence
of concurrent autonomic responses. In this connection it is interesting to
note that Gerall *et al.* agree that their study shows "... that a generalized fear reaction was modified ... rather than a specific light reflex."

Kendler further admits that Young is in a certain sense entitled to
accept his own definition of conditioning. But his definition leads to some
questions: Is his definition contrary to the conventional definitions of
conditioning? That is, in Pavlov's classical study was only the salivary
response occurring in the complete absence of other concurrent responses?
When a pupillary dilation response does occur, how can one be absolutely sure that no other generalized autonomic responses are occurring?

As frequently happens when one wishes to sharpen controversial
issues, Kendler takes a rather extreme position since no behavior occurs
in complete isolation nor need it to answer the questions raised. Further,
the controversy lies not in the definition of conditioning but rather in
the criteria of conditioning which are employed. Under what conditions
may we say that the pupil has been conditioned? There is no controversy

with respect to a pupillary constriction which occurs to a sound or similar conditioned stimulus which does not elicit such a response before conditioning occurs. The only controversy with respect to constriction concerns its actual demonstration since there have been no clear-cut, repeatable instances of pupillary conditioned constriction. On the other hand a number of investigators have found the pupillary dilation response to be conditionable. As Kimble puts it:

In the laboratory, the pupillary reflex is readily elicited either with a change in illumination or by administration of an electric shock. Although the division of studies on this basis is not perfect, success in conditioning the pupillary reflex has been notably better in experiments employing electric shock. It seems likely that the emotional accompaniments of the shock may have been important. (1961, p. 51)

Before examining these "emotional accompaniments" in more detail let us consider what takes place in a classical conditioning setup. In brief, two sources of stimulation are paired so that the corresponding stimuli are presented to an organism in a fixed and repeatable manner. One of these stimuli elicits a response which is sought by the investigator, the unconditioned response or reflex (UR), and is given the name unconditioned stimulus (US). The actual manner in which the US elicits the UR is of no immediate concern as long as the US is consistently followed by the desired response. The second stimulus may elicit a response or responses which are of no interest to the investigator and these are usually ignored, although in many cases they should not be ignored. Traditionally this second stimulus is called the conditioned stimulus (CS) since the investigator expects that it will eventually elicit, after enough pairings, the same response (UR) as the first stimulus elicits or, at least, a reasonable facsimile of the unconditioned response. He tests this hypothesis by omitting the unconditioned stimulus to see whether the unconditioned response will occur in the presence of the conditioned stimulus only or notes the occurrence of a response, an anticipatory response, before the occurrence of the unconditioned response. If either or both of these occur, the investigator concludes that a conditioned response or reflex has developed and classical conditioning has occurred. Here we have a factual description or an operational definition of classical conditioning but what this *means* depends not upon this definition but upon the characteristics of the observer.

In his preface to the first Russian edition of the Lectures on Conditioned Reflexes written in 1923 Pavlov says:

Some years after the beginning of the work with our new method I learned that somewhat similar experiments on animals had been performed in America, and indeed not by physiologists but by psychologists. Thereupon I studied in more detail the American publications, and now I must acknowledge that the honour of having made the first steps along this path belongs to E. I. Thorndike. By two or three years his experiments preceded ours, and his book must be considered as a classic, both for its bold outlook on an immense task and for the accuracy of its results. Since the time of Thorndike the American work (Yerkes, Parker, Watson, *et al.*) on our subject has grown. It is purely American in every sense—in collaborators, equipment, laboratories, and publications. The Americans, judged by the book of Thorndike, set out on this new path of investigation in a quite different manner from us. From a passage in Thorndike one may conjecture that the practical American mind applied to everyday life found that it is more important to be acquainted with the exact outward behavior of man than with guesses about his internal states with all their combinations and changes. With these considerations concerning man, the American psychologists proceeded to their laboratory experiments on animals. From the character of the investigations, up to the present, one feels that both the methods and the problems are derived from human interests.

I and my co-workers hold another position. As all our work developed out of physiology, so it has continued directly in that path. The methods and the conditions of our experimentation, as well as the scheme of the separate problems, the working up of the results, and finally their systematisation—all this has remained in the realm of the facts, conceptions and terminology of the central nervous system. This approach to our subject from both the psychological and the physiological sides enlarges the sphere of the phenomena under investigation. (Pavlov, 1928, pp. 39-40)

This long quotation points up the stimulus-response characteristic of much of the early and recent American work in conditioning. This concentration on the purely external aspects of the learning situation has led some investigators into theoretical positions which are unproductive if not actually meaningless. This may even be likened to failure to see the tree because of the leaves. While Pavlov's own "physiological" position replete with concepts such as irradiation, excitation, inhibition, concentration and induction suffers from an excess of unverified concepts, a position between these two extremes would enable a correlation of psychological and physiological approaches which would eliminate some of the confusion existing in both points of view.

Since the pure S-R approach represents the ultimate in molar approaches, it yields the least information for the energy expended although one does not go beyond the information directly available to the sense organs and thus remains purely objective. If one takes the position that observable stimuli and observable responses are associated or conditioned, it is possible to say that the pupillary dilation response is conditioned since the tone is followed by an increase in the diameter of the pupil. But if one asks what is conditioned in a classical conditioning setup and is willing to go beyond the observable stimuli and responses but not beyond physiological facts, rather interesting possibilities arise.

The simple reflex arc is usually considered to have three basic physiological components: a sensory component propagated over the afferent nerve fibers, a spinal or cortical connection between the sensory and motor components mediated by interneurons and a motor component propagated over the efferent nerve fibers (Ruch, 1960, p. 33). The observable stimulus activates a receptor which starts impulses moving up the sensory component toward the spinal cord and/or brain. These impulses make connections across the interneurons with the motor component which sends impulses to an effector which results in observable movement. If the complexity of this basic system is increased, neither the sensory nor motor aspects change, except that more fibers may become involved, but rather the change in complexity occurs primarily at the brain level. This discussion ignores the modifications in sensory input which occur at synapses such as has been demonstrated by Galambos *et al.* (1956) and by the *afferent neuronal habituation* phenomenon which has been elaborated by Hernández-Peón and Brust-Carmona (1961) since these modified inputs are received at the cortical level and must be approximated by direct cortical stimulation in order to develop a comparable conditioned response. The peripheral nervous system can transmit the characteristics of intensity, area and duration of a stimulus to a sensory projection area and the area involved likely determines the qualitative aspects of the stimulus, but it is unlikely that it can do anything other than this. Likewise the efferent aspect of the peripheral nervous system can transmit the same characteristics to the effector system and can probably not do anything else. These characteristics of the peripheral nervous system suggest that the stimulus and the response can be moved to central ends of these systems without changing the basic stimulus-response characteristics other than that we must now observe them with oscilloscopes and electrodes rather than with the unaided sense organs. From this it follows that the sensory receptor and the afferent nervous system are not basic to the conditioning process as long as a pattern of stimulation can be developed in the sensory projection area which is similar to that which is usually developed through the afferent nervous system. This conclusion applies to the unconditioned stimulus as well as to the conditioned stimulus, although available experimental evidence does not unequivocally support its application to the unconditioned stimulus. The early studies by Loucks (1936, 1938) and by Loucks and Gantt (1938) in which he used his technique of a chronically implanted coil activated by a primary coil located outside the skin (Loucks, 1934) to stimulate various parts of the cortex faradically as a conditioned stimulus demonstrated that it is possible to set up conditioned responses without activation of the peripheral afferent system. Thus he was able to set up a conditioned salivary response using a faradic stimulus applied to the visual sensory elements of the cortex as the CS and acid as the US, and a conditioned motor response using a shock to the *sigmoid gyri* as the CS and a shock to the foot as the US.

Supportive results were obtained by Martino (1939) in a series of studies using the blinking response in the dog. More recently Rutledge and Doty (1955); Doty, Rutledge, and Larsen (1956); and Doty and Giurgea (1961) have verified these findings with cortical stimulation of cats through implanted electrodes. Rutledge and Doty (1955) also compared the effect of chlorpromazine on conditioned responses set up to cortical stimulation of the visual and auditory areas with CRs set up to visual and auditory stimuli and found that chlorpromazine had little or no effect on the cortically established CRs but eliminated those to visual and auditory stimuli. The available experimental evidence unanimously supports the dispensability of the afferent circuit of the conditioned stimulus provided comparable cortical effects can be substituted.

The experimental evidence bearing on the substitution of cortical stimulation for peripheral stimulation as the unconditioned stimulus parallels that for the conditioned stimulus except that the more complicated locus of the neural activity associated with the US makes the substitution of cortical stimulation more difficult. Loucks (1936) and Loucks and Gantt (1938) attempted to condition a leg withdrawal movement elicited by cortical stimulation to a sound CS in dogs and were not successful in 600 trials. They conclude that cortical stimulation which results in movement but no pain or autonomic involvement is not adequate as an unconditioned stimulus. Since no cortical areas associated with pain have been located and the relationships between the somewhat diffuse structures extending through the brain stem from the medulla the diencephalon which are thought to be related to pain and the affective side of sensory experience and the cortex is unknown (Ruch, 1960, p. 377), it is not possible to elicit all the necessary components by cortical stimulation. The work which has followed the Olds and Milner (1954) discovery of areas of the old brain which lead to behavior when electrically stimulated suggests the possibility of a dual stimulation of cortical sensory areas and the brain stem which would duplicate the usual dual aspect of the unconditioned stimulus. That this dual aspect of the US is necessary for conditioning follows from Loucks' studies and studies on salivary conditioning using morphine and pilocarpine as unconditioned stimuli. Collins and Tatum (1925) and later Kleitman and Crisler (1927) have demonstrated that it is possible to condition the salivary reflex using morphine as the unconditioned stimulus. Crisler (1930) concludes that morphine apparently acts directly on the reflex center, and the afferent part of the unconditioned arc is not necessary for the development of a conditioned reflex. Since the injection of morphine in the dog is usually followed by nausea and other signs of discomfort, Loucks (1936) draws the conclusion that conditioning is established upon the basis of certain primitive urges, impulses, appetites—probably subcortical in character—and that it is the feeling of pain, hunger, nausea, etc. which is the significant factor rather than the reflex response which is merely one component in a complex pattern. Thus as long as the cortical and subcortical components of the US can be duplicated at the cortical and subcortical levels by shock, drugs or any suitable means, the unconditioned stimulus and the afferent system connected thereto may be dispensed with and conditioning is possible. Brogden and Gantt (1937) report a study in which a point in the lateral cerebellar lobe under weak faradization elicited an ipsilateral foreleg extension. When stimulated with a current level below that required to elicit struggling and signs of pain from the dog, this leg movement was as easily conditioned to an auditory stimulus as a leg movement resulting from a painful skin stimulus. Their conclusion is of interest, "The rapid formation and the stability of the conditioned reflex indicates that it was not elaborated to proprioceptive stimuli resulting from stimulation. In the light of this apparent integrative function of the cerebellum further researches will be directed to the relation of this organ to the higher nervous structures—viz., the thalamus and the cerebral cortex" (p. 278). Since the animal extended its foreleg in response to cerebellar stimulation, it received proprioceptive feedback from this movement. This feedback probably plays an important role in the learning described in the Brogden and Gantt study. Once the conditioned response has been established the unconditioned stimulus pathway may be abolished without affecting the operation of the CR (Settlage & Harlow, 1936).

The finding that direct cortical stimulation can be substituted for the usual afferent stimulation in the learning situation does not rule out the contribution of other cortical areas as suggested by Loucks and supported by Hernández-Peón and Brust-Carmona (1961). This finding does indicate that the connections between various areas of the brain are numerous and that some of these areas other than the cortex may contribute the "attention" factor which seems essential for learning (Galambos, 1961).

From an examination of some of the evidence which bears on the stimulus aspects of conditioning, we may turn to the response end and consider the effector system. A considerable number of studies have dealt with the effector aspect and with several notable exceptions all agree that the response is unnecessary for conditioning. One group of studies has dealt with a comparison of salivation when induced by morphine which has a central effect and pilocarpine which has a peripheral effect. All such studies (Collin & Tatum, 1925; Crisler, 1928, 1930; Kleitman & Crisler, 1927; Mulinos & Lieb, 1929) found that it is possible to set up conditioned salivation easily and rapidly in dogs or cats to subcutaneous injections of morphine sulphate. These injections are usually accompanied by nausea, vomiting and defecation. While the conditioned responses are long lived, four months or more without reinforcement, they are abolished or reduced more effectively by starvation (Kleitman, 1927) or withdrawal of water (Crisler, 1928) than are the unconditioned salivary responses to morphine or to pilocarpine. This may mean that thirst or starvation have an influence on the sensory components of the CR or differential influences on separate cortical or subcortical centers (Crisler, 1928). Several studies have also shown that the salivation response to morphine can be conditioned even though salivation itself is inhibited by atropine (Crisler, 1930; Finch, 1938; Mulinos & Lieb, 1929). On the other hand, most of the studies (Crisler, 1930; Kleitman, 1927; Mulinos & Lieb, 1929) which have attempted to set up CRs to pilocarpine nitrate or sulphate which has a peripheral effect on the salivary glands have been unsuccessful even though salivation is induced. The one exception is a study by Finch (1938) who used a technique capable of detecting extremely small fluctuations in amount of saliva produced. He found that there is some indication of a small increase in salivation to saline injections following conditioning injections of pilocarpine hydrochloride. He concludes that these results, while not *proving* that exercise of a response provides alone an adequate basis for conditioning that response, indicate that the question as to the efficacy of exercise in conditioning must be regarded as still open. These studies support the conclusion that the response is not necessary for the occurrence of conditioning and, probably, by itself is not capable of supporting conditioning.

A second group of studies has attempted to condition motor responses when the subject was prevented from making the response through the action of a drug or nerve damage or when the motor response was elicited by stimulation of the effector system only. The earliest of these studies was made by Harlow and Stagner (1933) in which they attempted to condition a gross motor avoidance response and the pupil under curare. The gross response involved jumping off an electrified grill. The animals were tested with a variety of stimuli to see how much time elapsed before they would jump off the grill when it was not charged. Once all animals had done this, a group of 7 cats and 12 dogs were used as experimental subjects. The animals were put under curare and artificial respiration and placed on their backs on the electrified grill. A series of 30 conditioning trials were presented and the animals were tested for learning after recovery from curare. While none of the animals showed any learning with respect to the gross jumping movement to avoid the grill after presentation of the CS, they were more tractable than before exposure to the training situation. In an unpublished study performed in our laboratory we shocked rats through an electrode fastened to the back. The response to this stimulation was to crouch as close to the floor as possible and remain motionless. It seems likely that the Harlow and Stagner animals learned to do the same since no other response was open to them. A conditioned pupillary dilation occurred to the severe shock used which could be extinguished only with great difficulty. This response will be considered in detail later on. Since the experimental conditions of this study are such as to preclude clear cut results, it contributes little to the evaluation of the role of the response in conditioning. With a more meaningful escape response Harlow later demonstrated conditioning under lower levels of curare in cats (Harlow, 1940). Girden (1940, 1942a, b, c) has carried out a series of studies in which dogs were subjected to mild doses of curare or of erythroidine and conditioned under this state. While these studies do not bear directly on the question as to whether conditioning can take place when no effector response is possible since the drug dose allowed some muscle movement, they do indicate that conditioning is possible and specific to the drug state since the CRs do not appear in the normal state. These studies also bear on the question of pupillary conditioning which will be considered later.

The recent studies by Black (1958) in which a conditioned avoidance response in dogs was partially extinguished while the animals were under complete curarization and by Black, Carlson, and Solomon (1962) which reports autonomic conditioning in dogs totally paralyzed with d-tubo-curarine support the hypothesis that the response is not essential in conditioning. Light and Gantt (1936) crushed the motor nerves to the rear leg and conditioned the dog using a shock to the foot of the same leg as the US and a buzzer as the CS. The UR or lifting of the leg could not be made. After recovery of the damaged motor nerve the animals were tested with the CS and the CR of leg lifting occurred. Loucks (1936) using a leg movement elicited by direct stimulation of the sigmoid gyri was not able to demonstrate conditioning even though the UR was elicited since no neural paths were involved. This conclusion is supported by a further study by Loucks (1937) which attempted to condition hyperglycemia using injections of epinephrine as the US and by a study by Katzenelbogen, Loucks and Gantt (1939) which attempted to condition gastric secretion to injections of histamine. In neither study was conditioning successful since the drugs used as unconditioned stimuli had a peripheral locus of action and no neural centers were involved.

The studies reviewed clearly support the hypotheses that neither the afferent nor the efferent systems are essential for conditioning as long as comparable neural activity can be elicited by other means. Further, they support the hypothesis that without neural representation at either the cortical or subcortical level or both no conditioning can occur. The evidence bearing on this latter hypothesis may be examined in more detail especially with regard to the neural level necessary for conditioning.

All the evidence presented so far indicates that in animals conditioning will occur as long as the cortical area and all lower centers are functioning normally. Evidence is also available to indicate that conditioning is possible in the decorticate animal although the level and type of conditioning is much grosser than that possible in the normal subject. Culler and Mettler (1934) demonstrated that it is possible to condition a foreleg withdrawal movement elicited by shock to a sound in a thalamic dog. Girden, Mettler, Finch, and Culler (1936) also demonstrated that in the decorticate dog it is possible to set up a variety of conditioned responses which are rather diffuse in character and not similar to the precise, controlled movements which may be conditioned in the normal dog. These responses could be conditioned to acoustic, thermal and tactile stimuli but not effectively to visual stimuli. These studies are supported by recent studies of conditioning in decorticate cats by Hernández-Peón and Brust-Carmona (1961).

Culler together with Shurrager extended the studies on decorticate dogs to spinal dogs and found evidence of conditioning which started a controversy lasting more than a decade. Using acute preparations of spinal dogs Shurrager and Culler (1938, 1940, 1941a, b) excised the semitendinosus muscles except for blood and nerve supply in both rear legs of the inverted dog and connected these by means of threads to recording pens on a kymograph. A shock to the pad of one of the feet was used as the UCS; three shocks to the tail presented one second apart with the last one coinciding with the US served as the CS. The UR was the reflex contraction of the leg to the food pad shock while the CR was the contraction of a small section of the semitendinosus muscle. Shurrager and Culler used four criteria for conditioning. First, the CR was not evoked by the CS prior to conditioning. However, as their published records show (Shurrager & Culler, 1940) the muscle did respond to the CS before conditioning but the magnitude of the response increased during the course of the conditioning procedure. Usually they found a larger response in one leg and attached the US to the leg which showed the smallest response. The response in this leg usually increased while the response in the other leg decreased as a result of conditioning (Shurrager & Culler, 1941a).

The second criterion required that the CR appear and become firmly established as conditioning was continued. Since the magnitude of the response in the muscle increased with conditioning, this criterion seems to have been met. The third criterion required that the CR be extinguishable. When the US was discontinued the magnitude of the muscle response decreased and returned to the original state. The fourth criterion was that the CR was not subject to spontaneous recovery. This is a rather unusual criterion for the CR since almost all investigators since Pavlov have found spontaneous recovery of some degree following extinction (Kimble, 1961, p. 284). The response of the semitendinosus muscle did not show spontaneous recovery after extinction. The lack of spontaneous recovery is not the only difference between their CR and the usual CR. The CS was presented three times and the CR occurred twice following each of the first two CSs but was not visible after the third CS since the response to the US also occurred. This relationship was invariant throughout the course of conditioning. Further the latency of the CR was very short (40 milliseconds in one dog and an average of 71 milliseconds over all dogs and trials). These extremely short latencies combined with the invariant characteristics of the response suggest that they were dealing with an unconditioned reflex rather than a conditioned reflex which usually shows changes in latency and shape as well as magnitude during conditioning. Shurrager and Shurrager (1946) considered this to be learning at a single synapse and attempted to construct the elemental learning curve on this basis. The results obtained by Shurrager and Culler may be an example of the enhancement phenomena which occur in muscles following tetanus as described by Guttman, Horton and Wilber (1937) combined with the habituation phenomenon of Griffith (1924), since the US, 60 cycle current, was always presented.

The spinal conditioning of Shurrager and Culler was disputed by Kellogg, Pronko, and Deese (1946); by Kellogg (1946); and by Kellogg, Deese, Pronko, and Feinberg (1947) who were not able to demonstrate a conditioned leg movement or muscle movement in intact chronic spinal dogs. Shurrager (1947) admitted that he had not been able to do this but had conditioned acute spinal dogs. Kellogg (1947) argued that if the phenomenon could only be demonstrated in acute dogs, it may be an artifact of the time involved after surgery or a muscle twitch to intense electrical stimulation. Deese and Kellogg (1949) attempted to duplicate the Shurrager and Culler (1940) study with acute animals and found that the CR is actually an unconditioned reflex to the electric shock applied to the tail. Pinot and Bromiley (1950) also tried to condition the spinal dog without success. In the light of other possible interpretations of the Shurrager and Culler response and the failure of other investigators to find acceptable evidence of conditioning in the spinal dog, it seems reasonable to conclude that conditioning does not occur without involvement of the central nervous system (Gantt, 1937).

What is conditioned, therefore, are the pathways or whatever, which exist in the brain between the sensory projection areas and subcortical areas and the motor areas of the cortex and cerebellum. These areas between the sensory end points and the motor beginning points must include the subcortical areas of the brain which are intimately related to cortical areas (Bykov, 1957; Hoff, Kell, & Carroll, 1963). Nor is it necessary to think in terms of specific sensory and motor areas in an anatomical sense since as Pribram (1958) has pointed out the amount of overlap in these systems is so great that it is not meaningful to speak of separate sensory and motor systems.

If one distinguishes sensory input and motor output for discussion purposes, several possibilities exist, e.g., (a) the CS input may be connected directly to the motor output, (b) the CS input may be connected indirectly to the motor output via the US input-motor output connection which is then modified, or (c) the CS input may be connected directly to the UR-feedback sensory input which depends upon induction of the UR by the US. The first alternative (a) is basically the simple SR formulation which would require no sensory component or feedback, while (b) and (c) are variants of an SS formulation. In (b) CS input is connected directly to the US input and thus indirectly elicits the UR. With further pairing some of the unused elements of the US drop out and the UR becomes modified into the CR. In (c) the CS input is connected directly to the UR feedback input and requires the operation of the CS only for the purpose of eliciting the UR and its attendant feedback. In effect (b) suggests the need for common elements in CS and US inputs whereas (c) does not require any communality.

This analysis may be carried further by use of an example. Pavlov discusses the relationship between the amount and the characteristics of the saliva produced when various types of substances such as hard food, soft food, acid, sand, and pebbles are introduced into the dog's mouth. He thought that special reflexes are involved in these cases which, thanks to the specific irritability of the peripheral endings of the centripetal nerves of the mouth (through various mechanical and chemical stimuli), condition the difference in the activity of the salivary glands when these stimuli are not in contact with the mouth, but are at some distance from the dog (Pavlov, 1928, pp. 61-65). The salivary response to the sight and sound of food is in itself a conditioned response based on unconditioned response of salivation to food in the mouth.

If the receptors in the various sensory systems in the mouth—tactual, chemical, thermal, olfactory, gustatory, kinesthetic, etc.—are anesthetized or otherwise cut off from the sensory projection areas before conditioning to visual stimuli has occurred, the animal will not salivate to objects placed in the mouth since there are no nerve impulses to indicate that objects are in the mouth. Under the assumption of an unconditioned reflex path, impulses from these sensory receptors go by way of the cranial nerves to the nuclei salivatorius inferior and superior in the reticular formation at the junction of the pons and the medulla oblongata from whence general visceral efferent fibers go to the parotid gland by way of the glossopharyngeal nerve or the salivary glands by way of the facial nerve (Ranson-Clark, 1953, p. 230).

In terms of the analysis presented earlier the conditioned salivary responses to the sight and sound of food may have resulted from a direct connection between the visual and auditory input and the nuclei salivatorius, from the operation of common sensory input such as olfactory and auditory components, or from a connection between the visual and auditory input and the sensory feedback from activity of the salivary glands themselves. A direct connection between visual and auditory input and the nuclei salivatorius amounts to a reflex arc so that no learning should be necessary. As a matter of fact Kuntz takes this position since he says, "The salivary glands react reflexly both to stimulation of the oral mucosa and strong stimulation of afferent nerves from other parts of the body, particularly the eyes, ears and nasal mucosa" (1945, p. 352). From this point of view the response to the sight and sound of food may be considered an unconditioned reflex. Further, the response to the bell may also be considered as a reflex since it involves stimulation from the ears. One might postulate that such connections are present but not operative and a certain amount of exercise is required for them to become operative. This position would be congruent with many types of conditioning situations as well as a strict S-R approach but would limit all learning to situations in which direct anatomical connections between input and output centers are present.

The widespread representation of sensory input in the cortical and subcortical areas of the brain and the relatively restricted representation of motor outflow areas suggest that there are many more opportunities to form sensory-sensory connections than sensory-motor connections. It is also difficult to conceive of a mechanism by means of which a new neural pathway could be established on the basis of function or repetition. A study carried out by Varga and Pressman and reported by Asratyan (1961) bears on this question. Dogs were placed in a harness similar to that used for leg-withdrawal avoidance training to shock. However, instead of shocking the dog the experimenter raised the hind leg just after a bell was sounded. Thus the leg was raised passively so that the dog received the kinesthetic feedback from the movements of the leg muscles and joints but there was no stimulation of motor outflow. In this situation a connection could be formed between the sensory input from the bell and the kinesthetic feedback from the passive movement of the leg but not between the sensory input from the bell and the motor output to the leg since the latter did not occur. When the bell was sounded without the passive lifting of the leg the dog actively lifted the leg but had not done so before training. These results would seem to support an S-S type of connection rather than an S-R connection, and suggest that common elements are not necessary for conditioning to occur. The Light and Gantt (1936) study discussed earlier obtained conditioning of leg withdrawal when no kinesthetic feedback was present as the motor nerve to the leg had been crushed. The foot of the damaged leg was shocked following presentation of the sound of a bell and presumably the dog received the sensory input from the shock. Since the lifting of the leg may be considered a reflex reaction to shock, the dog formed a connection between the shock input and bell input. Later, after regeneration of the motor nerve the dog responded to the bell by lifting the leg.

The assumption that the kinesthetic feedback is a true feedback to the nucleus giving rise to the motor outflow is necessary for this position since some connection between sensory input and motor outflow must exist anatomically in order to support learning. As far as the subject is concerned no response has occurred until this feedback has been received. Thus conditioning is assumed to represent the formation of connections between a new sensory input and the feedback input from a response. The response must be made before any learning can occur and the presence of common elements in the CS and US situation would likely improve learning but are not essential for learning. The exact mechanism of the formation of connections is not essential for this elaboration and most of the theoretical positions discussed by Galambos and Morgan (1960) would be applicable.

Pavlov (1928), p. 61) stressed the role of attention in conditioning and felt that it was only necessary to attract the *attention* of the dog to the CS (bell, for example) in order to condition salivation to the CS. The "attracting attention" may be essential to any form of conditioning and the hypothesis is advanced here that no conditioning can occur without this "attention." Attention refers to the orientation of the sense receptor system or systems including the cortical portions toward a particular stimulus or group of stimuli (English & English, 1958). It may be demonstrated behaviorally by the occurrence of a response to the stimulus such as moving the ears and head to the sound of a bell, raising the foot following a shock to the paw, or pressing a lever. If such responses do not occur, the conclusion does not follow that the subject did not attend to the stimuli. The "attention" may be demonstrated neurophysiologically in the absence of overt behavior by means of recording electrodes placed in the cortex. The orientation must be directed toward both the CS and the US in the classical conditioning setup in order for conditioning to occur.

In a recent study Smith, McFarland and Taylor (1961) found that rats failed to learn to turn a wheel to avoid shock when a light was used as the CS but learned this response rapidly when a buzzer was substituted for the light as the CS. Since the buzzer had a fairly high intensity (65 db) it may have been more effective in eliciting "attention" than the light and cannot be avoided by the animal whereas the light can be avoided by change of position. Attention is determined by the interaction between stimulus characteristics such as quality, intensity, duration, and the characteristics of the organism as determined by its drive state. A sufficiently intense stimulus such as a shock to the foot may elicit auto-nomic components and a startle or fear response. In this case the stimu-lus is capable of generating its own "attention." In the case of a weak stimulus such as the sensory characteristics of food, a hunger-drive state must be present in the animal before the orientation response toward food will occur. In this view the drive serves to elicit "attention" although it may also serve as a reinforcer through drive reduction. The former role is viewed as essential to learning and conditioning while the latter role may or may not be essential. The concept of attention which played an important role in the structural psychology of Titchner and in the conditioning reflexology of Pavlov continues to play an important role in modern physiological psychology. Studies such as the one by Hubel, Henson, Rupert, and Galambos (1959) provide an experimental support for this concept. The discussion by Lindsley (1961) is of interest.

Thus what is conditioned or associated are two sets of neural ac-tivity (including autonomic and kinesthetic components) resulting from stimulation of oriented sense organs. Further, this interpretation reduces the value of the distinction of two types of conditioned reflexes as has been proposed by Skinner (1937) and by Konorski and Miller (1937) and by Konorski (1950) since the function of the US in the classical design is to elicit the sensory impulses which are to be connected to the sensory impulses elicited by the CS. Konorski and Miller point out that classical or respondent conditioning may be used with striped muscles, smooth muscles, and glands, whereas operant conditioning may be used only with striped muscles. If the only requirement is to elicit sensory impulses there is no reason, other than the obvious difficulty of voluntarily elicit-ing activity in smooth muscles and glands, why operant conditioning may not be used with smooth muscles and glands. The essential requirement is the setting up of concomitant impulses in the cortex and subcortical areas from two sets of attended stimuli, and not whether these impulses occur spontaneously or are elicited by means of reflexes or prior condi-tioned responses. The differences between operant and respondent con-ditioning thus become differences in technique rather than differences in type of learning. The classical approach uses stimuli (US) which have developed strong "attention" value through past conditioning and thus the role of drive in the subject is minimized whereas with operant con-ditioning strong stimuli are not available and the orientation response must be developed on the basis of drive-states.

Turning to the specific case of pupillary conditioning, we may com-pare the conditioning situation existing here with that occurring in salivary and in avoidance conditioning. In salivary conditioning the cortical aspects of sensory impulses arising from the receptors in the mouth area including olfaction and vision are connected with the cortical aspects of sensory impulses arising from the sound of the bell. In the case of avoidance conditioning the cortical aspects of the total sensory pattern including the autonomic component elicited by the shock or other noxious stimulus are connected to the cortical aspects of the sensory impulses elicited by the buzzer. In both of these cases the US elicits sensory impulses which have strong attention value or elicit strong orientation responses in the animal. When pupillary constriction is elicited by an increase in light intensity, accommodation or convergence, the US does not elicit sensory impulses which have strong attention value. In fact it does not elicit any sensory impulses associated with the pupil at all. If the analysis presented in this paper is meaningful, then an essential component of conditioning (sensory feedback input) is missing in the pupillary-constriction situation and, therefore, pupillary-constriction conditioning cannot occur. The experimental evidence to date (Young, 1954, 1958) supports this conclusion.

The situation with respect to pupillary-dilation conditioning has a dual aspect which does not occur with pupillary constriction. While the same type of stimuli used in constriction training—changes in light intensity, decreases in accommodation and in convergence—are capable of eliciting pupillar dilation in a manner parallel to that resulting in constriction, pupillary dilation may also be elicited in an entirely different manner through the application of noxious stimuli such as shock which results in increased epinephrine output and a dilation of the pupil (Ury & Gellhorn, 1959; Lowenstein & Lowenfeld, 1952). The first group of stimuli elicit reflex dilation or constriction of the pupil itself, whereas the noxious stimuli elicit pupillary dilation as part of the fear or startle pattern. Lowenstein and Lowenfeld (1952) indicate that normal pupillary constriction and dilation to light is controlled by the parasympathetic system which may be overridden by the sympathetic system under stress to produce a dilation. Neither of these types of stimulus situations results in impulses which are associated with the pupil since there are no sensory fibers associated with the pupil. Further, the subject is not able to perceive the changes in illumination induced by changes in pupil size.

Since there is no evidence to support pupillary conditioning to an increase or decrease in light intensity or to an increase or decrease in accommodation and/or convergence, the only evidence for conditioning concerns the dilation of the pupil to a noxious stimulus as shown by Harlow and Stagner (1933), Girden (1940, 1942a, b, c), Gerall, Sampson and Boslov (1957), and by Young (1958). Since the pupil dilates as part of a generalized unconditioned response to shock or noxious stimuli, it is far more likely that the generalized response is conditioned to the CS than that the pupil itself is conditioned. The nature of the generalized response in terms of latency and magnitude is modified during the course of conditioning in the expected direction, so that comparable changes in the behavior of the pupil probably represent the changes occurring in the generalized response. This hypothesis may be checked through the use of some other measure of the generalized response such as the galvanic skin response or vasodilation response. If both measures, GSR and pupil, show the same changes in the same time relationships, it is far more likely that they represent the generalized response rather than specific conditioned responses.

Since many autonomic responses do not give rise to specific sensory impulses, it is very unlikely that they can be conditioned directly although they will show changes as part of a conditioned generalized autonomic response. Those aspects of autonomic behavior which do have neural sensory impulses of high attention value such as the heart should be directly conditionable without involvement of the generalized autonomic response. Razran's (1933) early review of conditioning of autonomic functions generally supports the hypothesis that conditioning requires unconditioned and conditioned stimuli which are represented by neural sensory impulses of high "attention" value. Conditioning is clear cut in such cases and nonexistent or doubtful in cases without such cortical representation. These conclusions support those reached by Kendon Smith (1954) concerning the conditionability of autonomic behavior.

References

ASRATYAN, E. A. Some aspects of the elaboration of conditioned connections and formation of their properties. In J. F. DELAFRESNAYE (Ed.), *Brain mechanisms and learning—A symposium.* Oxford: Blackwell Scientific Publications, 1961. Pp. 95-113.

BLACK, A. H. The extinction of avoidance responses under curare. *J. comp. physiol. Psychol.,* 1958, *51,* 519-524.

BLACK, A. H., CARLSON, N. J., & SOLOMON, R. L. Exploratory studies of the conditioning of autonomic responses in curarized dogs. *Psychol. Monogr.,* 1962, *76,* No. 29.

BROGDEN, W. J., & GANTT, W. H. Cerebellar conditioned reflexes. *Amer. J. Physiol.,* 1937, *119,* 277-278.

BYKOV, K. M. *The cerebral cortex and the internal organs.* New York: Chemical Publishing, 1957.

CLARK, S. L. *Ranson's anatomy of the nervous system.* 9th ed. Philadelphia, W. B. Saunders, 1953.

COLLINS, K. H., & TATUM, A. L. A conditioned salivary reflex established by chronic morphine poisoning. *Amer. J. Physiol.,* 1925, *74,* 14-15.

CRISLER, G. The effect of withdrawal of water on the salivary conditioned reflex induced by morphine. *Amer. J. Physiol.*, 1928, *85*, 324-331.

CRISLER, G. Salivation is unnecessary for the establishment of the salivary conditioned reflex induced by morphine. *Amer. J. Physiol.*, 1930, *94*, 553-556.

CULLER, E. A., & METTLER, F. A. Observations upon conduct of a thalamic dog. Hearing and vision in decorticated animals. *Proc. Soc. Exp. Biol. & Med.*, 1934, *31*, 607-609.

DEESE, J., & KELLOGG, W. N. Some new data on the nature of "spinal conditioning." *J. comp. physiol. Psychol.*, 1949, *42*, 157-160.

DOTY, R. W., & GIURGEA, C. Conditioned reflexes established by coupling electrical excitations of two cortical areas. In J. F. DELAFRESNAYE (Ed.), *Brain mechanisms and learning—A symposium.* Oxford: Blackwell Scientific Publications, 1961. Pp. 133-152.

DOTY, R. W., RUTLEDGE, L. T., JR., & LARSEN, R. M. Conditioned reflexes established to electrical stimulation of cat cerebral cortex. *J. Neurophysiol.*, 1956, *19*, 401-415.

ENGLISH, H. B., & ENGLISH, A. C. *A comprehensive dictionary of psychological and psychoanalytical terms.* New York: Longmans, Green, 1958.

FINCH, G. Pilocarpine conditioning. *Amer. J. Physiol.*, 1938, *124*, 679-682. (a)

FINCH, G. Salivary conditioning in atropinized dogs. *Amer. J. Physiol.*, 1938, *124*, 136-141. (b)

GALAMBOS, R. Suppression of auditory nerve activity by stimulation of efferent fibers to cochlea. *J. Neurophysiol.*, 1956, *19*, 424-437.

GALAMBOS, R. Changing concepts of the learning mechanism. In J. F. DELAFRESNAYE (Ed.), *Brain mechanisms and learning—A symposium.* Oxford: Blackwell Scientific Publications, 1961. Pp. 231-241.

GALAMBOS, R., & MORGAN, C. T. The neural basis of learning. In J. FIELD (Ed.), *Handbook of Physiology, Section 1: Neurophysiology,* Vol. 3. Washington: American Physiological Society, 1960. Pp. 1471-1499.

GANTT, W. H. Contributions to the physiology of the conditioned reflex. *Arch. Neurol. Psychiat.* (Chicago), 1937, *37*, 848-858.

GERALL, A. A., SAMPSON, P. B., & BOSLOV, G. L. Classical conditioning of human pupillary dilation. *J. exp. Psychol.*, 1957, *54*, 457-474.

GIRDEN, E. Cerebral mechanisms in conditioning under curare. *Amer. J. Psychol.*, 1940, *53*, 397-406.

GIRDEN, E. The dissociation of blood pressure conditioned responses under curare and erythroidine. *J. exp. Psychol.*, 1942, *31*, 219-231. (a)

GIRDEN, E. The dissociation of pupillary conditioned reflexes under erythroidine and curare. *J. exp. Psychol.*, 1942, *31*, 322-332. (b)

GIRDEN, E. Generalized conditioned responses under curare and erythroidine. *J. exp. Psychol.*, 1942, *31*, 105-119. (c)

GIRDEN, E., METTLER, F. A., FINCH, G., & CULLER, E. Conditioned responses in a decorticate dog to acoustic, thermal, and tactile stimulation. *J. comp. Psychol.*, 1936, *21*, 367-385.

GRIFFITH, C. R. A note on the persistence of "practice effect" in rotation experiments. *J. comp. Psychol.*, 1924, *4*, 137-149.

GUTTMAN, S. A., HORTON, R. G., & WILBER, D. T. Enhancement of muscle contraction after tetanus. *Amer. J. Physiol.*, 1937, *119*, 463-473.

HARLOW, H. F. The effect of incomplete curare paralysis upon the formation of conditioned responses in cats. *J. genet. Psychol.,* 1940, *56,* 273-282.

HARLOW, H. F., & STAGNER, R. Effect of complete striate muscle paralysis upon the learning process. *J. exp. Psychol.,* 1933, *16,* 283-294.

HERNÁNDEZ-PEÓN, R., & BRUST-CARMONA, H. Functional role of subcortical structures in habituation and conditioning. In J. F. DELAFRESNAYE (Ed.), *Brain mechanisms and learning—A symposium.* Oxford: Blackwell Scientific Publications, 1961. Pp. 393-412.

HOFF, E. C., KELL, J. F., JR., & CARROLL, M. N., JR. Effects of cortical stimulation and lesions on cardiovascular function. *Physiol. Rev.,* 1963, *43,* 68-114.

HUBEL, D. H., HENSON, C. O., RUPERT, A., & GALAMBOS, R. Attention units in the auditory cortex. *Science,* 1959, *129,* 1279-1280.

KATZENELBOGEN, S., LOUCKS, R. B., & GANTT, W. H. An attempt to condition gastric secretion to histamine. *Amer. J. Physiol.,* 1939-40, *128,* 10-12.

KELLOGG, W. N. A search for the spinal conditioned response. *Amer. Psychologist,* 1946, *1,* 274.

KELLOGG, W. N. Is "spinal conditioning" conditioning? Reply to "a comment." *J. exp. Psychol.,* 1947, *37,* 263-265.

KELLOGG, W. N., DEESE, J., PRONKO, N. H., & FEINBERG, M. An attempt to condition the *chronic* spinal dog. *J. exp. Psychol.,* 1947, *37,* 99-117.

KELLOGG, W. N., PRONKO, N. H., and DEESE, J. Spinal conditioning in dogs. *Science.* 1946, *103,* 49-50.

KENDLER, H. H. Learning. In P. R. FARNSWORTH (Ed.), *Annual review of psychology.* Palo Alto, Calif.: Annual Reviews, 1959. Pp. 43-88.

KIMBLE, G. A. *Hilgard and Marquis' conditioning and learning,* 2nd ed. New York: Appleton-Century-Crofts, 1961.

KLEITMAN, N. The influence of starvation on the rate of secretion of saliva elicited by pilocarpine and its bearing on conditioned salivation. *Amer. J. Physiol.,* 1927, *82,* 686-692.

KLEITMAN, N. The effect of conditioned stimulation and of sleep upon conditioned salivation. *Amer. J. Physiol.,* 1930, *94,* 215-219.

KLEITMAN, N., & CRISLER, G. A quantitative study of a salivary conditioned reflex. *Amer. J. Physiol.,* 1927, *79,* 571-614.

KONORSKI, J. Mechanisms of learning. In Vol. 4, *Soc. Exp. Biol. Symposium on physiological mechanisms in animal behavior.* New York: Cambridge University Press, 1950.

KONORSKI, J., & MILLER, S. On two types of conditioned reflex. *J. gen. Psychol.,* 1937, *16,* 264-272.

KUNTZ, A. *The autonomic nervous system,* 3rd ed. Philadelphia: Lea & Febiger, 1945.

LIGHT, J. S., & GANTT, W. H. Essential part of reflex arc for establishment of conditioned reflex. *J. comp. Psychol.,* 1936, *21,* 19-36.

LINDSLEY, D. B. Attention, consciousness, sleep and wakefulness. In J. FIELD (Ed.), *Handbook of physiology, Section 1: Neurophysiology,* Vol. 3. Washington: American Physiological Society, 1960. Pp. 1553-1593.

LOUCKS, R. B. Technique for faradic stimulation of tissues beneath the integument in the absence of conductors penetrating the skin. *J. comp. Psychol.,* 1934, *18,* 305-313.

Loucks, R. B. The experimental delimitation of neural structures essential for learning; the attempt to condition striped muscles responses with faradization of the sigmoid gyri. *J. Psychol.*, 1936, *1*, 5-44.

Loucks, R. B. Humoral conditioning in mammals. *J. Psychol.*, 1937, *3-4*, 295-307.

Loucks, R. B. Studies of neural structures essential for learning. II. The conditioning of salivary and striped muscle responses to faradization of cortical sensory elements and the action of sleep upon such mechanisms. *J. comp. Psychol.*, 1938, *25*, 315-332.

Loucks, R. B., & Gantt, W. H. The conditioning of striped muscle responses based upon faradic stimulation of the dorsal roots and dorsal columns of the spinal cord. *J. comp. Psychol.*, 1938, *25*, 415-426.

Lowenstein, O., & Lowenfeld, I. E. Disintegration of central autonomic regulation during fatigue and its reintegration by psychosensory controlling mechanisms. I. Disintegration. Pupillographic studies. *J. Nerv. ment Dis.*, 1952, *115*, 1-21.

Martino, G. The conditioned reflex of blinking. *J. Neurophysiol.*, 1939, *2*, 173-177.

Mulinos, M. G., & Lieb, C. C. Pharmacology of learning. *Amer. J. Physiol.*, 1929, *90*, 456-457.

Olds, J., & Milner, P. Positive reinforcement produced by electrical stimulation of the septal area and other regions of the rat brain. *J. comp. physiol. Psychol.*, 1954, *47*, 419-427.

Pavlov, I. P. *Lectures on conditioned reflexes.* New York: Liveright, 1928.

Pinto, T., & Bromiley, R. B. A search for "spinal conditioning" and for evidence that it can become a reflex. *J. exp. Psychol.*, 1950, *40*, 121-130.

Pribram, K. H. Neocortical function in behavior. In H. F. Harlow & C. N. Woolsey (Eds.), *Biological and biochemical bases of behavior.* Madison, Wis.: University of Wisconsin Press, 1958. Pp. 151-172.

Razran, G. H. S. Conditioned responses in animals other than dogs. *Psychol. Bull.*, 1933, *30*, 261-324.

Ruch, T. C., & Fulton, J. F. *Medical physiology and biophysics,* 18th ed. Philadelphia: W. B. Saunders, 1960.

Rutledge, L. T., Jr., & Doty, R. W. Differential action of chlorpromazine on conditioned responses to peripheral versus direct cortical stimuli. *Fed. Proc.*, 1955, *14*, 126.

Settlage, P., & Harlow, H. F. Concerning the sensory pathway in the conditioned reflex. *J. comp. Psychol.*, 1936, *22*, 279-282.

Shurrager, P. S. A comment on "an attempt to condition the *chronic* spinal dog." *J. exp. Psychol.*, 1947, *37*, 261-263.

Shurrager, P. S., & Culler, E. Conditioned extinction of a reflex in the spinal dog. *J. exp. Psychol.*, 1941, *28*, 287-303.

Shurrager, P. S., & Shurrager, H. S. Converting a spinal CR into a reflex. *J. exp. Psychol.*, 1941, *29*, 216-224.

Shurrager, P. S., & Shurrager, H. S. The rate of learning measured at a single synapse. *J. exp. Psychol.*, 1946, *36*, 347-354.

Skinner, B. F. Two types of conditioned reflex: a reply to Konorski and Miller. *J. gen. Psychol.*, 1937, *16*, 272-279.

Smith, K. Conditioning as an artifact. *Psychol. Rev.*, 1954, *61*, 217-225.

SMITH, O. A., JR., MCFARLAND, W. L., & TAYLOR, E. Performance in a shock-avoidance conditioning situation interpreted as pseudoconditioning. *J. comp. physiol. Psychol.*, 1961, *54*, 154-157.

URY, B., & GELLHORN, E. Role of the sympathetic system in reflex dilation of pupil. *J. Neurophysiol.*, 1939, *2*, 268-275.

YOUNG, F. A. An attempt to obtain pupillary conditioning with infrared photography. *J. exp. Psychol.*, 1954, *48*, 62-68.

YOUNG, F. A. Studies of pupillary conditioning. *J. exp. Psychol.*, 1958, *55*, 97-110.

DAVID ZEAMAN

ROBERT W. SMITH

University of Connecticut

19

Review of Some Recent Findings in Human Cardiac Conditioning

SCOPE OF THE PAPER

Some published and unpublished studies of human cardiac conditioning will be reviewed and analyzed, primarily those dealing
with the simplest operations of classical conditioning. Our major emphasis
derives from theory or mechanism of conditioning. At least three theoretical mechanisms have been proposed for classical cardiac conditioning, (1) stimulus substitution, (2) mediation, and (3) drive reduction.
Classical stimulus substitution theory holds that the temporal pairing of
CS and US permits CS to be substituted for US in its control of UR. It
would be expected, according to this view, that UR and CR would be
similar in form. Mediation theory maintains that the temporal pairing
of CS and US results in the association of CS with a mediating state or
response, which in turn affects some aspect of response, not necessarily
UR. Examples of mediating states are anxiety and expectancy; examples
of mediating responses in cardiac conditioning include responses of the
respiratory or skeletal musculature. According to this view the CR and
UR need not have similar topographies. Drive reduction theory states
that the particular aspect of responses occurring at the time of drive
reduction becomes associated with CS. This theory predicts that the
similarity in form of CR and UR is under the control of manipulable,
experimental conditions. Thus it can be seen that each of these three
theoretical positions has something different to say about the relationship
in form of CR and UR. Each also calls for somewhat different controls,
and makes differential predictions about the parameters affecting the
conditioning process.

With these theoretical distinctions in mind, we will review and analyze some recent studies of human cardiac conditioning. A good place to start is with the systematic series of studies by Bersh, Notterman, and Schoenfeld.

COLUMBIA STUDIES

General Description

A long series of cardiac conditioning studies has been done by Bersh, Notterman, and Schoenfeld using Columbia University students as subjects (Bersh, Notterman, & Schoenfeld, 1953; 1956a, b, c; 1957a, b, c; Notterman, Schoenfeld, & Bersh, 1952a, b, c). Most of the experiments employ a trace conditioning procedure: a brief tone or light CS followed in six seconds by a shock US. A decelerative cardiac CR is reported for the two heartbeats immediately preceding US onset.

A variety of basic conditioning processes has been reported using this technique, including acquisition, extinction, spontaneous recovery, reacquisition, reextinction (Notterman, Schoenfeld, & Bersh, 1952b), generalization (Bersh, Notterman, & Schoenfeld, 1956b) and discrimination (Bersh, Notterman, & Schoenfeld, 1957b). The effects of conditioning parameters have been explored, such as those of schedules of partial reinforcement (Notterman, Schoenfeld, & Bersh, 1952c), random variation in CS-US interval (Bersh, Notterman, & Schoenfeld, 1953), and US intensity. Their findings are largely those expected from conditioning studies with other than cardiac responses, with an occasional exception (e.g., they report stronger acquisition with partial rather than a regular schedule of reinforcement). A number of their studies (Bersh, Notterman, & Schoenfeld, 1956a, c; 1957a, c) has also dealt with the interaction of cardiac CR and motor responses of avoidance learning and motor skill learning.

Theory

Underlying theory for this series of studies, as given by Schoenfeld (1950), we classify as an instance of mediation theory. The sequence of a neutral stimulus S_1 and an aversive one S_2, operationally defines a state of anxiety intervening between S_1 and S_2. The mediating state of anxiety has autonomic consequences the nature of which is not related to theory, but is empirically determinable. The findings of the Columbia studies indicate cardiac *deceleration* as a consequence of anxiety. The fact that the cardiac UR to shock is observed to be accelerative rather than decelerative is not embarrassing to this theoretical formulation.

Controls. Notterman, Schoenfeld, and Bersh (1952c) provided a sensitization control by a series of shock-alone trials prior to exposure to CS. The need for a sensitization control arises from the fact that the tone CS initially elicits a slight decelerative cardiac response which although initially adapted out over a series of preconditioning trials with CS-alone, might have been sensitized back to suprathreshold level by nonassociative, sensitizing effects of shock. The absence of a decelerative cardiac CR to CS following shock-alone trials ruled out a sensitization mechanism for the cardiac changes in this series of experiments.

Controls for pseudoconditioning were not included, but these were not required since a pseudoconditioned response would have had the form of the UR, cardiac acceleration, which it did not. The possibility of mediating responses or states other than anxiety should be considered. Gross movements of the skeletal musculature may accompany warnings of impending shock. These were minimized by instructions to sit quietly, but here again the need for control is slight because movements create acceleration rather than deceleration.

The important controls missing from the set of Columbia studies are for respiration and nonanxious expectancy. Patterns of inhalation and exhalation reflexly control heart rate (sinus arrhythmia), and these can produce either cardiac acceleration or deceleration. Furthermore, it has been shown (Westcott & Huttenlocher, 1961) that respiratory changes often follow warnings of shock. Cardiac deceleration may also accompany anticipation of nonaversive stimulation. As early as 1910 Billings and Shepard (1910) showed cardiac deceleration in subjects who listened for the faint ticking of a watch. More recently Zeaman and Wegner (1956) have shown cardiac deceleration in Ss listening for tones at and below verbally reported auditory threshold. For a set of experiments designed to study the causes and effects of *anxiety generated by an aversive* S_2, a proper control for the Columbia studies would have included a replication of all procedures with a *nonaversive* S_2 replacing the shock. A study by Steward (1962) to be reviewed later in this paper does introduce such a control, with surprising results.

CONNECTICUT STUDIES

General Description

A series of classical cardiac condition studies has been carried out at the University of Connecticut, several of which are as yet unpublished doctoral dissertations. Early in the series a trace conditioning procedure was employed nearly identical to that of the Columbia studies. Later a long-delay conditioning procedure was adopted to allow greater opportunity for the form of the cardiac CR to manifest itself, a matter of some theoretical importance.

Trace Procedure Studies

Six-second shock duration. In the first paper of its series (Zeaman, Deane, & Wegner, 1954), a beat-by-beat analysis of the cardiac CR during its 6-sec. trace interval revealed evidence of a diphasic response, acceleration followed by deceleration. Figure 19-1 shows the forms of CR and UR. The acceleration component of the cardiac CR may have been missed in the Columbia studies because of recording difficulties. Their published cardiograph records show electrical interference for the first few seconds after CS onset, and their published CR measurements were restricted to the last two beats prior to shock onset. In contrast the beat-by-beat analysis of the complete CR and UR in the Connecticut studies showed this cardiac CR to resemble more closely in form (although not magnitude) the UR to shock, both showing an initial acceleration followed by deceleration. These results lend support to stimulus substitution theory. But there were individual differences in forms of both CR and UR such as to suggest the possibility that what the heart was doing at the time the shock went off might be determining the form of the CR, a drive

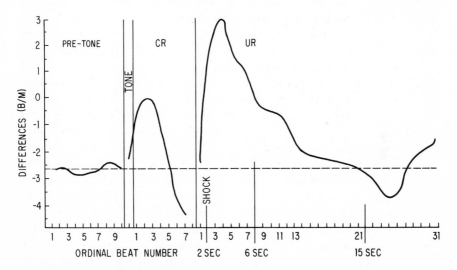

Fig. 19-1. The average beat-by-beat, corrected form of the cardiac CR and UR for 45 subjects. The ordinate has the dimension of average heart rate in beats per minute. The corrected measure is the difference in rate between that observed on initial control trials (tone alone) and all conditioning trials (tone-shock). The abscissa represents the ordinal number of heart beats counting forward from the tone and shock as successive reference points in the trial cycle. The abscissa also indicates the approximate duration in seconds of the four shock USs used by Zeaman and Wegner. The UR to shock did not vary systematically with variation in US duration. (Zeaman, Deane, & Wegner, 1954)

reduction explanation. As a test of these opposing explanations shock duration was manipulated experimentally to control heart rate at the time of drive reduction.

Two-second shock duration. The second study in the series (Zeaman & Wegner, 1954) replicated the first with shock US reduced in duration to two seconds. With two-second shock duration the heart is accelerating sharply at the moment the shock goes off. Figure 19-1 shows this clearly. If drive reduction corresponds with shock off, the drive reduction theory predicts an accelerative cardiac CR. The results with a two-second shock appear to confirm this—a greater tendency for accelerative CRs appeared with this shock duration than under the condition of six-second shock duration. The encouraging support thus given the drive reduction theory led to the arrangement of more critical tests of this notion.

One- and fifteen-second shock durations. The fact that the cardiac UR to shock remains approximately the same over a wide range of shock durations enabled two critical tests of the drive reduction view to be made. With a very brief shock (0.1 sec.) the shock has gone off before the heart has had the time to change its rate. With a fifteen-second shock, Figure 19-1 shows that the heart rate has returned to its pre-shock level. Drive reduction theory predicts for both of these shock durations the absence of conditioning, since at the moment of shock reduction the heart is neither accelerating nor decelerating with respect to pre-CS level. The results were clearly contrary to this theoretical prediction. Conditioning occurred with both shock durations. In fact, neither UR nor CR magnitude was systematically related to strength of conditioning for the range of durations, 0.1, 2, 6, and 15 seconds examined (Zeaman & Wegner, 1958). Fairly wide individual differences however, did appear in the accelerative and decelerative forms of cardiac CR. A correlational analysis of various aspects of UR and CR showed that subjects with the largest URs tended to have accelerative CRs; those with the weaker URs tended toward CRs with more decelerative components. These results did not accord well with drive reduction theory. They were related more readily to either a respiratory or anxiety mediation explanation to be elaborated on presently. To get a longer look at respiration and cardiac CR during a period of anxious waiting, a long-delay conditioning procedure was introduced.

Long-delay Conditioning Procedure: Deane and Zeaman Study

In order to prevent adaptation during a long-delay interval a series of numbers appearing one at a time in the window of a memory drum served as a long-delay CS in a study by Deane and Zeaman (1958). Since the process of acquisition was of less concern than the form of CR, Ss were told to expect shock during the number sequence. This allowed us to study cardiac CRs, transferred from previous experience, which appeared on the first trial. The results were unexpected. For the first time conditions were found that were reliably capable of producing both cardiac acceleration and deceleration in the same subjects under different experimental conditions.

Effects of instruction acceleration.   When subjects were told they would receive a mild electric shock when Number 15 appeared in the number series, the effect was a gradual rise in heart rate over a base level previously measured without threat of shock. Figure 19-2 shows the form of this response.

Effects of shock deceleration.   After being shocked at Number 15 the accelerative CR was lost on the next five trials of CS-US pairing. The numbers through 13 were accompanied by a rate not significantly different from base level. During Numbers 14 and 15, however, there occurred a sharp decelerative effect shown in Figure 19-2.

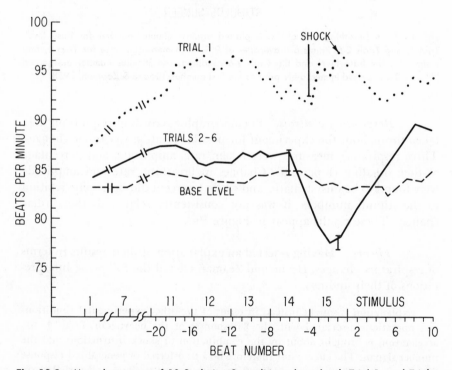

Fig. 19-2. Mean heart rate of 10 Ss during 3 conditions: base level, Trial 1, and Trials 2-6. The abscissa is a time line calibrated in terms of both the ordinal heart beat counting away from the end of the 15th number, and also the average stimulus number present during these beats. (Deane & Zeaman, 1958)

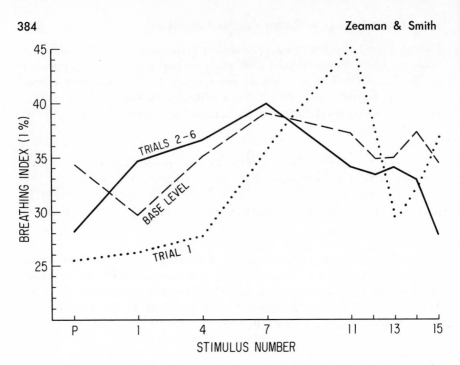

Fig. 19-3. A breathing index, 1%, is plotted against stimulus number for base level, Trial 1, and Trials 2-6. Points are averages of 9 Ss each measured once for Trial 1, and 5 times for the base level and the Trials 2-6 condition. The stimulus number designated "P" is a 3-sec. period immediately prior to the first number. (Deane & Zeaman, 1958)

Respiratory controls. Pneumographic records of respiration were taken throughout the experiment for possible relation to cardiac changes. Three respiratory measures were taken: rate, amplitude, and percentage of time inhaling (1 percent). Changes in breathing rate and amplitude were found to be unsystematic, and while 1 percent did bear some relation to the stimuli numbers, it was not consistently related to the cardiac changes. These results appear in Figure 19-3.

Theory. Having rejected an explanation of their results in terms of respiratory changes, Deane and Zeaman offered the following interpretations of their findings:

Explanation is sought instead in terms of the other experimental conditions and operations associated with the 2 responses of the heart. On Trials 1, the acceleration is brought about by the combination of shock instructions and the number signals. The effect must therefore be a transferred or generalized response dependent upon Ss previous conditionings with respect to shock and verbal warnings of shock. After Trial 1, the deceleration is apparently produced by the number signals after one experience with a brief shock, judged on the average to be mild. The shock, therefore, may be tentatively isolated as responsible for the change in form of cardiac response.

If this analysis is correct, the problem reduces to explaining the role of shock. We offer 2 speculations: the shock reduces anxiety or converts anxiety to fear.

The notion that shock reduces anxiety is not paradoxical. The intensity of the generalized, verbally-induced anxiety of Trial 1 could be greater than the anxiety generated in later trials by warnings of the impending, subjectively mild shock. Loosely speaking, Ss are relieved at discovering that the shock is no worse than it is. This notion, to account for the data, requires the auxiliary postulate that strong anxiety produces cardiac acceleration, and weak anxiety a deceleration, an assumption for which there is some independent evidence. Zeaman and Wegner (1957) found that Ss giving larger unconditioned responses to shock tended towards the accelerative type of heart CR.

The second speculation proposes a distinction between anxiety and fear with the following empirical significance. When warnings of approaching aversives are primarily response-produced (verbal) cues, the result is *anxiety,* a state with a diffuse temporal course and a physiological correlate of cardiac acceleration. When warning signals are external cues, the result is fear, a state with more well-defined temporal properties, and a physiological correlate of heart rate deceleration (Deane & Zeaman, 1958, pp. 105-106).

The Role of Instructions and Shock: The Deane Study

An extension of the Deane and Zeaman study was run by Deane (1961) as a dissertation problem designed to discover some of the controlling conditions of the two cardiac effects induced by signals of shock-to-come. The first question asked was whether the shock was a necessary condition for the disappearance of cardiac acceleration. To answer this question, conditions without shock were arranged.

Omission of shock. Following the general procedure developed in the previous experiment, Ss were told to watch the numbers 1-12 appear in the memory drum window. After a series of base level cardiac measurements, each S in Group A was told to expect a shock at Number 10 but not necessarily every trial, and each S in Group B was given exactly the same instructions. But only Group A received the shock (on Trial 1 only); Group B never received a shock. The results are shown in Figures 19-4 and.19-5. Group A showed acceleration in anticipation of shock on the first conditioning trial, and lost the acceleration on subsequent trials after having received the shock at the end of Trial 1. These results match those of the Deane and Zeaman study in which shock had been given on every trial. The results of omission of shock are shown in Figure 19-5 (Group B). Here the acceleration is maintained during all stimulus numbers except

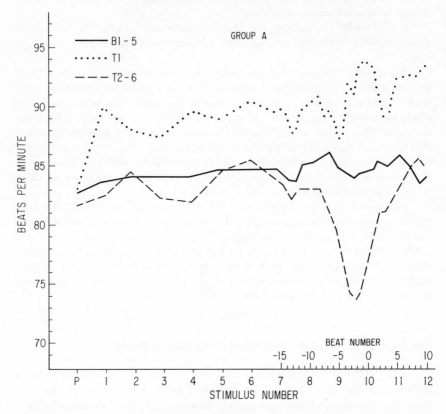

Fig. 19-4. Mean heart rate during the number stimuli with trials as the parameter: Group A. (The x axis is a time line calibrated in terms of both stimulus number and ordinal beat number—see text.) (Deane, 1961)

9 and 10, which are accompanied by a sharp deceleration. This figure established two points: (a) the shock appears to be a necessary part of the procedure for disappearance of acceleration; (b) instructions appear to be a sufficient condition for the occurrence of both the accelerative and decelerative effects.

Instructions to expect shock at a vague locus. After base level measurements, *S*s in Groups C and D were told to expect shock at *some* number during the 1-12 sequence, but not necessarily on every trial. The *S*s in Group C received shock at Number 10 on the first conditioning trial, none thereafter. The *S*s in Group D received no shock at all. The results are graphed in Figures 19-6 and 19-7. Anticipation of shock at an indefinite locus on Trial 1 produced the usual acceleration over base level. After having received the shock, *S*s in Group C lost their acceleration on subse-

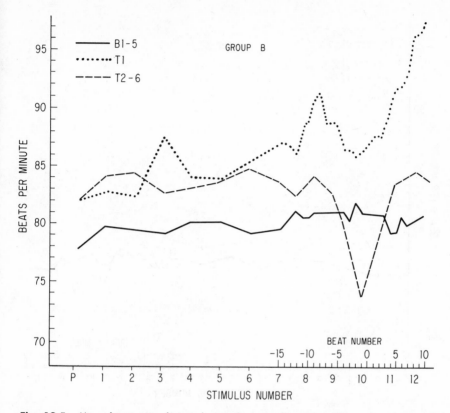

Fig. 19-5. Mean heart rate during the number stimulus with trials as the parameter: Group B. (Deane, 1961)

quent trials and showed a slight, but significant, deceleration in proximity to Number 10 where shock had been received on Trial 1. This establishes the new point that the decelerative effect at Number 10 can be produced by a shock at Number 10 without instructions to expect shock at this number. The Ss in Group D unshocked like those in Group B did not lose their acceleration. An unexpected decelerative effect showed up at Number 12 for this group. Presumably, Ss in Group D, told to expect shock at some number, inferred after 11 shockless numbers that the last number, 12, must be it.

Interpretations. In interpreting these results, Deane held to a dual mediation theory with different mediating states for the accelerative and decelerative effects. He says:

It might be speculated ... that these two cardiac effects are perhaps un-learned responses associated with what may be called anxiety and fear with the

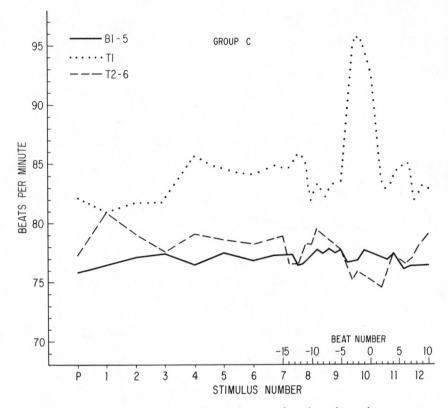

Fig. 19-6. Mean heart rate during the number stimuli with trials as the parameter: Group C. (Deane, 1961)

following empirical significance. When *S* expects a noxious stimulus of unknown strength, a state of anxiety with its associated response of cardiac acceleration is aroused a relatively long time before the stimulus is expected. In addition, if *S* expects the noxious stimulus at a particular instant in time, a state of fear with its associated response of cardiac deceleration is aroused immediately prior to and during the time the stimulus is expected. If the stimulus is found to be subjectively mild, the anxiety is reduced, but it is apparently the case that even experiencing the noxious stimulus as relatively mild is not sufficient to abolish the fear response at the expected locus of the stimulus (Deane, 1961, p. 493).

A crucial assumption of this theoretical account is the subjective mildness of the shock. Anxiety, with its accelerative correlate, is presumed to disappear because of the subjective mildness of shock. A direct experimental attack on this assumption was made in a dissertation study by Nolan (1961).

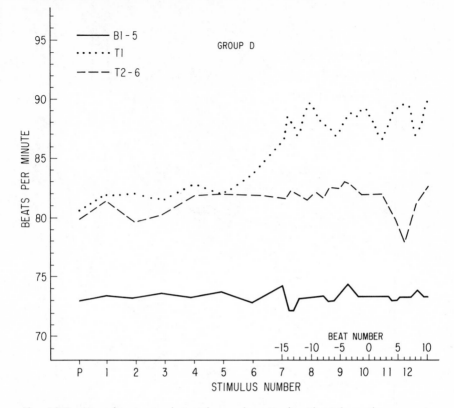

Fig. 19-7. Mean heart rate during the number stimuli with trials as the parameter: Group D. (Deane, 1961)

Long-delay Conditioning: Nolan's Study

Using the standardized techniques of long-delay conditioning developed in the previous studies in this series, Nolan designed his experiment to find out if a subjectively *strong* shock US would prevent the disappearance of cardiac acceleration during the early portions of the delayed CS. The experimental literature on the psychophysics of shock was thin, so Nolan first undertook to scale subjective shock intensity.

Shock psychophysics. A method of limits procedure was used to find the upper limit of tolerance to shock for 18 subjects. Beginning at a subthreshold level, AC, shock level was increased until the subjects refused to take any more despite strong encouragement by the experimenter to do so. The average maximum shock voltage was 43 VAC (range 28-49), which, delivered across the first two fingers of the left hand with electrodes (and electrode jelly), was accompanied by a mean milliamperage of 3.51.

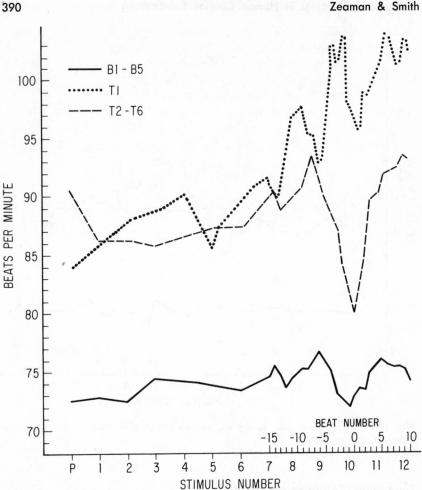

Fig. 19-8. Nolan's data. Form of the mean heart rate response during the number stimuli for the 9 Ss told to expect shock on Stimulus Number 10. The abscissa indicates both stimulus number, and ordinal heart beat number counting away from the moment of shock. The solid line is the mean of Trials B 1-5 (basal level); the dotted line represents T 1 (verbal shock-threat); the dashed line is the mean of Trials 2-6 (after one shock). (Nolan, 1961)

In the only other study on the human psychophysics of shock that could be found, one by Stevens, Carton, and Shickman (1958), it has been reported that currents approaching 1.0 milliamperes are "very disagreeable." Shock US levels in the previous Connecticut studies of cardiac conditioning were no more than 23 VAC, and in the Columbia studies, 30 VAC. To make sure that the shock to be used in his study would be subjectively strong, Nolan added 7 volts to the average maximum tolerable level, for a total of 50 VAC.

Strong shock condition. A group of 9 Ss was run under the same conditions as those in Deane's Group A, with instructions that shock would appear on some trials at Number 10, and with shock actually appearing on the first conditioning trial but not on the remaining five trials. The only differences in procedure were the promise of a *strong* shock and the use of a strong shock. The results are shown in Figure 19-8. The accelerative effect appears in response to the verbally threatened shock on the first trial, but does not disappear on the subsequent trials after Ss have received one strong shock at the end of the first trial. A sharp drop in rate occurs in the immediate vicinity of Number 10, but it is not great enough to bring rate below the base level.

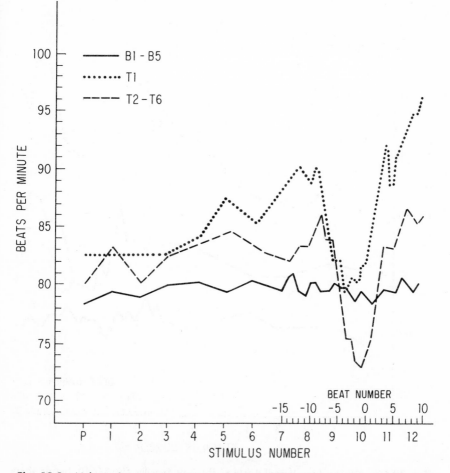

Fig. 19-9. Nolan's data. Form of the mean heart rate response during number stimuli of the 9 Ss threatened with shock on Trial 1, but never shocked. The coordinates and parameters of this figure are the same as those in Figure 8. (Nolan, 1961)

Threat of strong shock, but no shock.   This condition is analogous to Deane's Group B with the exception of instructions to expect a
strong shock (rather than mild) on some trials at Number 10. The results
appear in Figure 19-9, and do not differ greatly from Deane's results
shown in Figure 19-5. Threat of a strong shock has much the same effect
as threat of a mild shock provided that neither is received. The accelerative effect remains, with deceleration at about the time the shock is
expected.

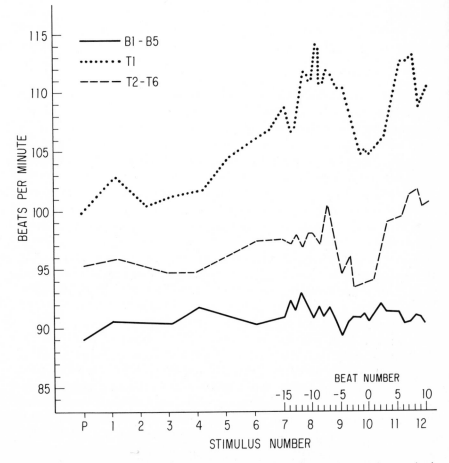

Fig. 19-10. Nolan's data. Verbal threat of shock at Stimulus Number 10, but no shock
given. Ss are those who had served in the psychophysical scaling procedures. (Nolan, 1961)

Replication with psychophysical Ss. The 18 Ss who had served in the psychophysical scaling procedures were available for a replication of the previous two conditions. After base level measurements these Ss were told that they would receive a stronger shock than any they had received in determining their maximum tolerance level, and that they would receive shock at Number 10 on some trials. Half the Ss did not receive any shock, and their data are graphed in Figure 19-10. Despite the already high base level rates, these Ss showed acceleration as high as 25 b/m on the first trial in anticipation of a shock stronger than any they had received during the psychophysical measurements. During Trials 2-6, an accelerative component remained, as in all previous conditions without shock although in this instance there was some loss. The usual decelerative tendency near Number 10 is clearly apparent.

Half the Ss who had served as psychophysical Ss were run under the conditioning procedures with one strong shock expected and given at Number 10. As shown in Figure 19-11, these Ss lost their accelerative component, while retaining the decelerative effect at expected shock locus.

Theoretical implications. If these results are to be interpreted in terms of anxiety and fear mediation, it must be assumed that a subjectively strong shock is capable of preventing adaptation of the anxiety state with its cardiac acceleration, but what would otherwise be a subjectively strong shock is not subjectively strong if Ss have recently received shocks almost as strong. Although the Ss in the last condition in Nolan's study received a shock stronger than one they could be coaxed to take in the psychophysical procedures, we reason, *post hoc,* that it was not subjectively strong enough (in relation to what they expected) to prevent adaptation of the anxiety generated by the warning signals (numbers). Adaptation to shock may have caused the adaptation of anxiety. Putting it loosely, when Ss are told to expect shock, they expect a mighty one. A 50 VAC shock averaging more than 3.5 ma. does not disappoint them unless they have recently experienced some shocks near this intensity and lived through them.

There is thus nothing in Nolan's data that puts a strain on the double mediation theory offered by Deane and Zeaman. When warnings of approaching aversives are primarily response-produced (verbal) cues, the result is anxiety, a state with a diffuse temporal course and a physiological correlate of cardiac acceleration. When warning signals are external cues, the result is fear, a state with more well defined temporal properties, and a physiological correlate of heart rate deceleration. To this must be added the assumption that anxiety quickly adapts unless the expected aversive is found to be subjectively strong. The fear state appears to be more resistant to adaptation.

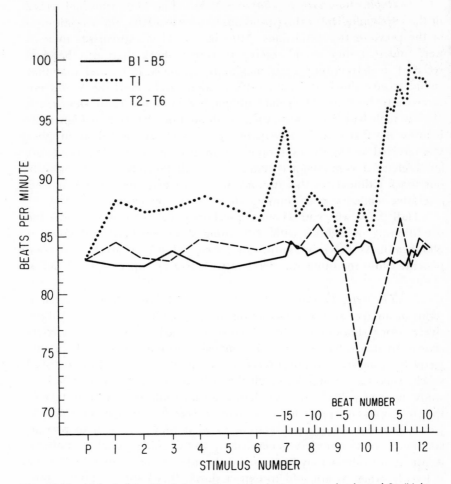

Fig. 19-11. Nolan's data. Shock-threat, but no shock given to psychophysical Ss. (Nolan, 1961)

While such theorizing may be weak on the grounds of parsimony, it can at least lay claim to the data. Stimulus substitution and drive reduction mechanisms on the other hand, cannot easily account for both the accelerative and decelerative forms of cardiac CR. Furthermore, not all of the properties of inferred mediating states need be assigned *post hoc;* having found them to be so in one experiment, they should be recoverable in another. For instance, if anxiety and fear can be generated by warnings by aversives *other than shock,* the accelerative and decelerative cardiac correlates should still be observed. Neither stimulus substitution nor drive reduction mechanisms predict that the form of CR should be independent of the nature of the US and the UR. An empirical test of these differential predictions has been made by Steward, with informative results.

Replacing Shock with Sound: Steward's Study

Under some conditions, auditory stimulation is accompanied by cardiac deceleration (Zeaman & Wegner, 1958), so threats of aversive sounds were used in this study to test the prediction of mediation theory that experimental results would be invariant with respect to the nature of US and UR. Seven conditions were arranged in this unpublished doctoral dissertation (directed by Dr. A. R. Rollin), represented by seven independent groups of nine subjects run under the long-trace conditioning procedures developed in the previous Connecticut studies. Two groups were threatened with an "annoying sound" (corresponding to Deane's mild shock); two groups were threatened with a "punishing sound" (corresponding to Nolan's strong shock); for each of the above pairs of groups, one would actually hear the sound promised, the other

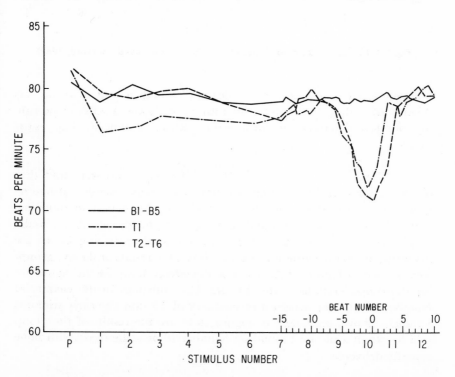

Fig. 19-12. Steward's data. Form of the heart rate response during the number stimuli of the 45 Ss who were told they would hear a sound (annoying, punishing, or pleasant). Coordinates and notation of this figure are the same as in previous figures. (Steward, 1962)

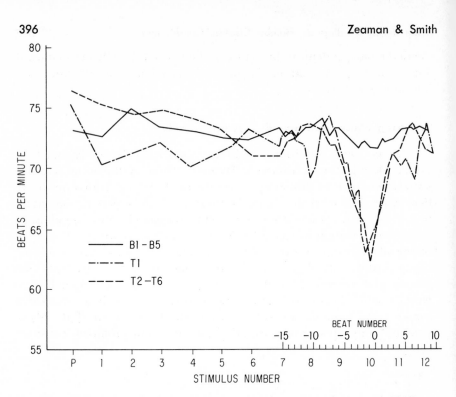

Fig. 19-13. Steward's data. Expectation of a pleasant sound. (Steward, 1962)

not; one group was promised a "pleasant" sound; a control group was threatened with a shock; and a final group was given a series of punishing sounds to determine the form of the UR to this stimulus. The results follow.

Expectation of a sound. The five groups who were told they would hear a sound at Number 10 showed the same average cardiac responses regardless of whether they were instructed to expect an annoying, a punishing, or a pleasant sound, and regardless of whether they actually heard the sound on the first trial. Statistical analyses having shown the difference among the groups to be unreliable, the results of the five groups were pooled in Figure 19-12. The reliable effects shown in this figure are the sharp decelerations of the T1 and T2-6 functions in the vicinity of Number 10, and the decelerative tendency of T1 over the early stimulus numbers. Shown separately in Figure 19-13 are the results of the group told to except a pleasant sound on Number 10 on some trials, with none actually delivered.

Control group results. To control for the possibility that some unknown novel features of the experimental conditions other than those

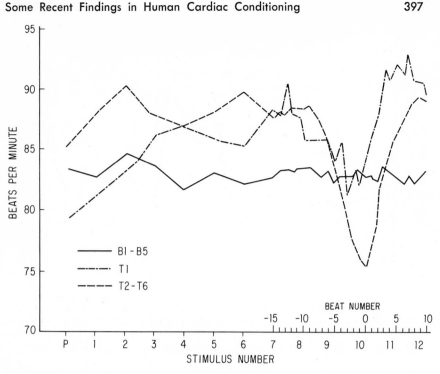

Fig. 19-14. Steward's data. Results of shock-threat with no shock given. (Steward, 1962)

purposefully manipulated might account for these unexpected results, a condition run by previous experimenters was included: subjects were instructed to expect a mild shock at Number 10 on some trials but were not given shock on any trial. The results, in Figure 19-14, correspond closely to those found by other investigators—acceleration in anticipation of shock, not lost over six shockless trials.

UR to "punishing" sound. The average cardiac response of 11 Ss to the punishing sound is shown in Figure 19-15. The sound was a 118 db, 1500 cycle tone delivered through earphones. The cardiac response to a sound of this magnitude was diphasic generally accelerative followed by deceleration and recovery.

Implications of decelerative effects. Mediation theories relating cardiac deceleration to either fear or anxiety are thrown into serious doubt by these findings. Expectation of a pleasant sound yielded as large a deceleration as expectation of annoying sounds, punishing sounds, or even shock. It appears not unlikely that anticipation of any stimulus may bring cardiac deceleration. After the fact, it seems surprising that none of the previous studies in the Columbia or Connecticut series included

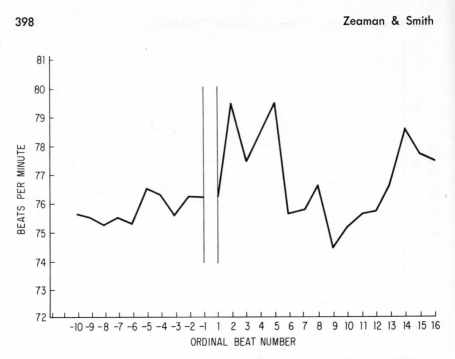

Fig. 19-15. Steward's data. Cardiac response to a loud sound. (Steward, 1962)

as a control, anticipation of a nonaversive stimulus. If there exists in humans a generalized anticipatory cardiac deceleration (an "attention" or "alertness" correlate) not specific to threats of aversive stimuli, then such controls are clearly necessary for conclusions to be drawn about such states as fear or anxiety.

It might be argued that all the subjects in Steward's experiment were afraid or anxious about receiving aversive stimulation despite contrary instructions and experimental arrangements. For this reason, subjects in all groups were given a formal interview in which they were asked to describe their expectations. The nine subjects in the group told to expect a pleasant sound used the following words to describe their expectations:

WORD	FREQUENCY OF OCCURRENCE
waiting	6
curiosity	5
listening	3
preparing	2
alertness	2
anticipation	2
attention	2
expectant	1
eager	1

Contrast these responses with those of the 36 subjects in the groups told that they would hear unpleasant (annoying or punishing) sounds:

WORD	FREQUENCY OF OCCURRENCE
scared	12
nervous	12
anxious	9
worried	9
tense	5
shook up	4
concerned	3
curious	3
uncomfortable	2
waiting	2
upset	2
fazed	1
disturbed	1
shaky	1
didn't care	1
sleepy	1

If (a) the absence of aversive stimulation, (b) instructions to expect pleasant sounds, and (c) subjective reports of nonanxious expectation are sufficient conditions for inferring absence of anxiety or fear in human subjects, then the results of Steward show that there are no clear grounds for inferring fear or anxiety from the observation of cardiac deceleration. If this is true, it does not simplify the theoretical picture. Regardless of whether we identify the decelerative CR with fear or simply anticipation or attention, the problem of accounting for its origins remains. We know from the Columbia and Connecticut trace conditioning studies that the decelerative effect appears as the result of paired presentations of CS and accelerative US, without instructions, and we know from the Connecticut long-delay conditioning studies that the effect appears as the result of instructions alone, presumably transferred from previous conditionings. If we assume that a state of attention (or simple anticipation) is classically conditioned, we still have the problem of determining the mechanism of conditioning. In short, why should anticipation of any stimulus bring a tendency for cardiac deceleration at the time of the expected stimulus? Steward speculates that the deceleration may be a psychological correlate of "attention" or "alertness." This response is not to be confused with what has been called an "orienting" reflex, i.e., a response accompanying reception of a stimulus, even a neutral one (Davis, Buchwald, & Frankmann, 1955); the attention response is anticipatory.

Implications of the absence of cardiac acceleration. The absence of cardiac acceleration during the early number portions of the CS in the groups waiting for an unpleasant sound was unexpected. The subjects certainly reported they felt anxiety after being told they would receive a "very punishing sound" at Number 10, but the acceleration found with shock threat was absent. It may be concluded (a) that threats of an aversive sound are not sufficient condition for cardiac acceleration, and (b) that verbal reports of anxiety are not sufficient conditions for cardiac acceleration.

The mediation theorist might explain these results by assuming that a supra-threshold amount of anxiety is required for cardiac acceleration. Such a conception would also handle the disappearance of acceleration in Deane's study after the subjects experienced the shock US as mild (generating anxiety below threshold of cardiac acceleration), and the results of Nolan's psychophysical subjects (adaptation of shock during the psychophysics reduced anxiety below threshold to cardiac acceleration during later conditioning).

Since the UR to loud sound is initially a cardiac acceleration, the absence of an accelerative cardiac CR also requires the stimulus substitution theorist to make additional assumptions. Since US intensity is a well known parameter of the conditioning process, it might be assumed that the loud sounds used as unconditioned stimuli were not intense enough to yield a conditioned accelerative CR. While the absence of an early accelerative effect may thus be explained by special assumptions, the appearance in Steward's study of an early, slight decelerative effect on Trial 1 alone is embarrassing to all the theoretical views considered. A later study by Deane throws some doubt on the reproducibility of this particular finding.

WESTCOTT AND HUTTENLOCHER STUDY

At about the time of these developments in the series of Connecticut studies, a study done in another laboratory called attention again to the role of respiration in cardiac conditioning. Westcott and Huttenlocher (1961) demonstrated reliable respiratory patterns (respiratory sinus arrhythmia), and cited some pilot research which suggests that respiratory changes occur during cardiac conditioning that could contaminate the form of the cardiac CR. An isolated gasp, they pointed out, produces a diphasic cardiac reflex response of acceleration followed by deceleration, similar in form to that observed in cardiac conditioning studies. The question was whether previous cardiac conditioning studies had succeeded in conditioning anticipatory gasps (with cardiac consequences) or had directly conditioned the heart.

Westcott and Huttenlocher carried out a direct experimental attack

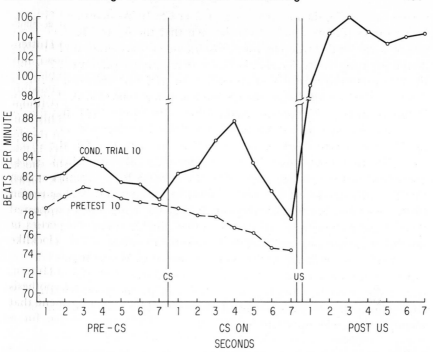

Fig. 19-16. Second-by-second cardiac activity on the last pretest and the last conditioning trial for all Ss with respiration held constant. (Westcott & Huttenlocher, 1961)

on the problem by controlling the rate and depth of respiration (by instructions to breathe shallowly in synchrony with a metronome) while simultaneously running a delayed conditioning procedure. A 7-sec. buzzer served as CS followed by a strong shock US (as strong as the subject would tolerate). The form of the uncorrected cardiac CR with respiration controlled is shown in Figure 19-16. The difference between the two functions of Figure 19-16 allows calculation of a corrected measure of conditioning shown in Figure 19-17, together with a comparison of the earlier data of Zeaman and Wegner (1957).

The disappearance of the decelerative effect in the corrected CR obtained by Westcott and Huttenlocher is attributed to their control of breathing. While it would be an attractive simplification to assume that adequate respiratory controls eliminate the diphasic nature of the cardiac CR, leaving just an acceleratory form, claimable by stimulus substitution theory, there are several counterarguments to be considered. First it should be pointed out that the term *deceleration* has at least three meanings used implicitly in this series of cardiac papers: (1) pre-CS deceleration—heart rate is below pre-CS level; (2) instantaneous deceleration—the slope of the rate curve is negative, i.e., the heart rate is decreasing below some maximum level during CS; (3) post-CS deceleration—the rate decreases during CS, then increases again after CS. In Westcott and Hutten-locher's data (Figure 19-17) it can be seen that the heart CR shows only one of these kinds of deceleration, instantaneous deceleration. This they do not interpret as deceleration but as recovery from acceleration. Possibly the interpretation is wrong. If an extinction trial had been run (without shock) a deceleration below pre-CS level may have developed. This con-jecture is supported by previous data. Observe in Figure 19-11 that the de-celerative tendency near shock locus in Nolan's data does not carry below pre-CS level before shock occurs and brings acceleration. On the shock-less trials to follow, however, the decelerative CR (near shock locus) appears in full magnitude, and well below pre-CS level. Another reason that the fully developed "attention" deceleration may not have appeared in Westcott and Huttenlocher's study is that the temporal properties of their 7-sec. buzzer were less easily discriminable than the clocklike number sequence used as CS in the Connecticut studies.

Despite the weakness of the evidence offered by Westcott and Hutten-locher for respiratory mediation of the decelerative CR, the hypothesis may nevertheless be true. It will be shown in the next experiment that with improved respiratory control there is additional evidence for a monophasic acceleratory CR.

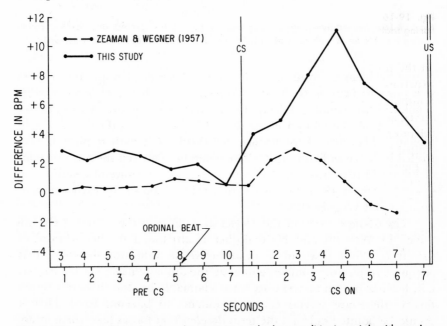

Fig. 19-17. Second-by-second cardiac activity on the last conditioning trial, with respira-tion held constant, corrected for cardiac activity on the last pretest. Each point is the difference between the rate on the last pretest and the rate on the last conditioning trial. Superimposed is a comparable curve with respiration uncontrolled, adapted from Zeaman and Wegner (1957, p. 131). (Westcott & Huttenlocher, 1961)

The respiratory controls produced by Westcott and Huttenlocher were not as strong as they might have been. It will be recalled that they controlled only rate and depth of acceleration. Recent analysis of the cardiac-respiratory reflex by Clynes (1960) has shown that a prime determinant of heart rate is respiratory *acceleration* (change in the rate of change of thoracic circumference). It is entirely possible that this respiratory factor (which is to some extent independent of rate and depth of respiration) was not controlled in the Westcott and Huttenlocher study.

CONNECTICUT STUDIES (continued): R. W. SMITH'S STUDY

To achieve as complete a control of respiration as seemed possible with human subjects short of curarizing them, Smith adopted the radical procedure of requiring his subjects to suspend their respiration completely for a time interval during which a long-delay cardiac conditioning trial was run. Four groups were run in this unpublished dissertation study, (1) a Sustained Inspiration, Classical Conditioning Group, (2) a Sustained Inspiration, Discriminative Conditioning Group, (3) a Normal Respiration Classical Conditioning Group, and (4) a Normal Respiration Discriminative Conditioning Group.

Sustained Inspiration, Classical Conditioning

Control measurements. Following measurement of basal heart rate, subjects were told to inhale when a red light began flashing, to hold their breath as long as the light continued to flash, and to exhale and resume normal breathing when the light stopped flashing. The light flashed for 30-sec. periods during which the subject sustained his inspiration and the experimenter recorded both cardiac and respiratory measures. Five such control trials were run with 1½-2 min. intertrial interval.

Shock-threat measurements. After the fifth control measurement the experimenter instructed the subject to continue the sustained inspiration procedure, but now at the 20th flash of light, a strong shock would occur. The subject was further instructed to *count* the flashes, for he would only be shocked on the 20th flash.

The light flashed about once every second, being triggered by the subject's heart beat. Each beat of the heart brought one flash. This arrangement provided a convenient overall measure of heart rate as the time required for 20 beats (the duration of the long-delay CS). The light continued to flash for 30 sec., well beyond the occurrence of the US, so that a respiration-free measure of cardiac response to shock might be obtained.

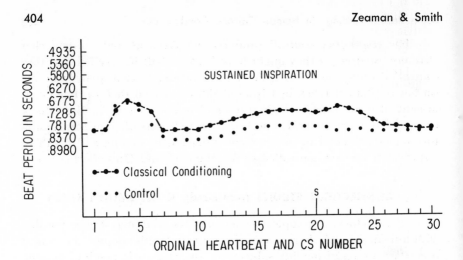

Fig. 19-18. Smith's data. Form of the mean heart rate during control and conditioning trials with sustained inspiration. The letter S denotes location of the shock. (Smith, 1963)

Results. The average results of 7 subjects over 5 trials are graphed in Figure 19-18. The reflex cardiac reaction following a sustained inhalation is shown by the control condition to be an acceleration followed by deceleration. The conditioning function shows some similar elements of general topography, with greater overall acceleration. A corrected measure of CR and UR is obtained from the difference between control and conditioning function and shown in Figure 19-19. The CR picture is one of gradually increasing acceleration up to the points of US, which brings further acceleration. No changes in CR were observed over trials.

Sustained Inspiration, Discriminative Conditioning

Control measurements. Procedure differed from that of the Classical Conditioning Group only in that on some trials, the flashing light (during which the subject held his breath) was white and on others, red.

Shock-threat measurements. Following basal and control measurements, 10 discrimination trials were run. Subjects were told that whenever the red light (CS+) flashed, they should continue to hold their breath, and on the 20th flash they would receive a strong shock. Whenever the white light (CS−) flashed, inspiration was to be sustained and no shock whatever would be administered. Five CS+ and 5 CS− trials were presented in random order.

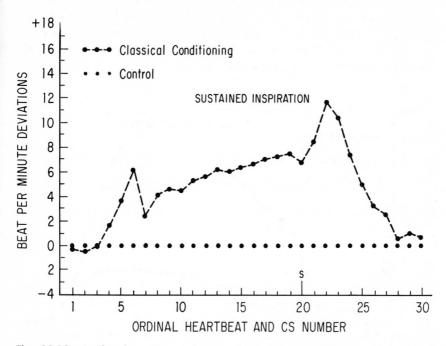

Fig. 19-19. Smith's data. Corrected form of CR during conditioning with sustained inhalation. (Smith, 1963)

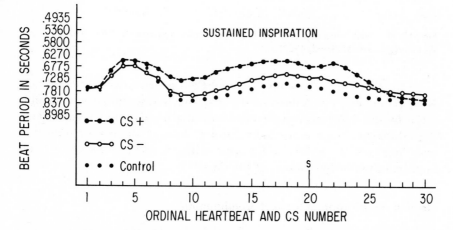

Fig. 19-20. Smith's data. Form of the response to the positive (CS+) and negative (CS−) discriminative stimuli, compared with that of the control condition. All observations have been taken with sustained inhalation. (Smith, 1963)

Results. The average forms of the uncorrected cardiac response to the positive and negative CSs and in the control condition are shown for 9 subjects in Figure 19-20. Respiratory sinus arrhythmia appears clearly in all three functions. Subtracting the control heart rate from the corresponding rates with positive and negative discriminative stimuli yields the corrected CRs of the Figure 19-21.

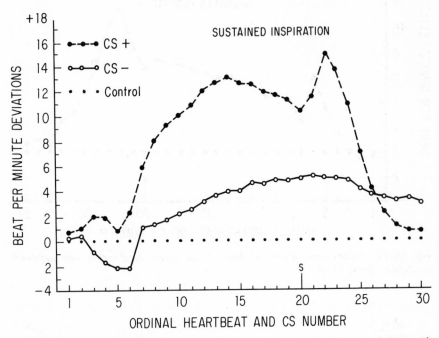

Fig. 19-21. Smith's data. Corrected forms of cardiac response to CS+ and CS— with sustained inhalation. (Smith, 1963)

Cardiac response to both CS+ and CS— is primarily accelerative, as is the response to US. A measure of the degree of discriminative control is given by the differences in heart rate during positive and negative CSs. This difference achieves a maximum of 11 b/m at about CS Number 14 and then falls off slightly as US approaches. A small decelerative trend appears in the early numbers of the CS—.

Normal Respiration, Classical Conditioning

Procedure. Experimental conditions for this group of 8 subjects were identical with those of the Sustained Inspiration, Classical Conditioning Group, with the exception of the omission of instructions to sustain inspiration during the flashing light.

Results. The average corrected CR for 8 subjects appears in Figure 19-22. A diphasic CR, initial acceleration followed by deceleration preceding US, can be observed; but the data are noisy and the magnitude of CR damped in comparison with those of Figure 19-19.

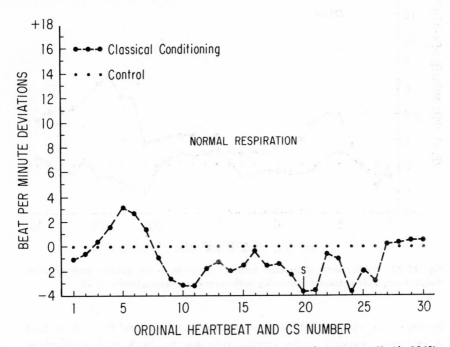

Fig. 19-22. Smith's data. Corrected form of CR during normal respiration. (Smith, 1963)

Normal Respiration, Discriminative Conditioning

Procedure. In this normal respiratory control condition, procedures paralleled those of the Sustained Inspiration Discriminative Conditioning Group, but respiration was not mentioned in the instructions.

Results. The average corrected CRs for 9 subjects with positive and negative discriminative stimuli are plotted in Figure 19-23. Again the data with normal respiration are irregular and the effects dampened. An accelerative CR+ is shown, but the CS− function is not significantly different from the control function.

Interpretations

True form of cardiac UR to shock. All previous measurements of the cardiac UR to shock have left respiration uncontrolled, allowing for the possibility that the accelerative response to shock was mediated

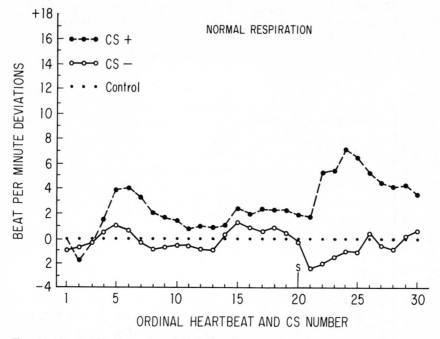

Fig. 19-23. Smith's data. Corrected form of response to the positive and negative stimuli during discriminative conditioning, with normal respiration. (Smith, 1963)

by respiratory changes following shock. Figures 19-19 and 19-21 show that acceleration remains as the cardiac response to shock with respiration held experimentally constant.

Monophasic or diphasic CR? It would appear from Figure 19-19 that with sustained inspiration the cardiac CR is monophasic-acceleration. Little evidence for the secondary deceleration can be seen in the locus of shock expectation. With discriminative conditioning, however, deceleration is present using one definition of deceleration—instantaneous deceleration, but not using the pre-CS definition of deceleration—a rate lower than pre-CS rate.

Although the data are not presented, shockless extinction trials were run after discrimination training and these showed neither a deceleration below pre-CS level nor a post-CS elevation in rate. The interpretation of the instantaneous deceleration is therefore one of recovery from acceleration and not of a diphasic CR.

Considering the array of data presented thus far the conclusion is suggested that as respiratory control is extended in stages from no control (Notterman, Schoenfeld, & Bersh, 1952a; Zeaman, Deane, & Wegner,

1954), to control of rate and depth (Westcott & Huttenlocher, 1961), to control with respiration constant (Smith, 1963), there is a progressive diminution of the deceleration portion of the cardiac CR, leaving a simple monophasic accelerative CR preceding an accelerative UR.

Role of respiration. The attenuated, accelerative CRs and URs obtained with the normal respiratory control groups led Smith to the conclusion that free respiration exerts a homeostatic influence on cardiac responding. The mechanism of this homeostatic control may be given by a set of transfer equations recently published by Clynes (1960) who has successfully used them with an analog computer to simulate heart rate output from a knowledge of respiratory movements as input. The use of Clynes' equations and computer methods may provide the best available method of controlling for respiratory artifacts and mediation in cardiac conditioning when it is desired to allow normal respiration during conditioning. Such studies are currently being undertaken by Zeaman and Smith.

Controls. In addition to providing control of respiration, Smith's unique demonstration of discriminative control of the accelerative CR provides good control for possibly nonassociative processes such as pseudoconditioning and sensitization.

Theory. Stimulus substitution: The similarity in form of the monophasic accelerative CR and the accelerative UR to shock (unmediated by respiration) makes the case for stimulus substitution stronger, but does not rule out alternatives. The locus of the maximum CR (just before shock in Figure 19-19) now resembles more closely the usual locus of delayed CRs (inhibition of delay) reported in the body of classical conditioning data that has in the past lent support to stimulus substitution theory.

Fear mediation: The earlier interpretation of the cardiac decelerative CR as an indicator of fear, having been made doubtful by Steward's data, is further weakened by Smith's. Despite the strong shock and large UR, no appreciable decelerative effects were observed on any trial with respiration controlled, although the subjects have as much reason to be afraid as in previous experiments.

Anxiety mediation: The hypothesis that warnings of aversive stimulation cause anxiety with its physiological correlate of cardiac acceleration is consistent with Smith's data. Inferring a gradually increasing anxiety from the gradually increasing heart rate in Figure 19-19 as shock approaches is consistent with subjective reports of anxiety under such conditions.

SMITH AND ZEAMAN STUDY

To extend the generality of Smith's findings of an accelerative CR with sustained inspiration, a follow-up study was done (as yet unpublished) by Smith and Zeaman with sustained exhalation.

Procedure. The details of Smith's long-delay classical conditioning procedure were adopted with a single change. The subjects were told to *exhale* when the signal light flashed (instead of *inhaling*, as in the previous study) and to sustain their exhalation for as long as the light

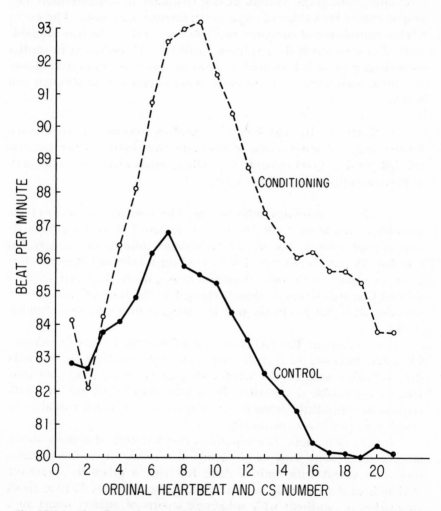

Fig. 19-24. The effects of sustained exhalation on heart rate are shown by the "control" function. During shock-threat trials the form of this cardiac-respiration reflex changes to that shown in the "conditioning" function.

flashed (20 sec.). Following basal and control measurement, the subjects were given shock-threat trials in which they were told that a shock would be administered on the 20th flash of the light. Shock was given on the 20th flash of each 5 trials.

Results. Control measures: The respiratory cardiac reflex associated with a sustained exhalation is plotted in Figure 19-24. The reflex is diphasic, acceleration followed by deceleration, and thus similar in form to the inspiratory reflex. However, the duration of each phase is considerably longer. With sustained inspiration the heart rate has returned to pre-inspiration level by the 14th beat; with sustained exhalation, the heart still deviates from pre-level 20 beats after the start of exhalation.

Shock-threat measure: Results of the shock-threat trials are plotted in Figure 19-24, and the differences between shock-threat and control measures are plotted in Figure 19-25 as a corrected measure of cardiac CR. The CR is accelerative, rising to a peak after nine beats and then falling off appreciably as shock approaches. The magnitude of the maximum CR (approximately 8 b/m) is about the same at that observed with sus-

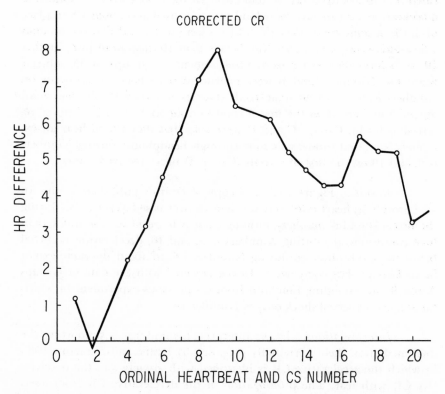

Fig. 19-25. The corrected form of the cardiac CR during sustained exhalation has been plotted as the difference between the control and conditioning function of Fig. 19-24.

tained inspiration (cf. Figure 19-19), but the location of the maximum CR is earlier in the CS-US interval, occurring on Beat 9 rather than Beat 19 as was observed with sustained inspiration. The form of CR resembles somewhat more closely the discriminative CR to CS+ shown in Figure 19-21.

Interpretations. The CR can again be interpreted to be monophasic in the sense that the rate does not return to pre-CS level, and the implications for stimulus substitution theory and mediation theory remain as before. It is not clear why the maximum CR should have changed its locus in the CS-US interval when the sustained respiration is exhalation rather than inhalation. The concept of inhibition of delay is of no explanatory help here.

OTHER STUDIES: A FOLLOW-UP BY JENKS AND DEANE

Procedure. The long-delay cardiac conditioning procedures used in the Connecticut studies and previously adopted by Deane were replicated in a follow-up study by Jenks and Deane (1963) with the following modifications: (a) an extremely loud tone was used as noxious US in place of shock in some conditions, (b) subjects were instructed that the noxious US would occur on Stimulus Numbers 8, 9, or 10 (instead of just Number 10, as before). Following basal measurements, 4 groups of 15 subjects were run: Groups A and B were instructed that shock would occur on Numbers 8, 9, or 10 on some trials (Group A received only one shock during Number 10 on the first 6 conditioning trials, Group B never received a shock); Groups C and D were told that they would hear an extremely loud and unpleasant tone through headphones during Numbers 8, 9, and 10 on the first of 6 trials (Group D never received a tone).

Results. Figure 19-26 is a copy of Deane's published results. In all 4 groups (a) heart rates were accelerated over base levels (B8-10) during the first 6 stimulus numbers, although much more so for the shock than tone conditions, (b) during Numbers 8, 9, and 10, deceleration occurred below the levels observed during Numbers 1-6, to about the same extent in all Groups. For comparison, Deane graphed with the data of Groups A and B corresponding functions from his previous experiment in which the subjects expected shock only at Number 10.

Interpretations. Deane interprets his findings as supporting the dual mediation theory originally proposed by Deane and Zeaman (1958), in which the accelerative CR is identified with anxiety and the decelerative CR with fear. The prolongation of the decelerative CR from 3-sec. duration in previous studies to 9 sec. in the present study he regards as evidence against respiratory mediation of the decelerative effect.

Other interpretations of his findings are possible. The fact that de-

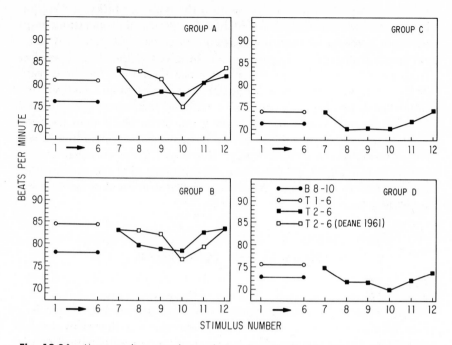

Fig. 19-26. Mean cardiac rate during the number stimuli with trials as the parameter. (Wenks & Deane, 1963)

celerative CR was of the same magnitude in all conditions regardless of the nature of the threat and whether or not it was carried out is consistent with the hypothesis that the decelerative CR is associated with some nonfear state such as simple attention. A control condition with warnings of nonaversive sound is missing.

The prolongation of the decelerative CR does not rule out respiratory mediation. It can be seen from Smith and Zeaman's Figure 19-24 that a sustained exhalation, for example, can create a heart rate deceleration as long as 15-20 beats later. Also, the prolongation of decelerative CR observed by Deane could have been produced by isolated gasps *on different trials* at Numbers 6-10. His analysis does not preclude this source of apparent time smear in the average taken over trials. It should be noted here that the definition of deceleration implied by Deane uses post-CS level as references. If not, he could not distinguish his decelerative CR from a simple recovery from acceleration.

The acceleration observed in response to warnings of a noxious sound raises no theoretical problems. It can be accounted for in stimulus substitution terms, since the UR to loud sound has been shown by Steward to be accelerative; or it can be treated in mediation terms, if it is assumed that anxiety produces cardiac acceleration.

There is some question, however, of the reproducibility of these findings, since Steward with almost identical experimental operations found
no acceleration in anticipation of sound, noxious or otherwise. A simple
explanation of this discrepancy would be given if the three basal level
trials (B8-10) chosen by Deane as reference level were for some reason
artifactually low for Groups C and D. In support of this conjecture, it
should be pointed out that the observed basal levels, averaging about 72
b/m for Groups C and D, are lower group basal levels than have ever
been observed by *any* of the previous investigators (including Deane)
whose work has been referenced in this paper. Note also that the sup-
posedly accelerated T 1-6 functions of Groups C and D average out *below*
the basal levels of Groups A and B. The answer to this puzzle awaits
more data.

GENERAL SUMMARY AND CONCLUSIONS

Findings

In response to warning signals of aversive stimuli, the human heart
rate has shown a diphasic reaction, an acceleration followed by deceleration. The decelerative reaction has been found in anticipation of nonaversive as well as aversive stimuli, and also been shown to be at least
partially under the control of respiration.

The accelerative cardiac response shows a tendency to adapt out over
trials if the aversive stimulus is subjectively weak, but it does not adapt
out readily if the threatened aversive is not delivered, of if it is very
strong. With normal respiration, both the accelerative and decelerative
cardiac responses have been observed during the CS-US interval of trace
or long-delay conditioning procedures. With increasing degrees of respiratory control, the decelerative CR is diminished leaving a monophasic
accelerative CR preceding an accelerative UR to shock.

Both accelerative and decelerative reactions occur in response to the
paired presentation of CS and US and in response to instructions of a
CS-US sequence. Phenomena of classical conditioning such as acquisition,
extinction and discrimination have been demonstrated with both.

Theory

Drive reduction. This mechanism of cardiac conditioning was
inferred to be unlikely after considering the results of experiments varying the duration of shock US. According to a drive reduction view, this
variable should have made a difference in form and magnitude of cardiac
CR, but it did not.

Stimulus substitution. This mechanism has little trouble accounting for the accelerative cardiac CR, since the UR to shock is also accelerative, with both normal and controlled respiration. If the anticipation of a loud sound produces a reliable accelerative CR, this too is consistent with stimulus substitution theory because the UR to loud sound is also accelerative. Since classically conditioned responses are known to be related to magnitude of US intensity, the adaptation of the accelerative CR is not unexpected, if the subjective intensity of shock is assumed to decrease with adaptation.

The big problem for stimulus substitution theory in cardiac conditioning is the origin of the decelerative CR. It may be that any change in a stimulus sequence is accompanied by respiratory changes, and that anticipation of a change results in the conditioning of the respiratory effects to warnings of the stimulus change. Respiratory changes can reflexly produce cardiac deceleration, but the mechanism of this control is subtle, requiring computer simulation for evaluation with normal respiration.

Mediation theory. The dual mediation theory relating the accelerative CR to anxiety and the decelerative CR to fear was weakened by the finding of a decelerative cardiac response in anticipation of non-aversive stimulation. Another dual mediation theory was proposed relating the decelerative CR to a state of simple anticipation or attention, and retaining the anxiety-acceleration notion. In paradigm form, the causal chains in this dual mediation hypothesis are shown below:

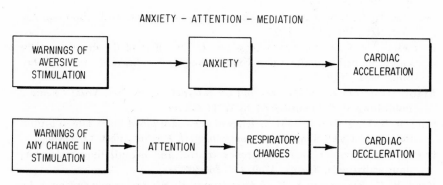

ANXIETY – ATTENTION – MEDIATION

Implications for further research. A critical test of stimulus' substitution theory (anxiety-attention) could be made if a noxious US could be found with a decelerative cardiac UR. Stimulus substitution theory would predict that classical conditioning with such a US would produce only decelerative CRs, whereas mediation theory would predict accelerative CRs. A search for such a US is under way.

References

BEIER, C. D. Conditioned cardiovascular responses and suggestions for treatment of cardiac responses. *J. exp. Psychol.*, 1940, *26*, 311-321.

BERSH, P. J., NOTTERMAN, J. M., & SCHOENFELD, W. N. The effect of randomly varying the interval between conditioned and unconditioned stimuli upon the production of experimental anxiety. *Proc. Nat. Acad. Sci.*, 1953, *39*, 553-570.

BERSH, P. J., NOTTERMAN, J. M., & SCHOENFELD, W. N. Extinction of human cardiac response during avoidance conditioning. *Amer. J. Psychol.*, 1956, *69*, 244-251. (a)

BERSH, P. J., NOTTERMAN, J. M., & SCHOENFELD, W. N. Generalization to varying frequencies as a function of intensity of unconditioned stimulus. *USAF Sch. Aviat. Med. Rep.*, 1956, No. 56-79. (b)

BERSH, P. J., NOTTERMAN, J. M., & SCHOENFELD, W. N. Relations between acquired autonomic and motor behavior during avoidance conditioning. *USAF Sch. Med. Rep.*, 1956, No. 56-80. (c)

BERSH, P. J., NOTTERMAN, J. M., & SCHOENFELD, W. N. A comparison of internal vs. external reinforcement in motor avoidance situations. *USAF Sch. Med. Rep.*, 1957, No. 57-27. (a)

BERSH, P. J., NOTTERMAN, J. M., & SCHOENFELD, W. N. The discriminative control of a conditioned heart rate response. *USAF Sch. Med. Rep.*, 1957, No. 57-29. (b)

BERSH, P. J., NOTTERMAN, J. M., & SCHOENFELD, W. N. The efficiency of pursuit-rotor performance during experimentally induced anxiety. *USAF Sch. Med. Rep.*, 1957, No. 57-28. (c)

BILLINGS, M. L., & SHEPARD, J. F. The change of heart rate with attention. *Psychol. Rev.*, 1910, *17*, 217-227.

BITTERMAN, M. E., REED, P., & KRAUSKOPF, J. The effect of the duration of the unconditioned stimulus upon conditioning and extinction. *Amer. J. Psychol.*, 1952, *65*, 256-262.

BYKOV, D. M. *The cerebral cortex and the internal organs.* New York: Chemical Publishing, 1957. (Transl. & ed. by W. H. GANTT)

CHURCH, R. M., & BLACK, A. H. Latency of the conditioned heart rate as a function of the CS-UCS interval. *J. comp. physiol. Psychol.*, 1958, *51*, 478-487.

CLYNES, M. Computer analysis of reflex control and organization: respiratory sinus arrhythmia. *Science*, 1960, *131*, 300-302.

DAVIS, R. C., BUCHWALD, A. M., & FRANKMANN, R. W. Autonomic and muscular responses, and their relation to simple stimuli. *Psychol. Monogr.*, 1955, *69*, No. 405.

DEANE, G. E. Human heart rate responses during experimentally induced anxiety. *J. exp. Psychol.*, 1961, *61*, 489-493.

DEANE, G. E., & ZEAMAN, D. Human heart rate during anxiety. *Percept. Motor Skills*, 1958, *8*, 103-106.

JENKS, R. S., & DEANE, G. E. Human heart rate during experimentally induced anxiety: A follow-up. *J. exp. Psychol.*, 1963, *65*, 109-112.

LACEY, J. I. Individual differences in somatic response patterns. *J. comp. physiol. Psychol.*, 1950, *43*, 338-350.

LACEY, J. I., & SMITH, R. L. Conditioning and generalization of unconscious anxiety. *Science*, 1954, *120*, 1045-1052.

NOLAN, R. E. Human cardiac conditioning during intense experimental anxiety. Unpublished doctoral dissertation, University of Connecticut, 1961.

NOTTERMAN, J. M., SCHOENFELD, W. N., & BERSH, P. J. A comparison of three extinction procedures following heart rate conditioning. *J. abnorm. soc. Psychol.*, 1952, *47*, 674-677. (a)

NOTTERMAN, J. M., SCHOENFELD, W. N., & BERSH, P. J. Conditioned heart rate responses in human beings during experimental anxiety. *J. comp. physiol. Psychol.*, 1952, *45*, 1-8. (b)

NOTTERMAN, J. M., SCHOENFELD, W. N., & BERSH, P. J. Partial reinforcement and conditioned heart rate response in human subjects. *Science*, 1952, *115*, 77-79. (c)

PETERS, J. E., & GANTT, W. H. Effect of graded degrees of muscular exertion on human heart rate and the role of muscular exertion in cardiac conditioned reflexes. *J. gen. Psychol.*, 1953, *49*, 31-43.

RAZRAN, G. H. S. Conditioning and attitudes. *J. exp. Psychol.*, 1939, *24*, 215-226.

SCHAEFER, H. Central control of cardiac functions. *Physiol. Rev.*, 1960, *40*, 213-230.

SCHOENFELD, W. N. An experimental approach to anxiety, escape and avoidance behavior. In P. H. HOCH & J. ZUBIN (Eds.), *Anxiety*. New York: Grune & Stratton, 1950.

SHEARN, D. Does the heart learn? *Psychol. Bull.*, 1961, *58*, 452-458.

SKAGGS, E. B. Changes in pulse, breathing and steadiness under conditions of startledness and excited expectancy. *J. comp. Psychol.*, 1926, *6*, 303-318.

SMITH, K. Conditioning as an artifact. *Psychol. Rev.*, 1954, *61*, 217-225.

SMITH, R. W. Simple and discriminative cardiac conditioning in humans with sustained inspiration as respiratory control. Unpublished doctoral dissertation, University of Connecticut, 1963.

STEVENS, S. S., CARTON, A. S., & SHICKMAN, G. M. Scale of apparent intensity of electric shock. *J. exp. Psychol.*, 1958, *56*, 328-334.

STEWARD, J. R. The effect on heart rate of warnings and receipt of pleasant and aversive auditory stimuli. Unpublished doctoral dissertation, University of Connecticut, 1962.

WEGNER, H., & ZEAMAN, D. Strength of cardiac conditioned responses with varying unconditioned stimulus durations. *Psychol. Rev.*, 1958, *65*, 238-241.

WESTCOTT, M. R., & HUTTENLOCHER, J. Cardiac conditioning: The effects and implications of controlled and uncontrolled respiration. *J. exp. Psychol.*, 1961, *61*, 353-359.

ZEAMAN, D., DEANE, G., & WEGNER, N. Amplitude and latency characteristics of the conditioned heart response. *J. Psychol.*, 1954, *38*, 235-250.

ZEAMAN, D., & WEGNER, N. The role of drive reduction in the classical conditioning of an autonomically mediated response. *J. exp. Psychol.*, 1954, *48*, 349-354.

ZEAMAN, D., & WEGNER, N. Cardiac reflexes to tones of threshold intensity. *J. speech and hearing disorders*. 1956, *21*, 71-75.

ZEAMAN, D., & WEGNER, N. A further test of the role of drive reduction in human cardiac conditioning. *J. Psychol.*, 1957, *43*, 125-133.

ZEAMAN, D., & WEGNER, N. Strength of cardiac conditioned responses with varying stimulus duration. *Psychol. Rev.*, 1958, *65*, 238-241.

INDEX